"DE ILLIS QUI FACIUNT PENITENTIAM"
THE RULE OF THE SECULAR FRANCISCAN ORDER

BIBLIOTHECA SERAPHICO-CAPUCCINA
39

ROBERT M. STEWART

"DE ILLIS QUI FACIUNT PENITENTIAM"

THE RULE OF THE SECULAR FRANCISCAN ORDER: ORIGINS, DEVELOPMENT, INTERPRETATION

ISTITUTO STORICO DEI CAPPUCCINI
ROMA 1991

Editor: VINCENZO CRISCUOLO

On the cover: Volterra, Biblioteca Guarnacci, MS 225 (Inv. 5230), f. 148r.

ISSN 0067-8163

Edizioni Collegio S. Lorenzo da Brindisi

Istituto Storico dei Cappuccini
Circonvallazione Occidentale 6850 (GRA km. 65) 00163 Roma (Aurelio)

ACKNOWLEDGMENTS

Both the writing of my dissertation and the subsequent redactional work in preparing it for publication in this series have been an experience of "doing penance" for me, a time of conversion which has brought a deepening realization of how our lives are worked out *in community*. A great many people have made this journey possible and have helped me to bring this work to completion through their guidance, support, encouragement, love, and prayer. Among the many people to whom I owe a debt of gratitude, I can mention but a few by name.

I would like to express my sincere gratitude to the members of my committee for their careful reading, probing questions, and constructive criticism: John Coleman of the Jesuit School of Theology who generously offered his time and encouragement; Regis Armstrong of the Franciscan Institute at Saint Bonaventure University who as mentor and friend enthusiastically encouraged me to pursue this topic right from its inception; Robert Brentano of the University of California at Berkeley who in offering intellectual guidance has inflamed within me a love of history and also presented me with a living embodiment of wisdom and grace; and Sandra Schneiders of the Jesuit School of Theology, the chairperson of my committee, whose interest in hermeneutics initially stirred my own interest in this topic and whose scholarship and commitment has been an inspiration for my own study and practice of Spirituality.

I would like to thank some of the people who offered technical assistance throughout this project: Carl Schafer who in his ever gracious manner offered invaluable assistance and support while I worked in the archives; my Capuchin brothers at the Collegio di San Lorenzo who allowed me the use of their library and who provided me with a powerful witness of Franciscan hospitality during my time at Rome; and my Franciscan brothers at the Istituto Storico for their assistance, guidance, and support in preparing this manuscript for publication, especially Vincenzo Criscuolo, Servus Gieben, and Pietro Maranesi.

I would also like to express my deepest gratitude to people whose prayer, love, and support have accompanied me throughout this journey: Stephanie Terril and other friends at Berkeley; my Franciscan brothers of Holy Name Province for their financial support, encouragement, and belief in me throughout this project; and my Franciscan classmates who have encouraged me both in my work and in my vocation.

But above all I would like to thank my family who, through their unconditional love and strength of faith, have been the presence of God for me in my life and have taught me to hope, to love, and to believe. With grateful heart, I dedicate this work to them and pray that each of them may be "happy and blessed" and that "*the Spirit of the Lord will rest upon them*"[1].

[1] *Earlier Exhortation*, 5-6.

CONTENTS

ABBREVIATIONS

Archives

GA Archives	Archives of the General Assistants to the Secular Franciscan Order Curia Generalizia dei Frati Minori Via S. Maria Mediatrice, 25 00165 - Roma, Italy
OFM Archives	Archives of the Order of Friars Minor Curia Generalizia dei Frati Minori Via S. Maria Mediatrice, 25 00165 - Roma, Italy
SFO Archives	Archives of the Secular Franciscan Order Curia Generalizia dei Frati Minori Via S. Maria Mediatrice, 25 00165 - Roma, Italy

Periodicals, Series, and Studies

AAS	*Acta Apostolicae Sedis*
AF	*Analecta Franciscana*
AFH	*Archivum Franciscanum Historicum*
Anal TOR	*Analecta Tertii Ordinis Regularis Sancti Francisci*
CF	*Collectanea Franciscana*
DIP	*Dizionario degli Istituti di Perfezione*
DSp	*Dictionnaire de Spiritualité*
FS	*Franciscan Studies*
MF	*Miscellanea Francescana*

Omnibus	*St. Francis of Assisi, Writings and Early Biographies: English Omnibus of the Sources for the Life of St. Francis,* edited by M. Habig, Chicago [4]1983.
Opuscula	*Opuscula Sancti Patris Francisci Assisiensis,* edited by C. Esser, Grottaferrata (Roma) 1978.

Medieval Biographies of Saint Francis

1 Cel	*Vita Prima S. Francisci* by Thomas of Celano
2 Cel	*Vita Secunda S. Francisci* by Thomas of Celano
L3S	*Legenda Trium Sociorum* (*The Legend of the Three Companions*)
LM	*Legenda Maior S. Francisci* by St. Bonaventure
Lm	*Legenda Minor S. Francisci* by St. Bonaventure
LP	*Legenda seu Compilatio Perusina* (*The Legend of Perugia*)

Writings of Saint Francis

Earlier Exhortation	The Earlier Version of the *Letter to All the Faithful* (*Epistola ad Fideles I*)
Later Exhortation	The Later Version of the *Letter to All the Faithful* (*Epistola ad Fideles II*)
RegB	*Regula Bullata,* The 1223 Rule of the Order of Friars Minor which received papal approbation
RnB	*Regula non Bullata,* The 1221 Rule of the Order of Friars Minor which did not receive papal approbation

Scripture

Scriptural quotations have been taken from the New Jerusalem Bible.

SELECTED BIBLIOGRAPHY

Allaire G. - Rossi J., *Des Laïcs dans L'Eglise: La Fraternité séculière de saint François*, Fayard (Belgium) 1987.

Approccio storico-critico alle Fonti Francescane, edited by G. Cardaropoli and M. Conti, Roma 1979.

Armstrong R. - Brady I., *Francis and Clare: The Complete Works* (Classics in Western Spirituality Series), New York 1982.

Asseldonk O. van, *Maria, Francesco e Chiara,* Roma 1989.

Assisi al tempo di san Francesco. Atti del V Convegno Internazionale, Società Internazionale di Studi Francescani (Assisi, 13-16 ottobre 1977), Assisi 1978.

Bartoli M., *Gregorio IX e il movimento penitenziale*, in *La "Supra Montem" di Niccolò IV*, 47-60.

Bartoli-Langeli A., *La realtà sociale assisana e il patto del 1210*, in *Assisi al tempo di san Francesco*, 271-336.

Bédrune L., *Ordine francescano secolare*, in *Dizionario Francescano*, Padova 1983, 1133-1166.

— *Regole dell'Ordine Francescano Secolare*, in *Dizionario Francescano*, Padova 1983, 1541-1556.

— *Les Travaux de la Règle*, in *Tertius Ordo* 35 (1974) 182-85.

— *L'Iter della Regola*, in *Tertius Ordo* 40 (1979) 8-10.

— *La Règle, une réponse aux attentes contemporaines*, in *Lettre aux assistents* (1980) n. 2, 20-28.

Bigi M., *Attualità, messaggio e missione dell'Ordine Francescano Secolare, sue incidenze nella pastorale vocazionale e nella formazione del Terz'Ordine Regolare*, in *Ritorno a Francesco*, 235-245.

Bolton B., *Innocent III's treatment of the Humiliati*, in *Popular Belief and Practice* (Studies in Church History, 8), edited by G. Cuming and D. Baker, Cambridge 1972, 73-82.

— *The Poverty of the Humiliati*, in *Poverty in the Middle Ages*, edited by D. Flood, Werl/Westf. 1975, 52-59.

Börner E., *Das Umfeld der Pönitentenbewegung*, in *Wissenschaft und Weisheit* 53 (1990) 106-141.

Brady I., *L'elaborazione storico-dottrinale in compilazioni biografiche posteriori*, in *Approccio storico-critico*, 125-37.
— *San Francesco: uomo dello Spirito*, Vicenza 1978.

Brooke R., *The "Legenda Antiqua S. Francisci" - Perugia Ms. 1046*, in *Analecta Bollandiana* 99 (1981) 165-68.
— *Recent Work on St. Francis of Assisi*, in *Analecta Bollandiana* 100 (1982) 653-76.
— *Scripta Leonis, Rufini, et Angeli, Sociorum S. Francisci*, Oxford 1970.

Callaey F., *The Third Order of St. Francis: A Historical Essay*, translated by J. Lenhart, Pittsburgh 1926.

Canonici L., *I Terziari francescani "fratelli e sorelle della penitenza"*, in *Quaderni di spiritualità francescana* 18 (1970) 148-171.

Carpaneto da Langasco C., *San Francesco, penitente*, in *L'Italia Francescana* 53 (1978) 417-426.
— *Lo Stato dei Penitenti nel "Corpus Iuris Canonici"*, in *I Frati Penitenti*, 9-19.

Casagrande G., *Il movimento penitenziale nel Medio Evo*, in *Benedictina* 27 (1980) 695-709.
— *L'Ordine Francescano Secolare nelle prime Fonti Francescane*, in *L'Italia Francescana* 55 (1980) 203-220.

Casolini F., *The History of the Third Order*, in *Franciscan Herald and Forum* 36 (1957) 257-264, 286, 304-305, 316-317, 329-332, 357-358; 37 (1958) 63-67, 132-135, 178-180, 202-205.
— *I Penitenti francescani in "Leggende" e Cronache del Trecento*, in *I Frati Penitenti*, 69-86.

Chenu M-D., *"Fraternitas": Évangile et condition socio-culturelle*, in *Revue d'Histoire de la Spiritualité* 49 (1973) 385-400.
— *Moines, Clercs, Laïcs au carrefour de la vie évangélique (XIIe siècle)*, in *Revue d'Histoire Ecclésiastique* 49 (1954) 59-89.
— *Nature, Man, and Society in the Twelfth Century: Essays on New Theological Perspectives in the Latin West*, translated by J. Taylor and L. Little, Chicago 1968.

Ciurana J., *La Orden de Penitencia de San Francisco: Notas sobre sus orígenes y desarrollo en el s. XIII*, in *Selecciones de Franciscanismo* 8 (1979) 19-54.

Conn W., *Bernard Lonergan's Analysis of Conversion*, in *Angelicum* 53 (1976) 362-404.
— *Christian Conversion: A Developmental Interpretation of Autonomy and Surrender*, New York 1986.
— *Conscience: Development and Self-Transcendence*, Birmingham 1981.
— *The Desire for Authenticity: Conscience and Moral Conversion*, in *The Desires of the Human Heart*, 36-56.
— *Moral Development: Is Conversion Necessary?*, in *Creativity and Method: Essays in Honor of Bernard Lonergan, S.J.*, edited by M. Lamb, Milwaukee 1981, 307-324.
— *Passionate Commitment: The Dynamics of Affective Conversion*, in *Cross Currents* 34 (1984) 329-36.

Conti M., *L'identità francescana dei fratelli e delle sorelle del Terzo Ordine Regolare di san Francesco: commento alla nuova Regola*, Bologna 1986.

Corstanje A. van, *The Third Order for Our Times*, Chicago 1974.

Cousins E., *Bonaventure* (Classics in Western Spirituality Series), New York 1978.

D'Alatri M., *Contrasti tra penitenti francescani ed autorità ecclesiastica nel Trecento*, in *I Frati Penitenti di San Francesco*, 101-110.
— *Eretici, penitenti e primi francescani*, in *L'Italia Francescana* 44 (1969) 357-361.
— *Francesco d'Assisi e i laici*, in *Ricerche Storiche* 13 (1983) 613-33.
— *Genesi della Regola di Niccolò IV: aspetti storici*, in *La "Supra Montem" di Niccolò IV*, 93-107.
— *I Minori e la "Cura Animarum" di fraternite e congregazioni*, in *I Frati Minori e il Terzo Ordine*, 143-170.
— *"Ordo Paenitentium" ed eresia in Italia*, in *CF* 43 (1973) 181-197.
— *Origin of the Rule of Nicholas IV: Historical Aspects*, in *Greyfriars Review* 4 (1990) n. 3, 107-118.
— *Il Terzo Ordine*, in *Francesco, il francescanesimo*, 119-129.

Dallen J., *The Reconciling Community: The Rite of Penance*, New York 1986.

Dal Pino A., *I Frati Servi di S. Maria dalle origini all'approvazione*, Louvain 1972.
— *Laicato italiano tra eresia e proposito pauperistico evangelico nei secoli XII-XIII*, Padova 1984.

Desbonnets T., *From Intuition to Institution: The Franciscans*, translated by P. Duggan and J. Du Charme, Chicago 1988.

Di Fonzo L., *L'anonimo Perugino tra le Fonti Francescane del secolo XIII: rapporti letterari e testo*, in *MF* 72 (1972) 117-483.

The Desires of the Human Heart: An Introduction to the Theology of Bernard Lonergan, edited by V. Gregson, New York 1988.

Dozzi D., *Tracce metodologiche in alcuni studiosi degli scritti di Francesco*, in *Laurentianum* 29 (1988) 199-222.

Duby G., *Les laïcs et la paix de Dieu*, in *I Laici nella "Societas Christiana"*, 448-486.

Elm K., *Francesco d'Assisi nella crisi spirituale e sociale del XII e XIII secolo*, in *Francesco, il francescanesimo*, 131-139.

Erba A., *Visione storico-antropologica della vita penitenziale nel primo Medioevo*, in *Ritorno a Francesco*, 103-134.

Esser K., *Un documento dell'inizio del Duecento sui Penitenti*, in *I Frati Penitenti di san Francesco*, 87-99.
— *A Forerunner of the "Epistola ad Fideles" of St. Francis of Assisi*, in *Anal TOR* 129 (1978) 11-47.
— *La Lettera di san Francesco ai fedeli*, in *CF* 43 (1973) 65-78.
— *Origins of the Franciscan Order*, translated by A. Daly and I. Lynch, Chicago 1970.
— *Repair My House*, translated by M. Meilach, Chicago 1963.
— *Gli Scritti di S. Francesco d'Assisi: nuova edizione critica e versione italiana*, Italian translation by A. Bizzotto and S. Cattazzo, Padova 1982.

Esser K. - Grau E., *Love's Reply*, translated by I. Brady, Chicago 1963.

Esser K. - Hardik L., *The Marrow of the Gospel: A Study of the Rule of Saint Francis of Assisi by the Franciscans of Germany*, translated and edited by I. Brady, Chicago 1958.

Faley R., *Biblical Considerations on Metanoia*, in *Anal TOR* 13 (1974) 13-33.
— *Visione biblico-teologica della penitenza e sua espressione oggi*, in *Ritorno a Francesco*, 89-102.

Favazza J., *The Order of Penitents: Historical Roots and Pastoral Future*, Collegeville 1988.

Flood D., *The Admonitions*, in *Haversack* 2 (1978-1979), n. 1, 13-15; n. 2, 20-23; n. 3, 19-21; n. 4, 16-19; n. 5, 20-22; n. 6, 18-22.

— *Assisi's Rules and People's Needs: The Initial Determination of the Franciscan Mission*, in *Franziskanische Studien* 66 (1984) 91-104.
— *The Commonitorium*, in *Haversack* 3 (1979-1980), n. 1, 20-23; n. 2, 20-23; n. 3, 21-23; n. 4, 20-24; n. 5, 19-24; n. 6, 21-23.
— *The Domestication of the Franciscan Movement*, in *Franziskanische Studien* 60 (1978) 311-327.
— *Franciscan Penitents*, in *Franziskanische Studien* 68 (1986) 272-277.
— *Franciscan Reading*, in *Haversack* 2 (1979), n. 6, 13-18.
— *Frère François et le mouvement franciscain*, Paris 1983.
— *Gospel Poverty and the Poor*, in *Concilium* 187 (1986) 63-69.
— *The Sacrum Commercium and Early Franciscan History*, in *Haversack* 1 (1977-1978), n. 1, 13-16; n. 2, 18-21; n. 3, 17-20; n. 5, 15-25; n. 6, 98-23.

Flood D. - Matura T., *The Birth of a Movement*, translated by P. La Chance and P. Schwartz, Chicago 1975.

Francescanesimo e vita religiosa dei laici nel '200. Atti del VIII Convegno Internazionale, Società Internazionale di Studi Francescani (Assisi, 16-18 ottobre 1980), Città di Castello 1982.

Francesco d'Assisi e Francescanesimo dal 1216 al 1226. Atti del IV Convegno Internazionale, Società Internazionale di Studi Francescani (Assisi, 15-17 ottobre 1976), Assisi 1977.

Francesco, il francescanesimo, e la cultura della nuova Europa, edited by I. Baldelli and A. Romanini, Firenze 1986.

The Franciscan Message in Authentic Texts, edited by M. Poppy, St. Louis 1941.

I Frati Minori e il Terzo Ordine: problemi e discussioni storiografiche. Convegno del Centro di Studi sulla spiritualità medievale (Todi, 17-20 ottobre 1982), edited by Stanislao da Campagnola, Assisi 1985.

I Frati Penitenti di san Francesco nella società del Due e Trecento. Atti del 2° Convegno di Studi Francescani (Roma, 12-14 ottobre 1976), edited by M. D'Alatri, Roma 1977.

Freeman G. P., *Supra Montem. Die Regel für die Pönitenten von Papst Nikolaus IV. (1289)*, in *Wissenschaft und Weisheit* 53 (1990) 142-156.

From Gospel to Life: The Rule of the Secular Franciscan Order, with Commentary, edited by B. Fonck, Chicago 1979.

Garberi T., *I vescovi e i movimenti penitenziali dal secondo concilio di Lione alla fine del '200*, in *La "Supra Montem" di Niccolò IV*, 133-45.

García y García A., *Génesis de la Regla de Nicolao IV: aspectos jurídicos*, in *La "Supra Montem" di Niccolò IV*, 109-131.

Gelpi D., *Committed Worship: A Sacramental Theology for Converting Christians*, unpublished manuscript, forthcoming Collegeville 1992.
— *The Converting Jesuit*, in *Studies in the Spirituality of Jesuits* 18 (1986) 1-38.
— *Experiencing God: A Theology of Human Emergence*, New York 1978.
— *Inculturating North American Theology: An Experiment in Foundational Method*, Atlanta 1988.
— *Religious Conversion: A New Way of Being*, in *The Human Experience of Conversion*, 175-202.

Grundmann H., *Movimenti religiosi nel Medioevo*, translated by M. Ausserhofer and L. Santini, Bologna 1974.

Habig M. - Hegener M., *A Short History of the Third Order*, Chicago 1963.

The Human Experience of Conversion: Persons and Structures in Transformation, edited by F. Eigo, Villanova 1987.

Hyde J. K., *Society and Politics in Medieval Italy: The Evolution of the Civil Life, 1000-1350*, New York 1973.

Iglesias F., *The Prophetic Originality of St. Francis*, in *Greyfriars Review* 2 (1988) 45-90.

Iriarte L., *Franciscan History: The Three Orders of St. Francis of Assisi*, translated by P. Ross, Chicago 1982.

Johnston T., *Franciscan and Dominican Influences on the Medieval Order of Penance: Origins of the Dominican Laity*, in *Spirituality Today* 37 (1985) 108-119.

I Laici nella "Societas Christiana" dei secoli XI e XII. Atti della settimana internazionale di Studio (Mendola 1968), edited by G. Lazzati and C. Fonseca, Milano 1968.

Lambert M., *Franciscan Poverty: The Doctrine of the Absolute Poverty of Christ and the Apostles in the Franciscan Order, 1210-1323*, London 1961.

Landini L., *The Causes of the Clericalization of the Order of Friars Minor: 1209-1260 in the Light of Early Franciscan Sources*, Ph.D. diss., Pontificia Universitas Gregoriana 1968.

— *The Historical Context of the Franciscan Movement*, in *Franciscan History: The Three Orders of St. Francis of Assisi*, Chicago 1982, 557-82.

Lapsanski D., *Evangelical Perfection: An Historical Examination of the Concept in the Early Franciscan Sources*, St. Bonaventure 1977.
— *The First Franciscans and the Gospel*, Chicago 1976.

Le Goff J., *Francis of Assisi between the Renewals and Restraints of Feudal Society*, in *Concilium* 149 (1981) 3-10.

Lehmann L., *Exsultatio et exhortatio de poenitentia. Zu Form und Inhalt der "Epistola ad fideles I"*, in *Laurentianum* 29 (1988) 564-608.
— *Exultation and Exhortation to Penance: A Study of the Form and Content of the First Version of the Letter to the Faithful*, in *Greyfriars Review* 4 (1990) n. 2, 1-33.

Lettura biblico-teologica delle Fonti Francescane, edited by G. Cardaropoli and M. Conti, Roma 1979.

Little L., *Religious Poverty and the Profit Economy in Medieval Europe*, Ithaca 1978.

Lombardi T., *Introduzione allo studio del Francescanesimo*, Assisi 1975.
— *Storia del Francescanesimo*, Padova 1980.

Lonergan B., *Method in Theology*, New York 1972.
— *Natural Right and Historical Mindedness*, in *A Third Collection: Papers by Bernard J.F. Lonergan, S.J.*, edited by F. Crowe, New York 1984, 169-83.

Maccarrone M., *S. Francesco e la Chiesa di Innocenzo III*, in *Approccio storico-critico*, 31-43.

Magli I., *Gli uomini della penitenza: Lineamenti antropologici del Medioevo Italiano*, Bologna 1967.

Manselli R., *Evangelismo e Povertà*, in *La concezione della povertà nel Medioevo*, edited by O. Capitani, Bologna 1974, 153-191.
— *La "Forma Vitae" di S. Francesco nell'esperienza dei suoi primitivi seguaci*, in *Lettura biblico-teologica*, 233-246.
— *Francesco d'Assisi e i laici viventi nel secolo: Inizio del Terz'Ordine?*, in *Prime manifestazioni*, 11-19.
— *From the Testament to the Testaments of St. Francis*, in *Greyfriars Review* 2 (1988) 91-100.
— *St. Francis of Assisi*, translated by P. Duggan, Chicago 1988.
— *San Francesco*, Roma [3]1982.

— *Il secolo XII: religione popolare ed eresia*, Roma 1983.
— *Il soprannaturale e la religione popolare nel Medio Evo*, Roma 1985.
— *La spiritualità francescana*, in *Francesco, il francescanesimo*, 219-225.

Marquard P., *Formation of Lay Franciscans*, Chicago 1973.

Martin P., *The Gospel in Action: The Third Order Secular of Saint Francis and Christian Social Reform*, New York 1932.

Matanić A., *Francesco D'Assisi: fattori causali della sua spiritualità*, Roma 1984.
— *Un incunabolo agiografico concernente l'Ordine Francescano Secolare*, in *Anal TOR* XIV/133 (1980) 771-782.
— *Introduzione allo studio della spiritualità francescana*, Roma 1971.
— *Legislazione propria dei penitenti francescani dal 1289 a tutto il secolo XIV*, in *I Frati Penitenti*, 51-67.
— *I penitenti francescani dal 1221 (Memoriale) al 1289 (Regola bollata) principalmente attraverso i loro statuti e le regole*, in *CF* 43 (1973) 41-63.
— *Problematica delle origini del Terz'Ordine Francescano*, in *Frate Francesco* 38 (1971) 241-246.

Mattesini F., *Le origini del Terz'Ordine Francescano: Regola Antiqua e vita del Beato Lucchese*, Milano 1964.

Mattioli M., *Estado actual de los trabajos de la nueva Regla de la Tercera Orden Franciscana*, in *Tertius Ordo* 35 (1974) 129-134.

McMullen P., *The Development of the New Third Order Regular Rule*, in *Anal TOR* XIX/143 (1987) 365-410.

Meersseman G., *Disciplinati e penitenti nel Duecento*, in *Il movimento dei disciplinati nel settimo centenario dal suo inizio (Perugia - 1260)*, Spoleto 1962, 43-72.
— *Dossier de l'Ordre de la Pénitence au XIIIe Siècle*, Fribourg 1961.
— *"Introduction" to Documentation on the Order of Penance in the 13th Century*, translated by G. Barth, in *Anal TOR* XVI/137 (1983) 271-315.
— *Ordo Fraternitatis: confraternite e pietà dei laici nel Medievo*, Roma 1977.
— *I penitenti nei secoli XI e XII*, in *I Laici nella "Societas Christiana"*, 306-345.
— *Penitents ruraux communautaires en Italie au XIIIe siècle*, in *Revue d'Histoire Ecclésiastique* 49 (1954) 343-390.
— *Premier Auctarium ou Dossier de l'Ordre de la Pénitence au XIIIe siècle*, in *Revue d'Histoire Ecclésiastique* 62 (1967) 25-32.

Metodi di lettura delle Fonti Francescane, edited by E. D. Covi and F. Raurell, Roma 1988.

Miskuly J., *Julian of Speyer: Life of St. Francis (Vita Sancti Francisci)*, in *Franciscan Studies* 49 (1989) 93-174.

Mollat M., *The Poverty of Francis: A Christian and Social Option*, in *Concilium* 149 (1981) 23-29.

Moorman J., *A History of the Franciscan Order from its Origins to the Year 1517*, London 1968.
— *Sources for the Life of Francis*, Manchester 1966.

Il Movimento francescano della penitenza nella società medioevale. Atti del 3° Convegno di Studi Francescani (Padova, 25-27 settembre 1979), edited by M. D'Alatri, Roma 1980.

Movimento religioso femminile e francescanesimo nel secolo XIII. Atti del VII Convegno Internazionale, Società Internazionale di Studi Francescani (Assisi, 11-13 ottobre 1979), Assisi 1981.

Nicolini U., *L'eremitismo francescano umbro nei secoli XIII-XVI*, in *Anal TOR* XIV/131 (1979) 425-442.
— *I frati della penitenza a Perugia alla fine del sec. XIII*, in *Il Movimento dei disciplinati nel settimo centenario dal suo inizio (Perugia - 1260)*, Spoleto 1962, 371-394.

Odoardi G., *L'Ordine della penitenza di san Francesco nei documenti pontifici del secolo XIII*, in *CF* 43 (1973) 79-115.

Olgiati F., *Commento alla Regola dell'Ordine Francescano Secolare*, Milano 1986.

Opuscula Sancti Patris Francisci Assisiensis, edited by C. Esser, Grottaferrata (Roma) 1978.

Opuscules de Critique Historique, Tome I, edited by P. Sabatier, Paris 1903. [Fasc. I: *Regula antiqua fratrum et sororum de Penitentia seu Tertii ordinis sancti Francisci*, 1-30. Fasc. IV: *Les règles et le gouvernement de l'Ordo de Poenitentia au XIIIe siècle*, 143-250].

L'Ordine della penitenza di san Francesco d'Assisi nel secolo XIII. Atti del [1°] Convegno di Studi Francescani (Assisi, 3-5 luglio 1972), edited by O. Schmucki, Roma 1973.

Papi M., *Il trattato del Terz'Ordine o vero "Libro come santo Francesco istituì et ordinò el tertio ordine de frati et sore di penitentia et della dignità et perfectione o vero sanctità sua" di Mariano da Firenze*, Roma 1985.

Pastor Oliver B., *Un precursor de la "Carta a los Fideles" de san Francisco de Asís (Códice 225 de la biblioteca Guarnacci de Volterra): Comparación con otros textos precedentes*, in *Anal TOR* XIV/133 (1980) 751-768.
— *The "State of Penance" and the beginnings of the Order of Brothers and Sisters of Penance*, in *Anal TOR* XIII/123 (1974) 35-72.

Pásztor E., *St. Francis, Cardinal Hugolino and the "Franciscan Question"*, in *Greyfriars Review* 1 (1987) 1-30.
— *The Sources of Francis's Biographies*, in *Greyfriars Review* 1 (1987) 31-40.
— *La "Supra montem" e la cancelleria pontificia al tempo di Niccolò IV*, in *La "Supra Montem" di Niccolò IV*, 65-92.

Pazzelli R., *Lineamenti di storia e spiritualità del movimento penitenziale francescano: le origini del Terz'Ordine*, Roma 1979.
— *Origini del movimento penitenziale francescano*, in *Ritorno a Francesco*, 139-156.
— *Penitenza*, in *Dizionario Francescano*, Padova 1983, 1271-1296.
— *Penitenza, Ordine della-*, in *Dizionario Francescano*, Padova 1983, 1297-1314.
— *Regola e vita dei fratelli e delle sorelle del Terzo Ordine Regolare di san Francesco*, Padova 1983.
— *Alla ricerca dei documenti primitivi riguardanti il Terz'Ordine*, in *Approccio storico-critico*, 179-206.
— *St. Francis and the Third Order: The Franciscan and pre-Franciscan Penitential Movement*, Chicago 1989.
— *San Francesco e il Terz'Ordine: Il movimento penitenziale pre-francescano e francescano*, Padova 1982.
— *The Title of the "Recensio Prior" of the Letter to the Faithful: Clarifications concerning Codex 225 of Volterra (cod Vo)*, in *Anal TOR* XIX (1987) 233-248; also in *Greyfriars Review* 4 (1990) n. 3, 1-6.

Pellegrini L., *Un secolo di "lettura" delle fonti biografiche di Francesco d'Assisi*, in *Laurentianum* 29 (1988) 223-250.

Peretto E., *Movimenti spirituali laicali del Medioevo: tra ortodossia ed eresia*, Roma 1985.

Philippart G., *Les Écrits des Compagnons de S. François: aperçu de la "Question Franciscaine" des origines à nos jours*, in *Analecta Bollandiana* 90 (1972) 43-66.

Pompei A., *Il movimento penitenziale nei secoli XII-XIII*, in *CF* 43 (1973) 9-40.
— *Terminologia varia dei penitenti*, in *Il Movimento Francescano della penitenza*, 11-22.

Poppy M. - Martin P., *Survey of a Decade: The Third Order Secular of St. Francis in the United States*, St. Louis 1935.

La povertà del secolo XII e Francesco d'Assisi. Atti del II Convegno Internazionale, Società Internazionale di Studi Francescani (Assisi, 17-19 ottobre 1974), Assisi 1975.

Prime manifestazioni di vita comunitaria, maschile e femminile, nel movimento francescano della penitenza (1215-1447). Atti del [4°] Convegno di Studi Francescani (Assisi, 30 giugno - 2 luglio 1981), edited by R. Pazzelli and L. Temperini, Roma 1982.

Quaglia A., *Storiografia e storia della regola francescana*, Ancona 1985.

La "Questione Francescana" dal Sabatier ad oggi. Atti del I Convegno Internazionale, Società Internazionale di Studi Francescani (Assisi, 18-20 ottobre 1973), Assisi 1974.

Raurell F., *Lettura plurale del testo: i metodi biblici*, in *Laurentianum* 29 (1988) 251-286.

Reinmann G., *The Third Order Secular of St. Francis*, Ph.D. diss., The Catholic University of America 1928.

Ricoeur P., *Hermeneutics and the Human Sciences*, edited and translated by J. Thompson, Cambridge/New York 1981.
— *Interpretation Theory: Discourse and the Surplus of Meaning*, Fort Worth 1976.

Rigon A., *Dalla Regola di S. Agostino alla Regola di Niccolò IV*, in *La "Supra Montem" di Niccolò IV*, 25-46.

Riley P. V., *Francis' Assisi: Its Political and Social History, 1175-1225*, in *Franciscan Studies* 34 (1974) 393-424.

Ritorno a Francesco. Atti del congresso sulla formazione francescana del Terzo Ordine Regolare di san Francesco (Assisi, 8-19 luglio 1979), (Acta Tertii Ordinis Regularis Santi Francisci, II, fasc. 7), Roma 1980.

Rivi P., *Le origini dell'O.F.S.: risveglio religioso e coscienza del laicato nella Chiesa dei secoli XII-XIII. Il contributo di Francesco d'Assisi*, Fidenza 1988.

Rodríguez Herrera I. - Ortega Carmona A., *Los Escritos de San Francisco de Asís*, Murcia 1985.

Roggen H., *The Franciscan Lay Movement*, in *Franciscan Herald* 50 (1971) 214-217, 225.
— *Les relations du premier Ordre franciscain avec le Tiers-Ordre au XIIIe siècle*, in *CF* 43 (1973) 199-209.
— *Spirit and Life: The Gospel Way of Life in the Writings of St. Francis and St. Clare*, Chicago 1970.

Rule and Constitutions: Franciscan Third Order, Chicago 1959.

The Rule of the Secular Franciscan Order, with a Catechism and Instructions, edited by Z. Grant, with Cathechism by C. Ramos, Chicago 1980.

The Rules of the Third Order of St. Francis, edited by M. Poppy, St. Bonaventure 1945.

St. Francis of Assisi, Writings and Early Biographies: English Omnibus of the Sources for the Life of St. Francis, edited by M. Habig, Chicago 1983.

Schillebeeckx E., *The Right of Every Christian to Speak in the Light of Evangelical Experience "In the Midst of Brothers and Sisters"*, in *Preaching and the Non-Ordained: An Interdisciplinary Study*, edited by N. Foley, Collegeville 1983, 11-37.

Schmucki O., *Der franziskanische Bußorden im Lichte der biografischen Quellen des 13. Jahrhunderts*, in *Wissenschaft und Weisheit* 53 (1990) 157-184.
— *Linee fondamentali della "Forma Vitae" nell'esperienza di san Francesco*, in *Lettura biblico-teologica*, 183-231.
— *Il T.O.F. nelle biografie di san Francesco*, in *CF* 43 (1973) 117-143.
— *The "Way of Life According to the Gospel" as It was Discovered by St. Francis of Assisi*, in *Greyfriars Review* 2 (1988) 1-56.

Schneiders S., *Feminist Ideology Criticism and Biblical Hermeneutics*, in *Biblical Theology Bulletin* 19 (1989) 3-10.
— *The Foot Washing (John 13:1-20): An Experiment in Hermeneutics*, in *The Catholic Biblical Quarterly* 43 (1981) 76-92.
— *From Exegesis to Hermeneutics: The Problem of the Contemporary Meaning of Scripture*, in *Horizons* 8 (1981) 23-39.
— *The Paschal Imagination: Objectivity and Subjectivity in New Testament Interpretation*, in *Theological Studies* 43 (1982) 52-68.

Scocca F., *L'evoluzione comunitario-regolare dei penitenti francescani dal sec. XIII al sec. XV*, in *Ritorno a Francesco*, 157-174.

Secondo L., *The Mission of the Third Order Regular of St. Francis in the modern world*, in *Anal* TOR XIV (1978) 139-156.

Sequeira J., *The Spirituality of the Secular Franciscans in the New Rule: A Study of the S.F.O. Rule of 1978 in the light of the Letter to the Faithful*, Licentiate Thesis, The Pontifical Athenaeum Antonianum 1986.

Short W., *Hagiographical Method in Reading Franciscan Sources: Stories of Francis and Creatures in Thomas of Celano's "Vita prima" (21:58-61)*, in *Laurentianum* 29 (1988) 462-495; also in *Greyfriars Review* 4 (1990) n. 3, 63-89.

Stanislao da Campagnola, *I Fedeli e i Frati Minori*, in *I Frati Minori e il Terzo Ordine*, 11-50.
— *Francesco d'Assisi e i problemi sociali del suo tempo*, in *Laurentianum* 26 (1985) 231-45.
— *Francesco D'Assisi nei suoi scritti e nelle sue biografie dei secoli XIII-VIV*, Assisi 1981.
— *Francis of Assisi and the Social Problems of His Time*, in *Greyfriars Review* 2 (1988) 133-144.
— *L'Ordo Poenitentium di san Francesco nelle cronache del Duecento*, in *CF* 43 (1973) 145-179.

La "Supra Montem" di Niccolò IV (1289): genesi e diffusione di una regola. Atti del 5° Convegno di Studi Francescani (Ascoli Piceno, 26-27 ottobre 1987), edited by R. Pazzelli and L. Temperini, Roma 1988.

Temperini L., *L'approvazione pontificia del Terz'Ordine Francescano e la Regola di Niccolò IV*, in *Anal* TOR XI (1968) 172-184.
— *Frate Francesco a tutti i suoi fedeli*, Roma 1987.
— *Ai fratelli e alle sorelle dell'Ordine della penitenza (Regola di Niccolò IV)*, Roma 1988.
— *Il penitente francescano nella società e nella chiesa, nei secoli XIII-XIV*, in *La "Supra Montem" di Niccolò IV*, 325-79.
— *Penitential Spirituality in the Franciscan Sources*, in *Anal* TOR XIV/132 (1980) 543-589.
— *The Rule of the Third Order Regular of Saint Francis from its Origins to the Present Day*, in *Anal* TOR XIII/123 (1974) 73-91.
— *Textus et Documenta Tertii Ordinis Sancti Francisci*, in *Anal* TOR XI (1968) 25-59.

Il Terzo Ordine Francescano: lezioni di storia, legislazione, spiritualità, apostolato, edited by L. Canonici, C. Sartorazzi and L. Mariani, Roma 1967.

Terz'Ordine francescano nel pensiero dei papi da Pio IX a Pio XII (1846-1943), edited by A. Peruffo, Rome 1944.

Testi e documenti sul Terzo Ordine Francescano (sec. XIII-XV). Originale latino e versione italiana, Roma 1991.

Tickerhoof B., *Francis's Volterra Letter: A Gospel Spirituality*, in *The Cord* 29 (1979) 164-175.

Vauchez A., *La spiritualité du Moyen Age occidental VIIIe-XIIe siècles*, Vendôme 1975.

Vogel C., *Il peccatore e la penitenza nella Chiesa Antica*, Torino 1967.
— *Le pécheur et la pénitence au Moyen Age*, Paris 1969.

Zaremba T., *Franciscan Social Reform: A Study of the Third Order Secular of St. Francis as an Agency of Social Reform according to Certain Papal Documents*, Ph.D. diss., The Catholic University of America 1947.

Zudaire J., *Espiritualidad seglar franciscana. Reflexiones sobre la Regla de la Orden Franciscana Seglar*, Buenos Aires 1979.

THE RULE OF THE SECULAR FRANCISCAN ORDER[1]

Prologue: Exhortation of Saint Francis to the Brothers and Sisters in Penance[2]

In the name of the Lord!

Chapter One: Concerning Those Who Do Penance

All those who love the Lord with their whole heart, with their whole soul and mind, with all their strength (cf. Mk 12:30), and love their neighbors as themselves (cf. Mt 22:39) and hate their bodies with their vices and sins, and receive the Body and Blood of our Lord Jesus Christ, and produce worthy fruits of penance:

Oh, how happy and blessed are these men and women when they do these things and persevere in doing them, because "the spirit of the Lord will rest upon them" (cf. Is 11:2) and he will make "his home and dwelling among them" (cf. Jn 14:23), and they are the sons of the heavenly Father (cf. Mt 5:45), whose works they do, and they are spouses, brothers, and mothers of our Lord Jesus Christ (cf. Mt 12:50).

We are spouses, when by the Holy Spirit the faithful soul is united with our Lord Jesus Christ, we are brothers to him when we fulfill "the will of the Father who is in heaven" (cf. Mt 12:50).

---

[1] This officially approved English translation is taken from *The Rule of the Secular Franciscan Order, with a Catechism and Instructions*, edited by Z. Grant, Chicago 1980, 21-35.

[2] This translation of Francis' *Exhortation to the Brothers and Sisters of Penance* (the so-called "Earlier version of the *Letter to All the Faithful*") was done by M. Habig, and is based upon the *Epistola ad Fideles I*, in K. Esser *Die Opuscula des Hl. Franziskus von Assisi*, Grottaferrata 1976.

We are mothers, when we carry him in our heart and body (cf. I Cor 6:20) through divine love and a pure and sincere conscience; we give birth to him through a holy life which must give light to others by example (cf. Mt 5:16).

Oh, how glorious it is to have a great and holy Father in heaven! Oh how glorious it is to have such a beautiful and admirable Spouse, the Holy Paraclete!

Oh, how glorious it is to have such a Brother and such a Son, loved, beloved, humble, peaceful, sweet, lovable, and desirable above all: Our Lord Jesus Christ, who gave up his life for his sheep (cf. Jn 10:15) and prayed to the Father saying:

"O holy Father, protect them with your name (cf. Jn 17:11) whom you gave me out of the world. I entrusted to them the message you entrusted to me and they received it. They have known that in truth I came from you, they have believed that it was you who sent me. For these I pray, not for the world (cf. Jn 17:9). Bless and consecrate them, and I consecrate myself for their sakes. I do not pray for them alone; I pray also for those who will believe in me through their word (cf. Jn 17:20) that they may be holy by being one as we are (cf. Jn 17:11). And I desire, Father, to have them in my company where I am to see this glory of mine in your kingdom" (cf. Jn 17:6-24).

Chapter Two: Concerning Those Who Do Not Do Penance

But all those men and women who are not doing penance and do not receive the Body and Blood of our Lord Jesus Christ and live in vices and sin and yield to evil concupiscence and to the wicked desires of the flesh, and do not observe what they have promised to the Lord, and are slaves to the world, in their bodies, by carnal desires and the anxieties and the cares of this life (cf. Jn 8:41):

These are blind, because they do not see the true light, our Lord Jesus Christ; they do not have spiritual wisdom because they do not have the Son of God, who is the true wisdom of the Father. Concerning them, it is said, "Their skill was swallowed up" (Ps 107:27) and "cursed are those who turn away from your commands" (Ps 119:21). They see and acknowledge, they know and do bad things and knowingly destroy their own souls.

See, you who are blind, deceived by your enemies, the world, the flesh, and the devil, for it is pleasant to the body to commit sin and it is bitter to make it serve God because all vices and sins come out and "proceed from the heart of man" as the Lord says in the gospel (cf. Mt 7:21). And you have nothing in this world and in the next, and you thought you would possess the vanities of this world for a long time.

But you have been deceived, for the day and the hour will come to which you give no thought and which you do not know and of which you are ignorant. The body grows infirm, death approaches, and so it dies a bitter death... no matter where or when or how man dies, in the guilt of sin, without penance or satisfaction, though he can make satisfaction but does not do it.

The devil snatches the soul from his body with such anguish and tribulation that no one can know it except he who endures it, and all the talents and power and "knowledge and wisdom" (2 Chr 1:17) which they thought they had will be taken away from them (cf. Lk 8:18; Mk 4:25), and they leave their goods to relatives and friends who take and divide them and say afterwards, "Cursed be his soul because he could have given us more, he could have acquired more than he did". The worms eat up the body and so they have lost body and soul during this short earthly life and will go into the inferno where they will suffer torture without end.

All those into whose hands this letter shall have come we ask in charity that is God (cf. 1 Jn 4:17) to accept kindly and with divine love the fragrant words of our Lord Jesus Christ quoted above. And let those who do not know how to read have them read to them.

And may they keep them in their mind and carry them out, in a holy manner to the end, because they are "spirit and life" (Jn 6:64).

And, those who will not do this will have to render "an account on the day of judgment" (cf. Mt 12:36) before the tribunal of our Lord Jesus Christ (cf. Rom 14:10).

Chapter One: The Secular Franciscan Order (S.F.O.)

1. The Franciscan family, as one among many spiritual families raised up by the Holy Spirit in the Church, unites all members of the people of God — laity, religious, and priests — who recognize that they are called to follow Christ in the footsteps of Saint Francis of Assisi.

In various ways and forms but in lifegiving union with each other, they intend to make present the charism of their common Seraphic Father in the life and mission of the Church.

2. The Secular Franciscan Order holds a special place in this family circle. It is an organic union of all Catholic fraternities scattered throughout the world and open to every group of the faithful. In these fraternities the brothers and sisters, led by the Spirit, strive for perfect charity in their own secular state. By their profession they pledge themselves to live the gospel in the manner of Saint Francis by means of this rule approved by the Church.

3. The present rule, succeeding "Memoriale Propositi" (1221) and the rules approved by the Supreme Pontiffs Nicholas IV and Leo XIII, adapts the Secular Franciscan Order to the needs and expectations of the Holy Church in the conditions of changing times. Its interpretation belongs to the Holy See and its application will be made by the General Constitutions and particular statutes.

Chapter Two: The Way of Life

4. The rule and life of the Secular Franciscans is this: to observe the gospel of our Lord Jesus Christ by following the example of Saint Francis of Assisi, who made Christ the inspiration and the center of his life with God and people.

Christ, the gift of the Father's love, is the way to him, the truth into which the Holy Spirit leads us, and the life which he has come to give abundantly.

Secular Franciscans should devote themselves especially to careful reading of the gospel, going from gospel to life and life to the gospel.

5. Secular Franciscans, therefore, should seek to encounter the living and active person of Christ in their brothers and sisters, in Sacred Scripture, in the Church, and in liturgical activity. The faith of Saint Francis, who often said "I see nothing bodily of the Most High Son of God in this world except his most holy body and blood", should be the inspiration and pattern of their eucharistic life.

6. Members of the Church through Baptism, and united more intimately with the Church by profession, let them be witnesses and instruments of her mission among all people, proclaiming Christ by their life and words.

Called like Saint Francis to rebuild the Church and inspired by his example, let us want to live in full communion with the pope, bishops, and priests, fostering an open and trusting dialogue of apostolic effectiveness and creativity.

7. United by their vocation as "brothers and sisters of penance", and motivated by the dynamic power of the gospel, let them conform their thoughts and deeds to those of Christ by means of that radical interior change which the gospel itself calls "conversion". Human frailty makes it necessary that this conversion be carried out daily.

On this road to renewal the sacrament of reconciliation is the privileged sign of the Father's mercy and the source of grace.

8. As Jesus was the true worshipper of the Father, so let prayer and contemplation be the soul of all they are and do.

Let them participate in the sacramental life of the Church, above all the Eucharist. Let them join in liturgical prayer in one of the forms proposed by the Church, reliving the mysteries of the life of Christ.

9. The Virgin Mary, humble servant of the Lord, was open to his every word and call. She was embraced by Francis with indescribable love and declared the protectress and advocate of his family. The Secular Franciscans should express their ardent love for her by imitating her complete self-giving and by praying earnestly and confidently.

10. United themselves to the redemptive obedience of Jesus, who placed his will into the Father's hands, let them faithfully fulfill the duties proper to their various circumstances of life. Let them also follow the poor and crucified Christ, witness to him even in difficulties and persecutions.

11. Trusting in the Father, Christ chose for himself and his mother a poor and humble life, even though he valued created things attentively and lovingly. Let the Secular Franciscans seek a proper spirit of detachment from temporal goods by simplifying their own material needs. Let them be mindful that according to the gospel they are stewards of the goods received for the benefit of God's children.

Thus, in the spirit of "the Beatitudes", and as pilgrims and strangers on their way to the home of the Father, they should strive to purify their hearts from every tendency and yearning for possession and power.

12. Witnessing to the good yet to come and obliged to acquire purity of heart because of the vocation they have embraced, they should set themselves free to love God and their brothers and sisters.

13. As the Father sees in every person the features of his Son, the firstborn of many brothers and sisters, so the Secular Franciscans with a gentle and courteous spirit accept all people as a gift of the Lord and an image of Christ.

A sense of community will make them joyful and ready to place themselves on an equal basis with all people, especially with the lowly for whom they shall strive to create conditions of life worthy of people redeemed by Christ.

14. Secular Franciscans, together with all people of good will, are called to build a more fraternal and evangelical world so that the kingdom of God may be brought about more effectively. Mindful that anyone "who follows Christ, the perfect man, becomes more of a man himself", let them exercise their responsibilities competently in the Christian spirit of service.

15. Let them individually and collectively be in the forefront in promoting justice by the testimony of their human lives and their courageous initiatives. Especially in the field of public life, they should make definite choices in harmony with their faith.

16. Let them esteem work both as a gift and as a sharing in the creation, redemption, and service of the human community.

17. In their family they should cultivate the Franciscan spirit of peace, fidelity, and respect for life, striving to make of it a sign of a world already renewed in Christ.

By living the grace of matrimony, husbands and wives in particular should bear witness in the world to the love of Christ for his Church. They should joyfully accompany their children on their human and spiritual journey by providing a simple and open Christian education and being attentive to the vocation of each child.

18. Moreover they should respect all creatures, animate and inanimate, which "bear the imprint of the Most High", and they should strive to move from the temptation of exploiting creation to the Franciscan concept of universal kinship.

19. Mindful that they are bearers of peace which must be built up unceasingly, they should seek out ways of unity and fraternal harmony through dialogue, trusting in the presence of the divine seed in everyone and in the transforming power of love and pardon.

Messengers of perfect joy in every circumstance, they should strive to bring joy and hope to others.

Since they are immersed in the resurrection of Christ, which gives true meaning to Sister Death, let them serenely tend toward the ultimate encounter with the Father.

Chapter Three: Life in Fraternity

20. The Secular Franciscan Order is divided into fraternities of various levels - local, regional, national, and international. Each one has its own moral personality in the Church. These various fraternities are coordinated and united according to the norm of this rule and of the constitutions.

21. On various levels, each fraternity is animated and guided by a council and minister (or president) who are elected by the professed according to the constitutions.

Their service, which lasts for a definite period, is marked by a ready and willing spirit and is a duty of responsibility to each member and to the community.

Within themselves the fraternities are structured in different ways according to the norms of the constitutions, according to the various needs of their members and their regions, and under the guidance of the respective council.

22. The local fraternity is to be established canonically. It becomes the basic unit of the whole Order and a visible sign of the Church, the community of love. This should be the privileged place for developing a sense of Church and the Franciscan vocation and for enlivening the apostolic life of its members.

23. Requests for admission to the Secular Franciscan Order must be presented to the local fraternity, whose council decides upon the acceptance of new brothers and sisters.

Admission into the Order is gradually attained through a time of initiation, a period of formation of at least one year, and profession of the rule. The entire community is engaged in this process of growth by its own manner of living. The age for profession and the distinctive Franciscan sign are regulated by the statutes.

Profession by its nature is a permanent commitment.

Members who find themselves in particular difficulties should discuss their problems with the council in fraternal dialogue.

Withdrawal or permanent dismissal from the Order, if necessary, is an act of the fraternity council according to the norm of the constitutions.

24. To foster communion among members, the council should organize regular and frequent meetings of the community as well as meeting with other Franciscan groups, especially with youth groups. It should adopt appropriate means for growth in Franciscan and ecclesial life and encourage everyone to a life of fraternity. This communion continues with deceased brothers and sisters through prayer for them.

25. Regarding expenses necessary for the life of the fraternity and the needs of worship, of the apostolate, and of charity, all the brothers and sisters should offer a contribution according to their means. Local fraternities should contribute toward the expenses of the higher fraternity councils.

26. As a concrete sign of communion and coresponsibility, the councils on various levels, in keeping with the constitutions, shall ask for suitable and well prepared religious for spiritual assistance. They should make this request to the superiors of the four religious Franciscan families, to whom the Secular Fraternity has been united for centuries.

To promote fidelity to the charism as well as observance of the rule and to receive greater support in the life of the fraternity, the minister or president, with the consent of the council, should take care to ask for a regular pastoral visit by the competent religious superiors as well as for a fraternal visit from those of the higher fraternities, according to the norm of the constitutions.

"May whoever observes all this be filled in heaven with the blessing of the most high Father, and on earth with that of his beloved Son, together with the Holy Spirit, the Comforter" (Blessing of St. Francis from the *Testament*).

INTRODUCTION

The Secular Franciscan Order, which prior to 1978 was called the Franciscan Third Order Secular, received a new Rule on June 24, 1978. The Decree of Promulgation, issued by Pope Paul VI states:

> The Seraphic Patriarch St. Francis of Assisi, during his life and even after his beautiful death, not only attracted many to serve God in the religious family founded by him, but also drew numerous members of the laity to enter his communities while remaining in the world (as far as possible)...
>
> With praiseworthy initiative and with common accord the four Franciscan families for ten years have striven to prepare a new rule for the Franciscan Third Order Secular, or as it is now called, the Secular Franciscan Order. This was necessary because of the changed conditions of the times and because of the teaching and encouragement given them by the Second Vatican Council. Therefore, our dearly beloved Sons, the four ministers general of the Franciscan Order, have requested that we approve the Rule presented to us[1]. Following the example of some of our predecessors, the latest being Pope Leo XIII, we have willingly decided to grant their request[2]. In this way, we nurture the hope that the

[1] In this instance "sons" refers appropriately enough to the four male ministers general of the four different branches of the Franciscan Order for men. However, with this first quotation, a brief explanation of the rule to be followed throughout this study with respect to the use of language would appear apropos. The main text and all translations by this author will use inclusive language. However, quotations taken from other authors and from official documents (including those documents promulgated in Latin but which have an officially approved English translation) will preserve the exact language of the text - even where male generic language, rather than inclusive language, has been used.

[2] The first official papally approved Rule for the Secular Franciscan Order was the *Supra Montem* issued by Nicholas IV in 1289. This Rule remained

form of life preached by that admirable man of Assisi will gain a new impetus and will flourish vigorously[3].

This new Rule thus claims to present, in the language and theology of the Second Vatican Council, the thirteenth century Rule[4] of the "Third Order" as "founded" by St. Francis[5].

---

in effect until 1883 when Leo XIII issued a new Rule with his Apostolic Letter, *Misericors Dei Filius*, which then remained in effect until Paul VI issued this new *Rule of 1978*. These three Rules, as well as other relevant documents, will be analyzed in *Chapter III* and *Chapter IV*.

[3] The official Latin text of Paul VI's Apostolic Letter, *Seraphicus Patriarcha*, with which he approved the new Rule of the Secular Franciscan Order may be found in *AAS* 70 (1978) 454ff, as well as in *Tertius Ordo* XXXIX (1978) 107-117. The official English translation may be found in *The Rule of the Secular Franciscan Order, with a Catechism and Instructions*, edited by Z. Grant, Chicago 1980, 1-35. The full text of the Rule has been included at the beginning of this volume, pp. 31-38.

[4] The papal bull, *Supra Montem*, promulgated by Nicholas IV on 18 August 1289, was the first "official" Rule for those penitents who eventually came to be known as the Franciscan Third Order Secular. However, the *Supra Montem* was not the earliest Rule. The origin and development of the Rule during the thirteenth century will be analyzed in detail in *Chapter III*.

[5] The terms "Third Order" and "founder" are laden with uncritical presuppositions and are, unfortunately, often used with imprecision. Although this Order of Penitents came to be known as the "Third Order" or the "Brothers and Sisters of the Third Order of St. Francis", the designation "Third Order" is a late development and postdates Francis by some fifty years. It appears in the 1280s when the brothers and sisters without distinction were said to be "of the third order" or "of penance", with these two designations at times being used together. But at the time of Francis these groups were *not* called "Third Order" but rather "penitents", "brothers and sisters of penance", "pinzocheri", "bizochi", and "vestite". In fact, this varied terminology continued even after the promulgation of *Supra Montem* in 1289 which spoke specifically about the Order of Penance founded by St. Francis. Cf. A. Pompei, *Terminologia varia dei penitenti*, in *Il movimento francescano della penitenza nella società medioevale*, edited by M. D'Alatri, Roma 1980, 13-14; and M. D'Alatri, *Il Terzo Ordine*, in *Francesco, il francescanesimo, e la cultura della nuova Europa*, edited by I. Baldelli and A. Romanini, Firenze 1986, 119-120.

Thus, this study will attempt to use the term "Third Order" with some precision, that is, only where this group of penitents is so designated and not

The hope clearly expressed in this decree of promulgation, the hope which motivated the formulation of this new Rule, is that this contemporary articulation of the way of life preached by Francis of Assisi in the thirteenth century will give a "new impetus" to the Secular Franciscan Order so that it might "flourish vigorously". The four Ministers General of the Franciscan family, in their letter which accompanies the new Rule, also speak of this hope:

> The hope of renewal hinges upon returning to the origins and to the spiritual experience of Francis of Assisi and of the brothers and sisters of penance who received from him their inspiration and guidance. This sentiment is also included in the prologue, "Letter to the Faithful" (recensio prior) and in the constant references to the teaching and example of St. Francis. This renewal also depends upon openness to the Spirit in the signs of the times[6].

However, more than ten years after the new Rule was promulgated, seemingly this hope has not been realized. While some fraternities of the Secular Franciscan Order have experienced growth and renewal, in general, the Secular Franciscan Order appears not to have gained a "new impetus".

Given that this hope remains frustrated, we might well ask why this renewal has not been effective or, at least, more effective and widespread. The fact that this new Rule has not attained its objective leads one to question if the Rule itself is not somehow flawed. Has it misinterpreted either the Franciscan charism or the "changed conditions of the times"? Or perhaps, has the Rule not yet been read and

---

in a generic fashion referring to the entire history of this movement or group. Similarly, prior to a detailed discussion in *Chapter II*, appropriate reserve will be exercised in speaking of Francis as "founder" of this group of penitents. The first official Rule, *Supra Montem*, clearly recognizes St. Francis as the founder of the Order of Penitents. However, as will be shown, in speaking of Francis as "founder" of the "First", "Second", and "Third" Orders, the term is used not in an equivalent but in an analogous sense. Thus, reserve will be exercised in the use of both terms, "founder" and "Third Order", until analyses in subsequent chapters allow for more precision and definition.

[6] *Letter from the four Ministers General of the Franciscan Family*, dated October 4, 1978. Cf. *The Rule of the Secular Franciscan Order, with a Catechism and Instructions*, edited by Z. Grant, 13-14.

understood correctly? Has this new Rule captured the essence of that "form of life preached by that admirable man of Assisi" in the thirteenth century? And if so, has it been articulated effectively within a contemporary theology and spirituality of the laity?

Since no critical work has yet been done on this new Rule, this study seeks to provide a critical analysis of the document as a basis from which to respond to these and other questions. This particular study draws upon Biblical methodologies for its analysis. The methods and results of historical criticism, literary criticism, and redaction criticism will be employed in our study of the relevant Franciscan texts. As Desbonnets points out, in terms of Franciscan origins,

> time in most instances has wiped out the fragile vestiges of what we would dearly like to know... we know history only through documents that, to a large extent, are more or less contemporary reports of events in which we are interested. Outside these documents the events do not exist. It helps, then, to put them into proper perspective so as to understand the reasons that caused them to be written, to penetrate the mental universe of their authors[7].

Thus, after exploring the exegetical and literary questions, we will consider the historical context of these thirteenth century documents. Finally, to move beyond the the exegetical, literary, and historical questions, we will follow a method suggested by the hermeneutical theory of Paul Ricoeur. We will utilize Ricoeur's approach to interpreting texts in order to move towards an interpretation of the 1978 Rule of the Secular Franciscan Order, to what the thirteenth century "form of life" preached by St. Francis means today.

Following the spirit of renewal engendered by the Second Vatican Council[8], and the challenge within this decree of promulgation which

---

[7] T. Desbonnets, *From Intuition to Institution: The Franciscans*, translated by P. Duggan and J. Du Charme, Chicago 1988, 2.

[8] According to the Decree of the Second Vatican Council, the "appropriate renewal of religious life involves two simultaneous processes: (1) a continuous return to the sources of all Christian life and to the original inspiration behind a given community and (2) an adjustment of the community to the changed conditions of the times". Cf. *Decree on the Appropriate Renewal of the Religious Life*, in *The Documents of Vatican II*, edited by W. Abbott, New York 1966, 468.

implicitly calls for a return to the original charism of the founder, this study seeks a *radical* understanding of the Order's purpose, meaning and charism[9]. To obtain this radical understanding we must explore the horizon of the "form of life" preached by Francis, the world from which the text emerged. But we must also explore the world which the text projects. We must ask what the text meant if we are to understand what the text means; we must understand who the Franciscan penitents were if we are to understand who the Secular Franciscans are. In order, then, to enter this dialogue, this study will examine cultural and religious context within which this Franciscan lay movement found its origin, came to its earliest expression, and later developed and was transformed.

More specifically, *Chapter I* will investigate the earliest sources concerning the origins of the Secular Franciscan Order. Informed by recent exegetical and literary analyses of the texts, we will examine the extant narrative accounts for historical information relative to the genesis and development of this "Third Order" of Saint Francis. Since these accounts claim that Francis gave a Rule or "norm of life" to his lay followers, the writings of Francis will then be explored in an attempt to identify this "primitive rule"[10].

---

[9] *Radical* is here intended in the literal sense, that is, a going to the root of the question, from the Latin, *radix*, meaning root.

[10] Unfortunately, any reference to the early Rule or Rules is confusing at best. While the first officially approved Rule of the Secular Franciscan Order dates from 1289 with Nicholas IV's promulgation of *Supra Montem*, there were in fact other "Rules" prior to 1289. Thus, our terminology needs to be clarified. In short, in this study we will use the term "primitive Rule" to indicate, in a very specific sense, the Rule (*norma vitae*) given by Francis himself to his lay followers according to the testimony of the early biographical sources. We will use the term "early rule" to refer, in a broader sense, to all of the documents which preceded and gave rise to the first "official" Rule of the Secular Franciscan Order given in 1289. A bit more specificity about the problem and our proposed designations will be offered here in the event it might prove helpful. However, all of the said documents and various terminology will receive detailed attention and further specification in subsequent chapters.

Scholars now generally concur that Francis' *Letter to the All the Faithful* represents the early "form of life" given to the penitents by Francis. Thus, we might be tempted to speak of this letter as the "first Rule". However, that terminology causes confusion since some speak of the *Supra Montem*, the

Chapter II, following an historical-critical approach, will attempt to identify the historical context of the "primitive rule" of this order of penitents. But before examining the cultural and religious context of the thirteenth century, this chapter will focus upon two distinct but related phenomena that affected the religious climate of the thirteenth century: the evolution of the Order of Penance and of the lay apostolic movements. The second chapter will attempt to illuminate the social

---

first official Rule, or at least the first papally approved official Rule, as the "first" Rule. Further complicating the issue, there are two versions of this so-called *Letter to All the Faithful*, and some debate concerning the chronology of the two versions. Even the traditional title of these two texts, *The Letter to All the Faithful*, misrepresents their content. Therefore, after a discussion of the nomenclature of these texts, this study will use the designations "*Earlier Exhortation*" and "*Later Exhortation*" to distinguish these two texts. The origin, content, and nomenclature of these two existing versions of the *Letter to All the Faithful*, as well as current theories and evidence as to the relationship between these two versions, will be examined in detail in *Chapter III*. However, to be more specific, "primitive rule", in its narrowest sense, here indicates the shorter version of the *Letter to All the Faithful*, the "*Earlier Exhortation*".

Beginning in 1221, many penitents adopted the *Memoriale propositi* (of which the earliest versions date from 1228 and which, in large part, is taken over into the first official Rule, Nicholas IV's *Supra Montem* of 1289). The *Memoriale propositi* (which in part parallels the way of life for the Humiliati, and which will be analyzed in *Chapter III*) approximated a "Rule" much more than did the *Earlier Exhortation* and thus this *propositum* could also be considered a "first Rule". The term "first Rule" will, therefore, be avoided. Rather, when speaking specifically about any one of these early documents which could in some way be assessed as a "first Rule", this study will use the particular identifying name of the document. However, given the fluidity of the period, the organic growth or evolution of the Rule from the *Earlier Exhortation* to the *Supra Montem* of 1289, we cannot speak with great precision about "the Rule" at a given particular moment. Thus, when speaking generally about the Rule in this period prior to the official promulgation of the *Supra Montem* in 1289, the term "early rule" will be used, in a broad sense, to designate both versions of the *Letter to All the Faithful* as well as the various versions of the *Memoriale propositi*. That is, the term "early rule" will be used to designate all of the documents, dating roughly from 1212 up to 1289, which present either Francis' guidance or specific legislation for these lay penitents which gave rise to and are later replaced by the first official Rule of the Secular Franciscan Order, the *Supra Montem* of 1289.

and religious context within which Francis lived and was formed, within which this lay Franciscan movement was born and took shape, in an attempt to understand not only Francis and his writings, but also to "shed light on the stimuli, dynamic, and choices of the first and second generation men and women who responded to Francis' message"[11].

Chapter III, drawing upon the historical analysis presented in the second chapter, will analyze Francis' guidance for these lay followers. Both versions of what has been traditionally known as the *Letter to All the Faithful* (the *Epistola ad Fideles I* and the *Epistola ad Fideles II* or the documents that we have designated as the *Earlier Exhortation* and the *Later Exhortation*) will be studied. This analysis will draw upon exegetical and historical research, as well as some structural analysis by literary critics. The third chapter will then review how the primitive Rule developed by analyzing the *Memoriale propositi* of 1221 and the officially approved *Rule of 1289*, the *Supra Montem*.

Chapter IV utilizes the approach of redaction criticism to study how the Rule of the Secular Franciscan Order developed from 1289 to 1978. The chapter will present a comparative study of the *Rule of 1289* and the *Rule of 1883*. However, the greater part of the chapter will be devoted to an analysis of the development of the new *Rule of 1978*. It will examine the redaction process from 1965 through 1978 through an analysis of the archival documents which preserve a record of that development.

Finally, after having analyzed the development of the new *Rule of 1978*, *Chapter V* will suggest an approach for interpreting the Rule. Building upon the foundation laid in the earlier chapters (utilizing the results of the relevant historical critical studies), *Chapter V* will propose a method for moving beyond those exegetical studies, for moving beyond what the Rule meant, to what the Rule means. Let us, then, begin the journey towards an interpretation of the 1978 Rule of the Secular Franciscan Order.

---

[11] L. Landini, *The Historical Context of the Franciscan Movement*, in *Franciscan History: The Three Orders of St. Francis of Assisi*, by L. Iriarte, Chicago 1982, 557-58.

CHAPTER I

THE EARLY SOURCES

Since our objective is to understand the "Rule of Life" given by Francis to his lay followers, the most obvious place to start our investigation would appear to be with this earliest Rule. Among the surviving documents which provide us with information about this man from Assisi and the early Franciscan movement, the accounts written by Thomas of Celano, Julian of Speyer, and Bonaventure of Bagnoregio give the clearest testimony that Francis did give the penitents a "Rule of Life"[1]. However, any attempt to derive historical information from medieval texts demands that we read and interpret them carefully.

PROBLEMS AND METHODS IN THE USE OF THE SOURCES

Statement of the Problem

The early biographies of Francis follow the conventions not of modern biography but of medieval hagiography. They do not present historical facts in a strict chronological order according to our contemporary understanding of biographical data. Rather, they present the spiritual life of the saint, that is, they proclaim how God acted in the saint's life and how that person imaged Christ. That is not to say that these

---

[1] A. Matanić, *I Penitenti francescani dal 1221 (Memoriale) al 1289 (Regola bollata) principalmente attraverso i loro statuti e le regole*, in *CF* 43 (1973) 44.

legends do not contain historical information. Medieval biography or hagiography, especially as influenced by the developing canonization process, became more personal and individualized[2]. While the biographers of Francis incorporate various hagiographical types, they nonetheless build their framework around an historical reality. These legends do furnish important historical data, but must be read carefully[3].

Of all these hagiographical works on Francis, the *Fioretti* or *Little Flowers of Saint Francis* continues to be the most widely read[4]. Written by an anonymous author in the fourteenth century, the *Fioretti* records the origin of the "Third Order" as follows:

> They [St. Francis and companions] arrived at a village called Cannara. And St. Francis began to preach, first ordering the swallows who were twittering to keep quiet until he had finished preaching. And the swallows obeyed him. He preached there so fervently that all the men and women of that village, as a result of his sermon and of the miracle of the swallows, in their great devotion wanted to follow him and abandon the village. But St. Francis did not let them, saying to them: "Don't be in a hurry and don't leave, for I will arrange what you should do for the salvation of your souls". And from that time he planned to organize the Third Order of the Continent for the salvation of all people everywhere[5].

A naïve reading of this account in the *Fioretti* has led to the popular notion that Francis founded the "Third Order". An uncritical reading of the early sources can lead to the erroneous belief that somehow the Order of Penitents began with Saint Francis, but the Order of

---

[2] A. Vauchez, *La Sainteté en Occident aux dernier siècles du Moyen Age, d'après les procès de canonisation et les documents hagiographiques*, Rome 1981.

[3] Unfortunately, the English term "legend" generally connotes an account that is imaginative and historically untrue. Throughout this study, "legend" will be used in its technical or hagiographical sense rather than its usual perjorative connotation, that is, as an account that was meant to be read publicly. (The Latin term *legenda* is derived from the verb *legere* meaning to read).

[4] In his introduction to the *Fioretti*, Raphael Brown makes the claim that the *Fioretti* has been the most widely read book about Francis for the last hundred years. Cf. *Omnibus*, 1269. For a general introduction to the work and an English translation of the text, cf. *Omnibus*, 1269-1530.

[5] *Fioretti* 16: *Omnibus*, 1335-36.

Penitents existed prior to Francis[6]. We must read each of these accounts within its historical context and in relation to other historical data.

Unfortunately, the early sources offer no easy access to historical information concerning the origins of the Secular Franciscan Order. This text from the *Fioretti* (a very late source in the tradition) cannot be read as a source for the life of Francis and the origins of the Franciscan movement. Critical studies have demonstrated that the text represents the mind of the friar community at La Verna in the fourteenth century[7]. When read critically, it does not provide us with historical information about the so-called "Third Order".

As William Short points out in his discussion of hagiographical method with respect to the early Franciscan sources, the "legends of Francis are meant to *edify*, both by exalting the figure of the new saint, and

---

[6] In 1963, Marion Habig wrote a history of the "Third Order" so that Secular Franciscans could "read and study it for themselves and learn the main historical facts about their 750-year-old order". In it he claims that it "is now historically certain that St. Francis is the true founder of the Order of Penance or Third Order, and also that he founded it before 1221, the year which has hitherto been regarded by most writers as the date of its founding". Cf. M. Habig - M. Hegener, *A Short History of the Third Order*, Chicago 1963, 7, 16-17.

Giovanna Casagrande represents an example of a more critical approach. In her study of the early sources relative to the origins of the Secular Franciscan Order, Casagrande notes that, while we know that Francis was concerned about the laity and suggested some norms for the penitential life, that seems insufficient to claim that he actually founded an Order of Penitents. The various biographies speak clearly about three orders, but without giving any precision or detail about this Rule or Form of Life given by Francis to the penitents. Casagrande's solution, therefore, is to speak about the existence of penitents before and during Francis' time of preaching, penitents who very naturally and spontaneously aligned themselves with Francis and the friars giving life *de facto* to the Secular Franciscan Order while *de iure* that life would have to await the *Supra Montem* of Nicholas IV. Casagrande therefore calls for more research in particular towns and cities, that is, more social history. Cf. G. Casagrande, *L'Ordine Francescano Secolare nelle prime Fonti Francescane*, in *L'Italia Francescana* 55 (1980) 216. We will address the topic of Francis' "founding" of the Secular Franciscan Order in *Chapter III*.

[7] A. Fisher, *A Reconsideration of the Fioretti, the Little Flowers of St. Francis*, in *CF* 57 (1897) 5-6.

also by encouraging people to seek his intercession"[8]. But these sources *are* about Francis and the Franciscan movement. We can derive historical information from the different accounts, but we must read these early biographies of Francis carefully. In attempting to discern the historical origins of the "Third Order" from the data provided in the early sources, we must read with an attentiveness to each work's genre and historical context.

These sources present an additional obstacle to our drawing historical information about the "Third Order" from them. Since they focus upon Francis and the foundation of the Order of Friars Minor, these sources contain very limited material concerning the origin of the Secular Franciscan Order. Thus, before considering the texts themselves, let us first identify the sources, the problems involved in the use of these texts, and a method for reading these early sources.

Identifying the Sources

The different sources for our understanding of Francis can be divided into three types: the writings of Francis himself, the early biographies, and the reminiscences of Francis' close companions[9]. In all three categories, the first task is to establish a critical text from which to work from among the extant manuscripts with their variant readings, due either to copyist error or subsequent editorial revision. Fortunately, critical editions of these early Franciscan documents have been established and published[10].

---

[8] W. Short, *Hagiographical Method in Reading Franciscan Sources: Stories of Francis and Creatures in Thomas of Celano's "Vita prima" (21:58-61)*, in *Laurentianum* 29 (1988) 468; also in *Greyfriars Review* 4 (1990) n. 3, 63-89. For a brief overview of some guidelines for the study of hagiographical legends, see pages 466-68.

[9] This division is suggested by R. Brooke in *Recent Work on St. Francis of Assisi*, in *Analecta Bollandiana* 100 (1982) 654; see also: E. Pásztor, *The Sources of Francis's Biographies*, in *Greyfriars Review* 1 (1987) 33.

[10] A precise reference to the critical edition of each text considered in this study will be cited in its corresponding note. However, in general, the critical edition for each of Francis' writings may be found in *Opuscula Sancti Patris Francisci Assisiensis*, edited by C. Esser, Grottaferrata (Roma) 1978. The critical editions of the early "Lives" of St. Francis may be found for the most part in volume X of the *Analecta Franciscana*. For an overview of the discovery and publication of these documents, cf. Pásztor, *The Sources*, esp. 31-32.

It is at the next level within the hermeneutical process, the historical-critical evaluation of the various legends and their interrelationships, that much remains to be done and where we move into the so-called "Franciscan Question" which has plagued all of Franciscan study for almost a century and which must, therefore, be addressed here briefly[11].

The "Franciscan Question"

The genesis of this term, the "Franciscan Question", can be traced back to the work of Paul Sabatier at the turn of the century, even though he himself did not use the term[12]. The *Franciscan Question* as a problem of historiography and of historical methodology arose shortly after and as a result of work in the Biblical field at the end of the nineteenth and the beginning of the twentieth centuries. As Biblical research began to focus upon the relationship between the historical Jesus and the Christ of faith, Sabatier, who published his biography of Francis in 1894, began to focus upon the difference between the historical Francis and the Francis of the early biographies and legends[13]. In 1898 Sabatier published a manuscript called the *Speculum Perfectionis* with the claim that he had discovered the original work of Francis' early companion, Brother Leo, in a document dating from 1227[14]. Later

---

[11] For treatment of the "Franciscan Question", cf. Brooke, *Recent Work*, 653-76; Desbonnets, *From Intuition to Institution*, 151-65; Pásztor, *The Sources*, 31-40; *La "Questione Francescana" dal Sabatier ad oggi, (Atti del I Convegno Internazionale della Società Internazionale di Studi Francescani)*, Assisi 1974.

[12] This term comes from an article written by S. Minocchi in 1902. Cf. S. Minocchi, *Storia della letteratura italiana* 39 (1902) 293. Desbonnets, in reflecting upon this unfortunate choice of a title, suggests that had the article been entitled *Research on the dating of some Franciscan documents of the Thirteenth century* rather than *The Franciscan Question*, the whole debate would have been confined to a small circle of specialists. However, in 1902 Minocchi wrote about the *Franciscan Question* and it has since ensnared every researcher. Cf. Desbonnets, *Saint François d'Assise - Documents*, 16.

[13] F. Raurell, *Linee tematiche: alla ricerca di un approccio molteplice alle Fonti Francescane*, in *Laurentianum* 29 (1988) 185-86.

[14] P. Sabatier, *Speculum Perfectionis seu S. Francisci Assisiensis Legenda Antiquissima Collection de documents pour l'histoire religieuse et littéraire du Moyen Age, I*, Paris 1898.

research revealed the *Speculum Perfectionis* to be a document dating from the fourteen century[15]. Nonetheless, even though the *Speculum Perfectionis* was shown to be a compilation dating from 1318 and thus not the work of Brother Leo, subsequent discoveries of manuscripts thought to be the source material for the *Speculum Perfectionis* led scholars to believe that it was possible to identify the stories of the early companions in their primitive form[16]. Thus, Sabatier's discovery and claim ignited a search for the earliest or most reliable sources for the life of Francis.

Initially, the *Franciscan Question* designated the search for the writings of Brother Leo and of the other early companions, writings considered to be free from an "official" bias and thus judged to be more historical or reliable. More generally, the *Franciscan Question* has been used throughout the century as a technical term to designate the problem of the chronological and literary relationships among the various legends, accounts, and biographies of Francis[17].

This study makes no claim to answer this *Franciscan Question* (which, at present, is not possible), nor even to present a comprehensive treatment of the history of the debate (which, though of scholarly interest, remains outside the scope of this study's immediate concerns). In fact, no adequate synthesis of that debate can be given because it has been conducted for almost a century in about six different languages and because there are fundamental points which are still disputed[18]. Just the enormity of the material (not only the diversity of the various medieval

---

[15] The subsequent discovery of another manuscript of the *Speculum Perfectionis* which was dated 1318 revealed that the date on the manuscript discovered by Sabatier was due to a scibal error, the substitution of an "X" for a "C" in the date: MCCXXVIII for MCCCXVIII. Although the date 1318 is not absolute (it appears on only one manuscript), it is quite probable. Cf. the *Introduction* to the *Mirror of Perfection*: *Omnibus*, 1105-1113.

[16] Brooke, *Recent Work*, 654. For a more complete discussion of Sabatier's discovery, cf. R. Brooke, *Scripta Leonis, Rufini, et Angeli, Sociorum S. Francisci*, Oxford 1970, 5-7.

[17] G. Philippart, *Les Écrits des Compagnons de S. François: aperçu de la "Question Franciscaine" dès origines à nos jours*, in *Analecta Bollandiana* 90 (1972) 143-66; Desbonnets, *From Intuition to Institution*, 151-65; L. Pellegrini, *Un secolo di "lettura" delle Fonti biografiche di Francesco d'Assisi*, in *Laurentianum* 29 (1988) 223-50.

[18] Brooke, *Recent Work*, 670.

legends, but also all of the subsequent scholarly research - relative to the ensuing *Franciscan Question*) could cause us to abandon our attempt to discern the historical origins of the "Third Order" from these sources.

But we are, in fact, in a good position to know about Francis, his relationship with the penitents, and the origins of that order. While the enormity of the research can be overwhelming, the fact remains that we have discovered a lot about Francis and the beginnings of the Franciscan movement. But, before we venture forth into the texts themselves, we do need to address the problematic and propose a methodology which will allow us to read the early sources appropriately.

Proposing a Method

Methodologically, we propose an inclusive reading of all of the early sources for the life of Francis which deal with the origin of the Secular Franciscan Order. We turn then to the texts themselves, not in search of the one sacred or most reliable witness, but rather to read each text as part of the history of the Franciscan movement. Each text will be examined, in light of its *Sitz im Leben* and literary genre, for information concerning Francis' role in the foundation of what came to be known as the "Franciscan Third Order". Margaret Carney, in speaking about an approach to the sources, defends this type of inclusive reading:

> Those familiar with the voluminous research on the textual intricacies of these sources, the questions of dating and authorship will smile at the naïveté of such a proposal. Perhaps it is, however, this very wealth of scholarship that emboldens us to hazard this reading. Whereas such a process would have certainly led to hopeless confusion a few decades ago, it can be attempted at this point in time precisely because we possess an adequate critique of the materials at hand. A judicious use of these critical materials allows us to use each of these major biographical sources in a way that does not lose sight of what strengths it brings to our topic and what inadequacies it entails... While, it would appear that there will always be room for more surprises in the study of the Franciscan sources, it would also appear that we are at a juncture at which we can assay this kind of reading with a modicum of confidence[19].

---

[19] M. Carney, *Francis and Clare: A Critical Examination of the Sources*, in *Laurentianum* 30 (1989) 30-31.

Thus we will survey the various accounts, reading them within their historical context, informed by recent research and various methodological analyses. Further, the information which emerges from these hagiographical writings will be supplemented with historical data furnished by "external" witnesses, that is, thirteenth century non-Franciscan sources such as historical annals and papal documents. Finally, after we have synthesized the results of this "inclusive" reading of the texts, we will then consider that testimony in connection with Francis' own writings.

However, a critical understanding of the early sources and Francis' own writings will necessitate a thorough examination of the historical context, that is, the Franciscan history from which each of these texts arose and to which each of them gives voice. Every effort will be made to read these texts within the context of the Franciscan movement and to analyze critically the "primitive Rule" within the context of Franciscan history[20].

This method will necessarily involve much material and span several chapters. We will begin, in this first chapter, with an inclusive reading of the early sources' portrayal of the origins of the "Third Order". We will then move, in the second chapter, to a more detailed examination of the historical context from which Francis and the Franciscan movement emerged. We will then be able, in the third chapter, to proceed to a critical analysis of the "primitive Rule". Let us begin, then, by turning to the early sources.

Thirteenth Century Sources on Francis and the Penitents

Francis of Assisi died on the evening of October 3, 1226. Less than six months later Cardinal Hugolino, whom Francis had chosen as Cardinal-Protector of his order, was elected as the successor to Pope Honorius III, taking the name Gregory IX. The new pope immediately started procedures to canonize Francis and, since a canonization presumes a biography of the saint, he commissioned Thomas of Celano to write a biography of Francis[21]. This work by Thomas of Celano

[20] D. Flood, *Franciscan Reading*, in *Haversack* 2 (1979) n. 6, 15.

[21] Gregory IX probably commissioned Thomas because of his writing ability. Thomas' education and training become evident in his eloquent style of writing in Latin. Cf. Desbonnets, *From Intuition to Institution*, 154.

presents the earliest narrative source on the life and work of Francis. Therefore, we will begin with Thomas' presentation of Francis' relationship with the early penitents. We will then consider other thirteenth century texts in a somewhat chronological order[22].

Thomas of Celano

Thomas of Celano wrote this officially commissioned biography sometime in 1228, the year of Francis' canonization, but two brief years after the death of the Poverello[23]. This biography came to be known as *The First Life of St. Francis*, or the *Vita prima*, to distinguish it from the *Second Life of St. Francis*, or the *Vita secunda*, which Thomas wrote in 1246 to supplement his first work[24]. Thomas' *Vita prima* consists of three books. Thomas himself, in the prologue, outlines the parts: Book I "follows the historical order", Book II focuses on the last two years of Francis' life, and Book III records miracles attributed to the saint[25]. However, even the so-called "historical" section follows the medieval hagiographic tradition and, in Thomas' own words, "is given over, for the most part, to the purity of his [Francis'] conduct and life, to his holy striving after virtue, and to his salutary teachings"[26].

Thomas places the text which concerns us right after the return of Francis and his early companions from Rome, where they had gone to obtain Innocent III's approval of their way of life. The pope gave his blessing to their project and instructed them to go forth and "preach penance to all"[27]. Thus, Francis "went about the towns and villages announcing the kingdom of God, preaching peace, teaching salvation

---

[22] Schmucki offers an extensive study of how the "Third Order" is presented in the early biographies of Francis. Cf. O. Schmucki, *Il T.O.F. nelle biografie di san Francesco*, in *CF* 43 (1973) 117-143.

[23] Thomas of Celano, though not one of the earliest companions of Francis, did know Francis personally, and quite probably was received into the order by Francis himself in 1215. Cf. Desbonnets, *From Intuition to Institution*, 153; and the *Introduction* to the works of Thomas of Celano: *Omnibus*, 179-212.

[24] Brooke, *Scripta Leonis*, 3.

[25] *Omnibus*, 227-28.

[26] *Ibid.*, 227.

[27] *1 Cel* 32-33: *Omnibus*, 254-56.

and penance unto the remission of sins"[28]. Francis' preaching had an effect. According to Thomas' account, those who were moved by Francis' preaching asked for his guidance, and Francis responded:

> Many of the people, both noble and ignoble, cleric and lay, impelled by divine inspiration, began to come to St. Francis, wanting to carry on the battle constantly under his discipline and under his leadership[29]. All of these the holy man of God, like a plenteous river of heavenly grace, watered with streams of gifts; he enriched the field of their hearts with flowers of virtue, for he was an excellent craftsman; and, according to his plan, rule, and teaching, proclaimed before all, the Church is being renewed in both sexes, and the threefold army[30] of those to be [saved] is triumphing[31]. To all he gave a norm of life, and he showed in truth the way of salvation in every walk of life[32].

Thomas attests clearly that many people were moved by Francis' word and example, and that they sought guidance from him for their own spiritual journeys. However, this textual witness, which is our earli-

---

[28] *1 Cel* 36: *Omnibus*, 258.

[29] Pazzelli suggests that Thomas' "*perpetuo militare*" (here translated as "to carry on the battle constantly") should be understood as wanting "to serve the Lord forever". Cf. R. Pazzelli, *Alla ricerca dei documenti primitivi riguardanti il Terz'Ordine*, in *Approccio storico-critico alle Fonti francescane*, edited by G. Cardaropoli and M. Conti, Roma 1979, 194.

[30] Casagrande notes that this "*trina militia*" is a literary type and does not necessarily imply a reference to "three orders", that is, to the founding of the "Third Order". Cf. Casagrande, *L'Ordine Francescano Secolare*, 219.

[31] The word "saved" replaces "served" to correct an apparent error in the English text. The English translation reads: "threefold army of those to be served is triumphing". However, the Latin text reads: "trina triumphat militia salvandorum".

[32] *1 Cel* 37: *Omnibus*, 260. The critical Latin edition reads: "Coeperunt multi de populo, nobiles et ignobiles, clerici et laici, divina inspiratione compuncti, ad sanctum Franciscum accedere, cupientes sub eius disciplina et magisterio perpetuo militare. Quos omnes Sanctus Dei, velut caelestis gratiae rivus uberrimus, charismatum imbribus rigans, agrum cordis ipsorum virtutum floribus exornabat: egregius nempe artifex, ad cuius formam, regulam et doctrinam, efferendo praeconio, in utroque sexu Christi renovatur Ecclesia et trina triumphat militia salvandorum. Omnibus quoque tribuebat normam vitae ac salutis viam in omni gradu veraciter demonstrabat". Cf. *AF*, X, 30.

est source relative to the "first Rule", merely claims that Francis did give some norm of life (*normam vitae*) to these followers. Unfortunately, Thomas does not offer any further information relative to the content of this "Rule" or when Francis gave this *normam vitae* to the penitents.

The chronology of Thomas' narrative suggests a very early date for this "Rule" since the account follows Francis' return from Rome, that is, around 1210. This judgment remains very tentative since Thomas does not always follow a chronological order. Nonetheless, given that Thomas inserts this account within the early development of Francis' small band of friar companions, it is reasonable to assume that this phenomenon of penitents following Francis and asking for his advice for their particular way of life occurred early in the history of the Franciscan movement[33].

Julian of Speyer

Julian of Speyer, who became a Franciscan somewhere between 1224 and 1227, was commissioned to write an official liturgical office, that is, prayers for celebrating the feast of St. Francis. Since Julian had studied music at Paris and had been the choirmaster of the French King's court it was natural that the task of writing a liturgical office should fall to him[34]. Julian's *Officium Rhythmicum Sancti Francisci*, written around 1231, clearly depends upon Thomas of Celano's *Vita prima* and Thomas' shorter *Legenda ad Usum Chori*[35].

A short time later (between 1232 and 1235), Julian also wrote a

---

[33] Schmucki, *Il T.O.F. nelle biografie*, 121.

[34] Bartholomew of Pisa, writing around 1398, attests to Julian's background in his *De conformitate vitae beati Francisci ad vitam Domini Iesu*. Cf. *AF*, IV, 308. Julian probably served under Philip II (1180-1223) and/or Louis VIII (1223-1226). Cf. Jason Miskuly, *Julian of Speyer: Life of St. Francis (Vita Sancti Francisci)* in *Franciscan Studies* 49 (1989) 93-94. In general, the information in this section concerning Julian of Speyer and his works depends upon Miskuly's *Introduction*.

[35] Miskuly, *Julian of Speyer*, 98-99.

biography of the saint, apparently to meet the needs of his community at Paris. As does his *Officium*, Julian's *Vita Sancti Francisci* also evidences strong literary dependence upon the earlier works of Thomas of Celano. Yet, Julian does add some interesting details[36]. In both his works Julian speaks of the three orders founded by Francis; he clearly interprets Thomas of Celano's *trina militia* to be three specific orders.

In his *Officium S. Francisci*, in a verse of a responsorial, there appears for the first time the typology of the three churches repaired by Francis[37] as a prophetic sign of the three orders to be founded by Francis[38]. The third antiphon for Lauds makes very explicit this idea, proclaiming:

> He [Francis] establishes three orders:
> the first he names [the Order] of Lesser Brothers,
> and the middle [Order] is made for the Poor Ladies,
> but the third [Order] of penitents includes both sexes[39].

In his *Vita Sancti Francisci*, Julian develops the themes and images set out briefly in his *Officium*. Julian again speaks of "three orders" and testifies that Francis offered the way to salvation and gave "to all a rule of life":

> Then, comforted in the Lord, blessed Francis began to act more confidently owing to the apostolic authority he had been granted, and going around through cities, towns and villages, he preached penance unremittingly.

---

[36] Pazzelli makes the claim: "The *Vita S. Francisci* of Julian of Speyer is important most of all because, even though it does depend greatly on the *Vita Prima* of Celano for its material, it clarifies some vague expressions used by Celano. Julian lived for many years with Celano and knew his thought well. His explanations can therefore be said to be not subjective, personal interpretations, but representations of Celano's own meaning". Cf. Raffaele Pazzelli, *St. Francis and the Third Order: The Franciscan and pre-Franciscan Penitential Movement*, Chicago 1989, 194, note 36.

[37] San Damiano, San Pietro della Spina, and Santa Maria della Porziuncola.

[38] The critical Latin text reads: "Sub typo trium Ordinum / Tres, nutu Dei praevio, / Ecclesias erexit". Cf. *AF*, X, 380.

[39] Translation by the author. The critical Latin edition reads: "Tres Ordines hic ordinat: / Primumque Fratrum nominat / Minorum, pauperumque / Fit Dominarum medius, / Sed Poenitentum tertius / Sexum capit utrumque". Cf. *AF*, X, 383.

He was particularly careful to show himself blameless in all things, lest he be thought to gloss over the truth with flattering words. Educated men marveled at the power of the words of him who had not been taught by man, and seeing the noble and the low born, the rich and the poor flood around him in bands, they ingeniously made their way to him as though to a new star rising in the darkness. In fact, he alloted patterns of salvation to all orders, conditions, ages and sexes alike giving to all a rule of life, and that it today holds sway over followers of both sexes in a triple knighthood of those destined for salvation, is a cause of joy to the Church.

For, as we mentioned above, he ordained three Orders; he himself considered the first preeminent by profession and habit, which, as he had written in the Rule, he called the Order of Friars Minor.

The second, moreover, which is also mentioned above, the Order of the Poor Ladies and Virgins of the Lord, took its happy beginning from him. The third, also, of no mean perfection, is called the Order of Penitents, which beneficially encompasses clerics and laity, virgins, and the unmarried and married of both sexes[40].

Julian of Speyer clearly testifies that Francis gave to all of these followers a rule (*vivendi regulam*). But he does not go beyond Thomas' account; he adds nothing to identify the text, its origin or its con-

---

[40] *Vita S. Francisci*, 23. Cf. Miskuly, *Julian of Speyer*, 134-35. The critical Latin edition reads, "Tunc sanctus Franciscus, in Domino confortatus, ex auctoritate apostolica fiducialius agere coepit, et per civitates villasque et castella circuiens, poenitentiam constantissime praedicavit. Curabat praecipue semetipsum irreprehensibilem in omnibus exhibere, ne veritatem cogeretur verbis adulatoriis palliare. Mirabantur viri litterati eius, quem non homo docuerat verborum virtutem, videntes ad ipsum nobiles et ignobiles divites et egenos turmatim confluere, eique, veluti novo sideri in tenebris orienti, sollerter intendere. Omni namque ordini, conditioni, aetati et sexui congruenter documenta salutis impendit; omnibus vivendi regulam tribuit, cuius hodie felicem ducatum in utroque sexu sequentium triumphare se gaudet Ecclesia triplici militia salvandorum. Tres enim, ut supra tetigimus, Ordines ordinavit; quorum primum ipse professione simul et habitu super omnes excellentissime tenuit, quem et Ordinem Fratrum Minorum, sicut in Regula scripserat, appellavit. Secundus etiam, qui supra memoratus est, pauperum Dominarum et virginum felix ab eo sumpsit exordium. Tertius quoque non mediocris perfectionis Ordo Poenitentium dicitur, qui clericis et laicis, virginibus, continentibus coniugatisque communis, sexum salubriter utrumque complectitur. Cf. *AF*, X, 345-46.

tent[41]. Through the poetic form of his *Officium* and the hagiographic style of his *Vita*, Julian of Speyer presents his conviction, or perhaps more precisely, repeats Thomas of Celano's conviction that Francis had indeed given guidance to these lay followers. We are led back to Thomas of Celano and thus left in uncertainty.

But even if Julian of Speyer offers no further precision with respect to this primitive Rule, his writings are important. His particular use of Thomas' works, his concern to edit Thomas' editorial comments and to present information relative only to Francis, evidences an interest in information about Francis himself[42]. Given this focus, his additions are all the more noteworthy. In his *Vita S. Francisci*, Julian states that Francis founded three orders, that the third group was an Order of Penance, and that it was open to all women and men. But even more importantly, these statements are contained in an antiphon in Julian's *Officium Rhythmicum Sancti Francisci* which about six years after Francis' death became the official liturgical text used for the feast of Francis. That is, shortly after the death of Francis, in celebrating his memory, the people celebrated his founding of three orders, the "third" being an order of penance[43].

---

[41] Another author makes the same claim as Julian. Vincent di Beauvais, a Dominican historian writing before 1244, includes a treatment of Saint Francis in his *Speculum historiale*. At the conclusion of his biographical notes on Francis, he adds the affirmation that Francis, "also established three orders, the first of which he certainly held to be the Friars Minor, the second was of the Poor Ladies and Virgins, and the third truly of Penance". (Translation by the author). The Latin text reads, "qui etiam tres ordines instituit, quorum primum ipse tenuit, scilicet fratrum minorum; secundus fuit pauperum dominarum ac virginum; tertius vero poenitentium". Cf. Stanislao da Campagnola, *L'Ordo Poenitentium di san Francesco nelle cronache del Duecento*, in *CF* 43 (1973) 154. However, this testimony does not hold value as an independent witness since, as Stanislao points out, the author here "blindly" (*pedissequamente*) follows Julian of Speyer's work, and di Beauvais' use of the word "also" (*etiam*) indicates that his concern focused not on the institutions but on the figure of Francis. Cf. Stanislao da Campagnola, *L'Ordo Poenitentium,* 154-55.

[42] Miskuly, *Julian of Speyer*, 101-102.

[43] We cannot determine how Francis' "founding" of these three orders was understood by thirteenth century hearers. Certainly in later centuries Francis' role as founder of these three orders has often been understood in an

A Letter from Gregory IX to Agnes of Prague

In a letter to Agnes of Prague in 1238, Gregory IX writes of Francis having established three orders: "they are designated the communities (*collegia*) of the Order of Friars Minor, of the Enclosed Sisters and of the Penitents"[44]. However, in his mention of three Orders (*ordinibus*), the pope names only the first as an "order" (*ordinis*) per se, that is, the *Order* of Friars Minor; the other two "orders" the pope names as "*collegia*": the *collegia* or communities of the Poor Sisters and the *collegia* or communities of the Brothers and Sisters of Penance. Thus, this letter does not present Francis as the founder of three orders in any equivalent sense, rather, it suggests only that Gregory IX attributed to Francis the same role in the foundation both of the Enclosed Sisters and of the Brothers and Sisters of Penance[45].

A Biography of Gregory IX

The testimony contained in the *Vita Gregorii IX papae*, an anonymous author's biography of Pope Gregory IX, stands in stark contrast to Gregory IX's own account. Writing about events in the life of Gregory IX before his election as Pope, the anonymous author notes that the then-Cardinal Hugolino, while bishop of Ostia,

---

equivalent sense. Schmucki, in discussing the significance of this testimony, notes that Julian of Speyer obviously used the term in an analogous and not equivalent sense. Schmucki argues that Julian of Speyer's silence concerning the role of Clare in the founding of the "second order" indicates that he used the term in an analogous sense. Cf. Schmucki, *Il T.O.F. nelle biografie*, 124. This question of the role of Francis as "founder" of the Order of Penitents will receive further attention at the end of *Chapter III*.

[44] institutis per ipsum, ...insignitum, per orbis latitudinem tribus ordinibus... *fratrum ordinis Minorum, sororum Inclusarum et Penitentium collegia designantur...*" For the full Latin text, cf. G. Meersseman, *Dossier de l'Ordre de la Pénitence au XIIIe Siècle*, Fribourg 1961, 52-53.

[45] It is also significant that in his letters to the Penitents Gregory IX never attributes the founding of the Order of Penance to St. Francis. Cf. G. Meersseman, *"Introduction" to Documentation on the Order of Penance in the 13th Century*, translated by G. Barth, *Anal TOR* XVI/137 (1983) 314, note 41.

established and carried forward to greatness the new orders of the Brothers [and Sisters] of Penance, and the Enclosed Sisters. He also guided the Order of Minors as it wandered uncertain at its beginnings by the giving over of a new Rule, and he gave shape to the shapeless order, putting Francis in charge of them as minister and head[46].

This biography, written around 1240, presents the first thirteenth century non-Franciscan source which registers together these three religious groups which the Franciscan tradition had attested as going back to Francis[47]. According to this account, Gregory IX acted only as a guide for the Order of Friars Minor, while it states clearly that with respect to the other two orders he acted as the founder, a role which Gregory himself had attributed to Francis.

This apparent contradiction can be explained in part by the author's certain exaggeration of the role played by the pope[48]. But in both cases, whether attributed to Francis or later to Hugolino, the role of the founder contains a distinction. Gregory IX spoke of Francis having founded an Order and two "collegia", from which we can infer a different role as founder. Similarly, Gregory IX's biographer speaks of the pope founding only the "Second" and "Third" Orders; the First Order he "guided with a new Rule". Thus, both accounts suggest that the role of "founder" be understood in an analogous, not equivalent sense with respect to these three Orders.

The Legend of the Three Companions

The *Legend of the Three Companions*, as a document, presents many problems. All of the extant manuscripts of this work contain a letter

---

[46] *Vitae pontificum romanorum*, ed. L.A. Muratori, in *Rerum Italicarum Scriptores*, III/1, 575. (Translation by the author). The Latin text reads, "cuius officii tempore Poenitentium fratrum et Dominarum inclusarum novos instituit ordines et ad summum usque provexit. Minorum etiam ordinem intra initia sub limite incerto vagantem novae regulae traditione direxit et informavit informem, beatum Franciscum eis ministrum praeficiens et rectorem". Cf. Stanislao da Campagnola, *L'Ordo Poenitentium*, 152.

[47] Stanislao da Campagnola, *L'Ordo Poenitentium*, 152.

[48] Pásztor notes this type of exaggeration in her study of how the different sources portray Gregory IX in his role as Cardinal-Protector of the Order. Cf. E. Pásztor, *St. Francis, Cardinal Hugolino and the "Franciscan Question"*, in *Greyfriars Review* 1 (1987) 1-29.

addressed to the minister general and signed by Brothers Leo, Angelo, and Rufinus (hence the traditional name of this document)[49]. The letter, dated 1246 from Greccio, states the companions' intention not to present a legend or chronological account. They claim, rather, to "have picked as it were from a field of flowers those we thought the most fair: we have not followed a continuous narrative, but have carefully omitted many events elegantly and accurately told in the *Legende*"[50]. Nonetheless, not the companions' reminiscences, but rather, a legend follows the letter[51]. This discrepancy sparked great debate over the still-unresolved questions of dating, authenticity, and literary relationship to other early sources. However, scholars now generally concur that chapters one through sixteen can be attributed to Francis' early companions and therefore merit attention[52]. Thus, without attempting to settle the many textual problems involved in this work, let us consider a passage from chapter XIV:

> Not only men, but also women and unmarried virgins were fired by the brothers' preaching, and, on their advice, entered the prescribed convents to do penance; and one of the brothers was appointed as their visitor and guide. Married men and women, being bound by the marriage vow, were advised by the friars to dedicate themselves to a life of penance in their own houses.
>
> Thus through blessed Francis' perfect devotion to the Blessed Trinity the Church of Christ was renewed by three new orders; and this had

---

[49] In fact, this letter has not been found attached to any other document. Cf. T. Desbonnets, *Legenda trium Sociorum: Edition critique*, in *AFH* 67 (1974) 86.

[50] Brooke, *Scripta Leonis*, 87-89.

[51] Since the manuscripts to which the letter is attached do exactly what the letter promises not to do, the text was considered mutilated. In the 1890s Sabatier searched for the "missing chapters" and found what seemed to be this material embedded within the *Speculum Vitae*, a work from 1509. His heuristic sense that parts of this later work reflected the early tradition of the three companions received confirmation in his subsequent discovery of a manuscript not only containing these chapters as a separate work but which included a title, author and date: the *Speculum Perfectionis* written by Leo in 1227. However, later research showed the *Speculum Perfectionis* to be a compilation dating from 1318. Cf. Brooke, *Scripta Leonis*, 5-6; and above page 52 note 15.

[52] T. Desbonnets, *La légende des trois compagnons. Nouvelles recherches sur la généalogie des biographies primitives de saint François*, in *AFH* 65 (1972) 66-106.

been prefigured through his previous reparation of three churches. His three distinct orders were each in due time approved[53] and confirmed by the sovereign pontiff[54].

Beyond adding a trinitarian motivation to the "three churches" typology, the early companions testify that the friars counseled married men and women to live a more intense Christian life within their own family situations. Clearly, they present the "Third Order" as comprised of married women and men who became penitents in their own homes.

The Anonymous of Perugia

The *Anonymous of Perugia* provides another textual witness from the thirteenth century, having been written between 1266 and 1270[55]. The designation "*Anonymous of Perugia*" resulted from the fact that its author was not originally identified and that the text, contained in a fifteenth century manuscript, was discovered in a Franciscan church in Perugia[56]. Authorship of the text is now generally attributed to

---

[53] The claim that the three orders were approved by the pope has brought the dating of this document into question since the "third order" received papal approbation only in 1289. However, the document is held to be earlier, around 1246, with the explanation that this "approval" references not the definitive approbation, but rather the bulls issued by Honorius III in favor of different groups of penitents. Cf. Schmucki, *Il T.O.F. nelle biografie*, 125.

[54] *L3S 60: Omnibus*, 944. The critical Latin edition reads: "Non solum autem viri sic convertebantur ad ordinem, sed etiam multae virgines et viduae, ad eorum praedicationem compunctae, secundum ipsorum consilium per civitates et castra monasteriis ordinatis recludebant se ad poenitentiam faciendam. Quibus unus ex fratribus constitutus fuit visitator et corrector earum. Similiter et viri uxorati et mulieres maritatae, a lege matrimonii discedere non valentes, de fratrum salubri consilio se in domibus propriis arctiori poenitentiae committebant. Et sic per beatum Franciscanum, sanctae Trinitatis cultorem perfectum, Dei Ecclesia in tribus ordinibus renovatur sicut trium ecclesiarum praecedens reparatio figuravit. Quorum ordinum quilibet tempore suo fuit a summo pontifice confirmatus". Cf. Desbonnets, *Legenda trium Sociorum: Edition critique*, in *AFH* 67 (1974) 134-35.

[55] L. Di Fonzo, *L'Anonimo Perugino tra le Fonti Francescane del secolo XIII: rapporti letterari e testo critico*, in *MF* 72 (1972) 381.

[56] *Ibid.*, 117-18.

Giles' companion, Brother John[57], who expressed in the prologue his intention of preserving the memory of the birth and foundation of the Order[58]:

> Servants of the Lord ought to know the way and the teachings of holy men, by which they can come to God. Therefore, for the honor of God and the edification of readers and listeners, I have told a few stories about our holy Father Francis and the brothers who came at the birth of the brotherhood. I witnessed their deeds. I shared their conversations. I myself was a disciple. And I have recounted the stories as the Lord has inspired me[59].

This early witness, who with an enthusiasm and an immediacy of style records the establishment of the Friars Minor, mentions briefly the two other "orders":

> Those whom the brothers would receive, they used to take to Blessed Francis, so that they could be invested by him.
>
> Something similar happened in the case of many unmarried women and girls. Having heard the brothers preach, they would come, pierced to the heart, and say: "And what are we to do? We cannot join you. So tell us how we can save our souls". To this end, the brothers made arrangements, in the different towns wherever it was possible, for enclosed monasteries, so they could do penance. They also appointed one of the brothers to be visitor and corrector for the ladies.
>
> Then too, the married men began to say: "We have wives. They will never let us divorce them. Therefore, teach us how we can walk in the path of salvation". And the brothers instituted an order for them.

---

[57] *Ibid.*, 372-78, esp. 373; 396-98.

[58] Desbonnets, *From Intuition to Institution*, 161.

[59] For the English translation, cf. Eric Kahn, *Anonymus Perusinus*, in *Workbook for Franciscan Studies: Companion Guide to the Omnibus of Sources*, edited by D. Isabell, Chicago 1979, 94. The critical Latin edition reads: "Quoniam servi Domini non debent ignorare viam et doctrinam sanctorum virorum, per quam ad Deum valeant pervenire, ideo ad honorem Dei et aedificationem legentium et audientium, ego qui actus eorum vidi, verba audivi, quorum etiam discipulus fui, aliqua de actibus beatissimi Patris nostri Francisci et aliquorum fratrum qui venerunt in principio Religionis narravi et compilavi, prout mens mea divinitus fuit docta". Cf. Di Fonzo, *L'Anonimo Perugino*, in *MF* 72 (1972) 435.

It is called the Order of Penitents. They had it confirmed[60] by the Supreme Pontiff[61].

The text reaffirms the witness of others: the people responded enthusiastically to the friars' preaching. That is, the friars' exhortation to penance figured causally in the people's entrance into the Order of Penance. But interestingly, this author attributes the founding of the "Third Order" to the friars generally, not to Francis specifically[62].

---

[60] Given that the official papal confirmation of the Rule for the Order of Pentitents was the bull *Supra Montem* given by Nicholas IV on August 12, 1289, this phrase would suggest that the *Anonymous of Perugia* was written *after* 1289. However, Di Fonzo claims that this sentence, "They had it confirmed by the Supreme Pontiff", is an addition made by a later redactor sometime between 1292-1296. Cf. Di Fonzo, *L'Anonimo Perugino*, 395.

[61] Eric Kahn, *Anonymus Perusinus*, 112. The critical Latin edition reads: "Illos autem quos fratres recipiebant, ad beatum Franciscum adducebant ut induerentur ab eo.

Similiter et multae mulieres virgines et non habentes viros, audientes praedicationem eorum, veniebant corde compuncto ad eos, dicentes: «Quid faciemus et nos? Vobiscum esse non possumus. Dicite ergo nobis quomodo salvare nostras animas valeamus». Ad hoc ordinaverunt per singulas civitates quibus potuerunt monasteria reclusa ad paenitentiam faciendam. Constituerunt etiam unum de fratribus qui esset visitator et correptor earum.

Similiter et viri uxores habentes dicebant: «Uxores habemus, quae dimitti se non patiuntur. Docete ergo nos quam viam tenere salubriter valeamus». At illi ordinaverunt ex ipsis ordinem, qui Paenitentium Ordo vocatur, facientes hunc a Summo Pontifice confirmari". Di Fonzo, *L'Anonimo Perugino*, in *MF* 72 (1972) 459-60.

[62] Esser notes that the testimony of the *Legend of the Three Companions* and the *Anonymous of Perugia*, which do not attibute the foundation of the Order of Penance explicitly to Francis alone, gain value in light of the fact that the authors every year on the feast of Francis sang the antiphon from Julian of Speyer's office: "He [Francis] established three orders: / the first he named [the Order] of Lesser Brothers, / and the middle [Order] was made for the Poor Ladies, / but the third [Order] of penitents included both sexes". Cf. K. Esser, *Un documento dell'inizio del Duecento sui penitenti*, in *I Frati Penitenti di san Francesco nella società del Due e Trecento*, edited by M. D'Alatri, Roma 1977, 95.

The Legend of Perugia

The *Legend of Perugia* (not to be confused with the *Anonymous of Perugia*) speaks briefly about the penitents at Greccio, recording the early friars' influence upon the people of that town. But the questions and controversy surrounding this text abound. Scholars have reached little consensus. Even the title, the *Legend of Perugia*, has been disputed given that the text is not a legend in the strict sense (since it does not follow a chronological order), but rather, a compilation without any particular order. It has, therefore, been variously designated as the *Legenda antiqua*[63], *Compilation of Assisi*[64], *Fiori dei tre Compagni*[65], and *Scripta Leonis, Rufini, et Angeli*[66]. The dating is likewise disputed.

Nonetheless, most scholars agree that the *Legend of Perugia* (ms. 1046) represents the best witness to the material written by Francis' companions between 1244-1246[67], material used by Thomas of Celano as a source for his *Vita Secunda*[68]. Let us then consider the early companions' testimony concerning Francis' followers at Greccio:

> St. Francis saw that the friary at Greccio was worthy and poor, and the men of the town, although they were very poor and simple, pleased him more than the other folk of the province; and he used often to stay and rest in that house, especially since there was a poor little cell there which was really remote, in which the holy father used to stay. Because of his and the friars' example and preaching, many of the men of the region by the grace of God entered the Order, and many women preserved their virginity wearing garments of religion while dwelling in their own homes, they lived a common form of life sincerely, afflicting their bodies with prayer and fasting. It seemed to men and to the friars that their life was not among laymen and their kindred but among the saintly and religious who had served God for a long time - although

---

[63] F. Delorme, *La "Legenda antiqua s. Francisci" du Ms 1046 de la bibliothèque communale de Pérouse*, in *AFH* XV (1922) 23-70, 278-332.

[64] M. Bigaroni, *"Compilatio Assiensis" dagli scritti di fr. Leone e compagni su S. Francesco d'Assisi*, Assisi 1975.

[65] J. Cambell, *I fiori dei tre compagni*, translated by N. Vian, Milano 1966.

[66] R. Brooke, *Scripta Leonis, Rufini, et Angeli, Sociorum S. Francisci*, Oxford 1970.

[67] Brooke, *Recent Work*, 655; and Pásztor, *The Sources*, 36.

[68] R. Brooke, *The «Legenda Antiqua S. Francisci» - Perugia Ms. 1046*, in *Analecta Bollandiana* 99 (1981) 166.

> in fact they were young and truly simple. So that St. Francis often used to say with joy about the men and women of that town: "There are not so many converted to penitence from any one great city as there are from Greccio, which is a little town". For often in the evening when the friars of the house were praising God, as the friars in many houses used to do at that time, the men of the town, small and great, would come outside and stand in the road in front of the town, making responses to the friars with a loud voice: "May the Lord God be praised". Even the little boys who had not yet learnt to speak properly, when they saw the friars, used to praise God as best they could[69].

While this account focuses only upon Greccio, it once again testifies that many men and women responded to the preaching of penance by Francis and the friars. This early recollection presents the people's dedication to a more intense Christian life as a direct result of the friars' preaching and manner of life. The text does not say anything about a rule for these penitents, however, Schmucki suggests that given the details of their life (a religious habit, chastity, some form of the common

---

[69] Brooke, *Scripta Leonis*, 147, 149. The critical Latin edition reads: "Videns etiam beatus Franciscus quod ille locus fratrum de Gretio esset honestus et pauper et quod homines illius castri, licet essent pauperculi et simplices, inter alios de illa prouincia placuerunt magis beato Francisco, ideo sepe quiescebat et morabatur in eodem loco, maxime quia erat ibi cella una paupercula, que erat ualde remota, in qua manebat sanctus pater. Vnde exemplo suo et predicatione et fratrum suorum, gratia Domini multi ex ipsis intrauerunt religionem, mulieres multe seruabant uirginitatem suam, permanentes in domibus suis indute pannis religionis. Et licet unaqueque maneret in domo sua, communi uita uiuebat honeste et affligebat corpus suum ieiunio et oratione, ut uideretur hominibus et fratribus earum conuersatio non inter seculares esse et consanguineos suos, sed inter sanctas personas et religiosas que longo tempore seruissent Domino, cum tamen essent iuuencule et simplices ualde. Vnde sepe dicebat cum letitia beatus Franciscus inter fratres de hominibus et mulieribus illius castri: « De una magna ciuitate non sunt conuersi tot ad penitentiam quot de Gretio, quod est ita paruum castrum ». Nam sepe cum in sero fratres de loco laudarent Dominum, sicut fratres in multis locis illo tempore solebant facere, homines illius castri, parui et magni, exibant foras stantes in uia ante castrum, respondentes fratribus alta uoce: « Laudatus sit Dominus Deus! » ita quod etiam pueri nescientes adhuc bene loqui, cum uiderent fratres, laudarent Dominum sicut poterant". Cf. Brooke, *Scripta Leonis*, 146, 148.

life, more intense prayer and fasting, and a rapport with the friars), it is likely they had some "rule of life"[70].

A Biblical Commentary

A commentary on the Book of Revelation written by Alexander Minorita di Brema in 1249 makes mention of the Order of Penitents. While this text, *Expositio in Apocalypsim*, does not add any further information concerning the penitents, their life, or the rule, it does evidence a growing diffusion of the view that Francis founded three orders. The commentary reads:

> the eleventh is hyacinth, which is of a sky-blue color, clouded in obscurity, and brilliant in the light. Therefore it is designated the Order of Penitents which is inserted in the eleventh place. For according to history, Saint Francis, after the Order of Friars Minor and that of the Poor Ladies, established the Order of these [Penitents][71].

A Thirteenth Century Chronicle

A chronicler known only as a Franciscan of Erfurt, writing between 1261 and 1266, after having listed the major events of Gregory IX's pontificate, goes on to say that

> this same Gregory IX approved the two orders which Saint Francis founded: the one of the consecrated Poor Ladies, and the other of the Penitents, which includes both sexes, and evidently, clerics, married people, virgins, and celibates[72].

---

[70] Schmucki, *Il T.O.F. nelle biografie*, 134.

[71] Translation by the author. The Latin text reads: "Undecimum iacinctus, qui est cerulei coloris, nubilus in obscuro et rutilat in sereno. Per istum designatur Ordo Paenitentium, qui undecimo loco inseritur. Nam secundum historias sanctus Franciscus post Ordines Fratrum Minorum Pauperumque Dominarum Ordinem istorum constituit". Cf. Schmucki, *Il T.O.F. nelle biografie*, 127, note 45.

[72] Translation by the author. The Latin text reads, "iste Gregorius IX duos ordines confirmavit, quos sanctus Franciscus ordinavit, unum pauperum dominarum sanctimonialium, alterum penitencium, qui sexum capit utrumque, scilicet clericos, coniuges, virgines et continentes". Cf. Stanislao da Campagnola, *L'Ordo Poenitentium*, 161.

While chronologically inaccurate, this account again portrays the involvement of both Gregory IX and Francis in the "Second" and "Third" Orders: Francis as the one who founded the two groups, Gregory IX as the one who gave papal approval to both[73].

Bonaventure of Bagnoregio

The Chapter at Rome in 1257, which elected Bonaventure of Bagnoregio Minister General, expressed the desire that another history or biography be written from the existing ones. At the following Chapter at Narbonne (1260), Bonaventure himself accepted the task and by 1263 had completed his text[74]. Bonaventure's Life of St. Francis later came to be known as the *Legenda maior* to distinguish it from a subsequent shorter version. Bonaventure wrote this shorter life of Saint Francis (which basically was a condensation of his "First Life" and which came to be known as the *Legenda minor*) for liturgical use during the octave celebration of the feast of Francis[75]. Bonaventure's theological portrayal of Francis supplanted the works of Thomas of Celano as the official biography of Francis. In fact, the General Chapter of Paris in 1266 ordered that all other existing legends be destroyed and that every Franciscan house be supplied with a copy of this new biography by Bonaventure[76].

---

[73] Although the chronicler claims that Gregory IX gave his confirmation to the Order of Penitents, it is more likely that this "confirmation" refers to interventions of a generic nature for "collegia" or communities of Penitents more than a specific *Order* of Penitents. Cf. Stanislao da Campagnola, *L'Ordo Poenitentium*, 161.

[74] For more information on Bonaventure and his works, cf. the introduction in E. Cousins, *Bonaventure*, New York 1978, 1-48; and the *Introduction* to the Major and Minor Lives of St. Francis: *Omnibus*, 615-23.

[75] Cousins, *Bonaventure*, 10.

[76] While in 1244 the General Chapter sought new material about Francis and welcomed new biographies, the mood changed dramatically with the General Chapter of 1260. All existing materials were to be destroyed and a new life, to be written by Bonaventure, was to replace all of them as the definitive life of Francis. The reasons for this reversal have not been fully explained. The simplest explanation given presents the Chapter's decision as a reflection of the ideological struggle within the order, however, there are probably other reasons also involved. Cf. Cousins, *Bonaventure*, 40-41; Fleming, *Introduction to Franciscan Literature*, 43-44; Di Fonzo, *L'Anonimo Perugino*, 247, note 49.

The works of Bonaventure are therefore very important for the ideas and images of Francis that they presented and propagated, almost without rival.

In the second chapter of the *Legenda maior*, Bonaventure writes:

This is the place
where the Order of Friars Minor was begun
by Saint Francis
under the inspiration of divine revelation.
For at the bidding of divine providence
which guided Christ's servant in everything,
he physically repaired three churches
before he began the Order
and preached the Gospel.
This he did
not only
to ascend in an orderly progression
from the sensible realm to the intelligible,
from the lesser to the greater,
but also
to symbolize prophetically
in external actions perceived by the senses
what he would do in the future.
For like the three buildings he repaired,
so Christ's Church-
with its threefold victorious army
of those who are to be saved-
was to be renewed under his leadership
in three ways:
by the structure, rule and teaching
which he would provide.
And now we see
that this prophecy has been fulfilled[77].

[77] *LM* II, 8. Cf. Cousins, *Bonaventure*, 197-98. The critical Latin edition reads, "Hic est locus, in quo Fratrum Minorum Ordo a sancto Francisco perdivinae revelationis instinctum inchoatus est. Divinae namque providentiae nutu, qua Christi servus dirigebatur in omnibus, tres materiales erexit ecclesias, antequam, Ordinem inchoans, Evangelium praedicaret, ut non solum a sensibilibus ad intelligibilia, a minoribus ad maiora ordinato progressu conscenderet, verum etiam, ut quid esset facturus in posterum, sensibili foris opere mysterialiter praesignaret. Name instar reparatae triplicis fabricae ipsius sancti viri ducatu, secundum datam

While Bonaventure's treatment of the by then well-known typology of the "three churches" recalls both Thomas' *Vita prima* and Julian's *Vita S. Francisci*, his development is almost pseudo-Dionysian in presenting these symbolic actions through which Francis perceived mysteriously through the senses what he would in fact accomplish in the future[78]. Bonaventure presents this theme again in his *Legenda minor* where he further elaborates the typology and develops it theologically:

> People eventually came to help him in their devotion to him, because they could see already that his was no ordinary holiness. With their cooperation he repaired the church of San Damiano and another dedicated to the Prince of the Apostles, followed by a third dedicated to the Blessed Virgin, all of which were abandoned and in ruins. In this way the work which God afterwards planned to accomplish through him on a spiritual plane was mysteriously foreshadowed in a visible, material fashion. Like the three churches he repaired, the universal Church of Christ was to be renewed in three different ways under his guidance and according to his directions, his rule and teaching. The voice which he heard from the Cross, which repeated the command to repair God's house three times, was a prophetic sign which we now see fulfilled in the three Orders which he founded[79].

Bonaventure had recorded Francis' experience before the crucifix in San Damiano in the *Legenda maior*, and had explained that Christ's command "go and repair my house" referred not to material buildings

---

ab eo formam, regulam et doctrinam Christi triformiter renovanda erat Ecclesia trinaque triumphatura militia salvandorum, sicut et nunc cernimus esse completum". Cf. *AF*, X, 566.

[78] For references concerning the influence of pseudo-Dionysius on Bonaventure, cf. Schmucki, *Il T.O.F. nelle biografie*, 128, note 48.

[79] *Lm* 1:9. Cf. *Omnibus*, 798. The critical Latin edition reads: "Devotione quoque sibi assistente fidelium, qui praeclaram in viro Dei iam coeperant nosse virtutem, non solum Sancti Damiani, verum etiam principis Apostolorum, et Virginis gloriosae ruinosas et derelictas resarcivit ecclesias, ut, quae per eum in posterum Dominus spiritualiter operari disponeret, sensibili foris opere mysterialiter praesignaret. Nam instar reparatae triplicis fabricae ipsius sancti viri ducatu, secundum datam ab eo formam, regulam et doctrinam Christi triformiter renovanda erat Ecclesia, sicut et vox ad eum facta decruce, tertio replicans de domus Dei reparatione mandatum, praeambulum exstiterat signum, et nunc in tribus ab eo institutis Ordinibus cernimus esse completum". Cf. *AF*, X, 658.

but to "that Church which Christ purchased with his own blood"[80]. However, only in the *Legenda minor* does he present this command as a symbolic prefiguring of the "three Orders"[81].

But Bonaventure goes beyond the mention and symbolic prefiguring of "three Orders". In the fourth chapter of the *Legenda maior* he offers some information about this Order of Penitents:

> Set on fire by the fervor of his preaching, a great number of people bound themselves by new laws of penance according to the rule which they received from the man of God. Christ's servant decided to name this way of life the Order of the Brothers of Penance. As the road of penance is common to all who are striving toward heaven, so this way of life admits clerics and laity, single and married of both sexes. How meritorious it is before God is clear from the numerous miracles performed by some of its members[82].

---

[80] The *Legenda maior* records the episode of the crucifix speaking to Francis in the church of San Damiano in chapter II, 1. Cf. Cousins, *Bonaventure*, 191-92.

[81] Bonaventure uses this typology also in one of his sermons. In his fourth sermon on St. Francis, preached at Paris in 1267 on the feast of St. Francis, Bonaventure said: "St. Francis also had three 'daughters'. At the outset of his religious life he repaired three churches: one dedicated to SS. Comas and Damian, another dedicated to St. Peter the Apostle and another to the Blessed Virgin Mary. It was in the last mentioned church that the Lord revealed to him the form of life he was to lead. Besides this, he founded three religious Orders: the first, the Order of Friars Minor; the second, the Order of the Sisters of St. Clare. Earlier these had been called the Poor Ladies of SS. Cosmas and Damian, but now, with St. Clare having been canonized, they are called the Sisters of St. Clare. The third is called the Order of Penitents, known as the Penitent Brethren. These Orders may be understood as his three 'daughters', and they were founded for the purpose of honoring God". Cf. *The Disciple and the Master: St. Bonaventure's Sermons on St. Francis of Assisi*, translated and edited by E. Doyle, Chicago 1983, 108.

[82] *LM* IV, 6. Cf. Cousins, *Bonaventure*, 210. The critical Latin edition reads: "Nam praedicationis ipsius fervore succensi, quam plurimi secundum formam a Dei viro acceptam novis se poenitentiae legibus vinciebant, quorum vivendi modum idem Christi famulus Ordinem *Fratrum de poenitentia* nominari decrevit. Nimirum, sicut in caelum tendentibus poenitentiae viam omnibus constat esse communem, sic et hic status clericos et laicos, virgines et coniungatos in utroque sexu admittens, quanti sit apud Deum meriti, ex pluribus per aliquos ipsorum patratis miraculis innotescit". Cf. *AF*, X, 573.

Bonaventure presents some very clear details: that the Order of Penitents resulted from the Francis' preaching, that Francis named the Order, and that he gave a Rule to the penitents. Bonaventure also offers an interesting theological note and an important pastoral observation. Theologically, Bonaventure notes that every Christian must live a life of penance to be saved. Pastorally, Bonaventure attests to the holiness of some penitents. Bonaventure's claim indicates that by 1263 people must have recognized some penitents who, in living that life of penance under the guidance or inspiration of Francis, were truly outstanding in holiness.

But once again, relative to this "primitive Rule" (*legibus*) or guidance given by Francis, we have no identifying detail, no descriptive clue. This "rule" remains enigmatic at best.

A Benedictine Treatise

The *Legenda Monacensis S. Francisci*, written by a Benedictine monk around 1275 records[83]:

> Moreover, he [Francis] instituted three orders in the Church... The third is said to be [the Order] of Penitents, which accepts people of both sexes, and is known to arise aptly enough for married people as well as celibates, clergy as well as lay people who do not yet renounce their property. Prompted by God, he restored three famous churches as a symbol of these three orders[84].

While the author adds only the detail that these penitents did not renounce all of their property, his account merits attention as a non-Franciscan witness[85].

---

[83] Schmucki dates the text between 1263 and 1282, claiming that it was probably written around 1275. Cf. Schmucki, *Il T.O.F. nelle biografie*, 129.

[84] *Legenda monacensis S. Francisci*, 14. (Translation by the author). The critical Latin edition reads: "Tres autem Ordines instituit in Ecclesia... Tertius dicitur Poenitentum, qui sexum capit utrumque et tam coniugatis quam continentibus, clericis et laicis etiam, qui proprietati nondum renuntiare praesumunt, apte satis noscitur provenire. Sub quorum trium typo Ordinum tres, nutu Dei praevio, memoratas ecclesias reparavit". Cf. *AF*, X, 699.

[85] Schmucki, *Il T.O.F. nelle biografie*, 129.

An Inquisition's Sentence against a Heretic

Another external witness bears mention, a testimony which holds significance precisely because of its connection with heresy. During an inquisition at the city of Orvieto between 1268 and 1269, two Franciscan inquisitors condemned some eighty-seven citizens as heretics or supporters of heresy[86]. The sentence condemning one Dominic di Pietro Rosse speaks of him as a member "of the most holy Order of Penitents founded by our blessed father Francis"[87]. As Mariano D'Alatri points out in his study, this text provides apodictic proof neither of the fact nor of the manner of Francis' "founding" of the Order of Penitents. It does, however, provide undeniable evidence that by 1269 the belief that Francis had founded this Order of Penitents was held as a fact, otherwise the Franciscan inquisitor would certainly have avoided making the claim that a heretic was a "son of Saint Francis"[88]. Further, the text attests to an established fraternity at Orvieto by the year 1269.

"Disputed Questions"

Determinationes quaestionum circa Regulam Fratrum Minorum, a pseudo-Bonaventurian treatise written by an anonymous author around 1275, offers another interesting testimony even though it does not deal directly with Francis' role in founding the Order of Penitents[89]. The text responds to various objections, one such objection being that the friars were not promoting the Order of Penitents. While the relationship between the friars and the penitents at that time remains beyond our specific concerns, the author's response is instructive. In response to

---

[86] M. D'Alatri, *Ordo Paenitentium ed eresia in Italia*, in *CF* 43 (1973) 181.

[87] Translation by the author. The Latin text reads, "sanctissimi Ordinis Penitentum a beato Francisco patre nostro conditi". Cf. D'Alatri, *Ordo Paenitentium ed eresia*, 181. For the full text of the sentenee, see the appendix to D'Alatri's article, pp. 196-97.

[88] D'Alatri, *Ordo Paenitentium ed eresia*, 182.

[89] The Latin text, that is, this particular section of the *Determinationes quaestionum circa Regulam Fratrum Minorum*, can be found in G. Meersseman, *Dossier de l'Ordre de la Pénitence au XIIIe siècle*, Fribourg 1961, 123-25. For a discussion of the dating of the document, cf. M. D'Alatri, *Francesco d'Assisi e i laici*, in *Ricerche storiche* 13 (1983) 625.

the question why the friars, as imitators of Francis in all things, do not minister to the Order of Penitents founded by Francis, the author presents twelve reasons or justifications. A seemingly irrefutable argument would have been to deny that Francis had founded the Order, thus removing the very foundation for the objection[90]. However, the author does not deny that Francis founded not only the Order of Friars Minor but also and the Order of Penitents. The text suggests, therefore, that by 1275 the role of Francis as founder of the Order of Penitents was held with such certitude that its denial was unthinkable.

Bernard of Bessa

Sometime after 1278, Bernard of Bessa wrote his *Liber de laudibus beati Francisci*. In speaking of the three orders founded by St. Francis, he writes:

> The fruit of the teaching of St. Francis shines forth to the greatest extent in the three orders established by him...
>
> The third is the Order of the Brothers and Sisters of Penance including clerics and lay people, virgins, widows and married people, whose *propositum* is to live respectably in their own homes, to practice works of compassion, and to avoid worldly ostentation. Thus, at times one may see among them renowned knights and other important people of the world wearing dark furs along with simple mantels, as humble in their mounts as in their clothing, living so moderately along with the needy that one does not doubt that they truly fear God. From the beginning a friar was assigned to them as Minister, but now they are directed to their own secular ministers, with the result that they are supported nevertheless by the friars with counsel and aid as brothers [and sisters] having the same father.
>
> In laying out the rules or forms of life for their Order, Pope Gregory of holy memory, united by a great friendship to blessed Francis, while

[90] Prospero Rivi makes this suggestion in his discussion of the text. Cf. P. Rivi, *Le Origini dell'O.F.S.: Risveglio religioso e coscienza del laicato nella Chiesa dei secoli XII-XIII - il contributo di Francesco d'Assisi*, Fidenza 1988, 172.

he was still established in a lesser office, devotedly supplied to this holy man, what was lacking in the knowledge of law[91].

Beyond his claim that Francis founded three orders, Bernard offers some interesting details. His description of this "Order of the Brothers and Sisters of Penance", as composed of all classes (with the first specific mention of the category of "widows"), attests that the members overcame the feudal distinctions of birth, power, and wealth.

His claim that "at the beginning a friar was assigned to them as Minister" presents historical difficulties. Juridical documents from that time indicate that a member of the local community, that is, one of the lay penitents, served as its minister[92]. Nevertheless, the account testifies to the close relationship between the friars and the penitents.

Further, we once again have mention of Hugolino's involvement in the writing of the Rule, a topic we will treat in our consideration of the *Memoriale propositi* in *Chapter III*.

What the Early Sources Reveal

All of the early narrative sources, beginning with the *Vita Prima* of Thomas of Celano, affirm a causal relationship between Francis and the lay penitential movement, often calling him its founder[93]. Thus it

---

[91] *Liber de laudibus beati Francisci*, VII. (Translation by the author). The critical Latin edition reads, "Doctrinae Francisci elucet maxime fructus in tribus ab eo statutis Ordinibus... Tertius Ordo est fratrum et sororum de poenitentia, clericis, laicis, virginibus, viduis et coniugatis communis, cuius propositum est in domibus propriis honeste vivere, operibus pietatis intendere, pompam saeculi fugere. Unde videas inter eos nobiles aliquando milites vel alios magnos secundum saeculum viros cum mantellis honestis nigris pellibus involutos, in humili tam veste quam equitatura cum indigentibus sic conversari modeste, ut eos vere Deum timentes non dubites. Istis a principio frater assignabatur Minister, sed nunc suis in terra dimittuntur Ministris, ut tamen a fratribus tamquam confratres et eodem patre geniti consiliis et auxiliis foveantur.

In regulis seu vivendi formis Ordinis istorum dictandis sanctae memoriae dominus Papa Gregorius in minori adhuc officio constitutus, beato Francisco intima familiaritate coniunctus, devote supplebat quod viro sancto iudicandi scientia deerat". Cf. *AF*, III, 679, 686.

[92] Schmucki, *Il T.O.F. nelle biografie*, 131.

[93] M. D'Alatri, *Il Terzo Ordine*, in *Francesco, il francescanesimo, e la cultura della nuova Europa*, edited by I. Baldelli and A. Romanini, Firenze 1986, 120.

is possible, even probable, that Francis provided guidance for a lay penitential group as he had done for his early friar companions[94]. The fact that early on Francis did write a Rule both for the friars and for the sisters would seem to make not only plausible but probable Thomas of Celano's claim that "to all he gave a Rule of life"[95]. Further, the evolution or development of the Rule both of the Friars Minor and of the Poor Ladies, lends plausibility to the suggestion that Francis' Rule for the penitents also underwent a similar process of adaptation and change. The indisputable evolution of the *Protoregula*[96] of the friars makes plausible the hypothesis that these "norms" for the penitents progressed from simple gospel texts[97], to more detailed directives occa-

---

[94] Schmucki makes this suggestion in his analysis of these early texts in *Il T.O.F. nelle biografie*, 120.

[95] Francis himself attests to the Rule for the friars in his Testament where he records, "And after the Lord gave me brothers, no one showed me what I should do, but the Most High Himself revealed to me that I should live according to the form of the Holy Gospel. And I had this written down simply and in a few words and the Lord Pope confirmed it for me". *Testament* 14-15. Cf. Armstrong, *Francis and Clare*, 154-55. In her Testament, Clare records not only that Francis gave them a Rule, but that he gave them many writings: "And afterwards he wrote a form of life for us, especially that we always persevere in holy poverty. While he was living he was not content to encourage us with many words and examples to the love of holy poverty and its observance, but he gave us many writings that, after his death, we would in no way turn away from it, as the Son of God never wished to abandon this holy poverty while He lived in the world. And our most blessed father Francis, having imitated His footprints, never departed either in example or in teaching from this holy poverty that he had chosen for himself and his brothers". *Testament of Saint Clare*, 33-36. Cf. R. Armstrong, *Clare of Assisi: Early Documents*, Mahwah 1988, 56.

[96] Though the rule of 1209/1210 is no longer extant, the *Regula non bullata* of 1221 evidences the process of change and development of this "primitive rule" prior to the papal approbation of the *Regula bullata* in 1223. In his study of the *Regula non bullata* Flood treats the evolution of this document, indicating the evidences of additions and changes. Cf. D. Flood and T. Matura, *The Birth of a Movement*, Chicago 1975.

[97] In line with this theory, Esser, a prominent Franciscan scholar, has presented the hypothesis, and argues convincingly, that the shorter and longer versions of Francis' *Letter to All the Faithful* should be understood as the "primitive rule". Cf. Esser, *Un documento dell'inizio*, 87-99; *A Forerunner of the "Epistola*

sioned by specific situations and changing conditions[98], gradually becoming more codified, and eventually resulting in a more juridical document[99].

But, however plausible these hypotheses appear, based upon the witness of the early biographical sources, they remain just that, hypotheses. As we have seen, these texts offer no specific testimony describing this "norm of life" or its contents; they reveal little or nothing about this "primitive rule".

Instead, the sources reveal how the tradition in the mid-to-late thirteenth century imaged and understood this "order" and its relation to Francis. Clearly, a very short time after Francis' death, the tradition presented Francis as having founded this "Third Order" and as having given its members a Rule. In fact, by the second half of the thirteenth century, even outside a strictly Franciscan context, the foundation of the Order of Penance was attributed to Francis[100].

An inclusive reading of these sources, while not producing specific details about the "primitive rule", does reveal certain consistencies in the various testimonies about this Order of Penitents[101]. We can affirm Schmucki's conclusions in which he delineates certain "convergences" which emerge within the tradition:

---

ad Fideles" of St. Francis of Assisi, in *Anal TOR* 129 (1978) 11-47; *La Lettera di san Francesco ai fedeli*, in *CF* 43 (1973) 65-78. *Chapter III* will discuss in depth these works of Esser, as well as other research with respect to the two versions of Francis' *Letter to All the Faithful.*

[98] David Flood, in his analysis of Francis' *Letter to All the Faithful*, discusses Francis' understanding of a *Rule* as "the literary correlate to the spiritual discernment in which the movement went its own way". Cf. D. Flood, *The Commonitorium*, in *Haversack* 3 (1979) n. 1, 20.

[99] Bernard of Bessa's testimony, given above pp. 76-77, states explicitly that Francis was aided by Cardinal Hugolino in the rule or form of living which he gave to the Penitents. D'Alatri notes that this testimony would therefore seem to equate the *Memoriale propositi* of 1221, rather than one of Francis' letters, with this "rule" of which these early sources speak. Cf. D'Alatri, *Il Terzo Ordine*, 122.

[100] Cf. discussion above, p. 74.

[101] The use of "testimonies" in the plural is deliberate. The textual witnesses do not present themselves merely as continued repetitions of Thomas of Celano. Cf. D'Alatri, *Francesco d'Assisi e i laici*, 622.

- the name of the order (most often *Ordo Poenitent[i]um*)
- its penitential character
- its lay structure
- its universal recruitment (men and women from all classes)
- its influence on the church and civil society
- Francis' having given a rule[102].

In a separate study of the early Franciscan sources, Giovanna Casagrande stresses that amidst these "convergences" one recurrent theme, one undeniable witness stands out and remains the most important: the laity were inflamed, empowered, inspired by the life and exhortation of Francis[103]. The inspiration of Francis and his influence upon the early penitents remains indubitable. Also incontestable is the fact that the sources made the claim, starting from 1228 at the latest, that this lay penitential group received from Francis not only inspiration but a "rule of life". But how do we move from these early testimonies about a "rule" to an actual document, or at least to more concrete data concerning Francis' guidance for these penitents? Given that our earliest source, the *Vita prima* of Thomas of Celano, offers only a vague reference to this "norm of life", must we then surrender our quest for this "primitive rule", for the way of life proposed by Francis for the members of the penitential group which has evolved into the Secular Franciscan Order? While, scholars have generally conceded the probability that Francis wrote the *Epistola ad Fideles* for penitents, until very recently most scholars have denied the possibility of knowing anything definite about the "primitive rule"[104].

However, recent research suggests the opposite. We can know something definite about this "primitive rule". The actual text has, in fact, been dis-covered among the extant writings of Francis.

The Writings of Francis

Many of the writings of Francis (including letters, prayers, rules, and testaments) have survived in medieval manuscripts. While only two

[102] Schmucki, *Il T.O.F. nelle biografie*, 135-140.

[103] Casagrande, *L'Ordine Francescano Secolare*, 216-20.

[104] For example, Casagrande emphatically states her belief that we can know nothing definite about the "Rule". Cf. Casagrande, *L'Ordine Francescano Secolare*, 219.

writings in Francis' own hand survive, some twenty-eight existing writings have been accepted as authentic, that is, as composed by Francis[105]. Much work has been done in the last century to establish critical editions of each of these writings from the variant manuscripts[106]. This research brought the discovery of some writings that had been unknown for centuries. One such discovery by Paul Sabatier in 1900 brought to light a manuscript which appeared to contain the "primitive rule" of the "Third Order", that is, the *norma vitae* given by Francis to the early penitents.

Sabatier's Discovery

Sabatier discovered the text in Codex 225 of the Guarnacci Library of Volterra and published it under the title of "*Haec sunt verba vitae et salutis quae si quis legerit et fecerit inveniet vitam et auriet salutem a domino*" (These are the words of life and salvation, which if anyone reads them and puts them into practice, that one will find life and attain the salvation of the Lord)[107]. Sabatier perceived a direct relationship between this Volterra document and the well-documented and authenticated writing of Francis known as the *Epistola ad Fideles*, or the *Letter to All the Faithful.* He believed the shorter Volterra document

---

[105] For a brief discussion of the meaning of "authenticity" with respect to these medieval documents, cf. Desbonnets, *From Intuition to Institution*, 151-52.

[106] Kajetan Esser produced a critical edition of the writings of Francis from 1,028 variant manuscripts. Esser's work has been published in two different editions: *Die Opuscula des Hl. Franziskus von Assisi*, Grottaferrata (Roma) 1976; and *Opuscula Sancti Patris Francisci Assisiensis*, Grottaferrata 1978. An English translation based upon Esser's critical edition of Francis' writings may be found in R. Armstrong and I. Brady, *Francis and Clare: The Complete Works*, New York 1982.

[107] P. Sabatier, *Fratris Francisci Bartholi de Assisio Tractatus de Indulgentia S. Mariae de Portiuncula Collection d'études et de documents sur l'histoire religieuse et littéraire du Moyen Age II*, Paris 1900, cf. *Appendice*, 132-36; for a complete description of the Volterra ms. 225, cf. pages CLIII-CLVI. As Esser points out, the Volterra manuscript is made up of parts which were written at different times, however, the part in question has been dated around the middle of the thirteenth century. Cf. K. Esser, *A Forerunner of the "Epistola ad Fideles" of St. Francis of Assisi*, in *Anal TOR* 129 (1978) 12, note 1.

not to be an extract, but rather, a "first draft" because of its "simplicity of design" and "intensity of vision"[108]. According to Esser, Sabatier's argument for the priority of this text evidenced a significant insight into the writing style of Francis[109]. Francis did return to his writings to rework and expand them as changed conditions demanded.

But if, as Sabatier suggested, the Volterra text was a "first draft" of the *Epistola ad Fideles*, then the possibility that this text represents the "primitive rule" becomes more probable. It is probable because, as Esser has shown in his study on the *Epistola ad Fideles*, the so-called "*Letter to All the Faithful*" is addressed not to Christians in general (as the title would seem to indicate), but rather, to "religious Christians", that is, to those living a more intense commitment to the Christian life according to the ecclesiastical forms of penance[110]. Esser even speaks of the *Epistola ad Fideles* as a "*forma vivendi*", that is, as a way of life for the early Franciscan penitents[111]. But then Sabatier's insight into Francis' manner of composing texts, his hunch that the Volterra text is a "first draft" of the *Epistola ad Fideles*, an earlier form of this "*forma vivendi*", suggests that the Volterra text could be the "primitive rule" of the penitents.

However, Sabatier's discovery and insight went largely unheeded. Walter Goetz, who published his critical research on the writings of Francis in 1904, disputed Sabatier's claim[112]. He expressed doubt about the title attributed to the work by Sabatier since many manuscripts

---

[108] P. Sabatier, *Deux nouveaux Opuscules de Saint François*, in *Collection d'études et de documents sur l'histoire religieuse et littéraire du Moyen Age II*, 134, note 1.

[109] Esser, *A Forerunner of the "Epistola ad Fideles"*, 14.

[110] K. Esser, *La Lettera di san Francesco ai fedeli*, in *CF* 43 (1973) 71-72.

[111] Esser points out that the *Memoriale propositi* of 1221, which parallels almost literally the rules of other medieval penitential groups, contains "little or nothing" specifically Franciscan. Therefore Esser argues that since Thomas of Celano states unequivocally that Francis gave the penitents a "*normam vitae ac salutis viam*", and further, since Julian of Speyer speaks of this "*vivendi regula*" making this group of penitents "*non mediocris perfectionis*", this text could be that "Rule". Cf. Esser, *Un documento dell'inizio*, 87-88. For a summary of Esser's conclusions, cf. Pazzelli, *St. Francis and the Third Order*, 104-106.

[112] Esser's article offers a brief summary of the history of the research on this document, including citations of the referenced critical studies. Cf. Esser, *A Forerunner of the "Epistola ad Fideles"*, 11-15.

gave that exact phrase as the conclusion of the *Admonitions*[113]. Given that in the Volterra manuscript examined by Sabatier the text in question follows immediately after the text of the *Admonitions*, Goetz suggested that Sabatier mistook the conclusion of the *Admonitions* to be the "title" of the letter[114]. Goetz, therefore, denied the priority given the text by Sabatier and suggested that it was merely an extract or an abbreviation of the *Letter to All the Faithful*. Unfortunately, later scholars accepted Goetz' position and while they referenced the Volterra manuscript in their discussion of the manuscript tradition, no further critical edition of the writings of Francis included the text discovered by Sabatier[115]. Thus, the text lay forgotten for almost seventy years.

Esser's Reconsideration of the Volterra Text

When all of the extant manuscripts for the *Letter to All the Faithful* were collated for a new critical edition about twenty years ago, it became evident that "the text of Vo[lterra] stood by itself in the whole textual tradition"[116]. Based upon the singularity of the document, Kajetan Esser began an exhaustive critical study of the text[117]. Up until that time, Esser had accepted the generally held belief that Sabatier's proposed title was actually the conclusion to the *Admonitions* and that

[113] Cf. *Opuscula*, 82, note 6.

[114] Pazzelli explains how, more probably, the opposite was the case. He suggests that the actual title of the letter became attached to the end of the *Admonitions* and then continued to be copied as such in the manuscript tradition. Cf. R. Pazzelli, *The Title of the "Recensio Prior of the Letter to the Faithful": Clarifications concerning Codex 225 of Volterra (cod Vo)*, in *Anal TOR* XIX (1987) 247-48, and in *Greyfriars Review* 4 (1990) n. 3, 1-6.

[115] L. Lemmens, *Opuscula Sancti Patris Francisci Assisiensis*, Grottaferrata (Roma) 1904, 182-85; H. Boehmer, *Analekten*, S. XIX, LVII: 49-57.

[116] Esser, *A Forerunner of the "Epistola ad Fideles"*, 15.

[117] Esser's original article, written in 1974, was first published as *Ein Vorläufer der "Epistola ad fideles" des hl. Franziskus von Assisi (Cod. 225 de Biblioteca Guarnacci zu Volterra)*, in *CF* 45 (1975) 5-37. It was later translated and published in both English and Italian: *A Forerunner of the "Epistola ad Fideles" of St. Francis of Assisi*, in *Anal TOR* 129 (1978) 11-47; *Un (Documento) precursore della "Epistola ad Fidelis" di San Francesco d'Assisi (Il Codice 225 della Biblioteca Guarnacci di Volterra)*, in *Anal TOR* 129 (1978) 11-47.

the Volterra text was, therefore, merely a later extract of the *Letter to All the Faithful*[118].

However, Esser's extensive study convinced him otherwise. Esser concluded that this Volterra text was "independent in itself and at the same time older than the rest of the tradition of the "*Epistola ad fideles*"[119]. Further, due to his extensive study of the extant manuscripts, Esser no longer accepted the contested phrase to be an authentic conclusion to the *Admonitions*, rather he judged it to be a later editorial addition[120]. But Esser still did not accept Sabatier's proposed title[121]. He considered the text to be untitled and therefore suggested a title based upon the content of the text:

> it becomes quite evident that this is a question of an earlier version of what we call today the *Epistola ad Fideles*. This aspect then should be clearly expressed in the title. Furthermore, it is clear that it is a matter of a directive for the Brothers and Sisters of Penance to whom Francis is giving admonition and encouragement for their life. Therefore it might be formulated thus:
>
> *EPISTOLA AD FIDELES (RECENSIO PRIOR)*
> *Exhortatio ad fratres et sorores de poenitentia*[122].

But, in that same study, Esser goes beyond his claim that this text is an "Exhortation to the Brothers and Sisters of Penance". Esser suggests that this text *could* be that "primitive rule", the *norma vitae* of which Thomas of Celano spoke. Esser writes:

> It is quite clear therefore that we have before us a written instruction directed toward persons who have joined the penance movement of the

---

[118] K. Esser and R. Oliger, *La tradition manuscrite des Opuscules de Saint François d'Assise*, Roma 1972, 93 note 355.

[119] Esser, *A Forerunner of the "Epistola ad Fideles"*, 33.

[120] *Opuscula*, 82.

[121] Esser, *Un documento dell'inizio*, 88, 97.

[122] Esser, *A Forerunner of the "Epistola ad Fideles"*, 42. This text has, therefore, come to be known as the "First Version" or "Prior Recension" of the *Letter to All the Faithful*. It has since generally been designated as *Epistola ad Fideles I* or *EpFid I*. Some of the problems associated with this traditional designation and a suggested alternative will be discussed in *Chapter III*.

> later Middle Ages, a movement to which Francis and his brotherhood were deeply attached and obligated. Sentence 48, however, clearly shows that the addressees are not the friars minor themselves. It therefore concerns "fratres et sorores de poenitentia in domibus propriis existentes", that is, those people who took on themselves a definite way of life in the year 1221, those to whom moreover, or at least to some individual groups among them, Francis gave a "forma vivendi", according to the testimony of his first biographers. Unfortunately we do not have detailed information on the content of this way of life. The biographers however do report that it was a "salutis via" suitable for leading its followers "ad perfectionis status". Our letter *could* be such a "documentum salutis"[123].

Based upon Esser's study and his extraordinary claim, most people identified this Volterra text, the *Recensio Prior,* as the "norm of life" given by Francis to the early penitents[124]. Raffaele Pazzelli, based upon his own recent examination of the Volterra codex, goes beyond Esser's suggestions and makes the astounding claim that this identification of the *Recensio Prior* with the form of life given by Francis to the penitents "is no longer merely an hypothesis, as has been commonly

[123] Esser, *A Forerunner of the "Epistola ad Fideles"*, 38-39.

[124] It might well be noted here, relative to our focus upon the 1978 Rule of the Secular Franciscan Order, that sometime between June and October 1977 the decision was made to add this *Recensio Prior* as a prologue to the proposed new Rule. While this decision was indeed extremely important, to my puzzlement, no document presenting reasons for this addition can be found within the archives. The Ministers General inserted the text into the Rule as a prologue without explanation. This single change, possibly the most significant change throughout the entire ten year redactional process, remains without any documented explanation. The most plausible explanation for this unexplained change in the proposed Rule would appear to be related to Esser's position (as published in 1975, amidst the latter part of the redactional process). Given that his hypothesis became so popularly accepted, I would guess that the incorporation of the text within the Rule appeared so obvious and appropriate to those involved in its formulation, that an explanation or justification of its addition was unnecessary. The significance of the decision to include this *Recensio Prior* as the prologue of the new Rule will be discussed further in both *Chapter IV* and *Chapter V*.

admitted up to this point after Esser's masterly study, but almost a certainty''[125].

Pazzelli's Re-examination of the Volterra Text

Since Pazzelli's discovery holds such great significance for our own study, we will consider his findings and arguments in some detail. In an article devoted to the defense of his thesis, which is based upon his own thorough examination of the actual Volterra manuscript, Pazzelli presents his startling position:

> we defend the position that the words ''Haec sunt verba vitae et salutis...'' are the correct original title of the ''*Recensio Prior* of the Letter to the Faithful''; we also claim that the same formulation shows that the *Opusculum* is addressed to the brothers and sisters of Penance and that, consequentially [*sic*], we are dealing with the *forma vitae* given by St. Francis to his penitents, according to the testimony of his first biographers[126].

Pazzelli's examination found that the Codex did not read, as Esser had claimed, ''Haec sunt verba vitae et salutis, quae, si quis legerit et fecerit, inveniet vitam et hauriet salutem a Domino. Amen''[127]. Rather, the text reads, ''haec sunt verba vitae et salutis quae si quis legerit et fecerit inveniet vitam et auriet salutem a domino *de illis qui faciunt poenitentiam*''[128]. Further, this whole phrase appears in red ink

---

[125] The author has here translated from the original Italian article to avoid the contradictory term ''precluded certainty'' given in the English translation of Pazzelli's article. The Italian reads: ''non è più dunque solo una ipotesi — come si ammetteva comunemente fino ad oggi, dopo lo studio magistrale dell'Esser, — ma pressoché una certezza''. Cf. R. Pazzelli, *Il titolo della ''Prima Recensione della Lettera ai Fedeli'': Precisazioni sul Codice 225 di Volterra (cod Vo)*, in *Anal TOR* XIX (1987) 238.

[126] Pazzelli, *The Title of the ''Recensio Prior''*, 243.

[127] *Opuscula*, 82, note 6.

[128] Emphasis added by the author. For Pazzelli's arguments supporting this phrase rather than the phrase given by Esser as the title, cf. Pazzelli, *The Title of the ''Recensio Prior''*, 244-45.

which indicates that it is, in fact, the title of the work[129]. While it seems odd that the other scholars could miss so obvious a clue, Pazzelli explains,

> it is our opinion that, among the five authoritative scholars who wrote about the *cod Vo* (namely Sabatier, Goetz, Lemmens, Boehmer, and Esser) only Sabatier examined the manuscript personally. The others dealt with either transcripts made by their collaborators or, more probably, with black and white photocopies or microfilms. This could explain the mistake. It is mainly because of the red ink and the parts written in red in the *cod. Vo* that the deductions we now present are apparent[130].

According to Pazzelli, this title well explains the content of the text that follows, that is, it introduces the "form of life" for those penitents who asked Francis for guidance. Further, the beginning words, "*haec sunt verba vitae et salutis*", call to mind the beginning words of the Earlier Rule of the Friars Minor, "*Haec est vita Evangelii*"[131]. Thus, Pazzelli concludes with "certainty" that the "*Recensio Prior* can be identified with the *forma vitae* given by St. Francis to the Penitents "according to the testimony of the earliest biographers"[132].

As the title of the work claims (less the conditional clause), we have the "words of life and salvation... concerning those who do penance".

---

[129] The cover of this volume presents a somewhat reduced, color reproduction of the manuscript. As Pazzelli points out, "In the part of the Volterra Codex containing the Opuscula of St. Francis (ff. 141r-155r) the only things written in red ink are the titles of the works and the first letter of each chapter and conclusions. In particular, in the "Recensio prior", that is in the work under consideration here, the only things written in red are: a) the title of the work, b) the "De illis qui non agunt poenitentiam" of the second part and c) the three initial letters, namely the I (In nomine domini), the O beginning the second section (Omnes autem illi et illae...) and the O of the conclusion (Omnes illos quibus...)". Cf. Pazzelli, *The Title of the "Recensio Prior"*, 244. Pazzelli's article includes a color plate of the page of the manuscript containing the title. Temperini's study includes color plates of the entire Voterra text, as well as a line by line transcription of the Latin script. Cf. L. Temperini, *Frate Francesco a tutti i suoi fedeli*, Roma 1987, 10-19.

[130] Pazzelli, *The Title of the "Recensio Prior"*, 247.

[131] *Ibid.*, 246.

[132] *Ibid.*, 246.

We have Francis' "Rule of life" for the penitents who sought his guidance. We have in the Volterra text that "primitive Rule" of the "Third Order"[133].

The Primitive Rule: An Exhortation to Penance

In order to understand this "primitive Rule", Francis' exhortation to penance, we must understand Francis' experience of penance. In his Testament, Francis speaks of how he began his life of penance:

> The Lord granted me, Brother Francis, to begin to do penance in this way: While I was in sin, it seemed very bitter to me to see lepers. And the Lord Himself led me among them and I had mercy upon them. And when I left them that which seemed bitter to me was changed into sweetness of soul and body; and afterward I lingered a little and left the world[134].

By Francis' own account, he embraced this penitential life after his conversion experience: "*parum steti et exivi de saeculo*"[135]. In the thirteenth century, "leaving the world" signified entering some form of religious life. But "religious life" designated not only monastic Orders but also the Order of Penance[136]. For Francis, "leaving the world" involved leaving only the worldliness of reality, not departing from civil society, in which Francis continued to live and to preach. The early sources and Francis' own writings concur: Francis embraced and preached a life of penance.

---

[133] The text of this "primitive Rule" will receive careful analysis in *Chapter III*.

[134] *Testament* 1-3. Cf. Armstrong, *Francis and Clare*, 154. The critical Latin edition reads: "Dominus ita dedit mihi fratri Francisco incipere faciendi poenitentiam: quia, cum essem in peccatis, nimis mihi videbatur amarum vider leprosos. Et ipse Dominus conduxit me inter illos et feci misericordiam cum illis. Et recedente me ab ipsis, id quod videbatur mihi amarum, conversum fuit mihi in dulcedinem animi et corporis; et postea parum steti et exivi de saeculo". Cf. *Opuscula*, 307-308.

[135] *Opuscula*, 308.

[136] The understanding of "leaving the world" and "religious life" will be discussed in detail in *Chapter II*.

When near the end of his life Francis reflected back on his conversion, he saw it as the work of God: "The Lord granted me..." In his later reflection, Francis understood his encounter with the leper as a critical moment in that conversion, as a moment of grace. In seeing the leper Francis began to see; in touching the leper Francis was touched. This holy exchange empowered Francis to exchange his former way of life for a life of penance[137].

Francis' dramatic experience of God, his being inspired by God "*incipere faciendi poenitentiam*"[138], becomes encoded in his "Rule of life" for the penitents[139]. In his exhortation to penance, Francis speaks of "those who do penance" and "those who do not do penance". Francis shares with others his new way of seeing; he contrasts sight and blindness. He presents the "*salutis via*", the only possible response to God, as a life of *penance*.

Clearly, to understand the primitive Rule we must understand the concept of penance. Before moving to an analysis of the primitive Rule,

---

[137] Most scholars (Meersseman, Pazzelli, D'Alatri, Pompei, etc.) interpret Francis' words and actions as his deliberate choice to enter the Order of Penitents, that is, to embrace a juridical state or condition. Raoul Manselli insists that one can understand Francis' life as a penitent only in light of the strong contrast between Francis who was "absolutely indifferent to formal juridical institutions", and a society for which these institutions had an "essential importance". According to Manselli, Francis changed his social state from that of a rich merchant to that of the poor and wretched, without juridical protection. Only later did the bishop and others push him to embrace a juridical state of penance. Cf. R. Manselli, *Francesco d'Assisi e i laici viventi nel secolo: Inizio del Terz'Ordine?* in *Prime manifestazioni di vita comunitaria, maschile e femminile, nel movimento francescano della Penitenza (1215-1447)*, edited by R. Pazzelli and L. Temperini, Roma 1982, 11-12.

This author finds Manselli's presentation convincing and agrees that Francis chose a social condition rather than a juridical state. However, given that Francis practiced and preached penance, our examination will pursue an understanding of this penitential life rather than delay over the question of Francis' intention, as over against the persuasion of Bishop Guido or other ecclesiastical figures, concerning the choice of a religious way of life or of a juridical state.

[138] *Opuscula*, 307.

[139] This point, already evident from the discussion of Esser's analysis of the text and suggested title (cf. above, p. 84), will be discussed in detail both in *Chapter III* and in *Chapter V*.

therefore, we will turn now in *Chapter II* to a discussion of "penance". We will consider how the understanding and practice of penance developed in the Church and how it had evolved in the thirteenth century. Then, after having examined the historical context and Francis' experience of penance more closely, we will turn in *Chapter III* to an analysis of the primitive Rule.

Chapter II

THE HISTORICAL CONTEXT

To penetrate Francis' words, his statements about his own conversion and his exhortations to penance, we need to explore Francis' own historical and theological context, the world from which he arose. This second chapter is dedicated, therefore, to an analysis of the context of Francis and the early penitents. But given that Francis embraced a life of penance and exhorted his followers "to do penance", prior to a consideration of Francis' more immediate context, we must examine the concept of "penance" itself.

We begin, therefore, with a survey of the development of the concept and praxis of "penance" in the Church up to the time of Francis[1]. We will then explore the dramatic changes and religious climate of the twelfth century which will lead to an examination of Assisi at the beginning of the thirteenth century, the immediate context from which emerge Francis and the Franciscan movement. Let us, then, first turn to a consideration of the historical development of penance to pro-

[1] For a brief, admittedly overly-simplified treatment of the development of "penance" and the history of the penitents, cf. B. Pastor Oliver, *The "State of Penance" and the beginnings of the Order of Brothers and Sisters of Penance*, in *Anal TOR* XIII/123 (1974) 35-72. For an excellent, more detailed study of the development of penance in the Church, offering an extensive treatment of the ancient, medieval and modern forms of penance, cf. J. Dallen, *The Reconciling Community: The Rite of Penance*, New York 1986. For an extensive treatment of the textual witness of the first three centuries with respect to the existence of an Order of Penitents prior to and distinct from the Order of Penitents within the later institution of canonical penance, cf. J. Favazza, *The Order of Penitents: Historical Roots and Pastoral Future*, Collegeville 1988.

vide a basis from which to understand the meaning of penance for Francis and his lay followers in the thirteenth century.

"Penance" in the Church

Although in contemporary parlance "penance" often connotes the "sacrament of confession" or "acts of mortification", both the Hebrew Scriptures and the Christian Scriptures present the notion of penance or repentance within the context of conversion[2]. No single term is used consistently in the Scriptures to designate this reality, nor is the biblical notion of conversion completely contained within one term. The Hebrew root *shub*, which basically means "to turn back" or "to return", forms a foundation for the biblical concept of repentance or conversion[3]. Its moral sense of turning from a sinful life to God becomes gradually more pronounced with the prophets. The New Testament further develops the concept of conversion, designated by the Greek term *metanoia* which signifies a radical change of heart, specifying the complete break with a sinful life as a radical new life in Christ which depends on faith[4].

Thus, the biblical notion of penance primarily involves an interior attitude. Although it does necessarily involve an external manifestation, in the Scriptures penance does not consist merely of external practices. Rather, penance essentially and more profoundly signifies a "change of heart" or a new way of living.

In the Old Testament

The Old Testament witnesses to the existence of a cultic-ritual form of repentance which included confession of sin and penitential prayer[5].

---

[2] For a discussion of the concept of "penance" in the Scriptures, cf. *DSp*, s.v. *Pénitence*, by P. Adnès, 944-52; R. Faley, *Biblical Considerations on Metanoia*, in *Anal TOR* 13 (1974) 13-33; and M. Crosby, *The Biblical Vision of Conversion*, in *The Desires of the Human Heart: An Introduction to the Theology of Bernard Lonergan*, edited by V. Gregson, New York 1988, 31-74.

[3] Faley, *Biblical Considerations on Metanoia*, 14.

[4] *DSp*, s.v. *Pénitence*, by Adnès, 943.

[5] Cf. *Leviticus* 5:5; 2 *Samuel* 12:13; and *Psalms* 6, 32, 38, 51, 102, 130, and 143.

This ritual expression of repentance became more specified in post-Exilic Israel and included practices such as the offering of sacrifice, fast and abstinence, the use of sackcloth and ashes, and almsgiving[6]. But the prophets criticized Israel's practice of repentance precisely because its main element, the interior change of heart, had for the most part been set aside[7]. In fact, the summons to a true repentance and a change of life on the part of Israel stands at the heart of the prophetic mission[8]. The prophets called Israel to a return to the covenant; they railed against empty ritualism. Yahweh demands acts of justice, love and mercy:

> Come, let us return to Yahweh.
> He has rent us and he will heal us;
> he has struck us and he will bind up our wounds;
> after two days he will revive us,
> on the third day he will raise us up
> and we shall live in his presence.
> Let us know, let us strive to know Yahweh;
> that he will come is as certain as the dawn.
> He will come to us like a shower,
> like the rain of springtime to the earth.
>
> What am I to do with you, Ephraim?
> What am I to do with you, Judah?
> For your love is like morning mist,
> like the dew that quickly disappears.
>
> This is why I have hacked them to pieces by means of the prophets,
> why I have killed them with words from my mouth,
> why my sentence will blaze forth like the dawn -
> for faithful love is what pleases me, not sacrifice;
> knowledge of God, not burnt offerings[9].

This call to conversion was first addressed by the prophets to the nation as a whole, but it became steadily more personalized and nu-

---

[6] *DSp*, s.v. *Pénitence*, by Adnès, 945-48.

[7] J. Bauer, *Encyclopedia of Biblical Theology: The Complete Sacramentum Verbi*, New York 1981, s.v. *Conversion*, by J. Bauer, 138.

[8] Faley, *Biblical Considerations on Metanoia*, 14.

[9] *Hosea* 6:1-6.

anced. Not just the nation as a whole, but each individual person was called to conversion, and this "return to Yahweh" implied a turning away from everything evil[10]. But the capacity to turn from evil to God exceeds any individual person's ability and depends upon the graciousness of God. It is Yahweh who declares: "Within them I shall plant my Law, writing it on their hearts. Then I shall be their God and they will be my people"[11].

Thus, in the prophets, conversion involves two inextricably interwoven elements: a "turning back" and "compassion". On the part of the person, conversion involves a turning away from sin, from that which is ungodly. On the part of God, there is compassion which expresses itself in forgiveness. The prophets proclaim that God will completely regenerate the chosen people *if* they repent; Yahweh will purify them from their sinfulness giving them a new heart and a new spirit, *if* they return to God with "faithful love". But this return to Yahweh, this living in the "knowledge of God", implied a life-long commitment to God's covenant. Conversion or repentance was therefore understood as "once and for all"; further recidivism was not envisioned. The new Israel, the one who had returned to Yahweh, lived in obedience to the law, lived a new life which would produce the fruits of justice[12].

In the New Testament

With the approach of the Christian era, prophetic eschatology gave way to apocalyptic expectations, heightening a sense of sin and encouraging an intense desire for moral purity[13]. Amidst this apocalyptic mentality both John the Baptist and Jesus preached repentance. Whereas the prophets warned of an infrahistorical judgment against those who refused to convert[14], and John the Baptist spoke of an imminent final judgment[15], Jesus did not threaten condemnation but proclaimed that

---

[10] *Encyclopedia of Biblical Theology*, s.v. *Conversion*, by J. Bauer, 138.
[11] *Jeremiah* 31:33.
[12] Faley, *Biblical Considerations on Metanoia*, 16-17.
[13] *DSp*, s.v. *Pénitence*, by Adnès, 948.
[14] For example, cf. *Isaiah* 5:25ff; 9:7ff.
[15] *Matthew* 3:10; *Luke* 3:9.

the Kingdom of God had already come and that the condition for entering into the Reign of God was conversion[16].

Jesus invited all people, especially sinners, to enter into the presence of God[17]. He called all people to conversion, and this conversion was, first and foremost, a turning of one's heart to God. But as Jesus the proclaimer became the proclaimed, this turning to God, the acceptance of faith and forgiveness of sin, became tied to the person of Jesus.

The Gospels proclaim boldly that Jesus forgave sinners who repented[18]. Even the passages in the New Testament which appear to indicate that there are certain sins that cannot be forgiven serve primarily to exhort the hearer to conversion[19]. These texts present the central salvific decision: to the extent that the person accepts or rejects the person and message of Jesus the Christ, to that extent he or she shares in the salvation offered by God through Christ[20]. The emphasis is, therefore, on the subjective response of the person. All things are possible for God; grace is decisive for conversion[21]. But the person must accept the forgiveness offered and so the Scriptures speak of the subjective behavior necessary for the forgiveness of sins.

The New Testament speaks of *metanoia*, of a change of heart which implied a dissatisfaction with one's former way of living[22]. This *metanoia* involved a commitment to change one's life, the decision to turn from sin and to live in Christ. But while the New Testament stresses the need for conversion or the demand to do penance, it offers little specific detail concerning the external actions involved in doing penance. Rather, the New Testament focuses upon the efficacy of the life, death, and resurrection of Jesus for the repentant sinner. However, one action is mentioned consistently as an external manifestation of the person's internal conversion: Baptism.

---

[16] *Mark* 1:15.

[17] *Luke* 5:32.

[18] For example, cf. *Matthew* 9:2; *Luke* 7:36-50; *John* 1:29.

[19] Cf. *Mark* 3:28-29; *Matthew* 12:31-32; *Luke* 12:10; *Hebrews* 6:4-6; 10:26-31.

[20] Favazza, *The Order of Penitents*, 70-71.

[21] *Luke* 18:27.

[22] Faley, *Biblical Considerations on Metanoia*, 27.

In Relation to Baptism

Both John the Baptist and Jesus preached a Baptism of repentance, however, the gospels distinguish clearly between John's Baptism with water and Jesus' Baptism with the Holy Spirit[23]. Evidently these passages reflect the early Christian communities' baptismal experience of the Spirit of the risen Jesus being conferred in Baptism[24]. The primitive Christian communties connected conversion with belief in the Lordship of Jesus. The immediate object of conversion to God was the faith-acceptance of Jesus as Lord and Messiah which brought the gift of the Holy Spirit. And the Spirit-directed movement toward Christ in conversion was symbolized, that is, both expressed and effected, in Baptism[25].

Thus, the early Christians understood Baptism to effect the forgiveness of sins, the beginning of a new life in Christ. There did not exist the more organized penitential institution which later evolved[26]. In Baptism the person died to a former way of life and became part of the new creation: "it is no longer I, but Christ living in me"[27]. Initiation into the community presupposed a total and absolute commitment; the *metanoia* it signified involved every aspect of the person's life. For the person whose sins were forgiven in Baptism and who had begun a life of holiness, sin remained outside the realm of possibility. And so, initially, forgiveness of postbaptismal sin remained a moot question.

However, the situation soon presented itself and the community had to decide how to deal with those who had sinned after Baptism. The idea and praxis of a second forgiveness of sin, of a "second penance" for postbaptismal sinners, gradually evolved. But this evolution was slow and uneven, not without controversy amidst the varying local traditions. Let us review briefly that evolution.

In the Apostolic Churches

The overwhelming witness of the New Testament confirms that the early Church communities offered reconciliation to *all* sinners who sin-

---

[23] *Mark* 1:8; *Matthew* 3:11; *Luke* 3:16; *Acts* 19:2-6.

[24] Faley, *Biblical Considerations on Metanoia*, 25.

[25] *Ibid.*, 30-31.

[26] *DSp*, s.v. *Pénitence*, by Adnès, 956.

[27] *Galatians* 2:20.

cerely repented[28]. While the New Testament does not present any evidence of an organized system within the earliest communities for the forgiveness of sin other than the Baptism of forgiveness, it does contain foundational elements for the practice which developed within the early communities. Sinners were exhorted to pray for forgiveness[29], and to perform works of charity for the forgiveness of sin[30].

Both sin and forgiveness were understood as communal realities. Just as sin damaged the whole community, so too, the entire community entered into the process of forgiveness. The entire community was exhorted to pray for the sinner, that is, to intercede before God on behalf of the sinner[31]. But the community also had the responsibility to call sinners to repentance:

> If your brother does something wrong, go and have it out with him alone, between your two selves. If he listens to you, you have won back your brother. If he does not listen, take one or two others along with you: *whatever the misdemeanour, the evidence of two or three witnesses is required to sustain the charge*. But if he refuses to listen to these, report it to the community; and if he refuses to listen to the community, treat him like a gentile or a tax collector.
>
> In truth I tell you, whatever you bind on earth will be bound in heaven; whatever you loose on earth will be loosed in heaven[32].

This Matthean procedure evidences that some members were segregated from the community for sin, but always as an exhortation to convert, as an attempt to coerce the sinner to repentance[33]. The community played a central role in the process of forgiveness, constantly exhorting the sinner to repentance[34]. And when repentance had been demonstrated by the sinner, forgiveness was effected by reconciliation with the community.

---

[28] Favazza, *The Order of Penitents*, 70-71.

[29] *Matthew* 6:12; *Acts* 8:22.

[30] *Luke* 7:47; *Acts* 26:20; *James* 2:24.

[31] *1 John* 5:15; *James* 5:16.

[32] *Matthew* 18:15-18.

[33] Favazza, *The Order of Penitents*, 81.

[34] *Galatians* 6:1-10; *2 Timothy* 2:25-26.

In the Second and Third Centuries

The postapostolic writings concerning the forgiveness of sin stand in continuity with the witness of the New Testament[35]. While there did exist rigorist tendencies within the early Church, nonetheless, the majority of local Christian communities offered reconciliation to any sinner who sincerely repented. The development within these postapostolic communities appears to be the link made between the public worship of the Church and observance of penitential practices. While they still followed the Matthean procedure of isolating sinners, the emphasis shifted from a social isolation from the community to a liturgical isolation of the sinner[36].

These earliest responses to the pastoral problem of postbaptismal sin were local and informal, and they evolved gradually. However, in general, the responses of those small close-knit communities reflected both their deep-felt faith experience of forgiveness offered by God through Christ and their unshakable conviction that sin destroyed the sinner's relationship both with God and the community. Thus, while the Church proclaimed the possibility of forgiveness in Christ she also molded an ecclesial practice which reflected the sinner's relationship with God and the community, a relationship damaged or broken by sin. And given that by Baptism one entered the community and in Eucharist the community symbolized its identity, the communities' penitential practices quite naturally evolved with respect to these two foundational faith experiences: Baptism and Eucharist[37].

Since Baptism established a person's relationship with the community of believers, groups were distinguished based upon their relationship to the community given by their baptismal status. A transitional "Order of Penitents" developed which paralleled the Order of Catechumens. Although this "Order of Penitents" only became more specified and defined as such in the fourth century, penitents did exist as a distinct group within the community of believers in the third century. Both the catechumens and the penitents were distinguished from the community of believers based upon their baptismal status, that is, either as not

---

[35] Favazza, *The Order of Penitents*, 81-96.

[36] *Ibid.*, 95-96.

[37] *DSp*, s.v. *Pénitence*, by Adnès, 944.

yet possessing or as having been dispossessed of their full baptismal status or full membership in the community[38].

In the first three centuries the most consistent sign of this segregation was exclusion from the Eucharist. Eucharist symbolized the believers' union with Christ and, therefore, exclusion from the Eucharist for postbaptismal sin was a natural consequence since sin fundamentally altered the sinner's relationship with God and so with the community of the faithful. But the penitents remained in relationship with the community. Their exclusion was not punitive but medicinal, that is, the purpose of their segregation was to facilitate their process of conversion[39].

The development of the Church's teaching on the forgiveness of postbaptismal sin cannot be understood apart from the crises which faced the early Church. As the bishop's authority within the community increased and the hierarchical structure developed within the Church (largely as a defensive response to the threat of heresy), so too the structure of ecclesial penance became more defined[40]. In confrontation with the rigorism of some of the early heresies (especially Montanism and Novatianism), the Church reaffirmed the efficacy of the community's prayer for serious sinners and her authority to offer reconciliation. But, in the face of these challenges the Church also imposed more stringent demands upon those who had committed serious postbaptismal sin. Given the evolving connection between Baptism and postbaptismal penance (that both forgave sin and led a person to new life), the idea was introduced in the mid-second century that postbaptismal penance could be received only once. Though this notion of the unrepeatability of penance was not universal in the first three centuries, it did significantly influence further developments in the ecclesial practice of forgiveness of postbaptismal sin[41]. But not only was penance unrepeatable, the imposed practices became more severe in the face of the rigorists' challenge, at least within the communites in the West[42]. The penance which sinners had to perform became more

---

[38] Favazza, *The Order of Penitents*, 238.

[39] *Ibid.*, 242-43.

[40] *Ibid.*, 64-65.

[41] *Ibid.*, 96-107.

[42] Although our focus is the development of penance within the West, it should be noted that the early practice of penance developed differently within the Church in the East. The writers of the early communities in the East emphasized the community's role, in addition to the bishop's role, in the care

specific. Postbaptismal sinners had to perform an *exomologesis* or public confession of sin which involved specific actions (for example: fasting, penitential garb) and which segregated them from the community while they attempted to demonstrate their repentance[43].

But the single, most significant sociological event influencing the development of ecclesial penance was the Edict of Toleration at the beginning of the fourth century. Given that it then became advantageous to become a Christian, the communities greatly increased in size. This growth resulted in the loss of personal contact between the bishop and the people and caused the institutionalization of ecclesial penance, known as "canonical penance"[44].

In the Fourth and Later Centuries

Not only were there many converts to Christianity after the Edict of 313, but many of those who had denied their faith to avoid torture or death amidst the persecutions (the so-called *lapsi*) wanted to return to the Church. The question of readmittance of the *lapsi* brought to a climax the struggle between the rigorists and those who advocated leniency for serious sinners. The resolution of this pastoral problem resulted in a penitential praxis which combined elements from both sides. Against the rigorists, the Church proclaimed forgiveness for all sinners who were repentant. But to avoid the rigorists' condemnation of laxity, the Church demanded effective penance, that is, specific harsh disciplines which led the sinner through the process of conversion.

The liturgical actions which marked the distinct stages within the

---

of sinners. A practice of "spiritual direction" developed in the East. The sinner not only prayed for forgiveness and received the prayer of the community for forgiveness; sinners also had to manifest their sin to "someone of God" who would accompany them on their journey of reconciliation with the community. This practice allowed the evolving form of penance in the East to avoid the rigorism that crept into the penitential institution of the West. For a discussion of the developments of penance in the East, cf. Favazza, *The Order of Penitents*, 121-70; and Dallen, *The Reconciling Community*, 44-49.

[43] For a treatment of these developments, especially as given in the works of Tertullian and Cyprian, cf. Favazza, *The Order of Penitents*, 187-232.

[44] Favazza, *The Order of Penitents*, 66.

Order of Penitents developed in the fourth century[45]. A rite of enrollment through the imposition of the hand (a rite which did not exist in the third century) developed which followed a private confession of faults to the bishop or his representative. This rite inititiated a time of segregation during which the person was excluded from the Eucharist, performed certain penitential practices, was relegated to a specific place at liturgical assemblies of the community, and in some cases wore a distinctive penitential garb. When the penitents had completed their penance and evidenced sufficient repentance (as determined by the bishop) they were reconciled to the community through the imposition of the hand by the bishop along with the prayer of the entire community[46].

But this gradual definition of liturgical rites brought with it juridical impositions: the unrepeatability of penance and a life-long commitment to the penitential practices rather than their cessation with the penitent's formal reconciliation with the community. While the notion of penance being unrepeatable existed earlier in the Church, in the fourth century the purpose of the mandated penitential practices was dramatically transformed. The original purgative intent of the imposed penance (to coerce the sinner to repentance) became subordinated to its punitive aspect by which the penitents were stigmatized for the rest of their lives. Though reconciled, the penitents remained second-class citizens within the Church[47]. With these fourth century developments, canonical penance became a clearly defined institution within the Church with various dimensions: juridical, in that it assigned an ecclesiastical status to the sinner; liturgical, in that it involved somewhat established rites celebrated by the bishop amidst the community; and pastoral, in that its members performed certain works of charity under the direction of the bishop[48].

By the fifth century the regime of the penitents consisted of certain practices and prohibitions: the adoption of a habit; a secluded life; the prohibition of attending popular feasts, shows, and banquets; renunciation of administrative, judicial and military functions; prohibition against practicing business; absolute continence even for married spouses; sobri-

---

[45] For a discussion of the development of canonical penance and its liturgy, cf. Dallen, *The Reconciling Community*, 56-88.

[46] Favazza, *The Order of Penitents*, 58.

[47] *Ibid.*, 59.

[48] *DSp*, s.v. *Pénitence*, by Adnès, 959.

ety in food and drink; and all of this until death[49]. At the end of their time of expiation, the bishop reconciled these sinners with the community. This reconciliation welcomed them back to the Eucharist, from which they were excluded during their time of performing penance, however, their penitential practices continued. They were condemned to a "quasi-monastic" life[50]. Thus, forgiveness of sin by entrance into the Order of Penance could not be repeated and it did not terminate the day the sinners were reconciled. In fact, excommunication was the penalty for abandoning the state of Penance, whether imposed upon the sinner or voluntarily embraced because of the person's desire for perfection[51].

From the fourth century onward, penance no longer connoted limited penitential practices performed by the members of the transitional Order of Penitents. Rather, canonical penance designated a "state" that the person entered. The Order of Penitents became an *ordo* within the Church in a more technical and defined sense, that is, the transitional Order of Penitents that existed in the third century was transformed into an "order" wherein the penitents had a specific permanent ecclesiastical status[52]. However, the sense of an "order" (*ordo*) within the Church developed. At this early stage *ordo* designated the religious "state" of these penitents rather than specific groups. Only in later centuries did the term *ordo* evolve to signify local federations of penitents, and eventually, specific groups affiliated with canonical religious "orders" (for example, the Franciscan Order of Penitents as opposed to the Dominican Order of Penitents)[53].

While the precise reasons for the increased severity of the juridical obligations connected with postbaptismal penance cannot be determined,

---

[49] It should be noted that these characteristics of the penitential life remained practically unchanged through the following centuries and, as we will see in our analysis in *Chapter III*, became codified in the rules of various penitential groups in the thirteenth century. Cf. G. Meersseman, *Ordo Fraternitatis: Confraternite e pietà dei laici nel Medievo*, Roma 1977, 268-69.

[50] *DSp*, s.v. *Pénitence*, by Adnès, 963.

[51] A. Pompei, *Il movimento penitenziale nei secoli XII-XIII*, in *CF* 43 (1973) 13.

[52] For a discussion of the development of the Order of Penitents as a specific *ordo* within the Church, cf. Favazza, *The Order of Penitents*, 234-53.

[53] G. Meersseman, *Disciplinati e penitenti nel Duecento*, in *Il movimento dei disciplinati nel settimo centenario dal suo inizio [Perugia - 1260]*, Spoleto 1962, 70-71.

the severity probably resulted from the laxity resulting from the Peace of Constantine[54]. The mass conversions to Christianity caused a breakdown of the catechumenate and "the understanding of baptism shifted from being a faith commitment to a kind of eschatological insurance policy"[55]. Hence the Church's development of a more severe penitential practice probably resulted from her concern to provide a structure to ensure interior conversion among her members, as the catechumenate had effectively done with smaller numbers of converts[56]. However, that hope became frustrated precisely due to the severity of canonical penance. That severity, in fact, led to the disintegration of the practice of canonical penance.

A New Form of Penance

Very early, for reasons that remain unclear, the Irish Church took shape as a monastic church[57]. The abbot played a more central role than the bishop and exercised jurisdiction over the people. As a consequence, monastic spirituality and practices influenced pastoral practice[58]. Within monastic tradition the monks observed the ascetical practice of confessing their faults or sins to the abbot or another monk in order to receive spiritual advice and some "penance" to aid them on their journey of conversion. After they had completed this penance they received absolution from the abbot. The monks carried this tradition into their pastoral practice.

Canonical penance, with its Order of Penitents and solemn liturgical rites, never became firmly established in the Irish Church[59]. Rather, the monastic practice of "confession" gradually became the general pastoral

---

[54] Dallen, *The Reconciling Community*, 63.

[55] Favazza, *The Order of Penitents*, 250.

[56] *Ibid.*, 250-51.

[57] J. Komonchak, ed. *The New Dictionary of Theology*, Wilmington 1987, s.v. *Reconciliation*, by R. Duffy, 833.

[58] *DSp*, s.v. *Pénitence*, by Adnès, 967-68; also cf. Dallen, *The Reconciling Community*, 102-110.

[59] Dallen, *The Reconciling Community*, 103.

practice[60]. Lay people were encouraged to confess their sins in private to a monk who would impose a penance determined by the gravity of the sins. The penitent would return after having completed the penance and, while there was no formal reconciliation with the community, the person was then allowed to receive communion[61]. Sinners could avail themselves of this form of penance as often as was necessary. This repeatability introduced a novel element into penance; the practice of a private repeatable penance did not exist in the Church, at least in the West, prior to the late fifth or sixth century[62].

But this new form of penance, which had originally been developed within monastic groups for people fully committed to interior conversion, could not fulfill its intended purpose when extended to nominally Christian groups. Further, in the absence of a rite of reconciliation, this form of penance lost almost all reference to the larger community[63]. But this penitential praxis of "private penance" spread throughout western Europe and, though initially rejected by the Church[64], quickly replaced the existent canonical penance[65].

> So far as the people were concerned, monastic penance seemed much like the canonical system that preachers urged them to enter. Both systems required severe mortification and made harsh demands; in both, *confessio* and *paenitentia* obtained God's forgiveness. The monastic system, however, was much more practical. It was private: social stigma could be avoided. It had no further consequences: penitents could return to a normal way of life. It was repeatable: sinners could turn to it again and again to be purified of their sins and freed from guilt and anxiety[66].

---

[60] This study will not treat the development of "confession" in our modern sense. That development is, however, much more complicated than the generally accepted and overly simplified view which attributes the origin of "confession" to this monastic practice. The Irish monks were *not* directly responsible for the medieval practice of private penance nor were they the originators of our modern form of the sacrament. For a discussion of the development of private penance, cf. Dallen, *The Reconciling Community*, 100-128.

[61] Dallen, *The Reconciling Community*, 103-107.

[62] Favazza, *The Order of Penitents*, 55.

[63] Dallen, *The Reconciling Community*, 108.

[64] Pazzelli, *St. Francis and the Third Order*, 16.

[65] Dallen, *The Reconciling Community*, 111-12.

[66] *Ibid.*, 110.

Public penance, which became the exception, took on two forms: "solemn" public penance indicated the ancient form of canonical penance, and "non-solemn" public penance consisted of penitential pilgrimages or the crusades[67]. Meanwhile, the increasingly common practice of private penance (which became more and more codified in the "penitentials" and further externalized through the introduction of the process of "substitution") caused the disappearance of the "spirit" of penance[68].

The Order of Penance in the Middle Ages

From the fourth century onward the penitential discipline became more severe with the result that fewer and fewer people entered the Order of Penance. Rather, they waited until the last days of their life to be reconciled to the Church[69]. The severity of this penitential expiation is evidenced by the fact that both martyrdom and penance were designated by the same image: "second baptism". The reference to penance, as well as martyrdom, as a "baptism by blood" not only reinforced the notion of penance as unrepeatable, it expressed the unfortunate reality that penance (that is, canonical penance) no longer presented itself as a viable option for the majority of sinners desirous of doing penance[70].

There were, however, two other ways that sinners could receive forgiveness of sins: by monastic profession or by becoming one of the so-called "*conversi*" (the converted ones). Monastic profession was an intensification of one's baptismal commitment. Thus, monastic profession, as a "second Baptism" entailing a life of constant penance, also offered forgiveness of sin[71]. Analogously, the life of the *conversi* became identified with the forgiveness of sin. Basically the *conversi* followed a monastic

---

[67] Pompei, *Il movimento penitenziale*, in 17.

[68] Dallen, *The Reconciling Community*, 106-107.

[69] *Ibid.*, 76-82.

[70] Pompei, *Il movimento penitenziale*, 12-14.

[71] *DSp*, s.v. *Perfection*, by K. Frank, 1119; Dallen, *The Reconciling Community*, 83.

way of life[72]. These men and women (who lived in a monastery, a solitary retreat, or in their own homes continuing their normal occupations) essentially lead a penitential life: a life of mortification, of chastity, and of continence[73]. Thus, conversion after a sinful life (becoming one of the *conversi*) or an intensification of one's baptismal commitment to conversion (by monastic profession) forgave a person's sins. However, these two alternatives to canoncial penance did not offer easier access to forgiveness. Rather, they represented equally severe alternatives which demanded a life-long commitment.

Thus, from the middle of the fifth to the beginning of the seventh century there was a progressive disintegration of the primitive penitential discipline[74]. Paradoxically, as a result of the severity, the Order of

[72] Unfortunately, the term *conversi* cannot be defined precisely. It is a very general term and its use with respect to the penitents varied throughout the Middle Ages. It was used at times to distinguish penitents from monks, that is, to designate the penitents who were attached to a monastery but who had not made a monastic profession. However, from the fifth to the eighth centuries both "*conversi*" and "religious" were used somewhat interchangeably in referring to people who had voluntarily committed themselves to some form of the penitential life, either by monastic profession or as voluntary penitents. In the eighth century the term "regulars" was introduced to signify those who lived in a monastery under a canonically approved rule. There were then two clearly defined groups: the regulars and the penitents. The two groups were alike in that they had "left the world". They were distinct from each other in that the former (monks and nuns) lived communally under an approved rule, while the individual penitents did not constitute a group, or *ordo*, as such. However, from the beginning of the twelfth century individual penitents tended to form groups or fraternities which, although not living together as monks or canons, adopted the same "*propositum*" or way of life: binding themselves to one another, accepting a certain control by the group, and making an act of commitment called a "profession". In 1221, Honorius III approved one of these "*propositi*" (that of the Humiliati), and thus, by then one can talk about an "Order of Penitents" in the same sense that one can talk about the "Order of Monks" or the "Order of Clerics". Cf. Pompei, *Il movimento penitenziale*, 17-19.

[73] Despite the resemblances between canonical penance and this "*conversio*", there remained great differences. While penitents were forbidden to become clerics, these *conversi* were seen to be at a higher state of perfection and in an appropriate condition for being admitted into the clerical state. Cf. Pompei, *Il movimento penitenziale*, 14-15.

[74] Pazzelli, *St. Francis and the Third Order*, 13-14.

Penitents came to be composed almost exclusively of people who, not because of serious sin but because of a desire for perfection or in preparation for death, freely asked to enter the Order of Penance. These "voluntary penitents" willingly embraced a life of rigorous penance as the means to Christian perfection[75]. These penitents became a kind of "Third Order before its time"[76].

One might imagine that this phenomenon of voluntary penitents would gradually subside, that people would turn exclusively to the evolving praxis of private penance. But on the contrary, it flourished and grew rapidly during the twelfth and thirteenth centuries. What caused such a resurgence of the Order of Penitents? What factors so readily disposed the people of the twelfth and thirteenth centuries to this penitential life with all of its severity? In an attempt to answer these questions and to move toward a critical understanding of the "primitive Rule" of the Franciscan penitents, we turn now to an examination of some of the events and conditions which nurtured the resurgence of voluntary penance.

The Resurgence of the Order of Penance

In the early Middle Ages the image of the monk somewhat shaped and expressed the popular religious imagination. While certainly there did not exist a single prototype for all spirituality, nonetheless, the monastic way of life was held up as an ideal[77]. For many believers, Christian perfection became identified with leaving the world, with entering a monastery[78]. To follow Christ fully was to become a monk. But this understanding of Christian perfection changed dramatically through the

---

[75] R. Pazzelli, *Alla ricerca dei documenti primitivi riguardanti il Terz'Ordine*, in *Approccio storico-critico alle Fonti Francescane*, edited by G. Cardaropoli and M. Conti, Roma 1979, 182.

[76] Pompei, *Il movimento penitenziale*, 14.

[77] M-D. Chenu, *Nature, Man, and Society in the Twelfth Century: Essays on New Theological Perspectives in the Latin West*, translated by J. Taylor and L. Little, Chicago and London 1968, 204.

[78] *DSp*, s.v. *Perfection*, by K. Frank, 1118.

eleventh and twelfth centuries. Those centuries witnessed an "awakening" of the consciousness of the laity[79]. In contemporary terms we would speak of this evolution as a growing awareness of the universal call to holiness. Gradually the the idea of Christian perfection broadened; increasingly the laity themselves became involved in the pursuit of holiness. Let us consider some of the factors involved in this evolution.

The Eleventh and Twelfth Centuries: A Time of Change

The eleventh and twelfth centuries witnessed many significant changes. The population in northern and central Italy greatly increased[80]. With the increased population came the reclamation of much land (swamps drained and forests cleared), an increase in agriculture, and a significant increase in trade. One consequence of these changes was the gradual evolution of the "commune" or the early urban centers. The population started to shift from rural areas to these developing places of trade. These trade markets, "fairs" of sorts, gradually became economic, political, and social centers.

The flourishing of trade resulted in both economic and social changes. The new forms of commerce created the need for a means of exchange or "money" and consequently new occupations for the "money handlers". But the new occupations (merchants, various craftsman, "money handlers") and the opportunity for economic advancement brought social changes as well. The social structure became more fluid; a person's class or rank was less determined by birth. Inequality remained. There were still the wealthy and powerful, but wealth and power were no longer tied firmly to nobility[81].

During these centuries there was a shift from the monasteries to these developing communes as the economic and cultural centers. The demographic, economic, and social changes created new religious needs within the people. New ways were therefore needed to address the reli-

---

[79] P. Rivi, *Le origini dell'O.F.S.: risveglio religioso e coscienza del laicato nella Chiesa dei secoli XII-XIII - il contributo di Francesco d'Assisi*, Fidenza 1988.

[80] It is estimated that the population doubled between the tenth and fourteenth centuries. Cf. D. Waley, *The Italian City-Republics*, New York [3]1988, 4-18.

[81] J. Le Goff, *Francis of Assisi between the Renewals and Restraints of Feudal Society*, in *Concilium* 149 (1981) 3-4.

gious needs of the people[82]. The attempts to reform the Church during these centuries can be understood as responses to these dramatic changes[83]. Let us consider some of those religious changes and the effects of those changes upon the self-consciousness and praxis of the laity.

The "Evangelical Awakening"

This time of great change ushered in a period of intense religiosity. The increasingly apparent desire to live the faith more fully or more authentically (the causes of which have not yet been fully explained) translated into a longing to return to the past, to the origins, which evidenced itself not only in the religious renewal but also in culture and literature[84]. Religiously, this return to origins meant a return to the Church of the apostles and martyrs. The ideal of the "*ecclesiae primitivae forma*" became the reference point for a new spirituality. Concretely, this desire for the purity or perfection of the primitive church, expressed as the "*vita apostolica*"[85], focused upon the model of the community at Jerusalem as presented in the *Acts of the Apostles*[86].

The Gregorian Reform (which reached its heights under Gregory VII but which exceeds the period of his pontificate, 1073-1085) expressed this desire to return to primitive Church. The Gregorian Reform aimed, in part, at the reform of the clergy. When the Synod of Rome (1059), in an attempt to reform the avarice and incontinence of the clergy, called clerics to live the common life, it proposed as the motivation a return to the gospel life, to the *vita apostolica*: "and we urge that they mightily desire the *apostolic*, namely the common,

---

[82] Lester Little's study of voluntary poverty as it relates to the new profit economy of Europe (approximately 1000-1300) basically analyzes the different responses to this new economy: those who avoided it (monks and hermits) and those who confronted it (canons regular, various lay groups, the mendicants). Cf. L. Little, *Religious Poverty and the Profit Economy in Medieval Europe*, Ithaca 1978.

[83] Le Goff, *Francis of Assisi*, 5.

[84] A. Vauchez, *La spiritualité du Moyen Age occidental VIIIe-XIIe siècles*, Vendôme 1975, 81-82.

[85] *Ibid.*, 81-83.

[86] *Acts* 2:42-47; 4:32-35.

life"[87]. This call to return to the origins of the Church invited ever-expanding reflection on the nature of the *vita vere apostolica*, the *truly* apostolic life.

Monks and canons debated what constituted the true apostolic life: the common life or apostolic ministry[88]. The reform efforts of some individual monks and canons gave birth to new orders[89]. The different reform movements, as well as the widening debate on the *vita vere apostolica*, had the effect, often unintended, of spreading a different vision. The evangelical life of the apostles came to be understood as a model and norm which was obligatory for *every* Christian believer - a central point for understanding the "new penitential climate" of the twelfth and thirteenth centuries. New groups broke from the traditional structures of medieval "orders". These new groups proclaimed that all believers could attain Christian perfection by living according to the Gospel in poverty and charity, and by practicing the characteristically more "lay" virtues of prudence, justice, and work for the common good[90].

> The new role of the laity was a logical and necessary outcome of the revolution in progress. Since the evangelical awakening took place not by a revision of existing institutions but by a return to the gospel that by-passed these institutions, one could predict what its dynamics had to be: witness to the faith, fraternal love, poverty, the beatitudes - all these were to operate more spontaneously and sooner among laymen than among clerics, who were bound within an institutional framework[91].

---

[87] The Latin reads, "Et rogantes monemus, ut ad *apostolicam*, communem scilicet, *vitam* summopere studeant" (emphasis added). Cf. *Sacrorum Conciliorum Nova et Amplissima Collectio*, edited by J. Mansi, Paris-Leipzig 1901-1927, XIX 873.

[88] Cf. D. Lapsanski, *Evangelical Perfection: An Historical Examination of the Concept in the Early Franciscan Sources*, St. Bonaventure 1977, 6-28; M.D. Chenu, *Moines, Clercs, Laïcs au carrefour de la Vie Évangélique (XIIe siècle)*, in *Revue d'Histoire Ecclesiastique* 49 (1954) 59-89.

[89] For a treatment of these new orders, cf. J. Leclerq, *The Spirituality of the Middle Ages*, New York 1968, vol. II, 137-56.

[90] Pompei stresses that this was *not* a social movement, that is, a struggle between classes. It was rather a religious movement that encompassed people of all classes who, within a changing socio-economic world, wished to renew a truly Christian life. Cf. Pompei, *Il movimento penitenziale*, 24.

[91] Chenu, *Nature, Man, and Society*, 219.

Stirrings among the Laity

The laity were taking an increasingly active part in religious life, that is, they desired and found ways to live their faith more fully. Various lay religious movements grew, and in fact, flourished. Two lay movements at the end of the eleventh century, while not as widespread as later apostolic movements, evidence the growing desire on the part of the laity to live the ideals of the early Church and thus deserve mention.

The first was a group of artisans and workers in Lombardy known as the Pataria. Led by a deacon Ariald, they fought against the immorality of the clergy. They struggled against simony and the power of governing bishops in order to bring the Church back to living gospel ideals[92]. While remaining more of a political than religious movement, the Pataria clearly evidence some of the presuppositions of the later apostolic movements: an emphasis on Scripture as the means to evaluate preaching and the clergy, the following of Christ, opposition to lax clergy, and the proposal of the poor, common life as remedy[93].

The second, known as the Hirsau reform, resulted from the evangelical efforts of some monks in southwestern Germany who preached the return to a life modeled on the early apostolic communities. Inspired by the preaching of these monks, many married people decided to live continent lives in a lay religious community headed by a monk or priest. These communities modeled themselves upon the early Church communities and had their life-style approved by Pope Urban II in 1091[94].

These groups evidence how the popular notion of the apostolic life was changing and developing over the course of the eleventh and twelfth centuries. The apostolic life came to be identified with the Christian life to which every believer was called. In the twelfth century we witness the evolution from the idea of the monastic vocation as *the* Christian vocation, to the belief that vocation included secular callings and states of life[95]. A new consciousness was gradually developing within the laity, inflamed in great part by itinerant preachers. The witness

---

[92] Lapsanski, *Evangelical Perfection*, 31.

[93] A. Dal Pino, *I Frati Servi di S. Maria dalle origini all'approvazione*, Louvain 1972, 519.

[94] Lapsanski, *Evangelical Perfection*, 32.

[95] Chenu, *Nature, Man, and Society*, 221-25.

of their lives, their rigorous adherence to the gospel, spoke to the hungers of the masses.

The Itinerant Preachers

Throughout the eleventh century, and even more so from the beginning of the twelfth, the spirit of renewal found expression in the hermits-turned-itinerant-preachers[96]. These wandering preachers, who proclaimed poverty as the best means for attaining salvation, gathered many followers and succeeded in spreading a lively and intense religiosity[97]. They identified the apostolic life with a life of poverty: the true apostle must be poor, as Jesus and the first apostles were poor. This idea that only those who are truly poor are worthy to preach so caught the people's imagination that it led to a loss of esteem for wealthy monks and clergy[98]. In fact, for some poverty became the criterion by which they as lay people claimed the right to preach[99].

The preaching and asceticism of these itinerant preachers had a deep impact on the people. They reflected a spiritual restlessness and the desire for a more intense religious experience[100].

They, as other reformers, were inspired by the discovery of *Christus pauper*, and sought to identify with the poor and suffering Christ: "*Nudus nudum Christum sequi*"[101].

> Both men and women eagerly listened to the preachers' message and admired their ascetical life to such an extent that many actually became members of these new communities. This certainly indicates a hunger on the part of the populace for new modes of Christian living, based on the literal observance of the evangelical ideals. This hunger traditional monasticism, often bound to landed estates and the power structure, could

---

[96] For a discussion of the itinerant preachers who appeared in France (Robert of Arbissel, Bernard of Thiron, Vitalis of Savigny, Gerald of Salles, and Norbert of Gennep), cf. Lapsanski, *Evangelical Perfection*, 18-28.

[97] R. Manselli, *St. Francis of Assisi*, translated by P. Duggan, Chicago 1988, 9.

[98] Chenu, *Nature, Man, and Society*, 215.

[99] Dal Pino, *I Frati Servi di S. Maria*, 530.

[100] Lapsanski, *Evangelical Perfection*, 28.

[101] *DSp*, s.v. *Perfection*, by K. Frank, 1124.

not quench. In part, therefore, the movement can be considered as a reaction to the general worldliness of the Church, particularly of the monks and clerics. At a time when the rapid growth of riches blinded many a Christian heart, the itinerants' example of voluntary poverty and even physical deprivation embodied an appropriate and needed form of Christian asceticism. All these factors, together with a fresh reading of the Gospel, gave birth in many Christian hearts to a burning desire to imitate the life of Christ and his apostles in a very literal fashion[102].

By appropriating for themselves and their followers the term *pauperes Christi*, these itinerant preachers helped to spread the Christian ideal of the *vita apostolica* among all of the laity[103]. Earlier, the apostolic life was identified with monastic or canonical life, that is, with the communal life wherein the members lived without individual property or possessions. The transfer to the poor and afflicted of the name *pauperes Christi*, until then reserved to monks, indicates a significant mental evolution[104].

More widespread, more influential within the Church, and more directly related to the later Franciscan penitential movement were the groups that came to be known as the Waldensians and the Humiliati[105]. They preached a return to the primitive Gospel and thus their lives and preaching took on a penitential character. In their attempt to be faithful to the Gospel and to preach clearly the content of the penitential message, they placed an emphasis on the most concrete and measurable aspect, namely, poverty.

The Waldensians

Around 1175, Peter Waldo, a rich merchant of Lyons, experienced a dramatic conversion allegedly triggered by his hearing the story of St. Alexis, a story about a wealthy man who chose to live as a poor

---

[102] Lapsanski, *Evangelical Perfection*, 28-29.

[103] Chenu, *Nature, Man, and Society*, 239-46.

[104] M. Mollat, *The Poverty of Francis: A Christian and Social Option*, in *Concilium* 149 (1981) 27.

[105] For a full discussion of these groups and movements, cf. the chapter *Ambiente religioso e politico-sociale (secc. X-XIII)* in Dal Pino, *I Frati Servi di S. Maria*, 451-758.

beggar[106]. Waldo thereupon sold his possessions, provided for his wife and children, and gave the rest to the poor. He made a vow to model his life after that of the early apostles and went about barefoot preaching the gospel. His example attracted followers who likewise gave their possessions to the poor and went about preaching penance. The group lived on alms and exhorted the people to conversion, to a life of poverty, to the following of the poor Christ.

> [T]he early Waldensians did not have a peculiar theology. The conversion of Waldes and his attracting several people to join him had nothing to do with doctrine. None the less, the Waldensians posed a serious challenge to the purpose, the utility, and the prerogatives of the clergy. As laymen, they led lives of Christian perfection - they had faith and they engaged in good works - and they were doing so apparently without clerical help. Pushed to a logical extreme, as it was by some, this suggested that Christian society could get along without priests[107].

This development brought the Waldensians to an inevitable conflict with clerical authorities. The bishop of Lyons forbade them to preach (possibly because they resembled disruptive heretics)[108]. The group, therefore, traveled to Rome in March 1179 to seek papal approval for their life. They did receive the pope's blessing and approval of their life of voluntary poverty, however, with the restriction that they could not preach without the permission of the local clergy. Nonetheless, the Waldensians remained under suspicion because of unauthorized biblical translations, unauthorized preaching, and secret meetings[109]. When Waldo was later accused of heresy, he made a solemn profession of faith. Waldo's solemn profession of faith becomes significant not in and for itself, but rather, as the instance in which the Church acknowledged the legitimacy of his *propositum*: to follow not only the precepts of the gospel (norms applicable to everyone), but also the counsels of the gospel (recommendations given for those seeking perfection)[110].

The Waldensians were in effect an order made up of two distinct

---

[106] For a description of the Legend of St. Alexis, cf. Little, *Religious Poverty*, 40-41.

[107] Little, *Religious Poverty*, 127.

[108] Lapsanski, *Evangelical Perfection*, 34-35.

[109] Little, *Religious Poverty*, 125.

[110] Manselli, *St. Francis*, 10.

groups: the *perfecti* and the *credentes*[111]. Entrance into the first group involved ordination to the diaconate along with vows of evangelical poverty, chastity and obedience to the leaders of the group. The *perfecti* went about preaching penance and living on alms. The latter group, the "believers", continued to live in their own homes, practicing a life of penance and supporting these preachers with alms[112].

The Humiliati

While the Waldensians were a group of wandering preachers in southern France, the Humiliati were a lay community in Lombardy, Italy. This group, which evolved into three integrated orders, cared for the poor and needy outside of their own order or group, and gave special attention to lepers. They often were engaged in the work of cloth-making, especially a type of cheap woolen cloth. The Humiliati were a response to the spiritual and social crisis provoked by the developing economy and urban life. They offered a new interpretation of the gospel, a way of life for lay people, that "gave meaning to their existence in Christian Europe's first commercial age"[113]. Basically their life and ideals were similar to those of the Waldensians and can be summarized: "to live according to the letter of the Gospel and to expound to the people the truths of faith as did the apostles"[114].

In 1179, the Humiliati sought papal approval for their way of life, which they received, but again with the prohibition against preaching in public. Since they ignored this restriction, this group was excommunicated by Pope Lucius III in 1184. However, the group sought reunion with the Church in 1199, and after two years of deliberation, Pope Innocent III approved their order saying that Christ had come to call all sinners to do penance[115]. The institute consisted of three orders: married people *not* obliged to continence (living in their homes), men and women with the vow of celibacy (living the common life in separate dwellings), and clerics in service to the other two orders. The pope

[111] Chenu, *Nature, Man, and Society*, 255-56.
[112] Lapsanski, *Evangelical Perfection*, 36-37.
[113] Little, *Religious Poverty*, 120.
[114] Lapsanski, *Evangelical Perfection*, 38.
[115] Meersseman, *Ordo Fraternitatis*, 299.

approved all three "orders" (though the pope reversed the position of the "first" and "third" groups)[116].

Though the constitutional relationships between these three orders were not detailed until 1246, the pope's approval of their Rule in 1201 made the Humiliati a religious order. For the first and second "orders", Innocent III approved a Rule based upon the Benedictine and Augustinian Rules which included elements from their earlier statutes. It stressed the common life and individual poverty of the members. The third "order" posed a problem, however, since for centuries the religious life had been identified with the common life. Rather than giving this third "order" a Rule as such, Innocent III approved their *propositum* which was largely a summary statement of their ideals based upon gospel texts[117]. In his letter, the pope exhorted the members of this third group, among other things:

> to be humble and obedient,
> to love God, neighbor, and enemy,
> to enter by the narrow gate,
> to repent or do penance,
> to be at peace with everyone,
> to return anything gained by usury or any other improper means,
> to make satisfactory amends for any wrong done to anyone,
> and not to love the world[118].

The Humiliati were called to live simple lives, but they were not obligated to dispense with all of their possessions. In fact, since they remained in their own homes, they could presumably continue in a comfortable setting. However, as Little points out, some of their number must have experienced a very marginal existence or their *propositum* would not have contained the provision for mutual aid. They cared for the poor and needy within their own group, and beyond their own group, giving special attention to lepers[119].

The most radical innovation, however, was the pope's approval of

---

[116] *Ibid.*, 299.

[117] For an English translation of the *propositum* of the Humiliati, cf. *Appendix I*. For the Latin text (dated June 7, 1201), cf. G. Meersseman, *Dossier de l'Ordre de la Pénitence au XIIIe Siècle*, Fribourg 1961, 276-82.

[118] For the complete text, cf. *Appendix I*, below pp. 365-371.

[119] Little, *Religious Poverty*, 117-118.

lay preaching[120]. He sanctioned their practice of gathering on Sunday to hear one of the lay members preach. However, this approval sanctioned only moral exhortation, not doctrinal preaching. Innocent III's approval was based upon the distinction in Scripture between "*aperta*, narrative and moralizing passages accessible to all, and *profonda*, dogmatic statements whose understanding and explanation were reserved to the clergy"[121].

The Evolving Consciousness of the Laity

The self-consciousness of the laity and the notion of "religious" evolved dramatically during the eleventh and twelfth centuries. Various reform movements engendered an evolving debate on the *vita vere apostolica*: monasticism placed the focus on the common life; canons regular identified it with the common life and pastoral activity; the itinerant preachers connected it to contact with the people and the following of Christ through a rigorous poverty. The second half of the twelfth century witnessed a vast religious awakening of the laity. The religious fervor engendered by the reform movements resulted in an increased awareness on the part of the laity that the *vita vere apostolica* was the vocation of every Christian believer[122].

The gradual broadening of the category of "penitents" both expressed and helped to effect this changing consciousness. The extension of the image of "penitent" to both the pilgrim and the crusader somewhat lessened some of the distinctions between cleric and lay; it also reinforced the understanding that lay people could be "religious" without entering monastic life[123].

---

[120] Cf. paragraph 15 of the *propositum* of the Humiliati in *Appendix I*, p. 370. For an historical study which presents the developments which led to preaching being connected with priestly ordination, cf. E. Schillebeeckx, *The Right of Every Christian to Speak in the Light of Evangelical Experience "In the Midst of Brothers and Sisters"*, in *Preaching and the Non-Ordained: An Interdisciplinary Study*, edited by N. Foley, Collegeville 1983, 11-37.

[121] Le Goff, *Francis of Assisi*, 8.

[122] *DSp*, s.v. *Perfection*, by K. Frank, 1124.

[123] The category of "religious" and the understanding of religious life was somewhat fluid in this period. Contemporary canonical distinctions between *cleric* and *lay* and between *religious* and *secular* do not neatly coincide with medieval distinctions and can lead, therefore, to confusion concerning the identity of

Making a pilgrimage to a sacred place had long been recognized as a penitential practice in the Church. The pilgrim came to be understood as a wandering hermit: leaving everything behind, entering a foreign land as a stranger, being itinerant and poor, and journeying in search of pardon. Thus, the pilgrim, like the the hermit, was considered a "penitent", as having a particular *status* in the Church, as participating

---

the penitents and of the present Secular Franciscans. The hierarchical view of reality prevalent in the Middle Ages was reflected in ecclesiastical and social structures. A basic distinction which existed throughout the Middle Ages separated people into two categories based upon office or function: "clergy" and "laity". The category of clergy included bishops and priests, the *perficientes* or those who were charged with the care of souls (*cura animarum*). All others were grouped together under the category of laity, the *perficiendi*. Thus, this broad category of "laity" included monks, nuns, friars, penitents, and all other Christians. Cf. M-D. Chenu, *Aspects ecclésiologiques de la querelle entre mendiants et séculiers dans la seconde moitié du XIIIe siècle et le début du XIVe*, in *Archives d'histoire doctrinale et litteraire du Moyen Age* 36 (1961) 114-45.

However, alongside this twofold division based upon order or function, a threefold division based upon state or condition of life obtained within the Church. This division of lay, cleric, and monastic - distinctions not strictly opposed to one another - led, by a process of assimilation of clerics to monks and of monks to clerics, to the twofold division of Christians into people of religion ("religious") and people of the world. Further, by the gradual identification of a life of penance with monastic profession, "penitents" came to be understood as "religious". Cf. Y. Congar, *Lay People in the Church: A Study for a Theology of Laity*, Westminster (MD) 1985, 3-27; *Dictionary of the Middle Ages*, s.v. *Church, Latin: 1054 to 1305*, by L. Little, 355-60.

Thus, within medieval categories the Franciscan penitents were understood as "religious". However, in terms of modern canonical distinctions, these early Franciscan penitents were *secular* and not *religious*. Unfortunately, this confusion with respect to the identity of Secular Franciscans was not dealt with adequately in the development of their new Rule. While Secular Franciscans are by definition "seculars", they do make a profession and live by a "Rule". Although the precise historical, theological, and canonical identity of the Secular Franciscans needs further study and clarification, this study will not attempt to resolve the complicated question of their identity. Our concern in this section is to explore how penance came to be understood as an appropriate expression of the Christian life.

in a higher level of perfection[124]. But just as eremitism tended to level the distinctions between clerics, monastics, and lay people (since anyone could become a hermit), so too did the phenomenon of voluntary pilgrimages[125].

In an analogous way, participation in the crusades also came to be understood and explained as a penitential practice. Various popes had enlisted the aid of selected preachers to promote each crusade. These preachers encouraged the people to join the battle against the infidels or heretics by inviting them to share in the sufferings of Christ. They spoke of the crusader's commitment to accept suffering and to risk life itself as an identification with Christ. To enter the crusade was to take up the cross. Gradually, because of this penitential imaging, both participation in a crusade and making a pilgrimage came to be understood as equivalent to entering monastic life[126].

The idea spread and took root that the laity could live fully religious lives as lay people. Both marriage and involvement in the developing economic system, which had been viewed as obstacles to the spiritual life, slowly began to be integrated into the framework of the spiritual life. At the beginning of the Middle Ages the religious life, as flight from the world, demanded a commitment to celibacy and excluded involvement in the social and economic affairs of the secular community. Marriage was understood only as a remedy for concupiscence, a concession to human weakness. But toward the end of the twelfth century continence was no longer obligatory for married penitents[127]. The increasingly positive view of marriage and work was advanced by the Innocent III's approbation of the Humiliati in 1201[128]. The pope not

---

[124] The the term "penitents" cannnot be defined with much precision within the context of the Middle Ages. It has varied meanings and designates very diverse groups. For a listing of the different types of penitents, cf. *DIP*, s.v. *Penitenti*, by A. Matanić, 1363. "Penitents" should be understood here in the broad sense suggested by Vauchez: all of the laity who sought to lead a more pious or perfect Christian life while not entering the traditional monastic life. Cf. *DSp*, s.v. *Pénitents au Moyen Age*, by A. Vauchez, 1010.

[125] Some did hold that to be valid the pilgrimage ought to flow into the monastic life. Nonetheless, the distinction between clergy and laity was somewhat lessened. Cf. Dal Pino, *I Frati Servi di S. Maria*, 516.

[126] Dal Pino, *I Frati Servi di S. Maria*, 520-21.

[127] Meersseman, *Ordo Fraternitatis*, 300.

[128] *Ibid.*, 304.

only approved an order of married penitents, but also exalted the place of work in the religious life, work for the sustenance of the community and to aid the poor[129].

These changes reflected a broadened understanding of "religious life". The ideal of "leaving the world" was interiorized as a struggle against sin in all its forms and, therefore, every Christian could be a "religious" in the broadest sense of the term[130]. Thus, by the thirteenth century non-monastic lay people had secured a place in religious life; and penance had become the central element in that religious expression[131].

The Choice of Penance

Vast numbers of the laity became voluntary penitents during the twelfth and thirteenth centuries, an intriguing phenomenon given the severity of the penitential life that they embraced. Why did these lay penitential movements flourish? The new social and economic structures of the developing urban centers, as well as the evolution of the concept of the *vita apostolica*, explain in part the fuller participation of the laity in the religious life. But what motivated this penitential fervor? Why did these believers choose such a rigorous life of penance, seemingly with such an urgency?

The choice of penance by vast numbers of the laity cannot adequately be explained solely in terms of an economic or social motivation[132]. No single motivation can explain the phenomenon of

[129] Lapsanski, *Evangelical Perfection*, 47.

[130] Vauchez, *La spiritualité*, 129.

[131] Dal Pino, *I Frati Servi di S. Maria*, 581.

[132] Meersseman suggests that one of the causes of such large numbers of penitents was probably economic, that is, many women drawn along with the currents of popular piety would have liked to join a monastery but lacked the necessary dowry. Since following the Augustinian or Benedictine rule was not suited to their non-cloistered living, they adopted the *Memoriale propositi fratrum et sororum de Penitentia in domibus propriis existentium*. Cf. Meersseman, *Ordo Fraternitatis*, 282. He also suggests that a further motivation could have been to overcome a feeling of religious inferiority. Meersseman notes that from the beginning of the thirteenth century there was a reaction in the inhabitants of the communes against their sense of inferiority with respect to the clergy. They did not share their prestige, possibly not even their economic level, and certainly

these voluntary penitents, but apparently this response on the part of the laity arose from a deep-felt, inner need[133]. The penitents' most profound motivation lies hidden in their faith-view of penance.

The growing penitential movement was basically an urban phenomenon[134]. Certainly many people experienced great conflict amidst the social and economic changes surrounding life in the evolving communes. Deep-felt religious needs often went unanswered by the official Church. People sought meaning in their changing world. The official Church's morality and praxis did not immediately respond to the new social and economic situations of the evolving communes. Initially, the Church neither accepted nor provided nurture for the people of this new "culture". For example, merchants, a category outside a feudal hierarchical and moral system, were generally viewed as damned[135]. The intensity of this conflict quite probably accounts for the renewed popularity of the ancient Legend of St. Alexis (the wealthy merchant who becomes a saint by choosing a life of poverty and penance), as well as the vast increase in penitents.

But for whatever reasons, and they must have been many and varied, the laity embraced penance as the way to God. To convert or to do penance appeared to be the only appropriate response for the person before God. As a sinner the only possible stance before God was that of repentance. The experience of God's love heightened the awareness of one's own profound sinfulness. Becoming a penitent meant recognizing

---

not their cultural superiority. This cultural inequality waned as more and more people learned to read and write. However, many people wished further to live a more intense religious life; many sought to obtain an ecclesiastical status without becoming clerics or monks. Meersseman suggests that the Order of Penance was the answer for some: being thus recognized as "religious" while retaining the advantages of being lay people "in the world". Cf. Meersseman, *Ordo Fraternitatis*, 428-29. While both of these are probable motivations, neither seems to address the more profound, deep-felt inner need of the people which brought them to the choice of entering the Order of Penance.

[133] R. Manselli, *Conclusione*, in *Il movimento francescano della penitenza nella società medioevale*, edited by M. D'Alatri, Roma 1980, 492-93.

[134] *Ibid.*, 492-93.

[135] For a discussion of the conflict between the developing economy and the official Church's moral position, cf. Little, *Religious Poverty*, 35-41; for the specific condemnation of merchants given in Canon law ("A merchant is rarely or never able to please God"), cf. page 38.

oneself as profoundly poor or wretched before God. The penitent sought "nakedness" and poverty not as an end in themselves but as an approach to God. Only by shedding one's sinfulness could one approach God and thus, the penitents sought to be simple and humble, to refuse the self-aggrandisement of power and wealth.

For Christians in the early thirteenth century, "doing penance" did not mean simply repenting of one's sins and receiving the sacrament of penance (which the Fourth Lateran Council of 1215 mandated as a yearly obligation). Penance was a state. They took quite literally the Gospel admonition "Repent, for the kingdom of Heaven is close at hand"[136]. The apocalyptic expectation of the imminent arrival of the kingdom was not uncommon[137]. Thus, there was an urgency connected with the call to repentance. Conversion, this response of repentance, was established, realized, and deepened throughout life in "penance".

This understanding of penance reflected the biblical notion of penance as conversion. Just as the penitents in the early Church were eventually reconciled with the community and again brought into living "in Christ", so too these voluntary penitents of the thirteenth century would be brought to union with God through these penitential practices. The penitents were, in effect, profoundly convinced that only through a painful expiation could they obtain remission of their sins[138]. They were profoundly convinced that there was no resurrection without the passion and, therefore, they attempted to identify with the suffering Christ so as to be identified with Christ in resurrection. They voluntarily embraced a rigorous life of penance in an attempt to make the power of God manifest in their lives[139].

---

[136] *Matthew* 4:17.

[137] A. Vauchez, *Les Laïcs au Moyen Age: pratiques et expériences religieuses*, Paris 1987, 108. This apocalyptic mentality is mentioned but not developed by Chenu. Cf. Chenu, *Nature, Man, and Society*, 246. Given the lack of plagues, the end of invasions, the population increase, and economic growth during this period, this apocalyptic expectation (which comes to full expression in Joachim of Fiore but which existed earlier and appears to have encouraged the embrace of penance) remains very puzzling and begs further study. For one such study, cf. B. McGinn, *Apocalyptic Traditions and Spiritual Identity in Thirteenth-Century Religious Life*, in *The Roots of the Modern Christian Tradition*, edited by E. Elder, Kalamazoo 1984, 1-26.

[138] Vauchez, *La spiritualité*, 62.

[139] *Ibid.*, 142.

They sought penance precisely because they sought contact with God. To avoid damnation they embraced the penitential life since there was the expectation that the penitential life in some way could facilitate a participation in the sacred. Penance was *the* way of salvation. To turn to God was to become the penitent. Let us turn then to a consideration of Francis' turn to God, his choice of penance.

Francis' Conversion and Life of Penance

If we are to understand Francis and the central motivation or inspiration for his life and work, we must attempt "a critical exposition of the bonds between [Francis] and the religious, political, and social reality that enveloped him"[140].

Assisi at the Time of Francis[141]

During the twelfth and thirteenth centuries, Assisi, not unlike other developing communes in northern and central Italy, underwent dramatic changes. Francis witnessed great changes in the city of his youth. Of course, Francis was not just observer but participant in these changes. As the son of a merchant, Francis participated in the changing economic order with its consequent social implications. As a youth filled with chivalrous dreams, Francis participated in military conflicts and battles. As a product of his time and culture, Francis had his religious imagination formed by popular images of salvation and damnation.

Throughout the twelfth century the control of Assisi had been contested by the pope and emperor. In 1160, while the city was effectively under imperial control, the emperor Frederick Barbarossa issued a rescript which granted Assisi a broad autonomy to control its own internal

[140] Manselli, *St. Francis*, vii.

[141] Cf. P. Riley, *Francis' Assisi: Its Political and Social History, 1175-1225*, in *Franciscan Studies* 34 (1974) 393-424; Le Goff, *Francis of Assisi*, 3-10; and *Assisi al tempo di san Francesco. Atti dell V Convegno Internazionale, Società Internazionale di Studi Francescani*, Assisi 1978.

development[142]. Essentially, it declared Assisi to be a free city under imperial protection. However, in that very year of the rescript Frederick had begun a repression of civil liberties in many northern Italian cities. Thus, the Assisians realized that if they were to retain their freedom they would have to fight the German and his armies. Many serfs or common people revolted against the nobles who were aligned with the emperor. They rejected the demands of their lords, deserted the manors, and took refuge in the city. And so, from 1164-1174, while technically Assisi remained an imperial city, it was in revolt.

Then, in 1174, Archbishop Christian of Mainz (who was aligned with the emperor and had been excommunicated by the pope), acting as deputy for Frederick Barbarossa, seized and destroyed Assisi[143]. The emperor and his court were officially installed in *La Rocca*, the fortress in Assisi, in 1178. Much unrest and a growing desire for liberty among the people of Assisi marked the years that followed.

In 1189, Frederick Barbarossa reconciled with Pope Clement III, signaling peace for the Italian cities. However, one year later Frederick died and once again the tide changed. Frederick was succeeded by his son, Henry VI. The new emperor returned to Italy battling and conquering many cities. Henry's campaign and conquests gave new hope to the imperially aligned nobles who began to reassert their power.

After Henry VI's death in 1197, Innocent III again made claim to Assisi. But the people who had opposed imperial rule also opposed papal authority because they would have had to accept, as a consequence, coming under the predominance of the papal city Perugia, Assisi's great rival[144]. Thus, although the city technically changed from imperial to papal control in 1198, the people of Assisi refused to hand over *La Rocca* to the papal representative and instead destroyed the fortress[145]. Thus, in 1198, when Francis was sixteen years old, Assisi was finally freed from imperial domination.

---

[142] Manselli, *St. Francis*, 20.

[143] Riley, *Francis' Assisi*, 399.

[144] Manselli, *St. Francis*, 21.

[145] In that same year, Innocent III sent a bull to Bishop Guido of Assisi declaring the city under "apostolic protection". The bull, *In eminenti Apostolicae Sedis*, dated May 28, 1198, is preserved in the communal archives of Assisi. The Latin text may be found in A. Fortini, *Nova Vita di San Francesco*, Assisi 1959, III 543-45.

The political struggles of Francis' youth cannot be separated from the social conflicts. In part, the political conflicts and military battles can be seen in terms of the opposing claims made to Assisi by both the pope and the emperor. But these battles also involved the evolving conflicts between the nobles and common people of Assisi. During this time, Assisi witnessed much violence, division and oppression. The new developing economic order did not eradicate divisions, but rather removed the traditional division based upon birthright[146]. The new economy of the communes brought not only new wealth to many citizens, but also a new brand of poverty[147]. There remained the "lower class", the *homines populi,* which included many poor. But there were others excluded even from this lower class, excluded from society, literally the "outcasts" of society who were forced to live outside the walls of the city.

The polarization and intense discord among the people at Assisi erupted in 1198 when the *homines populi* took over the city and destroyed the main fortress and the city dwellings of the *boni homines*[148]. The nobles fled either to their castles or to Perugia for refuge. This "discord" between two distinct groups within Assisi then expanded into a conflict between Assisi and Perugia which culminated in the battle of Collestrada in 1202 where the *homines populi* were defeated[149]. The Pact of 1203 which established "peace" between the *boni homines* and the *homines populi,* in fact, reestablished the dominion of the former

---

[146] Manselli, *St. Francis,* 14-15.

[147] *Ibid.,* 25; and Little, *Religious Poverty,* 19-29, esp. 28.

[148] We speak of these two distinct groups because they are so designated in the Pact of 1203, which refers back to this conflict. The group designated as the "*boni homines*" comprised those who had established ties with Perugia, who had had homes and goods within the city walls, whose residences were demolished by the *homines populi,* and those soldiers or knights aligned with the emperor. However, the group designated as the "*homines populi*" remains an anonymous collective entity. No specific information about individuals within this group exists; we cannot assume a uniformity or homogeneity. They are defined - as always is the case in oppressive systems - only in contradistinction to those in power, the *boni homines.* But the fundamental distinction between the *boni homines* and the *homines populi* was not based upon social and economic requirements as much as it was based upon a spacial or institutional battle: country versus city, feudal estate versus commune. Cf. A. Bartoli-Langeli, *La realtà sociale assisana e il Patto del 1210,* in *Assisi al tempo di san Francesco,* 287-95.

[149] *Ibid.,* 282-84.

over the latter. The members of the common people who had gained their freedom in 1198 or thereafter were once again subject to their lords[150].

Seven years later the situation changed. Once again two distinct groups, now designated as the *maiores* and *minores*, attempted to end their discord and arrive at a peace, but in 1210 they established a very different "peace"[151]. In 1203, the discord had ended with the defeat of the common people. The pact reestablished the former structures of power, the very situation which had led to the conflict of 1198. The Pact of 1210 did not, however, assert the dominion of the *maiores*, but rather integrated them into the whole. The Pact, in effect, abolished servitude[152]. It asserted the freedom of all the people, that is, instead of being "*homines alicuius*", all people were subject to the commune[153]. Thus, following upon and as the fruit of many years of struggle, the Pact of 1210 gave expression to a reality that had slowly and progressively taken form: the commune.

Francis himself, while not of nobility, enjoyed the lifestyle and status as a member of the *maiores*. His father, Pietro Bernardone, was

---

[150] The freedom was recognized only of those people who had been "*homines alicuius*" for a time but had been liberated prior to 1180. Any of the other people who owed service to a noble and had acquired their freedom after 1198 were once again acknowledged as *homines alicuius*. This pact was not, therefore, a declaration of the freedom for all people. It was a "treaty" which gave compensation to the displaced nobles. Cf. Bartoli-Langeli, *La realtà sociale assisana*, 297.

[151] While these two groups, the *maiores* and the *minores*, are analogous to the groups designated by the Pact of 1203 as the *boni homines* and the *homines populi* (for example, the *boni homines* would be included in the *maiores*), they should not be strictly identified. The distinction between the *maiores* and the *minores* (themselves heterogeneous groups) rested upon power. Cf. Bartoli-Langeli, *La realtà sociale assisana*, 314-15.

[152] The Pact did not establish some abstract or general "freedom". It declared an unconditional liberation for all those who had been part of the commune prior to the *captio capitalis* of 1173-1174. Those who had become "citizens" subsequently, could obtain freedom by paying a sum of money to their ex-Lord. Cf. Bartoli-Langeli, *La realtà sociale assisana*, 298-99.

[153] *Ibid.*, 310.

a merchant, a merchant of uncommon wealth with a great love of money[154].

> Francis was, then, a young merchant but capable in business, lover of pomp and luxury, given over to a demeanor that let him shine for his generosity, liberality of means, elegance, and "courtliness". His was the ambitious aspiration to come out ahead, to be above others. He thought he could do it with his wealth and with whatever wealth could give him, looking to a future of prosperity and grandeur[155].

In fact, Francis twice set out, equipped in a knight's finery, to obtain upon his victorious return a "noble's glory". Neither of these attempts led to that glory, however, and Francis instead experienced profound inner crisis. Let us then look more closely at the events in Francis' life which led to his conversion.

Francis' Conversion

Francis, who was born in 1181 or 1182, dictated a Testament shortly before his death in 1226. Let us turn again to Francis' own account of his conversion:

> The Lord granted me, Brother Francis, to begin to do penance in this way: While I was in sin, it seemed very bitter to me to see lepers. And the Lord Himself led me among them and I had mercy upon them. And when I left them that which seemed bitter to me was changed into sweetness of soul and body; and afterward I lingered a little and left the world[156].

Francis clearly distinguished two periods in his life: a time when he was "in sin", and a time of "doing penance". But, while he spoke of his own conversion in a clear and meaningful way, while he singled out his experience with lepers as a critical moment, the slow and gradual

---

[154] Manselli calls attention to the "fact of an uncommon wealth" as an important element in understanding the depth of Francis' conversion. Cf. Manselli, *St. Francis*, 29.

[155] *Ibid.*, 45.

[156] *Testament* 1-3. Cf. Armstrong, *Francis and Clare*, 154.

process of his conversion remains obscure. Francis' silence about other significant events in his life, about his own internal struggles and crises, prohibits any definitive explanation of his spiritual development. We cannot know precisely the origins of his spiritual vision or the meaning he perceived in the experiences which brought him to "doing penance". Rather, we can only examine the circumstances, the events which led to this conversion in an attempt to grasp more fully Francis' understanding of penance.

At the battle of Collestrada in 1202 Francis was taken prisoner. His imprisonment lasted for about a year, at which point he returned to Assisi[157]. We do not know about the extent of his suffering or the depth of his disillusionment. Having set out with hopes of knightly glory, Francis returned defeated. But while this experience must have stirred profound questions within him, Francis had not lost his former hopes. When presented with another opportunity to obtain "nobility" as a knight, Francis once again prepared himself for battle. In the spring of 1205 Francis set out with Count Gentile to join the forces of the renowned, almost idealized knight, Walter of Brienne[158]. At Spoleto, for reasons that remain unknown, reasons imaged hagiographically as a "dream", Francis decided to abandon his pursuit and return to Assisi[159].

---

[157] *L3S* 4: *Omnibus*, 893.

[158] *L3S* 5: *Omnibus*, 893-94.

[159] Francis' dream or vision at Spoleto, as described in the hagiographical sources, cannot be taken as an historical event in the literal sense. Rather, these dreams or visions are used in these legends to express the person's profound interior understanding of the will of God made manifest in their lives. For example, we find an analogous use of a "dream" at another point in the Franciscan legends. When Francis went to Rome in 1210 to gain papal approval of the primitive rule or his Gospel way of life, it is recorded that Pope Innocent III "recalled a certain vision he had a few days before, which, he affirmed, under the guidance of the Holy Spirit, would be fulfilled in this man. He had seen in his sleep the Lateran basilica about to fall to ruin, when a certain religious, small and despised, propped it up by putting his own back under it lest it fall". Cf. *2 Cel* 17: *Omnibus*, 377. Pazzelli points out that the "dream" or very same "vision" is attributed to Pope Innocent III with respect to St. Dominic in the *Vita* written by Constantine of Orvieto in 1244, which predates Thomas' attribution of the vision to Francis. Cf. Pazzelli, *St. Francis and the Third Order*, 84. For a brief discussion of hagiographical genre and methodology, as well as further bibliography, cf. Short, *Hagiographical Method*, 462-495; and G. Caprettini, *Agiografia francescana fra storia e semiotica: proposte metodologiche e analisi di un testo*, in *Laurentianum* 29 (1988) 496-533.

He then spent some months in a depression and a seemingly aimless wandering.

Francis found himself in a period of profound inner crisis. Due to his own silence, we cannot know the inner struggles, however, as Manselli points out, "the new and distinct trait seems to be the passage from a *courtly* generosity and liberality, practiced to demonstrate one's own nobility of soul, over to a *merciful* generosity, intended for the aid of the poor and needy"[160]. Certain gestures recorded in the sources indicated this change in Francis: giving his shirt away to a beggar, distributing bread to the poor, and making a pilgrimage to Rome[161].

Francis' attitudes and behavior changed, causing great confusion and anger in his father, resulting in puzzlement and rejection among his friends[162]. Whatever his inner struggles and insights, Francis eventually knew that he had to reorder his values. Francis' biographers record that during this time of inner search and struggle Francis had two other significant experiences: his exchange of clothes with a beggar at Rome and his encounter with the leper[163].

Things had changed for Francis; things had changed within Francis. Did he perhaps have a "near death" experience on the battlefield of Collestrada? Did the death of the great Walter of Brienne bring him closer to the realization of his own mortality or the futility of his pursuit of wealth and nobility? Did his experience of the pain and suffering of the poor and of the lepers bring him to an insight into his own internal struggle and pain? What factors most influenced Francis' imagination, his view of salvation? Did Francis consciously perceive the hand of God in his experience? Was he reflectively aware of those experiences as moments of grace?

Certainly, in retrospect, Francis perceived the graced nature of his encounter with the leper. In his Testament he speaks of that moment having brought him insight, of how the grace of that moment brought him to the realization of his former life as a "life of sin". In his Testament, with his own words,

---

160 Manselli, *St. Francis*, 50.

161 *L3S* 8-9: *Omnibus*, 897-98.

162 Manselli calls attention to the strong expectations on the part of the group at that time, the "*fama publica*". Cf. Manselli, *St. Francis*, 26.

163 *L3S* 10-12: *Omnibus*, 898-902; also cf. Manselli, *St. Francis*, 50-51.

> an entire life from infancy to maturity is condemned in a global manner. At the same time, his life has been marked by a providential sign in which he recognizes himself, not to say he identifies himself with it. Between his life of sin and life of penance he was given a sign of God's intervention that resulted in a decision to enter into a life that had already been ordained by God himself: the beginning of a life of penance.
>
> There is, then, a definite connection between sin and the bitterness of the horror inspired by the lepers. Nor should we be surprised if a connection is drawn between sin (as the leprosy of the soul) and the lepers themselves. Sin as the soul's leprosy was an interpretation current in the spirituality of that time. The lepers were the sign of contradiction in the solitude of Francis' soul, which did not realize, by any self-reflection, that it too was leprous, no more of less than those who were leprous in body. Lepers thus horrified him, although he experienced no horror at the moral leprosy that rendered him equally repulsive within[164].

Francis lived within a "penitential culture". Most probably he had heard the Legend of St. Alexis; surely he was aware of that official morality which preached condemnation for merchants and the evil of wealth. But how influenced was he by the sense of urgency in an "apocalyptic" mentality, by a loss of the sense of God's immediacy and a fear of the demonic? We cannot answer these questions. Francis' motivations remain hidden. But, as noted above, many people of his time "abandoned the world" for a life of penance. Many, whether to avoid damnation or to pursue perfection, sought contact with God through penance.

Had Francis experienced an abandonment by God in his "life in sin"? Did he experience this "contact with God" precisely in his "doing penance": suffering in prison, giving alms to the poor, making a pilgrimage, begging alms at Rome, suffering an encounter with a leper?

Much remains hypothesis and yet, Francis clearly did experience God. In fact, his experience of God was so tangible, so palpable that it transformed him. Francis made a very clear decision; he "lingered a little and left the world". This technically precise term signified a conversion, the beginning of a religious life, a life of penance. Francis abandoned the world he had known and the ways in which he had lived. He turned from merchant to pauper, from noble to outcast. He deliberately chose a life of penance. But while the choice was clear,

---

[164] Manselli, *St. Francis*, 34.

the pattern of his life in penance had not yet been formulated. The gradual process and maturation of Francis' conversion continued.

Amidst his spiritual restlessness, while in prayer before the cruxifix in the little country church of San Damiano, Francis had a mystical experience. The early sources record that Francis heard a voice: Francis heard the crucified Christ speak to him the words, "Francis, do you not see that my house is falling into ruin? Go, and repair it for me"[165]. As we have seen, Bonaventure offers a theological elaboration of this account. But setting aside the details of the presentations, the manner in which the episode is presented, and the theological imagery of Bonaventure, Francis' experience before the crucifix remains pivotal in his spiritual journey. As Manselli poignantly describes it, this experience

> signals a second stage in Francis' transformation, in which the meaning of his conversion is completed and deepened, tracing a clearer and more precise direction in his spiritual journey. His instinctive and generous choice on impulse had moved him to leave his own world in order to pass over to the lepers' side. This choice found its justification in what we could call his encounter with the crucifix. "In his soul", relates the *Legend* [*of the Three Companions*], "he truly felt that it was Christ crucified that had spoken to him". His conversion was centered upon Christ on the cross. In him Francis felt that the deepest and truest root of his choice was touched and made real. The suffering of Christ explained, illuminated, and justified all human suffering. People, however, with all their penance, could never by themselves have attained the value of the suffering of the Crucified. The reality of Francis' conversion fell in this way within the context and sphere of the suffering Christ. It shifted from being an individual and personal matter, even a private one, over to a single unifying moment of a reality that greatly transcended any one person. It became an effective sign for all those who, like Francis himself, wanted to abandon their sinful way of life in order to join themselves to Christ and in Christ. His conversion acted as a sign as well for those who were not on the cross but who still suffered from misery, pain, rejection, and abandonment.
>
> The crucifix at San Damiano made Francis aware of the suffering of Christ as a superhuman value in the reality of human existence. It was the only power able to give meaning and sense to human suffering, to the point of attracting people to seek this suffering and to accept it freely in order to come closer to Christ. The saint's religious severity

[165] *L3S* 13: *Omnibus*, 903.

had its origin in his insight into the meaning of the crucifixion of Christ. Its theological meaning was not what impressed him, but rather its power of example for each individual and for all who wanted truly to call themselves Christians[166].

Francis' life of penance became more clear to him though he would still work out the details of that life for the friars, the sisters, and the penitents in the years to come. But while his resolve had solidified, his "leaving the world" was to become even more definitive or absolute in the encounter with his father before the bishop of Assisi.

When his father had him summoned before the consuls of Assisi on the charge that he had taken his father's goods, they in response turned the case over to the bishop claiming that Francis was no longer in their jurisdiction. Then, when called by his father before the bishop, when confronted with his former life, confronted by family, friends and peers, Francis, in his own symbolic way, with a powerfully dramatic gesture, broke definitively with all former ties. He stripped naked before the crowd, returning not only the money but also all his clothes to Pietro, calling from that day foward, only God his "father"[167]. By this gesture, Francis repudiated his entire past and displayed his intent to "do penance". Nakedness was a form of humiliation practiced by public penitents. Francis expressed symbolically the rigorous goal of penance: the goal of following Christ in the ancient tradition of *Nudus nudum Christum sequi*[168].

Francis had become the penitent[169]. But this act, this conversion, for Francis, was "much more than a simple spiritual change; it was a choice of a specific social life"[170]. Francis' former life of wealth and pursuit of glory, that life he later described as when he "was in sin", had now been exchanged for a life in penance.

---

[166] Manselli, *St. Francis*, 54-55.

[167] *1 Cel* 14-15: *Omnibus*, 240-41; *L3S* 19-20: *Omnibus*, 908-910.

[168] Manselli, *St. Francis*, 59.

[169] This choice on the part of Francis to become a "penitent" should be understood not as the choice of a juridical state, but rather, as the choice of a social condition. Cf. above, page 89 note 137.

[170] Manselli, *St. Francis*, 63.

Francis' Understanding of Penance

By speaking of his former life as "when he was in sin" (*esse in peccatis*), Francis meant his whole life as lived selfishly, as lived independent of God. He did not intend to confess certain "sins" as opposed to others, but rather, a life condition of separation from God, that is, a life not consciously lived in response to God[171].

> As Francis looked back on his life towards the end of his days, he could distinguish in it two periods. One he describes plainly and concisely as "when I was in sin", the other as "doing penance". The beginning of this "doing penance" is in the obedience he gives to God's command which urges him to the care of lepers. Accordingly, in the life of the Saint, the period of sin, of disobedience to God, and the period of penance, of obedience rendered to God ever anew, stand opposed to each other. He no longer did what he wanted himself, but what God demanded of him: "that which seemed bitter to me". In the process, he came to experience a special grace, that his bitterness was "changed into sweetness of soul and body". Penance to him is thus the conversion of man from a life centered on the personal "I" to a life which is completely under the will and sovereign lordship of God. He expressly acknowledges that, after a certain time, it led him out of the "world", thus bringing him to a life outside the "saeculum"[172].

In the Middle Ages, this terminology "to leave the world" signified the beginning of a religious life. It connoted conversion or *metanoia* in the biblical sense. "To do penance" meant for Francis *metanoia*, a conversion to God[173]. This reversal of values involving a dissatisfaction with a former way of life, this turning from evil to do good as a loving response to God, was for Francis the only possible response. And so Francis embraced and preached to others this life of penance: not specific actions but a conversion of heart, not simply penitential practices but a life lived "in God".

> [I]t can be proved, above all by his writings, that, in the course of time, he wanted to mold his whole being and life according to the Gospel,

---

171 *Ibid.*, 41.

172 K. Esser, *Origins of the Franciscan Order*, translated by A. Daly and I. Lynch, Chicago 1970, 204.

173 *Ibid.*, 207.

> and that he also expected and required of all those who joined him in his fraternity this "evangelical form of existence".
>
> Something very important, perhaps even decisive, is here expressed about the original intention of St. Francis. He was not concerned primarily with some kind of external activity in the service of the Church perhaps, nor in any pressing way with the realization of this or that "virtue" as the first principle of the Order; neither was he concerned with "ideals" of some kind or another, but with a *life*, or rather, with *the* life according to the form of the Gospel[174].

Let us, then, turn to a consideration of that life, the way of life Francis offered to the laity in the "primitive rule".

[174] *Ibid.*, 213.

Chapter III

THE PRIMITIVE AND EARLY RULES

Before beginning our analysis of the way of life that Francis proposed for the penitents in the primitive Rule, we need to clarify some terminology with respect to the various texts. While alternate designations of these early documents by some scholars can be confusing, more significantly, the commonly accepted designations have been shown to be both inappropriate and misleading. The text in the Volterra codex 225, which was identified by Pazzelli as the primitive Rule[1], and which had earlier been designated by Esser as the "*Epistola ad Fideles (Recensio prior): Exhortatio ad fratres et sorores de poenitentia*", has come to be known generally (following the original publication of Esser's study in 1975)[2] as the "*Recensio prior*" or the "*First Version of the Letter to All the Faithful*"[3]. The later document, the so-called "*Letter to All the Faithful*", had long been established as an authentic writing of Francis and although one of the oldest manuscripts preserves the text with the title "A Reminder and Exhortation" (*commonitorium et exhortatorium*)[4], the text came to be known in the tradition as the *Letter to All the Faithful*[5].

---

[1] Pazzelli, *The Title of the "Recensio Prior"*, 246.

[2] K. Esser, *Ein Vorläufer der Epistola ad Fideles des hl. Franziskus von Assisi (Cod. 225 der Biblioteca Guarnacci zu Volterra)*, in *CF* 45 (1975) 5-37.

[3] Armstrong, *Francis and Clare*, 62.

[4] K. Esser, *Gli Scritti di S. Francesco d'Assisi: nuova edizione critica e versione italiana*, translated by A. Bizzotto and S. Cattazzo, Padova 1982, 227.

[5] Cf. the Introduction to the *Letter to All the Faithful* in the *Omnibus*, 91-93.

Based upon Esser's extensive analysis of the Volterra text, most scholars accept the chronological priority and the literary connection of the Volterra text with respect to the so-called *Letter to All the Faithful*[6]. Thus, the Volterra text, the text which has now been identified as the primitive Rule, has generally been designated as the earlier version (*Recensio prior*) of the *Letter to All the Faithful*. However, recent analyses of the form and content of these two documents have shown that the common designation "*Letter to All the Faithful*" is, at best, misleading.

An Overview of the Thirteenth Century Documents

Nomenclature of the Documents

The *Letter to All the Faithful* (that is, the later or longer version), as other letters written by Francis, came to be designated by its recipients[7]. The manuscript reads: "*Universis christianis religiosis clericis et laicis masculis et feminis omnibus qui habitant in universo mundo*"[8]. And so it was thought to be written to all Christians. However, as Esser stressed, the words "*christianis religiosis*" cannot be separated; in fact, some of the early manuscripts lack the word "*christianis*"[9].

In order to make the sense of the Latin more apparent, in his critical edition of the text Esser added punctuation and argued that the Latin text should read: "*Universis christianis religiosis, clericis et laicis, masculis et feminis, omnibus qui habitant in universo mundo*"[10]. The letter is not, therefore, addressed to all Christians, that is, to "all the

---

[6] The notable exception is David Flood who still maintains that the Volterra text is a later extraction or abbreviation of the *Letter to All the Faithful*. Cf. D. Flood, *The Commonitorium*, in *Haversack* 3 (1979) n. 1, 22-23.

[7] After the thirteenth century the text came to be known as the "*Letter to All the Faithful*". Cf. D. Flood, *Frère François et le mouvement franciscain*, Paris 1983, 162.

[8] K. Esser, *La Lettera di san Francesco ai fedeli*, in *CF* 43 (1973) 66.

[9] Esser, *La Lettera di san Francesco ai fedeli*, 67.

[10] *Opuscula*, 114.

faithful", but rather, to "all *Christian religious*: clergy and laity, men and women, and to all who live in the whole world"[11]. The recipients are not "all the faithful", but rather, those Christians living in the world who have committed themselves to living more intensely their baptismal commitment through a life of penance[12].

Unfortunately, in his critical edition of the writings of Francis, Esser continued to use the traditional designation of the text, Francis' *Letter to All the Faithful*, and thus in establishing the critical texts for the earlier and later versions he identified them as the *Epistola ad Fideles I* and the *Epistola ad Fideles II*[13]. Since Esser's critical edition has been recognized world-wide as the most definitive work on Francis' writings to date, most scholars have continued to identify these two texts as different versions of the "*Letter to All the Faithful*", although this designation does not appropriately convey either the recipients or the contents of the texts.

This commonly accepted title implies that Francis intended his message for all Christians in general, rather than the specific group to which it was directed. Francis addressed his words to the brothers and sisters of penance who, within the medieval understanding of states within the Church, were considered "religious"[14]. Further, the designation "*Letter to All the Faithful*" does not describe the contents of Francis' message. While this generic title might suggest a general exhortation to traditional Christian morality, in fact, the letter presents the "discernments and precisions of the movement's way and purpose" for the women and men who became voluntary penitents under the guidance of Francis and the friars[15].

In his study on the "*Letter to All the Faithful*", David Flood discusses the problems associated with this designation and suggests an alternative. He writes:

> the early manuscript tradition calls it an *opusculum* (a brief text) and the late tradition a letter; the early tradition qualifies *opusculum* with *commonitorium* and *exhortatorium*, whereas the late tradition completes the

---

[11] Armstrong, *Francis and Clare*, 67, note 3 (emphasis added).

[12] *Ibid.*, 66, note 2.

[13] The abbreviated designations are respectively *EpFid I* and *EpFid II.*

[14] Meersseman, *Ordo Fraternitatis*, 431.

[15] Flood, *The Commonitorium*, in *Haversack* 3 (1979) n. 1, 21.

> title by designating the recipients of the letter. The key term in the early tradition, the difficult word abandoned in the course of transmission, is *commonitorium*. It reveals the nature of Francis' message.
>
> This does not mean that Francis used the term to designate this communication. Francis did not give his pieces titles - even the titles of the chapters in the rule [of 1221] came later. It means that in the early codification of Francis' writings, as the compilers designated the components of the collection, they qualified one long passage with the word *commonitorium*. They had their reasons for doing so, of which the foremost was that it is a *commonitorium*. The word does Francis' composition justice. The term deserves to replace the title by which the message has been known till now[16].

In medieval Latin the term *commonitorium* signified a letter which was both an exhortation and a reminder in order that a commitment be followed[17]. In giving these two texts to his followers as a "Rule of life", Francis offered the penitents a reminder of the life they had professed and exhorted them to that life of penance[18]. Thus, the designation "*Commonitorium et Exhortatorium*" does more accurately describe the content of the "letters" and more appropriately indicates Francis' purpose in preparing the texts for his followers. But since "*commonitorium*" loses much of its power in the English equivalents of "warning" or "reminder", and since *commonitorium* does also connote exhortation, we will adopt simply the "*Exhortatorium*" as the designation for the *Letter to All the Faithful*, that is, simply the "Exhortation" rather than the "Reminder and Exhortation". We will designate the shorter version of the *Letter to All the Faithful* as the *Earlier Exhortation* and the longer or later version of the *Letter to All the Faithful* as the *Later Exhortation*.

These designations have been chosen in an attempt to offer both a more appropriate and a sufficiently concise descriptive title for Francis'

---

[16] *Ibid.*, 21-22.

[17] The definition of *commonitorius* is given as "monitory, conveying a reminder, exhortation or warning". Cf. *Dictionary of Medieval Latin from British Sources* (1981), s.v. "*commonitorius*". The dual sense of "*commonitorium*" as both reminding and enjoining a person to something is even more clearly expressed by Du Cange in his ten volume Medieval Latin Glossary: "Epistola qua aliquid praecipitur, qua quis *Commonetur* ut rem mandatam exequatur". Cf. *Glossarium Mediae et Infimae Latinitatis*, 1954 ed., s.v. "*commonitorium*".

[18] Flood, *The Commonitorium*, 3 (1979) n. 1, 22.

address to the penitents. Thus, throughout this study we will designate the primitive Rule as the *Earlier Exhortation* rather than the appropriate but cumbersome designations of Lehmann ("exultation and exhortation concerning penance")[19] and Pazzelli ("These are the words of life and salvation concerning those who do penance")[20].

With respect to the later Rules of the Secular Franciscan Order, this study will designate those texts according to the year in which each was promulgated: the *Rule of 1289*, the *Rule of 1883*, and the *Rule of 1978*. Many authors refer to these Rules as the *Nicholas Rule*, the *Leonine Rule*, and the *Pauline Rule* given that respectively Nicholas IV, Leo XIII and Paul VI promulgated these later Rules. Interestingly, the *Regula bullata* of the Friars Minor, their officially approved Rule of 1223, is *not* designated as the *Honorius Rule*, although it was promulgated by Honorius III. The terms used to identify this Rule (the *Regula bullata* or the *Rule of 1223*) always indicate it as the Rule of the Friars Minor, not as the work of the pope. Therefore, to emphasize the later Rules of the penitents as the Rules of the Secular Franciscan Order, we will avoid the common pontifical designations and will always identify each of these later Rules according to the year of its promulgation: the *Rule of 1289*, the *Rule of 1883*, and the *Rule of 1978*.

Having added precision to the designations of the early documents, we can now define more specifically the terms first suggested in the *Introduction*[21]. Throughout this study the term "primitive Rule" will be used specifically to indicate the earlier version, that is, the *Earlier Exhortation*. The term "early Rule" will be used in a much more general sense, given the evolution of the Rule and the coexistence of distinct versions of the Rule prior to 1289, to indicate and to include all those extant documents which led to the officially approved Rule of 1289: the *Earlier Exhortation*, the *Later Exhortation*, and the *Memoriale propositi*.

The Dating of these Documents

Only one of these three documents can be dated with certainty: the *Memoriale propositi* of 1221. However, this "Memorial of the Man-

---

[19] Cf. the discussion below, pp. 162-168, esp. 166.
[20] Cf. the discussion above in *Chapter I*, pp. 86-88.
[21] Cf. note 10 of the Introduction, p. 43.

ner of Life of the Brothers and Sisters of Penance", which was orally approved by Pope Honorius III in 1221, is no longer extant as such. The *Memoriale propositi* has been preserved in four medieval codices which contain versions which date from 1228. The four versions have been designated the Venice Rule, the Königsberg Rule, the Capistrano Rule, and the Mariano rule[22]. All of the four extant manuscripts which contain the *Memoriale propositi* attest that it was written in 1221[23]. However, while these four versions differ little, the manuscripts do include changes which were incorporated into the text between 1221

---

[22] The "Venice Rule" was discovered in Codex 225-226 of the library of Landau at Florence. It was designated the Venice Rule because Mandonnet had first found the rule listed and described in an 18th century catalog at a Dominican library at Venice. The manuscript dates back to the fourteenth or possibly the thirteenth century but preserves a text of the *Memoriale propositi* dating from around 1228. Cf. *AFH* XIV (1921) 109-21. An English translation of the Venice Rule may be found in the *Omnibus*, 168-75.

The "Königsberg Rule" was edited by L. Lemmens from a manuscript found at Königsberg, Germany. The manuscript dates from the second half of the fourteenth century but preserves a version of the *Memoriale propositi* dating around 1228. Cf. *AFH* VI (1913) 242-50.

The "Capistrano Rule" was discovered in the Franciscan friary of Capistrano in Abruzzi, Italy. The first twelve chapters of the *Memoriale propositi* in the Capistrano codex date from 1228 at the latest. The text was edited by Paul Sabatier in 1901. Cf. *Opuscules de critique historique I*, Paris 1901, 17-30. A literal English translation can be found in T. Zaremba, *Franciscan Social Reform: A Study of the Third Order Secular of St. Francis as an Agency of Social Reform according to Certain Papal Documents*, Ph.D. diss., The Catholic University of America 1947, 114-21. Another English translation of this text, though not a literal translation, can be found in *The Rules of the Third Order of St. Francis*, edited by M. Poppy, St. Bonaventure 1945, 24-31.

The "Mariano Rule" was reconstructed by A. Van der Wyngaert from an early 16th century manuscript which contained a treatise on the Third Order written by Mariano of Florence. Cf. *AFH* XIII (1920) 3-77; and M. D. Papi, *Il trattato del terz'Ordine o vero "Libro come santo Francesco istituì et ordinò el tertio ordine de frati et sore di penitentia et della dignità et perfectione o vero sanctità sua" di Mariano da Firenze*, Roma 1985. However, this text is not as early a witness as the other versions; it dates from 1234 or later.

For a brief discussion of the various manuscripts containing the *Memoriale propositi*, cf. Zaremba, *Franciscan Social Reform*, 111-13.

[23] *Omnibus*, 165-68.

and 1228, since only after 1228 was the text considered "unchangeable"[24].

Unfortunately, the exact text of the *Memoriale propositi* as it existed in 1221 cannot be definitively reconstructed. But, the versions of the *Memoriale propositi* which have been preserved in these manuscripts do include the 1221 text, that is, as it had evolved up to 1228. And it was this version of the *Memoriale propositi* which remained officially in force as the Rule of the penitents for some sixty years: 1228-1289. Thus, our analysis will focus upon the 1228 version of the *Memoriale propositi* as given in the so-called "Capistrano Rule".

The precise dates that the *Earlier Exhortation* and the *Later Exhortation* were written cannot be determined, although quite plausible hypotheses have been proposed which suggest probable dates for each. Francis' mention of his infirmities, which forced him to write his message rather than to visit the penitents personally[25], suggests that the *Later Exhortation* comes from the later years of Francis' life, since Francis' serious illnesses began in 1220-1221[26]. Thus, many scholars accept the hypothesis that the *Later Exhortation* was written around 1221, that is, around the time of the *Regula non bullata* and the *Memoriale propositi*[27]. However, Esser suggested that the text could have been written as early as 1216 since Francis was sick at other times in his life also[28].

The dating of the *Earlier Exhortation* remains even less clear and hypotheses continue to be debated. Esser convincingly argued that the Volterra text was written prior to the *Later Exhortation*. But based solely on textual analysis we can claim only that the Volterra text predates the *Later Exhortation*[29]. We cannot assign the text a precise date, although Esser does hypothesize that it must have been written some years prior to 1221[30]. In fact, comparative analysis of the *Earlier Exhortation* with other writings of Francis known to be early, as well as historical analysis of its content relative to the decrees of the Lateran

---

[24] Meersseman, *Dossier*, 84.

[25] *Later Exhortation*, 3.

[26] Pazzelli, *St. Francis and the Third Order*, 115.

[27] *Ibid.*, 113.

[28] Esser, *Gli Scritti di S. Francesco d'Assisi*, 260.

[29] Esser, *A Forerunner of the "Epistola ad Fideles"*, 45.

[30] Esser, *Un documento dell'inizio*, 96.

Council IV, offer compelling (though not definitive) arguments that the text predates 1215[31].

Nonetheless, while the precise dates of these two documents remain uncertain, the scholarly hypotheses offer sufficient precision for our analysis[32]. Thus we will proceed with an analysis of these two Rules based upon the general hypothesis that the *Later Exhortation* was written by 1221 at the latest, and the *Earlier Exhortation* some years prior.

Analysis of the Earlier Exhortation

While many manuscripts preserve the *Later Exhortation*, the Volterra text remains the only extant copy of the earlier version. To explain the surprising absence of the *Earlier Exhortation* in later manuscripts, Esser suggests that "following the appearance of the longer version and its dissemination, the text contained in *Vo* [the Volterra manuscript] was no longer of interest"[33]. While the *Later Exhortation* states Francis to be the author, the Volterra text does not explicitly name Francis as the author. In fact, the epilogue uses the plural form "*rogamus*". However, in his painstaking analysis of the Volterra text and his comparison of that text with the *Later Exhortation*, Esser has clearly demonstrated the authenticity of the text, that is, Francis' authorship, and suggests that the plural "we" (*rogamus*) in sentence 19 indicates either Francis' desire to include himself with the brother who took dictation,

[31] Cf. L. Lehmann, *Exsultatio et exhortatio de poenitentia. Zu Form und Inhalt der "Epistola ad fideles I"*, in *Laurentianum* 29 (1988) 567-601, now translated into English as *Exultation to Penance: A Study of the Form and Content of the First Version of the Letter to the Faithful*, in *Greyfriars Review* 4 (1990) n. 2, 1-33; W. Viviani, *L'ermeneutica di Francesco d'Assisi: indagine alla luce di Gv 13-17 nei suoi Scritti*, Roma 1983, 321-23; Esser, *Un documento dell'inizio*, 91; and Esser, *A Forerunner of the "Epistola ad Fideles"*, 35.

[32] For example, Armstrong suggests a range of dates for both documents: 1213-1221 for the *Earlier Exhortation*, and 1219-1221 for the *Later Exhortation*. Cf. Armstrong, *Francis and Clare*, 9. Temperini, in his most recent work on the *Rule of 1289*, gives the date of the *Earlier Exhortation* as 1215 and the date of the *Later Exhortation* as 1221. Cf. L. Temperini, *Ai fratelli e alle sorelle dell'Ordine della penitenza (Regola di Niccolò IV)*, Roma 1988, 7.

[33] Esser, *A Forerunner of the "Epistola ad Fideles"*, 33.

or possibly that Francis worked with others in the composition of the text. Nonetheless, the text clearly preserves Francis' thought and admonitions[34].

Esser's historical-critical analysis of the text brought this long forgotten document to the attention of the Franciscan world. Let us, therefore, begin with a consideration of Esser's analysis of the primitive Rule.

An Historical-Critical Analysis of the Primitive Rule

Esser established a critical text and then compared that text with the longer version, the *Later Exhortation*. The English translation of both of these texts is given below in parallel columns[35]. The arrangement of the texts is based upon and reflects Esser's comparative analysis of the Latin texts[36]. However, to supplement Esser's critical analysis and to explain more fully the original meaning of the words and the sense of the text, some notes have been added from a philological commentary on the writings of Francis[37].

Let us then turn to the text itself; let us consider the text of the primitive Rule, the *Earlier Exhortation*, given in the left column:

---

[34] *Ibid.*, 11-45.

[35] The English translations are based upon Esser's critical Latin edition of the texts. The translations of both the *Earlier Exhortation* and the *Later Exhortation* have been taken from Armstrong, *Francis and Clare*, 63-65; 67-73.

[36] Esser, *A Forerunner of the "Epistola ad Fideles"*, 16-21. It should be noted that the numbering of the sentences in Esser's article differs from the numbering of those same sentences in his later critical edition. Cf. *Opuscula*, 108-28. The numbers within the English texts given below reflect the numbering in the critical English edition which preserves the numbering given in Esser's critical edition of the Latin text. Cf. Armstrong, *Francis and Clare*, 63-73.

[37] I. Rodríguez Herrera, and A. Ortega Carmona, *Los Escritos de San Francisco de Asís*, Murcia 1985, 206-53.

Earlier Exhortation	*Later Exhortation*
These are the words of life and salvation concerning those who do penance: whoever reads them and puts them into practice will find life and attain salvation from the Lord[38].	
In the name of the Lord!	1. In the name of the Father and of the Son and of the Holy Spirit. Amen. To all Christian religious: clergy and laity, men and women, and to all who live in the whole world, Brother Francis, their servant and subject, offers homage and reverence, true peace from heaven and sincere love in the Lord.
	2. Since I am the servant of all, I am obliged to serve all and to administer to them the fragrant words of my Lord[39].
	3. Therefore, on reflecting that, since I cannot visit each one of you in person because of the infirmity and weakness of my body, I have proposed to set before you in this present letter and message the words of our Lord Jesus Christ, Who is the Word of the Father, and the words of the Holy Spirit, which *are spirit and life*.

---

[38] This title does not appear in the English translation given by Armstrong since he depends upon the critical Latin edition of Esser who considered the title to be a later addition to the *Admonitions*. However, given Pazzelli's convincing demonstration that this phrase was indeed the title of the Volterra text, it has been included here and throughout this study as the actual title of the text. Cf. *Chapter I* for a complete discussion of these arguments and Pazzelli's "discovery", above, pp. 86-88.

[39] A special bond is here indicated between Francis and the recipients of the text. Cf. Armstrong, *Francis and Clare*, 67, note 4.

Earlier Exhortation

Later Exhortation

4. Through his angel, Saint Gabriel, the most high Father in heaven announced this Word of the Father - so worthy, so holy and glorious - in the womb of the holy and glorious Virgin Mary, from which He received the flesh of humanity and our frailty[40].

5. Though *He was rich* beyond all other things, in this world He, together with the most blessed Virgin, His mother, willed to choose poverty[41].

6. And, as the Passion drew near, He celebrated the Passover with His disciples and, taking bread, gave thanks, and blessed and broke it, saying: *Take and eat: this is My Body.*

7. *And taking the cup* He said: *This is My Blood of the new covenant which will be shed for you and for many for the forgiveness of sins.*

8. Then He prayed to His Father, saying: *Father, if it is possible, let this cup pass from me.*

9. *And His sweat became as drops of blood falling on the ground.*

---

[40] Here Francis adopts an "energetic posture against the Cathars and the Albigensians". Cf. Rodríguez Herrera, *Los Escritos*, 237-39; and Armstrong, *Francis and Clare*, 67, note 5.

[41] Rodríguez suggests that the correct punctuation of the Latin should read "*cum dives esset, super omnia voluit,*" that is, not that he "was rich beyond all things", but rather, that "though he was rich in the world... he *willed above all* to choose poverty" (emphasis added). Cf. Rodríguez Herrera, *Los Escritos*, 239.

Earlier Exhortation	Later Exhortation
	10. Nonetheless, He placed His will at the will of the Father, saying: *Father, let Your will be done; not as I will, but as you will.*
	11. And the will of the Father was such that His blessed and glorious Son, Whom He gave to us and Who was born for us, should, through His own blood, offer Himself as a sacrifice and oblation on the altar of the cross:
	12. not for Himself through Whom all things were made, but for our sins,
	13. leaving us an example that we should follow in His footprints[42].
	14. And the Father wills that all of us should be saved through Him and that we receive Him with our pure heart and chaste body.
	15. But there are few who wish to receive Him and be saved by Him, although His *yoke is sweet* and His *burden light.*
	16. Those who do not wish to taste how *sweet the Lord is* and love *the darkness rather than the light*, not wishing to fulfill the commands of God, are cursed;

[42] In his analysis, Esser notes that in "this text [verses 4-13], directed against the Docetistic falsifications of the Cathari, the central mysteries of Christian belief are presented in graphically concrete expressions, leading to the conclusion that Christians are called to follow the footsteps of Christ, a basic concern of St. Francis". Cf. Esser, *A Forerunner of the "Epistola ad Fideles"*, 35.

Earlier Exhortation	*Later Exhortation*
	17. of them the prophet says: *They are cursed who stray from your commands.*
1. All those who love the Lord	18. But Oh, how happy and blessed are those who love God and do as the Lord Himself says in the Gospel: *You shall love the Lord your God*
with their whole heart, with their whole soul and mind, with their whole strength and love their neighbors as themselves	*with all your heart and all your mind, and your neighbor as yourself.*
2. and hate their bodies[43] with their vices and sins,	[cf. 37]
	19. Let us love God, therefore, and adore Him with a pure heart and a pure mind because He Who seeks this above all else has said: *The true worshipers will adore the Father in spirit and in truth.*
	20. For all those *who worship Him* are to worship Him *in the spirit* of truth.
	21. And let us praise Him and pray to Him *day and night*, saying: *Our*

[43] The term "body" (here "*corpora*", from *corpus, corporis*) as used in medieval Latin and in Francis' writings does at times designate the physical body in the sense of a "cadaver", however, in medieval Latin "*corpus*" also signifies the whole person. Francis here uses "body" in the Pauline sense of "*sarx*" or "flesh". Thus, when Francis speaks positively of those who "hate their bodies" he means those who hate or turn from their own self-centeredness, from egotistical desires and concerns. Francis is *not* speaking of hate for the "body" understood in a physical sense, that is, as a constitutive element of the human person. Cf. Rodríguez Herrera, *Los Escritos*, 212-14. Faley also calls attention to the expression "those who hate their bodies with their vices and sins" as a strictly medieval expression which connotes the reality of knowing oneself as a sinner and the need for God's mercy. Thus, this disposition of "hating one's body" is the point of departure for conversion or a life of penance. Cf. Faley, *Visione biblico-teologica*, 93.

Earlier Exhortation	*Later Exhortation*
	Father Who art in heaven, since *we should pray always and never lose heart.*
	22. We must also confess all our sins to a priest[44].
3. and receive the Body and Blood of our Lord Jesus Christ,	and receive from him the Body and Blood of our Lord Jesus Christ.
	23. He who does not eat His flesh and does not drink His Blood *cannot enter the Kingdom of God*
	24. Yet let him eat and drink worthily, since he who receives *unworthily eats and drinks judgment to himself, not recognizing* - that is, not discerning - *the Body of the Lord.*
4. and produce worthy fruits of penance:	25. Moreover, let us perform *worthy fruits of penance.*
	26. And let us love our neighbors as ourselves.
	27. And if there is anyone who does not wish to love them as himself, at least let him do no harm to them, but rather do good.
	28. But those who have received the power to judge others should exercise judgment with mercy as they themselves desire to receive mercy from the Lord.
	29. *For judgment will be without mercy* for those *who have not shown mercy.*

[44] This directive can be understood against the heretical position of the Waldensians. Cf. Rodríguez Herrera, *Los Escritos*, 241; and Armstrong, *Francis and Clare*, 68, note 6.

Earlier Exhortation	*Later Exhortation*
	30. Let us then have charity and humility; let us give alms since this washes our souls from the stains of our sins.
	31. For people lose everything they leave behind in this world; but they carry with them the rewards of charity and the alms which they gave, for which they will have a reward and a suitable remuneration from the Lord.
	32. We must also fast and abstain from vices and sins and from any excess of food and drink, and be Catholics[45].
	33. We must also visit churches frequently and venerate and show respect for the clergy, not so much for them personally if they are sinners, but by reason of their office and their administration of the most holy Body and Blood of Christ which they sacrifice upon the altar and receive and administer to others.
	34. And let all of us firmly realize that no one can be saved except through the holy words and Blood of our Lord Jesus Christ which the clergy pronounce, proclaim and minister[46].

[45] Here again (as in the following sentences), Francis directs his words against abuses found in the Cathars and Waldensians. Fasting and abstaining should not be practiced because of a dualistic concept of the world which sees the body and material things as evil. The penitents are to fast according to the directives of the Church. Cf. Rodríguez Herrera, *Los Escritos*, 242; and Armstrong, *Francis and Clare*, 69, note 7.

[46] With these three verbs, "*dicunt, annuntiant et ministrant*", Francis emphasizes that only ordained ministers can consecrate the Eucharist, preach the Word, and administer the sacraments. Cf. Rodríguez Herrera, *Los Escritos*, 242.

Earlier Exhortation	*Later Exhortation*
	35. And they alone must administer them, and not others[47].
	36. But religious especially, who have left the world, are bound to do more and greater things without however leaving these undone.
	37. We must hate our bodies with their vices and sins, because the Lord says in the Gospel: All evils, vices, and sins proceed from the heart.
	38. We must love our enemies and do good to those who hate us.
	39. We must observe the commands and counsels of our Lord Jesus Christ.
	40. We must also deny ourselves and place our bodies[48] under the yoke of service and holy obedience, as each one has promised to the Lord.
	41. And no one[49] is to be obliged to obey another in anything by which a sin or a crime is committed.
	42. The one to whom obedience has been entrusted and *who* is esteemed

[47] This sentence clearly addresses the heretical position of the Waldensians who claimed that the power to consecrate the Eucharist and to administer the sacraments was based not upon ordination but rather upon the worthiness of the person. Cf. Rodríguez Herrera, *Los Escritos*, 242; and Armstrong, *Francis and Clare*, 69, note 8.

[48] Body here signifies the whole person. We must place ourselves under the yoke of service and holy obedience, that is, we must overcome self-centeredness. Cf. Rodríguez Herrera, *Los Escritos*, 243.

[49] The "*nullus homo*" used here is stronger than "*nemo*" found in sentence 34. Cf. Rodríguez Herrera, *Los Escritos*, 243.

Earlier Exhortation | *Later Exhortation*

as *greater* should be as *the lesser* and the servant of the other brothers[50].

43. And he should use and show mercy to each of his brothers as he would wish them to do to him were he in a similar position.

44. Nor should he become angry with a brother because of a fault of that brother, but with all patience and humility let him admonish him and support him.

45. We must not be wise and prudent according to the flesh; rather, we must be simple, humble, and pure.

46. And let us hold ourselves in contempt and scorn, since through our own fault all of us are miserable and contemptible, vermin and worms, as the Lord says through the prophet: *I am a worm and no man, the scorn of men and the outcast of the people.*

47. We must never desire to be over others; rather we must be servants and subject *to every human creature for God's sake.*

[50] While the Volterra text speaks only of a profession (cf. *Earlier Exhortation* II,4), this later text evidences developments in the organizational structure of the penitential communities. This expansion of the Volterra text's simple mention of the person's obedience to what they have professed presupposes communities which are structured with a vow of obedience and which need, therefore, to guard against the abuse of obedience and of office. Cf. Esser, *Un documento dell'inizio*, 91.

[51] Here "*corpora nostra*" (literally, "And let us hold *our bodies*") signifies the personal "I", the egotistical self. Cf. Rodríguez Herrera, *Los Escritos*, 243.

Earlier Exhortation	*Later Exhortation*
5. Oh, how happy and blessed[52] are	[cf. 18]
these men and women[53] when they do these things and persevere in doing them,	48. And upon all men and women, if they have done these things and have persevered to the end,
6. since *the Spirit of the Lord will rest upon them* and He will make His home and *dwelling among them*.	*the Spirit of the Lord will rest* and He will make His home and *dwelling among them*.
7. They are children of the heavenly Father whose works they do,	49. They will be children of the heavenly Father whose works they do.
and they are spouses, brothers, and mothers of our Lord Jesus Christ.	50. And they are spouses, brothers, and mothers of our Lord Jesus Christ.
8. We are spouses when the faithful soul is joined to our Lord Jesus Christ by the Holy Spirit.	51. We are spouses when the faithful soul is joined to Jesus Christ by the Holy Spirit.
9. We are brothers to Him when we *do the will of* *the Father Who is in heaven*.	52. We are brothers when we do *the will* of His *Father Who* is in heaven.
10. We are mothers when we carry Him in our heart and body through divine love and a pure and sincere conscience and when we give birth to Him	53. We are mothers when we carry Him in our heart and body through love and a pure and sincere conscience; we give birth to Him

[52] Francis uses the term *beatus* (here "*beati*") within an eschatological perspective, analogous to the use of "blessed" in the Beatitudes of the Gospel. Cf. Rodríguez Herrera, *Los Escritos*, 214.

[53] Both here and in sentence 48 of the later redaction, explicit mention of both men and women is made: "*illi et illae*".

Earlier Exhortation	*Later Exhortation*
[by our holy manner of living[54]], which should shine before others as an example.	[by our holy manner of living[55]], which should shine before others as an example.
11. Oh, how glorious it is, how holy and great, to have a Father in heaven![56]	54. Oh, how glorious it is, how holy and great, to have a Father in heaven!
12. Oh, how holy, consoling, beautiful and wondrous it is to have such a Spouse!	55. Oh, how holy, consoling, beautiful, and wondrous it is to have a Spouse!

---

[54] The author here disagrees with Armstrong's English translation which reads: "we give birth to Him through *His holy manner of working*" (emphasis added). Given the context of the Latin phrase "*parturimus eum per sanctam operationem*", the sense indicates that we give birth to Him by *our holy manner of living.* This reading of the text would appear to be supported by both the Italian and Spanish critical editions. The Italian reads: "*lo diamo alla luce per mezzo delle azioni sante*". Translated by A. Bizzotto and S. Cattazzo in K. Esser, *Gli Scritti di S. Francesco d'Assisi: nuova edizione critica e versione italiana*, Padova 1982, 217. The critical Spanish edition reads: "*lo diamos a luz por la santa operación*". Cf. Rodríguez Herrera, *Los Escritos*, 209.

[55] See prior note.

[56] Rodríguez Herrera points out the ambiguous grammatical construction of this sentence in Latin: *O quam gloriosum est, sanctum et magnum in caelis habere patrem*! The phrase could be as given above if *sanctum* and *magnum* are taken to be neuter and not masculine. However, if *sanctum* and *magnum* are masculine accusatives agreeing with Father, the phrase would be read: "Oh, how glorious it is to have a holy and great Father in heaven"!

Given that sentences 11, 12, and 13 have parallel constructions, and given that the adjectives in numbers 12 and 13 cannot all be either neuter or masculine accusative (for example, *admirabilem* and *humilem* can only be masculine accusatives), Rodríguez Herrera proposes this alternative reading: 11. Oh how glorious it is to have a holy and great Father in heaven! 12. Oh, how holy to have such a consoling, beautiful and wondrous Spouse! 13. Oh, how holy and how loving to have such a pleasing, humble, peaceful, sweet, lovable, and above all things desirable, Brother and such a Son: our Lord Jesus Christ"! Cf. Rodríguez Herrera, *Los Escritos*, 209, 214-15.

Earlier Exhortation	*Later Exhortation*
13. Oh, how holy and how loving, pleasing, humble, peaceful, sweet, lovable, and desirable above all things to have such a Brother and such a Son: our Lord Jesus Christ, Who gave up His life for His sheep and who prayed to the Father saying:	56. Oh how holy and how loving, pleasing, humble, peaceful, sweet, lovable, and desirable above all things to have such a Brother and Son, Who laid down His life for His sheep and Who prayed to the Father for us saying:
14. *O Holy Father, protect those in your name whom you have given to me in the world;*	*Holy Father, protect those in your name whom you have given to me.*
	57. Father, all *those whom you gave me in the world were yours and you have given them to me.*
they were yours and you have given them to me.	
15. And *the words which you gave to me, I have given to them, and they have accepted them and* have believed *truly that I have come from you and* they have known *that you sent me.*	58. And *the words which you gave to me I have given to them; and they have accepted them and truly know that I came from you and they have believed that you have sent me.*
16. I pray for them and *not for the world.*	59. I pray for them and *not for the world;*
17. Bless and *sanctify them and I sanctify myself for them.*	bless and *sanctify them, and I sanctify myself for their sakes.*
18. *Not only for these do I pray, but for those who through their words will believe in me*[57],	
so that they may be made holy *in being one as we are one.*	so that they may be holy in being one as we are.

[57] Given that the later version so closely parallels the *Earlier Exhortation* in this section, the omission of this phrase in the *Later Exhortation* would appear significant. While we cannot know definitively the reason for the omission of this sentence in the later redaction, Esser suggests a very plausible explanation based upon the historical situation. There were many questions and conflicts concerning the role of the lay preachers within the penitential movement, many had claimed the right to preach. Esser suggests that this verse was omitted to avoid its possible misinterpretation as a support of non-authorized lay preaching. This explanation for the deliberate omission of the phrase accords with

Earlier Exhortation	*Later Exhortation*
19. *And I wish, Father, that where I am they also may be with me so that they may see my glory in your kingdom.* Amen.	60. And I wish, Father, *that where* I am *they also may be with me so that they may see my glory in your kingdom.*
	61. Let *every creature in heaven, on earth, in the sea* and in the depths, give praise, *glory, honor, and blessing* to Him Who suffered so much for us, Who has given so many good things and Who will continue to do so for the future.
	62. For He is our power and strength, He Who *alone is good,* Who is most high, Who is all-powerful, admirable, and glorious; Who alone is holy, praiseworthy, and blessed throughout endless ages. Amen.
Concerning those who do not do penance[58]	
1. All those men and women who are not living in penance	63. All those, however, who are not living in penance
2. and do not receive the Body and Blood of our Lord Jesus Christ;	and do not receive the Body and Blood of our Lord Jesus Christ;

the view (implicit here and consistent throughout this later redaction) that the proclamation of the Word of God belongs only to clerics. Verses 34-35 state this position very explicitly: "And let all of us firmly realize that no one can be saved except through the holy words and Blood of our Lord Jesus Christ which the clergy pronounce, proclaim and minister. And they alone must administer them, and not others". Cf. Esser, *A Forerunner of the "Epistola ad Fideles"*, 27.

[58] The titles which appear in the Volterra document (this title, as well as the title at the beginning of the text) do not appear in any of the manuscripts containing the later redaction. Cf. Esser, *A Forerunner of the "Epistola ad Fideles"*, 28.

Earlier Exhortation	*Later Exhortation*
3. who practice vice and sin and follow the ways of *wicked concupiscence* and *the desires of the flesh*;	64. who practice vice and sin and walk the paths of *wicked concupiscence* and evil desires;
4. who do not observe what they have promised to the Lord,	65. who do not observe what they have promised
5. and bodily[59] serve the world by *the desires of the flesh*, the anxieties of the world and the cares of this life:	and bodily serve the world by the *desires of the flesh*, the cares and anxieties of this world, and the preoccupations of this life:
6. such people are held fast by the devil, whose children they are and whose works they perform.	66. such people are deceived[60] by the devil, whose children they are and whose works they perform.
7. They are blind, since they do not see the true light, our Lord Jesus Christ.	They are blind because they do not see the true light, our Lord Jesus Christ.
8. They do not have spiritual wisdom, since they do not possess the Son of God, Who is the true wisdom of the Father.	67. They do not shave spiritual wisdom because they do not have within them the Son of God Who is the true wisdom of the Father.

---

[59] The term "bodily" (*corporaliter*) should not be understood in the narrow sense of "physically". Rather, it signifies in a fuller sense: "completely or actually with body and soul" serve the world. Cf. Rodríguez Herrera, *Los Escritos*, 215.

[60] The word "*detenti*" has been changed to "*decepti*". In suggesting a probable cause for the change, Esser notes that "detenti is certainly to be understood here from the Italian detenere (= tenere in prigione, dominare, etc.), it follows the sense of the general concept of being possessed. However such a meaning might have seemed too severe in this context and was perhaps theologically unsatisfactory; hence its force was weakened to the more acceptable decepti". Cf. Esser, *A Forerunner of the "Epistola ad Fideles"*, 29.

Earlier Exhortation	*Later Exhortation*
9. It is said of these people: *Their wisdom has been swallowed up*[61], and: *Cursed are those who turn away from Your commands.*	Of these people it is said: *Their wisdom has been swallowed up.*
10. They see and acknowledge, they know and do evil deeds, and, knowingly, they lose their souls.	68. They see and acknowledge, they know and do evil, and, knowingly, they lose their souls.
11. See, you blind ones, you who are deceived by our enemies: by the flesh[62], the world, and the devil; because it is sweet to the body to commit sin and it is bitter for it to serve God;	69. See, you blind ones, you who are deceived by our enemies, the flesh, the world, and the devil. For it is sweet to the body to commit sin and bitter to it to serve God,
12. and because all vices and sins come forth and *proceed from the heart of man*, as the Lord says in the Gospel.	because *all evils*, vices, and sins come from and *proceed from the heart of men*, as the Lord says in the Gospel.
13. And you have nothing in this world or in the world to come.	70. And you have nothing in this world or in the world to come.
14. And you think you possess the vanities of this world for a while, but you are deceived, since the day and the hour will come to which you give no thought, of which you have no knowledge, and of which you are ignorant.	71. You think that you possess the vanities of the world for a while, but you are deceived, since the day and the hour will come to which you give no thought, of which you have no knowledge and of which you are ignorant.

[61] This biblical quotation offers an example of the use of different psalters in the earlier and later redactions, another indication of the priority of the Volterra text. As Esser points out, the "citation of Ps. 106:27 is quoted from the Psalterium Romanum in *Vo*: «deglutita est», while in all the others «devorata est», from the Psalterium Gallicanum, is used... Precisely here, therefore, it is evident that in *Vo* the older form of the text has been preserved". Cf. Esser, *A Forerunner of the "Epistola ad Fideles"*, 29-30.

[62] Rodríguez Herrera calls attention to Francis' ordering of the three enemies of the soul. Significantly, in both versions Francis first mentions the "flesh". Cf. Rodríguez Herrera, *Los Escritos*, 215.

Earlier Exhortation	*Later Exhortation*
The body becomes sick, death approaches,	72. The body grows weak, death approaches, family and friends come, saying: "Put your affairs in order".
	73. See, his wife and his children, relatives and friends pretend to cry.
	74. Looking at them, he sees them weeping and is moved by an evil impulse. As he thinks to himself, he says: "Look, I put my soul and body, as well as everything I have, into your hands".
	75. Certainly, that man is cursed who confides and entrusts his soul and body and all his possessions into such hands;
	76. for, as the Lord says through the prophet, *Cursed is the man who confides in man.*
	77. And immediately they summon the priest to come. The priest says to him: "Do you wish to receive pardon for all you sins?"
	78. He responds: "I do". "Do you wish to make restitution as far as you can from your substance for all that you have done and for ways in which you have defrauded and deceived people?"
	79. He responds: "No".
	80. And the priest asks: "Why not?" "Because I have placed everything in the hands of relatives and friends".

<table>
<tr><th>Earlier Exhortation</th><th>Later Exhortation</th></tr>
<tr><td>and this man
dies a bitter death.</td><td>81. And he begins to lose the power of speech and thus that miserable man dies.</td></tr>
<tr><td>15. And no matter where or when or how a man dies in guilt of sin
without doing penance and satisfaction,
if he is able to perform some act of satisfaction and does not,
the devil snatches up his soul from his body[63] with so much
anguish and tribulation that no one can know it unless he has experienced it.</td><td>82. But let everyone know that whenever or however a person dies in mortal sin
without making amends
when he could have done so
and did not,
the devil snatches up his soul out of his body with so much
anguish and tribulation that no one can know it unless he has experienced it.</td></tr>
<tr><td>16. And every talent and power and knowledge and wisdom which they think they possess will be taken away from them.</td><td>83. And every talent and power and knowledge[64] which he thinks he possesses will be taken away from him.</td></tr>
<tr><td>17. And they leave their substance to their relatives and friends, and these have taken and divided the inheritance among themselves and afterwards they have said: "May his soul be cursed since he could have acquired more and given more to us than he did"!</td><td>84. And whatever he leaves his
relatives and friends
they will snatch up and divide
among themselves. And afterwards they will say: "May his soul be cursed since he could have acquired more and given us more than he did".</td></tr>
</table>

---

[63] While Francis does not generally distinguish clearly between *suus* and *eius*, in this case he does. The phrase, "*rapit animam suam de corpore eius*", denotes that the devil snatches or takes what is his own. The soul submerged in sin, by definition, belongs to the devil. Thus, the soul, which because of sin already belongs to the devil, is taken by the devil from the body of the sinner. Cf. Rodríguez Herrera, *Los Escritos*, 216.

[64] Rodríguez Herrera suggests that, given the symbolism of the number three, "*talenta et potestas et scientia*" signifies the total loss of all things. Cf. Rodríguez Herrera, *Los Escritos*, 250.

Earlier Exhortation	*Later Exhortation*
18. Worms eat the body. And so they have lost body and soul in this passing world, and both will do down to hell where they will be tormented without end.	85. Worms eat his body. And so he loses body and soul in this brief life, and will go down to hell where he will be tormented without end.
	86. In the name of the Father and of the Son and of the Holy Spirit. Amen.
19. In the love which is God, we beg all those whom these letters reach to accept with kindness and a divine love the fragrant words of our Lord Jesus Christ which are written above.	87. I, Brother Francis, your little servant, ask and implore you in the love which is God and with the desire to kiss your feet, to receive these words and others of our Lord Jesus Christ with humility and love, and observe them and put them into practice[65].
20. And those who do not know how to read should have them read to them frequently.	[some manuscripts contain an alternate ending which parallels this phrase][66].

---

[65] According to Rodríguez Herrera, the Latin construction places emphasis upon the verb "*observare*" which has the sense both of persevering in and being attentive to the words or the "way". Cf. Rodríguez Herrera, *Los Escritos*, 251.

[66] The alternate ending, given in some of the manuscripts, reads: "In that love which is God, I, Brother Francis, the least of your servants and worthy only to kiss your feet, beg and implore all those to whom this letter comes to hear these words of our Lord Jesus Christ in a spirit of humility and love, putting them into practice with all gentleness and observing them perfectly. Those who cannot read should have them read to them often and keep them ever before their eyes, by persevering in doing good to the last, because they are *spirit and life*. Those who fail to do this shall be held to account for it before the judgment-seat of Christ at the last day. And may God, Father,

Earlier Exhortation	*Later Exhortation*
21. And, since *they are spirit and life*[67], they should preserve them together with their holy manner of working[68] even to the end.	88. And to all men and women who will receive them kindly and understand their meaning and pass them on to others by their example: *If they have persevered in them to the end*, may the Father and the Son and the Holy Spirit bless them. Amen.
22. And whoever shall not have done these things *will be held accountable* on the day of judgment *before the tribunal* of our Lord Jesus *Christ*.	

Esser's analysis demonstrates that the *Earlier Exhortation* contains the main points of the gospel life and provides testimony that Francis and his companions looked after some of the people in the penitential movement. In fact, Esser claims that what Francis and his brothers offer in the *Earlier Exhortation* "effectively constitutes the *marrow of the Gospel*, the heart of a *life according to the form of the holy Gospel*"[69].

Son, and Holy Spirit, bless those who welcome them and grasp them and send copies to others, if they persevere in them to the last". Cf. *Omnibus*, 98-99. Although Esser does not present this alternate ending for the *Epistola ad Fideles II* in his criticial edition of the works of Francis, he does offer a comparison of the Latin in this alternate ending and in the ending of the *Recensio Prior*. Cf. Esser, *A Forerunner of the "Epistola ad Fideles"*, 20-21.

[67] Pazzelli believes that is was this expression, "to conserve these words... because they are spirit and life", that led the copyist of the Volterra manuscript, or the document from which it was copied, to entitle the work "These are the words ...". Cf. Pazzelli, *St. Francis and the Third Order*, 196, note 12.

[68] According to Rodríguez Herrera, "*cum sancta operatione*" indicates instrumental cause. Francis wanted them to preserve the words of this text by their good works, that is, to preserve united the text and good works. Cf. Rodríguez Herrera, *Los Escritos*, 217-18.

[69] Esser, *Un documento dell'inizio*, 97.

But, as Leonhard Lehmann points out, Esser bases his interpretation on the history of the Franciscan movement and thus risks the danger of reading certain elements into the text[70]. To avoid this risk, Lehmann performs a literary-structural analysis of the text[71]. His thorough analysis of the speech, the literary construction, and the forms contained within the text offers further insights into this primitive Rule. We turn, therefore, to a consideration of Lehmann's work.

A Literary-Structural Analysis of the Primitive Rule

Esser divided the primitive Rule into two chapters since the text in the Volterra manuscript contains an obvious division into two distinct parts: Concerning those who do penance, and Concerning those who do not do penance[72]. But Lehmann's literary analysis of that same text revealed that it actually contains three distinct parts. Sentence 19 of Chapter II begins a new theme, changing from the third person singular to the first person plural. In fact, only here in the last four sentences can the whole text be recognized as a letter because of the "*istae letterae*":

> In the love which is God, we beg all those whom these letters reach to accept with kindness and a divine love the fragrant words of our Lord Jesus Christ which are written above[73].

Since the last four sentences refer to the text as a whole, requesting that the words be read and obeyed, Lehmann suggests that this last section should be understood as an epilogue, that is, as separate from the rest of Chapter II. Thus, he divides the text into three parts[74]:

Part 1: Concerning those who do penance (I, 1-19)
Part 2: Concerning those who do not do penance (II, 1-18)
Part 3: Epilogue (II, 19-22)

---

[70] Lehmann, *Exsultatio et exhortatio de poenitentia*, 568.
[71] *Ibid.*, 564-608.
[72] Esser, *Un documento dell'inizio*, 91.
[73] *Earlier Exhortation*, II: 19.
[74] Lehmann, *Exsultatio et exhortatio de poenitentia*, 570.

Lehmann then subdivides Part 1 into sections with the same sense[75]:

Part 1a) 1-7: Blessed are the ones who do penance
(written in the third person)

1-4: These verses offer a description and enumeration of the way of penance. The subject (*omnes*) is divided over five relative parts which describe the "doing of penance": love of God, love of neighbor, overcoming self-centeredness, receiving Eucharist, and producing the "fruits of penance".

5-7: These verses, in the form of an exclamation, speak of the Beatitude or Blessing of penance, that is, the blessing on those who perform the penance described in the prior verses. The effects of performing penance are so wonderful (the person who does penance is intimately related to God) that they can only be expressed with exclamation. Thus, the descriptive style changes to an exclamation of joy.

Part 1b) 8-13: Exultation of our relationship with God
(written in the first person plural)

8-10: These verses offer an explanation of how we are related to God. The construction of the three sentences is parallel: each sentence begins with the relation ("spouses", "brothers", and "mothers"), followed by the explanation (*quando*).

11-13: Here the text changes from a description of the conditions for this relationship (*quando*) and moves into exclamation about the triune God (*O quam*).

Part 1c) 14-19: Prayer to the Father
(first person address to God)

14-19: These sentences evidence a dramatic change from the prior sentences. Francis here begins a prayer addressed to the Father, a prayer which ends with Amen.

[75] *Ibid.*, 570-73.

Part I of the *Earlier Exhortation* moves from a brief description of penance, to the blessing of penance, to an exclamation of joy over this intimate relationship with God, and finally, to a prayer addressed to God. Francis' increasing joy or ecstasy, which results from a mystical experience of Christ, culminates in his use of Jesus' high-priestly prayer. Here, at the point of prayerful union where human words fail, the words of Christ become the prayer of Francis[76]. Thus, given that this section (sentences 1-19) begins with "*In nomine Domini*" and ends with "*Amen*", and given that it is a prayer of praise with exclamations of joy, Lehmann characterizes this section as an "*exultatio*" of penance[77].

Lehmann then goes on to subdivide Part 2 into sections with the same sense[78]:

Part 2a) 1-10: The Lost or Blind are those who do not do penance (written in the third person plural)

1-5: These verses present the contrast. This section parallels the structure of the beginning of the first chapter. Here *omnes* is followed by six verbs connected by "*et*" which describe more carefully those who do *not* do penance.

6-10: These verses explain the reason these people are blind. Here again the structure parallels that of the the first chapter. The "Beatitude" of the first chapter changes to a lamentation for those "held fast by the devil". The two different groups are described with the same verbs but in opposite ways.

Part 2b) 11-18: Admonition to convert

11-14: These verses present a call to the people described in the previous section (with the use of the second person plural). The call ends with the somber droning: "the body becomes sick, death approaches, and this man dies a bitter death".

15-18: These final verses present a generalized warning (as seen in the words *ubicumque, quandocumque, qualitercumque*) in which can be found the meaning of the whole section.

---

[76] *Ibid.*, 573.
[77] *Ibid.*, 573-75.
[78] *Ibid.*, 575-77.

While the first part moves to joy and then praise, the second part builds from a reproach to a warning of damnation. In the first half the imperatives are directed to God, in the second half to the readers. The first part, being formulated in a positive sense, concludes in the prayerful union of the speaker with Jesus. The second part ends with the dreadful image of a bitter death: the body being eaten by worms and the person condemned to eternal torment. Given the parallel structure of the two sections of the Volterra text, with the second presenting the negative or opposite of the first, Lehmann suggests that second part is best characterized as a contrast to the first. Francis describes what will happen to the person who does not do penance in order to forewarn the reader or hearer[79]. Thus, Lehmann characterizes Part II as an "exhortation" (the title suggested by Esser for the entire text), but cautions that the word fails to capture the full force of the text. He emphasizes that the designation "exhortation" must be understood as a "lamentation" and "awakening call" for those who do not do penance[80].

The last four sentences, while not further subdivided, do constitute a distinct part of the text[81]:

Part 3: The Epilogue (written in the first person plural)

19-22: These sentences present the request that the "text" be received, preserved, and lived.

Lehmann thus offers this overview of the text[82]:

Chapter I *EXULTATION OF THE WAY OF PENANCE*	*Chapter II* *REMINDER TO THOSE ON THE WAY OF SIN*
1-7 : *Blessed are those who do penance*	1-10 : *The blind or those who do not do penance*
1-4 : The Way of Penance	1-5 : The Way without Penance

---

[79] *Ibid.*, 576.
[80] *Ibid.*, 579.
[81] *Ibid.*, 579-80.
[82] *Ibid.*, 580.

5-7 : The Blessing of Penance	6-10 : The Tragic Consequences
8-13 : Exultation over our relationship with God	*11-18 : Exhortation to Convert*
8-10 : Explanation	11-14 : Call in Direct Address
11-13 : Astonished Exclamation	15-18 : Generalization
14-19 : Prayer to the Father	
19 : The Glory in the Kingdom of God	18 : The Pain in Hell
	19-22 : EPILOGUE

After having divided the text into three rather distinct parts, Lehmann searches for that which gives the text unity. Based upon parallel constructions, common semantic characteristics, and the most important sense lines, Lehmann concludes, not surprisingly, that the sections are connected by the subject of penance[83]. But this literary analysis of the text shows that the three parts, more than just being connected by the subject of penance, are held together by "*facere*" and other similar verbs. That is, the entire text seeks to bring people to action. The recipients are exhorted not just to "accept" and to "preserve" the words, but to "do" them, to realize these "words" in their lives[84].

Having completed his analysis, Lehmann ventures to title the text from a literary perspective. While "penance" connects the parts, the literary forms of the various sections of the text differ greatly. The first part takes the form of a meditation or praise of penance. The second part, which is threatening and serious, takes the form of a lamentation or exhortation for those who do not do penance. Given these two very different moods, it is difficult to give to the text one title which expresses the whole. Lehmann therefore suggests as an appropriate title: "exultation and exhortation concerning penance". Lehmann maintains that when Esser gave the title "exhortation to the brothers and sisters of penance" he did not sufficiently acknowledge the praise character of the first chapter. Further, Lehmann claims that Esser's designation

[83] *Ibid.*, 581-92.
[84] *Ibid.*, 582.

"brothers and sisters of penance", while possibly suggested by an historical analysis, is not warranted by a literary analysis of the text; it unnecessarily restricts the group of recipients[85]. However, given Pazzelli's more recent work which indicates that this text represents the primitive Rule of the "brothers and sisters of penance", Esser's restriction remains applicable.

Although Lehmann based the title "exultation and exhortation concerning penance" solely upon internal textual criteria, he points out that an analysis based upon external criteria, that is, comparison of this text with other writings of Francis, yields the same result[86]. Both chapters XXI and XXII of the *Regula non bullata* (the 1221 Rule of the Friars Minor) present obvious parallels and are closely related to the Volterra text. Chapter XXI, "The Praise and Exhortation Which All the Brothers Can Offer", reads:

1. And whenever it may please them,
   all my brothers can proclaim this or a like exhortation and praise
   among all the people with the blessing of God:
2. Fear and honor, praise and bless, give thanks and adore
   the Lord God Almighty in Trinity and in Unity,
   the Father and the Son and the Holy Spirit
   the Creator of all.
3. Do penance, performing worthy fruits of penance
   since we will soon die.
4. *Give and it shall be given to you.*
5. *Forgive* and you shall be forgiven.
6. And if you do not forgive men their sins,
   the Lord *will not forgive you your sins.*
   Confess all your sins.
7. Blessed are those who die in penance,
   for they shall be in the kingdom of heaven.
8. Woe to those who do not die in penance,
   for they shall be the children of the devil
   whose works they do,
   and they shall go into the eternal fire.
9. Beware and abstain from every evil
   and persevere in good till the end[87]

[85] *Ibid.*, 598.
[86] *Ibid.*, 598-603.
[87] Armstrong, *Francis and Clare*, 126.

The primitive Rule is very similar to the sermon presented in chapter XXI of the *Regula non bullata*. While this "praise and exhortation" treats several themes and the Volterra text treats only the theme of penance, both proclaim the blessedness of those who do penance. This model sermon reflects the same scheme found in the Volterra text, even in the same order: first comes "praise", then "exhortation". The texts differ in that the *Regula non bullata* does not move from praise to exultation, while the Volterra text moves to the mystical prayer of Jesus. But this distinction further confirms for Lehmann that the title of the Volterra text should read: "*exultation* and exhortation to penance"[88].

Lehmann had based his literary analysis upon the critical text given by Esser which began "In the name of the Lord". Since the results of Pazzelli's study concerning the title of the Volterra text were published immediately prior to the publication of his own article, Lehmann compared the results of Pazzelli's research with the results of his own study in an epilogue appended to his article. Pazzelli's examination of the original Volterra manuscript revealed the original title of the text to be "These are the words of life and salvation concerning those who do penance: whoever reads them and puts them into practice will find life and attain salvation from the Lord". According to Lehmann, this title confirms and advances his own conclusions: it confirms his rejection of the title proposed by Esser and more definitively identifies the Volterra text as the primitive Rule, that is, Francis' message for the penitents[89].

Thus, Lehmann's literary analysis corroborates Pazzelli's claims as well as the conclusions of Esser's historical-critical analysis: the Volterra text presents its hearers or readers with an exultation of and exhortation to a life of penance. Let us then examine more fully the content of that Way of Life presented in the *Earlier Exhortation*.

The Way of Penance in the Primitive Rule

The Way of Penance expressed in the *Earlier Exhortation* must be understood from the perspective of Francis' understanding of penance.

---

[88] Lehmann, *Exsultatio et exhortatio de poenitentia*, 600; emphasis added to reflect Lehmann's insistence that "exhortation" alone is insufficient to describe the text.

[89] *Ibid.*, 607.

Therefore, let us again consider Francis' own account of his conversion to a life of penance:

1. The Lord granted me, Brother Francis, to begin to do penance in this way: While I was in sin, it seemed very bitter to me to see lepers.
2. And the Lord Himself led me among them and I had mercy upon them.
3. And when I left them that which seemed bitter to me was changed into sweetness of soul and body; and afterward I lingered a little and left the world[90].

In these brief words Francis expresses his understanding of penance:

1. The life of penance is a gift from God;
2. God helps the person to accept the way of conversion; and
3. the way of penance entails a total change and a new way of perceiving reality.

In the primitive Rule Francis exhorts his followers to a life of penance. Again with brief words, but with a focused clarity, Francis presents what it means "to do penance" in the opening verses of the *Earlier Exhortation*:

1. to love God (1a);
2. to love our neighbor (1b);
3. to resist the sinful tendencies of our fallen nature (2);
4. to partake of the Body of Christ (3);
5. to act or to live in conformity with our conversion (4).

This conversion or life of penance expresses itself externally: blessed are those who "produce worthy fruits of penance". But Francis clearly places the action of God and the interior attitude or change within the person before the visible manifestation of penance. This recognition, at the heart of Francis' understanding of penance, remains crucial for any articulation of a Franciscan penitential spirituality. Francis does not suggest simply the adoption of norms and practices of penance; he does not suggest that one begin with the "fruits of penance". Rather, for Francis a life of penance begins with God's action.

---

90 *Testament* 1-3. Cf. Armstrong, *Francis and Clare*, 154.

The beginning of both the *Testament* and the *Earlier Exhortation* reveal the central dynamic of conversion or *metanoia*: the radical turning from self to God[91]. For Francis, penance is the only possible response to a loving God. The way of penance is a means to freedom, the way to mystical union with God. For Francis, the way of penance is the radical choosing of God's love, the constant seeking after God, a "thirsting after fullness of mystical experience"[92].

The "exultation and exhortation concerning penance" which the *Earlier Exhortation* presents must be understood first as a call to an intimacy with God. For Francis, penance begins with a mystical experience, that is, an experience of God that radically changes the person. And Francis found this intimacy with God in and through Christ. For Francis, Christ remains the focus of the penitential life; identification with Christ *is* the way of penance.

> Francis passes from the word of God to the Word of God par excellence, that is, the Word Incarnate. The principal mysteries of Christ are the continual object of attention, meditation and fascination.
>
> The Poverello feels the person of the Son of God made man vibrating in the Gospels; he perceives the message and senses the living and personal presence there. It is as if he saw Him, as if he listened to His voice and had direct experience of Him. Thinking of Christ, he meditated and imitated, was moved to tears and prayed, abandoning himself in ecstasy.
>
> The life of penance finds in Christ the way that leads to God, invisible and inaccessible[93].

An analysis of the primitive Rule can easily focus upon "doing penance", the works of penance. However, the key to this "*exultation* and exhortation to penance" is the experience of God given in and through Christ. In the *Earlier Exhortation* Francis calls people to that intimacy with God. Clearly, this intimacy begins with God's initiative, but this intimacy with God also demands the person's response. Francis experienced a deepening of that intimacy with God in and through a life of penance and thus exhorts others to that path.

---

[91] R. Faley, *Visione biblico-teologica della penitenza e sua espressione oggi*, in *Ritorno a Francesco*, Roma 1980, 93-94.

[92] L. Temperini, *Penitential Spirituality in the Franciscan Sources*, in *Anal TOR* XIV/132 (1980) 555.

[93] *Ibid.*, 566-67.

In exhorting people "to do penance", Francis implicitly exhorted people to embrace the penitential practices of the Order of Penance. These practices included the "works of penance", however, we must remember that in the Middle Ages people embraced the penitential life, they began doing penance, as a vehicle through which to experience the divine[94]. The way of penance was the way to God. In a sense, the way of penance was the way of the mystic.

While various scholars call attention to Francis' mystical experience and its expression within the *Earlier Exhortation*, this insight seems lost in their focus upon "penance". Esser claims that the text, which presents Francis' understanding of the "religious life" or the life lived more intensely in God, touches at times the "depths of theology and mystical life"[95]. Yet, he entitles the text simply the "Exhortation to the Brothers and Sisters of Penance". Similarly, Rodríguez Herrera claims that both the *Earlier Exhortation* and the *Later Exhortation*, while presenting ideas common to other writings of Francis (especially the *Admonitions* and the *Regula non bullata*), offer a rare view into the spiritual and mystical life of Francis[96]. Yet, he remains content with the designation "*Letter to All the Faithful*". Lehmann comes closer to acknowledging this call to intimacy with God, or at least Francis' mystical experience and expression, in his insistence that the text be designated "*exultation* and exhortation concerning penance". Lehmann examines the Johannine influence on the *Earlier Exhortation* and concludes that the goal of doing penance is, for Francis, being with the Father together with Jesus: "And I wish, Father, that *where I am they also may be with me so that they may see my glory in your kingdom*" (I:19)[97].

We must not, therefore, lose sight of the key to understanding the way of penance, that is, the basis for performing the works of penance. Francis exhorted people to penance and they embraced the penitential life as a way to deepen their experience of God, as a means to a deeper intimacy with God. This motivation for doing penance becomes more obvious in Francis' use of the Gospel of John in the primitive Rule.

---

[94] Cf. the discussion above, *Chapter II*, pp. 120-123.

[95] Cf. Esser's introduction to the critical edition of the *Recensio prior*: *Opuscula*, 107.

[96] Rodríguez Herrera, *Los Escritos*, 206.

[97] Lehmann, *Exsultatio et exhortatio de poenitentia*, 584.

As Bernard Tickerhoof points out in his study of the spirituality of the Volterra text, there is a definite pattern to Francis' use of the Johannine Gospel[98]. The first chapter of the primitive Rule contains an extensive paraphrase of the priestly prayer of Jesus in *John* 17[99]. The second chapter of the primitive Rule contains references drawn from the eighth and ninth chapters of the Gospel of John[100]. The use of the Johannine material in Chapter I is positive, in Chapter II decidedly negative.

In *John* 17, Jesus addresses a prayer to the God he knows intimately as "Father". He speaks of his mission and prays for his disciples, the true believers, concluding:

> I have made your name known to them
> and will continue to make it known,
> so that the love with which you love me may be in them,
> and so that I may be in them[101].

In the *Earlier Exhortation*, Francis could speak of the "words of our Lord Jesus Christ" as "*spirit and life*" because he had come to know that intimate and loving God in and through Christ[102]. Francis claims that those who do penance as the "spouses, brothers, and mothers of our Lord Jesus Christ"[103]. He explains those relations:

> We are spouses
> when the faithful soul is joined to our Lord Jesus Christ by the Holy Spirit.
> We are brothers to Him
> when we *do the will of the Father Who is in heaven.*
> We are mothers

[98] B. Tickerhoof, *Francis's Volterra Letter: A Gospel Spirituality*, in *The Cord* 29 (June 1979) 164-75. For a more extensive discussion of the use of the Gospel of John in the writings of Francis, cf. O. van Asseldonk, *San Giovanni Evangelista negli Scritti di San Francesco*, in *Laurentianum* 8 (1977) 225-55; and W. Viviani, *L'ermeneutica di Francesco d'Assisi: indagine alla luce di Gv 13-17 nei suoi Scritti*, Roma 1983.

[99] *Earlier Exhortation*, I: 14-19.

[100] *Later Exhortation*, 5-7, 10-11.

[101] *John* 17:26.

[102] *Earlier Exhortation*, I: 19, 21.

[103] *Earlier Exhortation*, I: 7.

> when we carry Him in our heart and body
> through divine love and a pure and sincere conscience
> and when we give birth to Him through our holy manner of living,
> which should shine before others as an example[104].

Thus, for Francis, the true believer has come to know God through the Word which is Christ. And these penitents, as true believers are "mothers" both by bearing Christ within their hearts and by giving birth to Christ by their example. By moving from this description of the penitents' relationship with Christ to the use of Jesus' priestly prayer, Francis demonstrates the true nature of belief and of discipleship. The penitents not only have received the Word and come to believe, but by their example will lead others to believe and "to do penance"[105].

In the second chapter concerning those who do not do penance, Francis presents the contrast with the true believers. The Johannine references turn from the disciples of Jesus to the "Jews" who represent those who do not truly believe[106]. Here Francis speaks of those who are "blind", who "are held fast by the devil, whose children they are and whose works they perform"[107]. Francis uses this reference to describe those who claim to believe but refuse the radical call of Christ, who claim to be Christian but refuse to embrace the penitential life. They are spiritually blind because they refuse to see the truth which is Christ.

Thus, Francis' use of Johannine imagery in the *Earlier Exhortation* reveals his understanding of faith and its connection to the life of penance:

> For Francis following Christ is not simply a matter of degrees. The penitent is not just a little farther along the road. In a sense there is for Francis no middle way; the issue at stake is too important. And the issue, simply stated, is one's belief in God. The penitent has shown himself willing to put his faith into practice by undergoing conversion of life. The one who does not undertake conversion shows himself to be no better than the unbeliever. The penitent through his or her life-style demonstrates true discipleship. But the one who is so proud and

---

[104] *Earlier Exhortation*, I: 8-10.
[105] Tickerhoof, *Francis's Volterra Letter*, 173.
[106] *Ibid.*, 174.
[107] *Earlier Exhortation*, II: 6-7.

avaricious as to feel no need for repentence has already been cut off from God. Such an understanding of the penitential life is indeed radical, but no more radical than John's: *If you were blind there would be no sin in that, "But we see", you say, and your sin remains* (Jn 9:41). No greater gift can be given to a person than the gift of faith, and for Francis it was the penitent who showed what it truly meant to believe[108].

Analysis of the Later Exhortation

A Comparative Analysis of the Earlier Exhortation and the Later Exhortation

The primitive Rule that Francis had given to the penitents changed and developed. Clearly, the rule or this "way of Penance" evolved[109]. Some years after Francis had given his followers this "*normam vitae*", he again presented in writing his message for the penitents. Francis elaborated on the way of penance, his guidance preserved in the document we have designated as the *Later Exhortation*. The text of this later Rule has been given above in the second column of the comparative analysis in order to demonstrate clearly the evolution of the primitive Rule[110].

However, the *Later Exhortation* is not simply a systematic development or expansion of the *Earlier Exhortation*. Francis, unfortunately or fortunately, was more a poet than a systematician. Thus, he did not analyze, but rather, further expressed his experience of God and the life of penance. Even a cursory comparison of these two documents (as provided above in the parallel arrangement of these two texts) reveals that almost all of the expansion or additions occur in Part I of the *Earlier Exhortation*: Concerning those who do penance. While verses 72-80 expand the image of the person dying a bitter death (given in verse 14 of the *Earlier Exhortation*), presenting a type of "sermon exemplum", almost all of the other additions occur within the section which presents the way of penance[111].

---

[108] Tickerhoof, *Francis's Volterra Letter*, 175.

[109] Esser, *Un documento dell'inizio*, 90.

[110] The text of the *Later Exhortation* is given in the right column of the comparative analysis above, pp. 144-161.

[111] Esser, *A Forerunner of the "Epistola ad Fideles"*, 30-31.

Structurally, the *Later Exhortation* has changed from the paralleled presentation of the "exultation and exhortation to penance", that is, from the two somewhat-balanced chapters concerning those who do penance and those who do not do penance. Thus, we cannot impose the structure of the *Earlier Exhortation* onto the *Later Exhortation*. The attempt to parallel the sections reveals a disproportionate expansion of Part I from 19 verses to 59 verses. That is, while the other sections remain relatively unchanged quantitatively, Part I triples in size:

	Earlier Exhortation	*Later Exhortation*
Introduction		1-3
Concerning those who do penance	I:1-19	*4-62*
Concerning those who do not do penance	II:1-18	63-86
Epilogue	II:19-22	87-88

The emphasis has shifted somewhat in the *Later Exhortation*. Francis describes in much greater detail the way of penance for his followers. Most of the development in the *Later Exhortation* concerns elements which characterized the penitential movement in the Middle Ages, among others: charity, humility, service, prayer, fasting and abstinence, and the restitution of goods unjustly acquired. In part, these emendations can be attributed to Francis' concern to keep the movement orthodox, that is, to avoid the heretical positions to which some of the other thirteenth century penitential movements had evolved[112]. In fact, given that Francis uses the strong injunction "we must" (*debemus*) in speaking of these obligations[113], Esser suggests that Francis must have been addressing abuses that had crept into the movement[114]. But for whatever reasons,

[112] Esser, *A Forerunner of the "Epistola ad Fideles"*, 37; *Un documento dell'inizio*, 90.

[113] Francis uses "*debemus*", a strong juridical prescriptive, eleven times in this latter version: verses 22, 32, 33, 37, 38, 39, 40, 45, and 47 (with a double occurrence, a negative and postive form, in the last two sentences). Cf. Esser, *Opuscula*, 114-28.

[114] Esser, *Un documento dell'inizio*, 90.

in this later text Francis continues to exult and to exhort others to penance by becoming more specific concerning the life of penance.

In the *Later Exhortation*, Francis expresses the essence of the Franciscan vision and life. Francis announces what he and his followers had learned of the way of penance as the movement evolved. They expressed their experience of God, their new vision of reality, and thus, their new mode of living in the world[115]. Let us, then, consider this "expanded" or "more fully expressed" experience and vision that Francis gives his penitents in the *Later Exhortation*.

An Historical-Structural Analysis of the Later Exhortation

David Flood analyzed the text of the *Later Exhortation* within the socio-economic context of the Franciscan movement around 1221[116]. His proposed structure of the text, based mainly upon an historical rather than literary analysis, offers important insights into the text. Flood divides the *Later Exhortation* into five separate sections[117]:

Introduction (1-3)
Part I: God's Call to Life in Jesus Christ (4-21)
Part II: The Way and Blessing of Penance (22-62)
Part III: A Warning against Willful Blindness (63-86)
Conclusion (87-88)

Briefly stated, Flood has divided the section of the *Later Exhortation* which parallels the first chapter of the *Earlier Exhortation* into two distinct parts. According to Flood, the Introduction itself suggests this division by presenting a distinction between the words of Jesus Christ and the words of the Holy Spirit:

> I have proposed to set before you in this present letter and message the words of our Lord Jesus Christ, Who is the Word of the Father, and the words of the Holy Spirit, which *are spirit and life*[118]

[115] Flood, *The Commonitorium*, 3 (1979) n. 1, 22.
[116] Flood, *The Commonitorium*, 3 (1979) n. 1, 20-21; and *Frère François*, 161-62.
[117] Flood, *The Commonitorium*, 3 (1980) n. 2, 20.
[118] *Later Exhortation*, 3.

The words of Jesus Christ represent the wisdom and reality of God as given in the Gospel and the words of the Holy Spirit indicate the words of the Gospel realized in the life of believers[119]. Flood therefore divides the chapter "concerning those who do penance" into two parts: Part I summarizes the words of Jesus, the Good News of salvation; Part II describes the way of penance, the words of Jesus received and lived which thereby become "the words of the Holy Spirit, which *are spirit and life*". In Part I, Francis first recounts the words of Jesus Christ or the Good News of the Gospel. The Word confronts the hearers with a decision and thus separates them into two groups: those "who wish to receive Him and be saved" and those who "love the darkness rather than the light". Francis then recounts the "blessedness" which results from receiving the words of Jesus Christ, the beatitude of putting them into practice as the words of the Holy Spirit which are "spirit and life". Flood writes:

> Francis' words do not function within the sociocultural context of his audience; they function within the context of the Franciscan movement; on the basis of Franciscan experience, they summon the men and women who hear to quit the one context in order to live out the other, a new and different, an enlivening and promising context. Instead of contributing to the development of the social consensus, the usual function of the human message, Part One purports to give rise to (to originate) a new mind in its addressees. Its pedigree is Jesus' proclamation of the good news...
>
> In Part One Francis extends to others the possibility of knowing life as he and his friends do. The movement was a new social system, and not, as perceived by those outside it, a novel encouragement to traditional morality... It explains how an end can come to the spiritual blindness which holds men and women back from "true peace in the spirit"[120].

According to Flood's reading of the text, Francis then shifts from the "possibility" to the reality. Flood therefore distinguishes this section as Part II. While the distinction between the first and second parts is not as clear as the distinction between the second and third parts, Flood marks the division with the word "*siquidem*" (verse 22). At this point the text moves from possibility to reality, that is, the word *siquidem*

---

[119] Flood, *The Commonitorium*, 3 (1980) n. 2, 23.

[120] Flood, *The Commonitorium*, 3 (1980) n. 3, 23.

(indeed) must here be understood to mean that "*if* this is the reality, *then* these are the consequences for our life"[121].

These "consequences" describe how the penitent makes the possibility a lived reality. Part II of the *Later Exhortation* elaborates on the way of penance presented in the *Earlier Exhortation*; Francis articulates with greater detail the words of our Lord Jesus Christ as put into practice. This part of the *Later Exhortation* "spells out the ways in which the men and women live their lives, once they have shifted the context of the life from Assisi's instructions to Jesus' words become spirit"[122].

Part III (which closely parallels the second chapter of the *Earlier Exhortation*, "concerning those who do not do penance") then presents an exhortation to the hearers in the form of a graphic warning against willful blindness. Not a simple moral exhortation, this section presents "an historically dialectical challenge to a spiritually reluctant age"[123]. Francis reminds those who live under the illusion of being rich and powerful that the moment of truth comes at death. Francis thus invites those who live in blindness into the way of penance which is "spirit and life".

The Conclusion then simply adds the request that those who hear these words of our Lord Jesus Christ "observe them and put them into practice... and pass them on to others by their example"[124].

The following structural outline of the *Later Exhortation* highlights Flood's analysis which places the emphasis of the text on the summary section[125]:

---

[121] Flood, *Frère François*, 163.

[122] Flood, *The Commonitorium*, 3 (1980) n. 3, 23.

[123] Flood, *The Commonitorium*, 3 (1980) n. 6, 21.

[124] *Later Exhortation*, 87-88.

[125] While Flood does not offer a schematic presentation of his structural analysis, this outline presents a summary of that analysis as interpreted by the author. In a separate study of the *Later Exhortation*, Esser confirms, at least in part, Flood's emphasis on verses 45-47. While Esser does not subdivide sentences 45-62, as does Flood, into a "summary" followed by the "blessing of penance", Esser does claim emphatically that this section represents the heart of the text. Cf. Esser, *La Lettera di san Francesco ai fedeli*, 73.

1-3: Introduction
4-21: God's Call through Jesus Christ
22-44: The Way of Penance
45-47: SUMMARY
48-62: The Blessing of Penance
63-85: Warning against Willful Blindness
86-87: Conclusion

Though he does not so name it, Flood has rightly judged an important hermeneutical key to this text to be the distinctive lifestyle of the Franciscan penitents and their experience of God precisely in and through that shared life of penance. More succinctly put, "the words of the Holy Spirit" offer a hermeneutical key for understanding the *Later Exhortation*. We turn, therefore, to a more thorough study of the central part of the text, that is, Francis' more detailed expression of the "way of penance", the words of Jesus Christ made spirit.

The Way of Penance in the Later Exhortation

As we have already noted in our consideration of Flood's analysis, Part II of the *Later Exhortation* expands greatly upon the "way of penance" in the primitive Rule. In this section of the later text Francis uses the strong injunction "*debemus*":

[Indeed] *we must* confess all our sins to a priest, and receive from him the Body and Blood of our Lord Jesus Christ...
We must also fast and abstain from vices and sins and from any excess of food and drink, and be Catholics.
We must also visit churches frequently and venerate and show respect for the clergy
We must hate our bodies with their vices and sins...
We must love our enemies and do good to those who hate us.
We must observe the commands and counsels of our Lord Jesus Christ.
We must also deny ourselves and place our bodies under the yoke of service and holy obedience, as each one has promised to the Lord[126].

[126] *Later Exhortation*, 22, 32, 33, 37, 38, 39 and 40 (emphasis added).

But these directives should not be understood merely as regulations describing the penitential life. Rather, they describe the experience of Francis and his followers; these words sum up their experience of God and their response to that love. In his analysis of the text, Flood proposes that here Francis

> does not explain how to become Franciscan; rather, he explains what one does once one has heard Jesus' word and crossed over from darkness into light - he explains how one lives and what one does once one has become Franciscan.
>
> Franciscanism is not a set of ascetical disciplines. It is a way of dealing with the universe. One does not bend oneself to law and rule; one catches onto the rhythm of things... Francis runs through the motions of Franciscanism. People have changed because they engage in them; by doing them they change. One goes through the steps in order to dance; and soon one is dancing and forgets the steps... Francis emphasizes doing. Consciousness changes in doing the truth[127].

This sense of doing was also emphasized by Lehmann in his analysis of the *Earlier Exhortation*[128]. Francis and his followers had experienced the blessedness which resulted from *doing penance* and thus he invited others to enter this new consciousness by *doing penance*. "Francis is not describing two modes of behavior within one cognitive schema... but two distinct cognitive systems, one the sociocultural system of the day and the other the achievement of the Franciscan movement"[129].

This section leads to a summary statement, in verses 45-47, of the Franciscan way of penance. While these sentences follow upon the series of injunctions which begin with "*debemus*", structurally sentences 45 and 47 are emphasized by the use of *debemus* twice in each phrase, both in a negative and positive form:

> *We must not* be wise and prudent according to the flesh; rather, *we must* be simple, humble, and pure.
>
> And let us hold ourselves in contempt and scorn, since through our own fault all of us are miserable and contemptible, vermin and worms, as the Lord says through the prophet: *I am a worm and no man, the scorn of men and the outcast of the people.*

---

[127] Flood, *The Commonitorium*, 3 (1980) n. 2, 20.

[128] Cf. the above discussion of Lehmann's analysis, p. 166.

[129] Flood, *The Commonitorium*, 3 (1980) n. 4, 23.

> *We must never* desire to be over others; rather *we must* be servants and subject *to every human creature for God's sake*[130].

According to Flood, these verses contain a summary of the Franciscan experience or way of penance. Here Francis explains that "those who do penance" live by a different wisdom, engage in a different struggle, and have a different understanding of power[131]. These verses might well be understood as an explanation of the the phrase in the *Earlier Exhortation*: "See, you blind ones, you who are deceived by our enemies: by the *flesh*, the *world*, and the *devil*..."[132] Francis emphasized the struggle against the flesh by placing it first[133]. In the *Later Exhortation*, Francis speaks of overcoming these enemies (here the order being the devil, the flesh, and the world) by living with a different wisdom, by engaging in a different struggle, and by embracing a different sense of power. Again, the struggle against the flesh receives emphasis by being placed at the center of the summary; the primary struggle for the penitent is against self-centeredness, the struggle to turn from self to God.

Rather than living according to the flesh, the penitent lives "in contempt and scorn" of that self-centeredness. Rather than being deceived by the devil or a false wisdom, the penitent lives humbly and simply in the wisdom of God. Rather than being deceived by the worldly sense of power as dominion over others, the penitent finds true greatness or "blessedness" in being servant and subject to all. Flood describes the wisdom of the Franciscan way as portrayed in this summary thus:

> Francis and his friends do not subject people and things they encounter to their own lives. They do not reach around others to gather them in and fashion them to their interest. They do not diminish others' identity to build up their own. They extend people and things understanding. They give of themselves instead of taking for themselves. They serve rather than rule. Francis nurtures the promise within the universe instead of claiming it to his advantage. The Franciscans celebrate God's presence

---

130 *Later Exhortation*, 45-47 (emphasis added).

131 Flood, *The Commonitorium*, 3 (1980) n. 4, 22.

132 *Earlier Exhortation*, II: 11 (emphasis added).

133 Rodríguez Herrera, *Los Escritos*, 215.

in his world instead of ordering the world to their mind and interest. A social extrapolation of this principle of interaction exorcises the spirit of profit and leads to a distinctively Franciscan socialism.

Francis sums up the cognitive and moral map of the movement in this brief passage. He explains that he and his friends live by another wisdom. They are committed to another struggle, with the social identity of the outcast Christ as consequence. They initiate an encounter pattern at sharp odds with normal ways[134].

The text then moves to a description of the blessing of this way of penance. Verses 48-62 very closely parallel the "*exultatio*" of the *Earlier Exhortation*. Francis reports his and the penitents' experience of the "visitation" of God[135]. Francis describes the blessedness which results from this way of penance, the experience of an intimacy with God.

Quite clearly, Fancis speaks here of a new consciousness, a consciousness which so many people seek but which remains so elusive within the confining wisdom of the world. Francis speaks ecstatically of the new life and new consciousness wrought by a life of penance. Francis invites others to share his experience of God; Francis challenges his hearers to the radical demands of the Gospel, to a radical *metanoia*, to a life of penance. And this "doing penance" essentially involves replacing the "spirit of the flesh" with the "Spirit of the Lord", overcoming self-centeredness which leads to division and violence by realizing our relatedness and equality in God[136]. In this sense Francis exhorted his followers to penance.

Part III, the Warning against Willful Blindness, also expresses, though indirectly, this new consciousness or vision. Flood insists that this third part must be understood against the background of the Pacts made in Assisi in 1203 and 1210 which expressed and sanctioned the right of proprietorship. The "blindness" or sin resulted from an improper understanding of goods, an understanding of goods as individual possessions which sanctioned their protection, the use of power, and the exploitation of others[137]. Francis' clarity of vision came in seeing Christ in the leper, in the most outcast. This "sight" allowed Francis and his follow-

---

[134] Flood, *The Commonitorium*, 3 (1980) n. 4, 24.

[135] Flood, *Frère François*, 169.

[136] Esser, *La Lettera di san Francesco ai fedeli*, 73-75.

[137] Flood, *Frère François*, 170-71.

ers to "see" the value of service rather than goods, for all else "*will be taken away*"[138]. And so Francis, even in this condemnation of blindness, exhorts his hearers to penance, from blindness to sight, from appropriation to service, from self-centeredness to self-denial, from fear to love, from violence to peace.

But in 1221, this early Rule for the Franciscan penitents took a very different form in the *Memoriale propositi*. Let us, therefore, turn to a consideration of that next stage in the evolution of the Rule and life of the penitents.

ANALYSIS OF THE MEMORIALE PROPOSITI

The Authorship of the Memoriale propositi

While Francis presented an exhortation to penance, the *Memoriale propositi* presents juridical norms regulating the life of penance for these followers of Francis. Apparently the *Memoriale propositi* was the official Church's response to the need for more organizational structure and control among these penitential groups[139]. Prior to the approval of the *Memoriale propositi* for Franciscan penitents, other "rules" or the "Way of Life" of other penitential groups had received papal approval. In fact, the text of the *Memoriale propositi* for the Franciscan penitents evidences a dependence upon the *propositum* of the Humiliati (1201), of the Poor Catholics (1206) and their Penitents (1212), and of the Poor Lombards (1210, 1212)[140].

Thus, no serious scholar today would attribute the authorship of the *Memoriale propositi* to Francis. Most scholars assume that the text

---

[138] *Later Exhortation*, 83.

[139] Pazzelli, *St. Francis and the Third Order*, 130.

[140] M. D'Alatri, *Genesi della Regola di Niccolò IV: aspetti storici*, in *La "Supra Montem" di Niccolò IV (1289): genesi e diffusione di una regola*, edited by R. Pazzelli and L. Temperini, Roma 1988, 98; now translated into English as *Origin of the Rule of Nicholas IV: Historical Aspects*, in *Greyfriars Review* 4 (1990) n. 3, 107-118.

comes from the hand of Cardinal Hugolino or a group of jurists connected with Hugolino[141]. However, the authorship remains uncertain; the only certain fact is that the *Memoriale propositi* became firmly established as a Rule for the penitents during the early years of the pontificate of Gregory IX[142].

Cardinal Hugolino, himself a jurist and the Cardinal-Protector of the Friars Minor, played centrally in the juridical development of the various Franciscan Rules. Thus, it is likely that Hugolino, if he did not author the text, did at least have some part in its composition. What remains certain is that Hugolino approved of the text as a Way of Life for the penitents and thus it would be helpful to read the text in light of aims of Cardinal Hugolino who, in March of 1227, became Pope Gregory IX.

Scholars have long debated the relationship between Francis and Cardinal Hugolino, especially in terms of Hugolino's role in the formulation of the various Franciscan Rules. Some have argued that the later Rules (the *Regula bullata* of the Friars Minor and the *Memoriale propositi*) do not reflect the thought of Francis, but rather the mind and wishes of Cardinal Hugolino. However, the early sources do not support that position[143]. Thus, we will proceed with our analysis based upon the supposition that the later Rules for the penitents were not without Francis' influence and inspiration. We will, however, attempt to examine how Francis' vision evolved and how Hugolino influenced that transformation.

Cardinal Hugolino and the Memoriale propositi

In 1221 Cardinal Hugolino was a powerful and influential figure; he was both a papal legate of Honorius III and an imperial representative of Frederick II. The political project of Hugolino was fairly simple: to settle the controversies within and between Italian cities and to direct their military strength against other forces by calling everyone to the

---

[141] *Ibid.*, 97.

[142] M. Bartoli, *Gregorio IX e il movimento penitenziale*, in *La "Supra Montem" di Niccolò IV (1289)*, 54.

[143] E. Pásztor, *St. Francis, Cardinal Hugolino and the "Franciscan Question"*, in *Greyfriars Review* 1 (1987) 25.

crusade[144]. When Cardinal Hugolino became Pope Gregory IX in 1227, he continued this program through his papal legislation. Gregory IX attempted to reestablish the freedom of the Church (freeing clerics from the power of civil courts), and to create civil harmony by directing the people's struggle against two constant enemies: externally against the Saracens, and internally against the heretics[145].

By 1227 the penitential movement had assumed national dimensions and Gregory IX was well aware of the importance that the movement had taken on politically. Thus, after only two months of his pontificate Gregory IX sent the bull *Detestando humani* in which he recalled the interventions of Honorius III on behalf of the penitents, confirming their exemption from military service and ordering local authorities not to burden the penitents with extra taxes because of their condition[146]. These aims help to explain some of the changes within the Rule as it changed from the *Later Exhortation* to the *Memoriale propositi* in 1221.

Gregory IX's attempt to regulate and control the commumities of Franciscan penitents would appear analogous to the treatment of the Humiliati by Innocent III, who in 1201 brought this earlier penitential movement under the auspices of the official Church by approving Rules for each of the three distinct groups within the Humiliati.

> He had demonstrated his practical concern by allowing the Tertiaries to preach and by rewarding the devotion not only of men but of women. Yet he sowed the seeds of their destruction as a primitive evangelical movement. Outside the church, they were valuable critics, and their emphasis on communal work and the family unit put them in a strong position to convert. Once they had shown they could win adherents, Innocent, with his love of institutions, disciplined, regulated and absorbed this spontaneous lay movement into the church. After 1201, they were forced into a diocesan structure which led to the ultimate vitiation of their early form... But this is not to underrate Innocent's achievement: from an undifferentiated *corpus* of religious sentiment, he enabled distinctive and valuable movements to emerge and ensured that they were perpetually harnessed in the service of the church[147].

---

[144] Bartoli, *Gregorio IX e il movimento penitenziale*, 48.
[145] *Ibid.*, 48.
[146] *Ibid.*, 55-56.
[147] B. Bolton, *Innocent III's treatment of the Humiliati*, in *Popular Belief and Practice*, edited by G. Cuming and D. Baker, Cambridge 1972, 82.

Cardinal Hugolino's attempts to regulate the spontaneous Franciscan penitential movement would appear also to have changed its early form, a change which becomes much more specific in the *Rule of 1289*. Let us, therefore, consider this evolution and turn to the text of the *Memoriale propositi*[148].

A Comparative Analysis of the Memoriale propositi

While in both the *Earlier Exhortation* and the *Later Exhortation* Francis used biblical language to present the the way of penance to his followers in terms of an exultation and exhortation, the *Memoriale propositi* presents the life of penance in terms of juridical prescriptions concerning:

- modesty in dress and appropriate entertainment
- abstinence and fasts
- the life of prayer, including confession and communion
- reconciliation with others
- the prohibition against bearing arms and taking oaths
- the monthly meeting
- the care of the sick and the dead
- the role of the minister
- admission and perseverence in the fraternity
- the avoidance of heresy and dissension
- the election of officers
- the obligation of the norms

Clearly, the *Later Exhortation* and the *Memoriale propositi* differ greatly, at least in style. In fact, the *Memoriale propositi* much more closely parallels the style and content of the *propositum* of the Humiliati. In order to demonstrate graphically both the similarities and differences between these texts, a comparative analysis follows in which the three texts have been arranged in parallel columns: the *Later Exhortation*, the *Memoriale propositi*, and the *propositum* of the Humiliati.

---

[148] Having noted that Cardinal Hugolino was guided by the legislation of the Fourth Lateran Council, our analysis of the *Memoriale propositi* will note parallels between that text and the canons of the Fourth Lateran council as given in H. Schroeder, *Disciplinary Decrees of the General Councils: Text, Translation and Commentary*, St. Louis 1937.

The first twelve chapters of the *Memoriale propositi* as found in the Capistrano Rule are given in the center column[149]. The thirteenth chapter has been omitted from this analysis since it represents local statutes appended sometime after 1228[150]. Given the great dissimilarity between the *Later Exhortation* and the *Memoriale propositi*, the entire text of the *Later Exhortation* has not been repeated here. Rather, in an attempt to present those ideas which have been incorporated into the *Memoriale propositi*, only those sentences which suggest an accord in content, however much they differ in style, have been included. Similarly, the entire text of the *propositum* of the Humiliati (which contains many biblical quotations) has not been recorded here, but rather, only those sections which demonstrate obvious parallels with the text of the *Memoriale propositi*[151].

One further comparative element has been added. Given that Hugolino was guided in his legislation by the decrees of the Fourth Lateran Council of 1215[152], the decrees of that Council which parallel the content of the *Memoriale propositi* have been given in the notes within the comparative analysis[153]. Let us then consider the Rule of the penitents as given in the *Memoriale propositi* with respect to these other documents, after which we will proceed to a discussion of how its content compares with the way of penance in the *Later Exhortation*.

---

[149] The Latin text of this *Memoriale propositi*, the Capistrano Rule, can be found in *Opuscules de critique historique* I: 17-30. The English text, which represents a literal translation of that Latin edition, comes from Zaremba, *Franciscan Social Reform*, 114-21.

[150] Zaremba, *Franciscan Social Reform*, 112.

[151] The sections of the *propositum* of the Humiliati which have been included in this comparative analysis have been arranged according to the structure of the *Memoriale propositi* and are *not*, therefore, in their proper order. The Latin text of this *propositum* may be found in Meersseman, *Dossier*, 276-82. Since the *propositum* of the Humiliati has not been published in English, the entire text has been included in *Appendix I*. The text of the English translation, as given in the Appendix and from which the excepts below are taken, was provided by Maurice Sheehan, of the Franciscan Institute at St. Bonaventure University, New York. However, the author of the translation is not known.

[152] Pazzelli, *St. Francis and the Third Order*, 133.

[153] Within the analysis of the *Memoriale propositi*, all of the references to specific canons refer to decrees from the Fourth Lateran Council of 1215 as given in Schroeder, *Disciplinary Decrees*.

Later Exhortation	*Memoriale propositi*	*Humiliati's Propositum*
	The Rule and Life of the Brothers and Sisters of Penance begins	
	In the name of the Father, the Son, and the Holy Spirit. Amen.	
	Memorial of the manner of life of the Brothers and Sisters of Penance living in their own homes, begun in the year of our Lord 1221. In the time of the lord Pope Gregory IX, 13th day of June, the first indication is such.	[Bull of approbation given by Innocent III, 7 June 1201]
	I. On the Manner of Dress	
	1. Let the men of this fraternity wear garments of ordinary colorless cloth the price of which shall not exceed six soldi of Ravenna money per yard, unless from this they shall be dispensed for a time because of an evident and necessary cause. The width and length of the cloth shall be included in the said price.	
	2. Let them have cloaks and furred outer garments without any opening at the neck, fastened or in one piece, and not buckled as the seculars wear, and with closed sleeves[154].	
	3. Let the sisters wear cloaks and tunics of ordinary cloth of the same price, or at least with the cloak let them have black or white skirts or dresses or a roomy linen robe without plaits whose cost is not more than 12 denarii of Ravenna money per yard.	
	4. According to the state of each woman and the local custom they may be dispensed from the price and manner of outer garments.	

[154] Canon 16 reads: "Their [clerics'] garments must be worn clasped at the top and neither too short nor too long... in public they must not appear with open mantles, but these must be clasped either on the back of the neck or on the bosom". Cf. Schroeder, *Disciplinary Decrees*, 257.

Later Exhortation	*Memoriale propositi*	*Humiliati's Propositum*
45. We must not be wise and prudent according to the flesh; rather, we must be simple, humble, and pure.	5. Let them not wear silk or colored ribbons or cords, and let the brothers as well as the sisters have furs of lambskin only. 6. It is unlawful to have other than leather purses and the thongs sewn without silk. Other ornaments let them put away at the judgment of the visitor.	11. Your clothes ought to be neither too elegant nor too shabby, but of a kind that have no irreligious note about them, for neither affected dirtiness nor shabbiness nor exquisite neatness and elegance are suitable for a Christian.
	7. Let them not attend shameful entertainments, theatres, or dances, and let them give nothing to actors and prohibit that anything be given by their family[155].	6. *"Do not love the world, brethren, nor those things which are in the world..."*
	II. On Abstinence	
32. We must also fast and abstain from vices and sins and from and excess of food and drink...	1. Let all abstain from meat except on Sundays, Tuesdays, and Thursdays, unless because they are ill, weak, been bled (in which case they are excused) for three days, or in journey, or	7. Unless prevented by sickness, debility, or labor, each one should fast on Wednesdays and Fridays,
	2. because of a special solemnity occurring, namely, for thee days at the Nativity of our Lord, the new year, Epiphany, for three days at Easter, the apostles Peter and Paul, the nativity of John the Baptist, the glorious Assumption of the Virgin Mary, the feast of All Saints and St. Martin.	excepting the days of Pentecost, and from Christmas to Epiphany, and other solemn days.
	3. On the other days of non-fasting it is lawful to eat cheese and eggs. But when with the religious in their convents it shall be lawful for them to eat what is set before them.	

[155] Canon 16 reads: "Clerics shall not hold secular offices or engage in secular and, above all, dishonest pursuits. They shall not attend the performances of mimics and buffoons, or theatrical representations..." Cf. Schroeder, *Disciplinary Decrees*, 257.

Later Exhortation	*Memoriale propositi*	*Humiliati's Propositum*
	4. And let them be content with dinner and supper, excepting the sick, weak and those travelling. Let the healthy be moderate in food and drink.	8...they should be content with lunch and dinner, and food and drink should be moderate and temperate.
	5. Before dinner and supper let them say once the Our Father and after eating, one Our Father and give thanks to the Lord. Other times let them say three Our Fathers.	9. When you come for meals, before you eat say the Lord's Prayer, and do the same after your meal.
	6. From Easter to All Saints let them fast on Fridays. From All Saints to Easter they shall fast on Wednesdays and Fridays, observing notwithstanding other fasts which may be indicated by the Church in general observance.	
	III. Concerning Fasts	
	1. During the Lent from the feast of St. Martin to Christmas and during the greater Lent from Sunday of Carnival to Easter let them fast continually unless dispensed because of illness or some other necessity.	
	2. Until their purification pregnant sisters may abstain from all bodily mortifications except those pertaining to dress and prayer.	
	3. It is lawful for those who perform hard work to eat three times a day from Easter to the feast of St. Michael.	
	4. It shall be lawful for those who work for others to eat of all things set before them except on Fridays and fast days generally appointed by the Church.	

Later Exhortation	*Memoriale propositi*	*Humiliati's Propositum*
	IV. On Prayers	
19. Let us love God, therefore, and adore Him with a pure heart and a pure mind... *21.* And let us praise Him and pray to Him *day and night,*	1. Daily let all say the seven canonical hours, that is Matins, Prime, Terce, Sext, None, Vespers, and Compline[156].	10. You ought to observe the seven canonical hours, namely, matins, prime, terce, sext, none, vespers, and compline so that you may praise the Lord seven times a day, as the Prophet said.
	2. The clerics according to the order of the clerics; let those who know the psalter say for prime (Psalm 53) *Deus in nomine tuo* and (Psalm 118, verses 1-32) *Beati immaculati* as far as *Legem pone*, and the other psalms of the hours with the Glorys.	
	3. But when they do not go to church, let them say for Matins the psalms said by the Church, or at least some other 18 psalms or at least the Our Fathers, just as the illiterate.	
saying: *Our Father Who art in heaven,* since *we should pray always and never lose heart...*	4. All the others must say for the hours: 12 Our Fathers for Matins, and 7 Our Fathers for each of the other hours together with the Glory after each one.	At each of the hours you should say the Lord's Prayer seven times on account of the seven gifts of the Holy Spirit.
	5. Let those who know the Creed and (Psalm 50) *Miserere mei Deus*, say them at Prime and Compline. If they have not said them at the constituted hours, let them say the Our Father. Let the infirm not say the hours unless they wish to.	At prime and compline, however, you should say the Symbol, that is, *Credo in Deum.*

[156] Canon 17 reads: "[We] strictly command in virtue of obedience that they celebrate diligently and devoutly the diurnal and noctural offices so far as God gives them strength". Cf. Schroeder, *Disciplinary Decrees*, 257.

Later Exhortation	*Memoriale propositi*	*Humiliati's Propositum*
	V. When They Must Go for Matins	
33. We must also visit churches frequently...	1. Let all go for Matins during the Lent of St. Martin and the greater Lent, unless an inconvenience of persons or things would result.	
	VI. On Confession, Communion, Restitution, Not Bearing Arms and Not taking Oaths	
22. We must also confess all our sins to a priest, and receive from him the Body and Blood of our Lord Jesus Christ.	1. Let them confess their sins three times a year and receive Communion on the Nativity of the Lord, Resurrection Sunday and Pentecost[157].	
	2. Let them make satisfaction for past tithes and make ready for the future.	4. Give back interest monies and all ill-gotten things; for the sin is not remitted unless the restitution is made. And make satisfaction for other wrongs. So the Lord in the gospel: "If you are offering your gift at the altar..."
26. And let us love our neighbors as ourselves. 27. And if there is anyone who does not wish to love them as himself, at least let him do no harm to them, but rather do good.	3. Let them not take up lethal arms against anyone or carry them with themselves.	1...Charity must also be shown to enemies, for the Lord says: "*Do good to those... 3...* "*[Be at] peace with [everyone]*". (Rm 12:18).

[157] Canon 21 reads: "All the faithful of both sexes shall after they have reached the age of discretion faithfully confess all their sins at least once a year to their own (parish) priest and perform to the best of their ability the penance imposed, receiving reverently at least at Easter the sacrament of the Eucharist". Cf. Schroeder, *Disciplinary Decrees*, 259.

Later Exhortation	*Memoriale propositi*	*Humiliati's Propositum*
41. And no one is to be obliged to obey another in anything by which a sin or a crime is committed.	4. Let all refrain from solemn oaths unless forced by necessity in the cases excepted by the Sovereign Pontiff in his indulgence, namely, for peace, faith, calumny and testimony.	2. Furthermore, "*above all, brothers, do not swear, neither by heaven, nor by earth, nor by any manner of oath...*
	5. And in their speech as much as possible let them avoid oaths. Those who by a slip of the tongue shall unwarily have taken oath, as it happens in much talking, that same day at evening when they must recall what they did, let them say three Our Fathers for such oaths.	
	6. Let everyone encourage his family in serving God.	
	VII. Concerning the Monthly Mass and Meeting	
34. And let all of us firmly realize that no one can be saved except through the holy words and Blood of our Lord Jesus Christ...	1. Let all the brothers and sisters in every city and locality gather each month whenever it shall appear expedient in a church announced by the ministers and there hear the divine word.	15. As for the rest, it will also be your custom to come together every Sunday in a suitable place to hear the word of God...
30. Let us then have charity and humility; let us give alms...	2. And let each one give to the treasurer one of the usual denari which he shall collect and on the advice of the ministers distribute among the poor brothers and sisters, and mostly to the infirm and those who would not have funeral services. Finally let him offer of that money to the other poor and to that Church.	5...the Lord says in the gospel: "*But yet what is left over, give alms...*
	3. And then, if they conveniently can, let them have one religious, instructed in the word of God, who	15... one or several of the brethren of proven faith and religious experience who are powerful in work and speech will, with the

Later Exhortation	*Memoriale propositi*	*Humiliati's Propositum*
25. Moreover, let us perform *worthy fruits of penance*.	would admonish and encourage them to penance, perseverance and the performance of works of mercy[158].	permission of the diocesan bishop, propose a word of exhortation to those who have gathered to hear the word of God. The speakers should admonish [and] lead them to an upright life and works of piety, and do this in such a manner that they should not speak about the articles of faith and the sacraments of the Church.
	4. And, except the officials, let them be silent during the Mass and preaching, attentive to the Office, prayer, and sermon.	
	VIII. Concerning the Works of Mercy, Wills, and the Settling of Discords	
	1. When any of the Brothers or sisters might happen to take ill, let the ministers, if informed of this by the sick one, either themselves or through others visit the sick, excite him to penance and provide from the common fund for his bodily needs as they shall see fit.	12. Because it is your custom, you should know how to come to the aid of any member of your fellowship who is in need of temporal things or is laid

[158] Canon 10 reads: "Among other things that pertain to the salvation of the Christian people, the food of the word of God is above all necessary... Wherefore we decree that bishops provide suitable men, powerful in work and word, to exercise with fruitful result the office of preaching; who in place of the bishops, since these cannot do it, diligently visiting the people committed to them, may instruct them by word and example". Cf. Schroeder, *Disciplinary Decrees*, 251-52.

Later Exhortation	*Memoriale propositi*	*Humiliati's Propositum*
		up with sickness; help them in their temporal need or in taking the necessary care of them.
	IX. Concerning the Dead Brothers	
	1. And if any sick brother or sister shall depart from this life, let it be announced to the brothers and sisters who are present in the city or locality, so that they gather at his funeral and let them not depart until Mass has been celebrated and the body given burial.	13. If any of your members shall have died, announce this to the brethren and let each one come to the funeral,
	2. And after that let each one, within eight days of the death itself, say for the soul of the departed, the priest a Mass, those who know how, fifty psalms; and the others fifty Our Fathers together with the Eternal rest after each.	and let each say twelve times the Lord's Prayer and *Miserere mei, Deus* for the soul of the deceased, seeing that you intend and arrange, with the help of the Lord, to remain and persevere in the order and your way of life.
	3. Besides this during the year let a priest say three Masses for the welfare of the brothers and sisters, living and dead; he who knows the psalter let him say it, and let the rest say a hundred Our Fathers together with the Eternal rest at the end of each. Otherwise let them duplicate.	
	X. On Making a Will	
	1. Let all who by right can do so, make a testament and dispose of their things within three months after their profession so that none of them die intestate.	

Later Exhortation	*Memoriale propositi*	*Humiliati's Propositum*
	2. Let it be as it shall appear to the ministers concerning peace among the brothers and sisters or outsiders causing discord; counsel also may be had of the diocesan bishop if it appears necessary.	
47. We must never desire to be over others; rather we must be servants and subject *to every human creature for God's sake*.	3. If the right or privileges of the brothers and sisters are molested by the authorities or governors of the places in which they live, let the local ministers, with the counsel of the lord Bishop do what shall appear necessary.	
42. The one to whom obedience has been entrusted... should be as *the lesser* and the servant...	4. Let everyone on whom the office of minister or the other offices here mentioned fall, accept and faithfully perform them, though anyone may vacate an office after a year.	
43. And he should use and show mercy...	5. When anyone shall petition to enter this fraternity, let the ministers inquire into his condition and office and let them explain to him the duties of this fraternity and most of all the restitution of the goods of others.	
	6. And if he shall be pleased with the aforementioned rule, let him be vested, and let him satisfy his creditors either by money or by a given security. Let him be reconciled with his neighbors and pay his tithes.	
	7. A year after this is fulfilled, he may, on the advice of some discreet brother, if he shall appear fit to them, be received in this manner:	
	8. that he promise to observe all that is here written or should be written or taken away, according to the Council of the brothers, all the time of his life, unless some time it should occur by the permission of the minister.	1... Hence the apostle: "*Obey those put in charge of you...*"

Later Exhortation	*Memoriale propositi*	*Humiliati's Propositum*
	9. And that if he do anything against this manner of life, questioned by the minister he shall make satisfaction according to the will of the visitor.	
	10. And let him make a public promise in writing thereto.	
	11. Let no one be received in any other way, unless it shall appear otherwise to them, considering the condition and dignity of the person.	
	12. Let no one depart from this fraternity or from what is here contained unless to enter into religion.	
	XI. Concerning Contempt and Distrust of Heretics	
32. We must ... be Catholics.	1. Let no heretic or one accused of heresy be received. If, however, he was only suspected of it, he may be admitted if, cleared before the bishop, he is fit in other respects[159].	
	2. Women having husbands shall not be received unless with the consent and permission of their spouses.	
	3. Incorrigible brothers and sisters expelled from the fraternity shall in no wise be again received, unless it should so please the more prudent part of the brothers.	

[159] Canon 3 reads: "We excommunicate and anathematize every heresy that raises itself against the holy, orthodox and Catholic faith which we have above explained; condemning all heretics under whatever names they may be known... Those condemned, being handed over to the secular rulers or their bailiffs, let them be abandoned, to be punished with due justice..." Cf. Schroeder, *Disciplinary Decrees*, 242.

Later Exhortation	*Memoriale propositi*	*Humiliati's Propositum*
	XII. Concerning the Declaration of Faults	
28. But those who have received the power to judge others should exercise judgment with mercy...	1. Let the ministers of each city and place declare the manifest faults of the brothers and sisters to the visitor for punishment[160].	
44. Nor should he become angry with a brother because of a fault of that brother, but with all patience and humility let him admonish him and support him.	2. And if anyone show himself incorrigible, let the visitor be informed of him through the ministers on the advice of some discreet brothers and expel him from the fraternity and let it be announced in the congregation.	
	3. Furthermore, if it is a brother, let him be denounced to the local authority or governor.	
	4. If one should know of some scandal concerning the brothers or sisters let him make it known to the ministers and he ought to inform the visitor, but they are not bound to denounce anything between husband and wife.	
	5. The visitor has the power to dispense all the brothers in all these things when he shall see fit.	
	6. Let the ministers with the counsel of their brothers after a year elect two other ministers, and a faithful treasurer who would provide for the necessities of the brothers and sisters and the other poor, and messengers who, at their bidding, should announce the things said and done by the fraternity.	

[160] Canon 7 reads: "By an irreragable decree we ordain that prelates make a prudent and earnest effort to correct the excesses and reform the morals of their subjects..." Cf. Schroeder, *Disciplinary Decrees*, 247.

Later Exhortation	*Memoriale propositi*	*Humiliati's Propositum*
36. But religious especially, who have left the world, are bound to do more and greater things without however leaving these undone.	7. In all the aforesaid let none be obliged under sin but to the punishment, so that if twice admonished by the minister he neglects to perform the imposed punishment or that which must be imposed, let him be obliged under sin as one who is contumacious.	17. Therefore, beloved sons and daughters in the Lord, "*with pure heart and good conscience and sincere faith*" (1 Tm 1:5) may you observe the form of living which we have taken care diligently to examine, prudently to correct, and beneficially to approve, so that you may return home to receive the everlasting reward from him who is the rewarder of merits and the searcher of hearts.

The Way of Penance in the Memoriale propositi

The profoundly biblical tone of the *Later Exhortation* clearly distinguishes it from the *Memoriale propositi* of the penitents which contains instead many juridical norms. This disparity, coupled with the *Memoriale propositi*'s similarity to the *propositi* of other penitential groups, led Esser to claim that there is little or nothing specifically "Franciscan" about the text[161]. At the other extreme, Pazzelli claims that the *Memoriale propositi* reflects perfectly the spirit of the *Later Exhortation*; the two documents differ only in style, with the *Memoriale propositi* codifying the spirit of the *Later Exhortation*[162]. The truth would appear to lie somewhere between these two extremes.

As demonstrated by its comparison with the text of the *propositum* of the Humiliati, the *Memoriale propositi* does evidence a dependence

[161] Esser, *Un documento dell'inizio*, 87.
[162] Pazzelli, *St. Francis and the Third Order*, 113-14.

upon other *propositi* which, prior to 1221, had been promulgated for other penitential groups. But at least some similarity between the Franciscan Rule and other *propositi* would be expected since Francis did indeed exhort his followers to a life of voluntary penance and hence to a life similar to other penitential groups. Clearly, both documents or Rules, the *Later Exhortation* and the *Memoriale propositi*, propose the life of penance as the Way of Life for the early Secular Franciscans, the latter according to the existent norms for voluntary penitents.

The Rule or Way of Life of Francis and his early followers did have roots in preceding religious experiences and expressions: eremitism and penance, solidarity with the lepers, and itinerant preaching[163]. The novelty, that which made this way of penance "Franciscan", was Francis' insistence on a radical *metanoia* combined with an absolute fidelity to the Church[164]. And, as Antonio Rigon points out in his study on the genesis of the Rule, the later legislation of the Order of Penitents did not lose all traces of its original evangelical matrix: the commitment to non-violence, the refusal to bear arms, the prescriptions for making peace within and beyond the limits of the fraternity, and the attempt to insure solidarity in life and in death[165].

Much of the life to which Francis exhorted the penitents can be found in the *Memoriale propositi*. His exhortations to be simple, to love and praise God, to fast and abstain, and to love one's neighbor have been translated into prescriptions concerning modesty in dress, times and manners of prayer, fasting and abstinence, restitution of goods and the prohibition against bearing arms. These prescriptions reflected the regime of the canonical Order of Penance as it had evolved in the thirteenth century. Many of the disciplines were originally formulated for public sinners as both punitive and preventative. But over the centuries these regulations had been modified. The extreme demands of fasting and abstinence had been simplified[166]. The prohibition against bearing arms, which originally intended to keep public sinners from shedding blood,

---

[163] Cf. A. Rigon, *Dalla Regola di S. Agostino alla Regola di Niccolò IV*, in *La "Supra Montem" di Niccolò IV (1289)*, 25-46; see also the discussion of this developing involvement of the laity in the Order of Penance during the twelfth and thirteenth centuries in *Chapter II*, above pp. 107-120.

[164] Rigon, *Dalla Regola di S. Agostino*, 43.

[165] *Ibid.*, 46.

[166] Meersseman, *Ordo Fraternitatis*, 290-91.

became for the voluntary penitents a freely accepted humiliation since the sword had become a symbol of the free person. But with the later growth of the communes and the resultant need for citizens to defend and protect those communes, this exemption from military service became an ecclesiatical privilege of the penitents which the popes and bishops attempted to preserve[167]. Thus, in becoming more structured the penitential movement in general and, more specifically, the Franciscan penitential movement as given in the *Memoriale propositi* lost some of the original intent and spirit.

Unfortunately, codification of religious experience and its expression often brings the loss of its true spirit. We have reviewed how the evolution of penance in the Church with the introduction of "private penance" brought a loss of the spirit of repentance[168]. The *Memoriale propositi*, as a codification of Francis' call to radical conversion, risked the loss of the true spirit of penance proposed by Francis. If the *Memoriale propositi* is understood apart from a radical *metanoia* grounded in an identification with the poor and suffering Christ (that is, apart from seeing with a radically different wisdom, engaging in a fundamentally different struggle, and living from a profoundly different sense of power), then the *Memoriale propositi* loses that which makes it specifically "Franciscan".

The *Memoriale propositi* expresses the Franciscan way of penance only insofar as it is read and understood through the lens of the primitive Rule or the *Later Exhortation*, only insofar as the life of penance begins with the experience of God which leads the person to a true sense of repentence which leads to self-denial, to humility and simplicity, to service and love of others. The *Memoriale propositi* presents the "Franciscan" way of penance only insofar as it empowers the penitents to seek reconciliation with God and neighbor, only insofar as its prescriptions for the life of penance suggest the way of a different wisdom, struggle and power. Unfortunately, the process of codification of the vision caused the loss, at least in part, of the radical nature of Francis' call to conversion.

But this way of penance changed even more significantly in the first formally approved Rule of the Secular Franciscans, the *Rule of 1289*. Let us, therefore, turn to a consideration of that later Rule and how the life of the Franciscan penitents evolved.

---

[167] *Ibid.*, 290.

[168] Cf. the discussion in *Chapter II*, above pp. 103-105.

Analysis of the Rule of 1289

Nicholas IV and the Rule of 1289

Nicholas IV became the first Franciscan pope on February 15, 1288. Shortly after his election to the papacy, he received requests from some local communities of penitents that he grant his official approval to their Rule[169]. Thus, on August 18, 1289 he issued the bull *Supra Montem* which contained the Rule for Franciscan penitents[170]. However, not all the penitents were equally disposed to accept Nicholas IV's bull "blindly"[171]. Some of the penitents refused to accept the changes introduced by Nicholas IV's bull. For example, Nicholas IV declared that the visitor to the communities of penitents had to be chosen from among the Friars Minor. Obviously this innovation was not generally accepted because on August 8, 1290 Nicholas IV issued another bull, *Unigenitus Dei Filius*, in which he reasserted that the visitors to this Order "begun by Francis" must be taken from the Friars Minor[172]. Nonetheless, the text of the *Supra Montem*, the *Rule of 1289*, was eventually accepted universally, and in fact, remained in effect as the official Rule of the Secular Franciscan Order until 1883. Let us, then, turn to an analysis of that first officially approved Rule[173].

---

[169] D'Alatri, *Genesi della Regola di Niccolò IV*, 100.

[170] Pásztor points out that the *Supra Montem* was registered among the common letters of Nicholas IV; it was not included within the curial letters, that is, as an *ex officio* document. The bull was, therefore, in response to a specific request rather than at the initiative of the Roman curia. Thus, the *Supra Montem* was considered equivalent to other letters written at the request of certain groups, for example, dispensations, concessions, indulgences. Cf. E. Pásztor, *La "Supra montem" e la cancelleria pontificia al tempo di Niccolò IV*, in *La "Supra Montem" di Niccolò IV (1289)*, 66-67.

[171] *Ibid.*, 71.

[172] Pazzelli, *St. Francis and the Third Order*, 151.

[173] It should be noted that we do not possess the original of the bull, although the extant copies do date from the thirteenth century. Cf. Pásztor, *La "Supra montem" e la cancelleria pontificia*, 71; and L. Temperini, *Ai fratelli e alle sorelle dell'Ordine della penitenza (Regola di Niccolò IV)*, Roma 1988, 8.

A Comparative Analysis of the Rule of 1289 and the Memoriale propositi

The *Rule of 1289* closely parallels the *Memoriale propositi*. In fact, while the *Rule of 1289* rearranges the contents of the *Memoriale propositi* to reflect the general order of prescriptions in other religious Rules, this first formally approved Rule of the Secular Franciscan Order contains most of the material found in the *Memoriale propositi*. Thus, rather than repeating the full text of each Rule in this analysis, we will focus here upon the significant points of comparison[174].

Although at first glance the *Supra Montem* appears only to rearrange the contents of the *Memoriale propositi*, as D'Alatri notes, Nicholas IV's bull does, in fact, contain numerous and significant changes[175]. Let us therefore consider the *Rule of 1289* in relation to the *Memoriale propositi*.

As already noted, much of the content remains essentially unchanged. In fact, some of the paragraphs are almost verbatim, for example:

Memoriale propositi	*The Rule of 1289*
I. On the Manner of Dress	*III. On the Manner of Dress*
2. Let them have cloaks and furred outer garments without any opening at the neck, fastened or in one piece, and not buckled as the seculars wear, and with closed sleeves.	1. Let the above mentioned brothers also have cloaks and furred outer garments without an opening at the neck, divided or in one piece, and not open but fastened together as becomes modesty, and let the sleeves be closed.
5. Let them not wear silk or colored ribbons or cords, and let the brothers as well as the sisters have furs of lambskin only.	4. Let the brothers and sisters, however, not use ribbons or silk cords. Let them have furs only of lambskin...

---

[174] The full text of the *Memoriale propositi* has already been given in the above analysis, pp. 188-199. The full text of the *Rule of 1289* is included in the comparative analysis at the beginning of *Chapter IV*, pp. 223-237. However, in the event that it might prove helpful to the reader, the full texts of both documents have been arranged in a comparative table given in *Appendix II*, pp. 373-388. The English text of the *Rule of 1289*, which represents a literal translation from the Latin, has been taken from Zaremba, *Franciscan Social Reform*, 123-31.

[175] D'Alatri, *Genesi della Regola di Niccolò IV*, 101.

Memoriale propositi	*The Rule of 1289*
II. On Abstinence	*V. On Abstinence and Fasting*
1. Let all abstain from meat except on Sundays, Tuesdays, and Thursdays, unless because they are ill, weak,	1. Let all abstain from meat on Monday, Wednesday and Saturday, unless a condition of sickness or weakness would suggest otherwise.
been bled (in which case they are excused) for three days,	Let meat, however, be given on three successive days to those who have been bled, and it should not be denied
or in journey...	to those making a journey...
5. Before dinner and supper let them say once the Our Father and after eating, one Our Father and give thanks to the Lord. Other times let them say three Our Fathers.	Dinner or supper should not be eaten until the Lord's Prayer has been said once; after the meal it should be repeated together with "Thanks be to God". But if it is omitted, then let three Our Fathers be said.
IV. On Prayers	*VIII. On Prayer*
1. Daily let all say the seven canonical hours, that is Matins, Prime, Terce, Sext, None, Vespers, and Compline.	Let all say the seven canonical hours daily, namely, Matins, Prime, Terce, Sext, None, Vespers, and Compline.

Where minor changes do occur, they often can readily be explained by the differing nature of the two documents. Whereas the *Rule of 1289* attempted to legislate the life of the Franciscan penitents in general, the *Memoriale propositi* had been adopted and redacted (at least up until 1228) by individual local Fraternities. Therefore, in those places where the *Memoriale propositi* reflects local customs, the *Rule of 1289* has stated these provisions in more generally applicable language. For example, the local monetary designation of "Ravenna" has been omitted in the later text:

Memoriale propositi	*The Rule of 1289*
I. On the Manner of Dress	*III. On the Manner of Dress*
1. Let the men of this fraternity wear garments of ordinary colorless cloth the price of which shall not exceed six soldi of Ravenna money per yard, unless from this they shall be dispensed for a time because of an evident and necessary cause. The width and length of the cloth shall be included in the said price.	1. Let the brothers of this fraternity be clothed alike in cloth of low price and of a color neither entirely white nor entirely black, unless, for a legitimate and apparent reason the visitors, upon the advice of their ministers, have temporarily dispensed someone with regard to the price.

Similarly, the mention of the feast of St. Francis occurs in the the *Rule of 1289* which post-dates his canonization:

Memoriale propositi	*The Rule of 1289*
III: 3. It is lawful for those who perform hard work to eat three times a day from Easter to the feast of St. Michael.	*V*: 3. Workers, on account of the demands brought on by fatigue, may licitly take food three times a day on any day they are engaged in labor from Easter until the Feast of St. Francis.

However, Nicholas IV introduced "Francis" into this Rule in other ways, ways which had profound effects upon the Order in terms of both its structure and function. In the preamble the pope explicitly named Francis as the "Founder of this Order"[176]. This claim is not so significant in and of itself; but the implications of this understanding played crucially in some of the changes made by Nicholas IV. Both the *Memoriale propositi* and the *Rule of 1289* speak of the penitents having a "religious", that is, a person who would offer spiritual guidance:

---

[176] The text of this part of the preamble, the *narratio*, is given below, p. 207. The *Rule of 1289* is the first official ecclesial document to make the claim that Francis founded this Order of penitents.

Memoriale propositi	*The Rule of 1289*
VII: 3. And then, if they conveniently can, let them have one religious, instructed in the word of God, who would admonish and encourage them to penance, perseverance and the performance of works of mercy.	*XIII*: 3. And then, if they can do so conveniently, they should have a religious, one ably instructed in the word of God, who will earnestly exhort, admonish and arouse them to penance and the exercise of the works of mercy.

The *Memoriale propositi* did not specify who the "religious" or the "visitor" was to be. Originally the visitor would have been designated by the bishop, although at times the penitents elected their own visitators[177]. The *Rule of 1289*, on the other hand, demands that the visitor be taken from the Friars Minor:

> *XVI*: 2. Because this present form of life took its origin from the aforementioned Blessed Francis, We counsel that the visitors and instructors should be taken from the Order of Friars Minor, whom the custodes or guardians of the same Order shall appoint, when they have been requested in the matter. However, We do not want a congregation of this kind to be visited by a lay person.

Thus, some of the differences can be explained by the nature of *Supra Montem* as a formal Rule, that is, the text could no longer contain regulations tied to particular localities. Other changes result from Francis' canonization and immediate popularity. Indeed, prior to the *Rule of 1289*, the penitents had found it prestigious and advantageous to claim their origin in Francis. Nicholas IV, at least in part, only acknowledged the phenomenon and therefore legislated a closer bond with the Friars Minor. However, while having a saint as their founder might have increased their prestige, not all of the penitents were willing to accept being placed under a clerical order. The penitents at Lombardy refused to accept this mandate from Nicholas IV and continued to elect

[177] Pazzelli, *St. Francis and the Third Order*, 144-145.

a lay person as their visitor[178]. But Nicholas IV made other even more significant changes, changes which evidence his concerns as legislator. Based upon her meticulous study of the *Supra Montem*, Edith Pásztor suggests that Nicholas IV defined the identity of the penitents[179]. Pásztor calls attention to Nicholas IV's preamble to the Rule. Here the pope presented a particular understanding of the faith and Francis' role in the preservation of that faith. After the inscription or address, the preamble presents an "*arenga* and *narratio*", a declaration concerning the Catholic faith and a narrative explaining Francis', and by extension his followers', devotion to that same faith. It reads:

> Nicholas, Bishop, Servant of the Servants of God. To our beloved sons and our beloved daughters in Jesus Christ, the Brothers and Sisters of the Order of Penance, present and to come, Health and Apostolic benediction:
>
> Not to be shaken by any storms or shattered by any waves of tempests, the solid foundation of the Christian religion is known to be placed on the rock of the Catholic faith which the sincere devotion, glowing with the fire of charity, of the disciples of Christ taught by solicitous preaching to the nations walking in darkness, and which the Roman Church holds and preserves. For, this is the right and true faith without which no one is rendered acceptable, no one appears pleasing in the eyes of the Most High. It is this faith which prepares the way to salvation and promises the rewards and joys of an eternal happiness.
>
> Wherefore the glorious Confessor of Christ, Blessed Francis, the founder of this Order, showing by words as well as by example the way leading to God, instructed his children in the sincerity of the same faith, and wished them to confess it boldly, retain it firmly and fulfill it in deed, so that as they profitably advanced along its path, they might merit, after the imprisonment of the present life, to be made possessors of eternal beatitude.

Pásztor suggests that the bull *Supra Montem* not only rearranged the content of the *Memoriale propositi* but also, and more significantly, through the *arenga* and *narratio*, gave the Order of Penance a function and particular finality within society. The Church needed not only theologians and trained jurists to meet the demands of the inquisition, but

---

[178] Meersseman, *Ordo Fraternitatis*, 433.

[179] Pásztor, *La "Supra montem" e la cancelleria pontificia*, 65-92, esp. 75.

also a social and Christian witness at the level of a popular religiosity, for which the Church enlisted the Franciscan penitents[180].

But then the *arenga* and *narratio* present the lens through which the document must be understood. Pásztor's insight has offered scholars an important hermeneutical key for understanding the changes introduced by Nicholas IV into the Way of Life for the penitents. The distinction, given its subtlety, could easily be overlooked.

Francis did, in fact, instruct the penitents "in the sincerity of the same faith" by exhorting them to "be Catholics"[181]. However, Francis' great faith as expressed in his devotion to the Church and even his veneration of the clergy must be understood in terms of his experience of God in and through Christ. His great devotion to the Word and Eucharist as the very presence of Christ on earth brought him to a veneration of the Church's ministers of the sacraments[182]. Francis' exhortations served not to control heresy, not to preserve orthodoxy, but rather, to bring others to the experience of God in and through Christ. Thus, in the *Rule of 1289* Nicholas IV brought a very different emphasis to Francis' exhortation that the penitents "be Catholics".

This insight given by Pásztor is confirmed and its implications made more specific in a separate study of the *Supra Montem* by Mariano D'Alatri. Based on his own expert analysis of the text, D'Alatri claims that, although not mentioned explicitly in the preamble, the *Supra Montem* presents the Order of Penance primarily as "orthodox" and "at the service of orthodoxy in the Roman Church". He calls attention to the significant changes made by the *Rule of 1289* which support this understanding:

- the document names the visitator rather than the bishop as guardian of orthodoxy
- the text demands more severity in confronting heresy and heretics than did the *Memoriale propositi*
- the penitents are given an active role in the repression of heresy which becomes more obvious in the exceptions noted concerning the use of arms: for the defense of the Church and the faith[183].

---

[180] *Ibid.*, 75-76.

[181] *Later Exhortation*, 32.

[182] Cf. *Later Exhortation*, 33.

[183] D'Alatri, *Genesi della Regola di Niccolò IV*, 101-103.

The relevant passages which present these crucial redactions of the text of the *Memoriale propositi* follow:

Memoriale propositi

The Rule of 1289

I. On the Manner of Examining Those Desirous of Entering the Order.

We, therefore, honoring this Order with fitting favors and very readily attending its growth, decree that

1. All who may happen to take upon themselves the observance of this form of life, before the undertaking or their reception, be subjected to a diligent examination on the Catholic faith and their obedience to the aforesaid Church. And if they have firmly their faith and obedience and truly believe in them, they may safely be admitted or received to it.

Memoriale propositi

XI. Concerning Contempt and Distrust of Heretics

1. Let no heretic or one accused of heresy be received.

If, however, he was only suspected of it, he may be admitted if, cleared before the bishop, he is fit in other respects.

The Rule of 1289

2. Solicitous precautions must be taken, however, lest any heretic or one suspected of heresy, or even one of ill-repute be in any way admitted to the observance of this life.

3. And if it happen that such a one was found to have been admitted, he should be turned over to the inquisitors as quickly as possible, to be punished for heretical depravity.

Memoriale propositi	*The Rule of 1289*
	VII. On not Bearing Arms
VI: 3. Let them not take up lethal arms against anyone or carry them with themselves.	Let the brothers not carry offensive weapons with themselves, unless in defense of the Roman Church, the Christian faith, or their country, or with the permission of their ministers.

As evidenced by this comparison, the *Rule of 1289* did introduce some very significant changes. Not only were heretics treated more severely, but the penitents themselves were engaged in the struggle against heresy. Whereas the *Memoriale propositi* definitively prohibited the bearing of arms, the *Rule of 1289* greatly mitigated that prohibition. The *Later Exhortation*'s demand that the penitents live by a different wisdom, engage in a different struggle, and refuse dominion over others, had been translated into an absolute prohibition against bearing arms in the *Memoriale propositi*. However, the *Rule of 1289*, precisely through the exceptions it introduced into the prohibition against arms, drew the penitents themselves into ecclesial and political struggles.

An Appraisal of the Rule of 1289

The claim that the *Rule of 1289* is "more Franciscan" than the *Memoriale propositi* denies the subtle but critical changes introduced by the later document[184]. Admittedly, the *Supra Montem* tied together more closely two groups of followers of Francis: the penitents and the friars. However, that same document introduced a different finality for the "Franciscan Order of Penitents".

Certainly many of the virtues proposed by Francis are also embodied within the life presented in the *Rule of 1289*: simplicity, charity,

---

[184] In his analysis of the *Rule of 1289*, Pazzelli writes that the "Rule of Nicholas IV is, most of all, more « Franciscan » [than the *Memoriale propositi*] because it affirms that « the present way of life (of the penitents) had its beginning in blessed Francis »". Cf. Pazzelli, *St. Francis and the Third Order*, 151.

prayer, and fasting. The *Rule of 1289* continues Francis' exhortation to the penitents that they persevere in penance and the works of charity, that they seek reconciliation. However, the charism of penance as "the particular way of freeing oneself toward Love"[185] has here been transformed to the service of orthodoxy.

As we have seen in our analysis of the primitive Rule and the *Later Exhortation*, for Francis "doing penance" was the way and means to God.

> The spirit of love, which continuously grows in the heart of the penitent is a part of the new concept of the "life of penance" discovered by Francis. For him there is only one reality: God who loves on the one hand, and the whole world, including mankind, in a penitent stance in the face of this love - an attitude of absolute humility, of total recognition of the relationship between God the Creator and the world his creature. It is this relationship of love between God and man, between God and creation, which is for Francis the only light, the only reality, a relationship of love which only the gospel, that is, the call to *metanoia*, makes possible. This love is augmented and deepened to the measure in which we accept and respond to it, in the measure in which we put the call to conversion into practice. Francis is the man of penance in the sense that he accepted the gospel as a message to live in the world. For him, the gospel was first of all an interior state; it gave meaning to his life and it showed him the proper attitude towards life[186].

But then the Franciscan penitent lives the gospel life, not as the means to preserve orthodoxy, but as a response to the God who is Love. For Francis *facere poenitentiam* meant and implied, most of all, loving God. But that brought Francis and his followers to a different vision of reality, to a radical *metanoia*. They "left the world" in terms of its ways and wisdom and lived the ways and wisdom of God as given in Christ.

> Francis refers to the "spiritual knowledge" which the enslaved of the world so sadly lack. As some work their way into obfuscation, so others accede to clarity. The task of the movement and the function of the writings consisted in inducing spiritual knowledge. How quit the ways

---

[185] Temperini, *Penitential Spirituality*, 549.

[186] Pazzelli, *St. Francis and the Third Order*, 121.

> of social injustice and stride the roads of Jesus' struggle unless we see those roads? The writings reflected and explained the ways of wisdom. The men and women in the movement did the disciplines whereby they threw off the age's blinders and trained the inner eye to see the spirit's action in history[187].

If we admit that this radical conversion, this new way of envisioning reality and treating others, was indeed the heart of the way of penance which Francis presented in the *Earlier Exhortation* and again in the *Later Exhortation*, then the *Rule of 1289* appears, in part, to have misinterpreted the Way of Life of the Franciscan penitents.

We will turn now, in *Chapter IV*, to a study of how the Rule developed through the centuries. However, given the above analyses of these early documents and the Francis' involvement with the penitents, we are now able to address the question of Francis as "founder" of this Order of Penitents. Thus, we will here consider Francis' role as founder and then continue our discussion of the development of the Rule of the penitents.

Excursus: Francis as "Founder" of the "Third Order"

From the fourteenth century onward the Secular Franciscan Order had been referred to as the "Third Order of St. Francis", and thus, the question of Francis' role as founder, for the most part, remained moot. However, Meersseman ignited an impassioned discussion with his bold claim that Francis was not, in fact, the founder[188]. Based upon his extensive research on the documentation from the thirteenth century concerning the Order of Penance, Meersseman concluded:

---

[187] Flood, *The Commonitorium*, 3 (1980) n. 6, 22.

[188] For a brief discussion of various theories concerning Francis as "founder" of the "Third Order" and for further bibliographical references, cf. L. Iriarte, *Franciscan History: The Three Orders of St. Francis of Assisi*, translated by P. Ross, Chicago 1982, 482-84.

It is clear that in the expression, *St. Francis, founder of the order of Penance*, the words *founder* and *order* do not mean the same thing as in the expression, *St. Francis founder of the order of Minors*. Certainly St. Francis and his first companions gave a *thrust* to the order, that is, to the penitential state, among the laity. But St. Francis did not invent this state; it existed before him; he himself embraced it before founding the order of Minors. If *order* is taken to mean a structured organization, then Francis cannot be given the title of founder of the order of Penance, for no document, no narrative text written during his time describes Francis as establishing a local fraternity of Penitents or grouping fraternities into provinces giving them a written rule - which is exactly what he did for the order of Minors[189].

As we have seen in our examination of the early sources, the early narrative accounts do affirm a causal relationship between Francis and the Order of Penitents, even calling him their founder at times. However, it cannot be denied that the Order of Penance existed prior to Francis and that the *Rule of 1289* is the first pontifical document concerning a *Franciscan* Order of Penance[190]. We cannot, therefore, naïvely claim that Francis founded the Secular Franciscan Order. What then does it mean to claim that Francis is the "founder"?

Admittedly, Francis and the friars had a relationship with the penitents, however, this relationship was not one of legislative or juridical authority but of a social and spiritual nature[191]. Initially, the Visitors, Directors and Ministers were lay people. Later legislation introduced the demand that these positions be filled by priests or religious, and finally, with the *Rule of 1289*, that the religious be chosen from the Friars

---

[189] G. Meersseman, *"Introduction" to Documentation on the Order of Penance in the 13th Century*, in *Anal TOR* XVI/137 (1983) 313. While this translation of the Introduction to Meersseman's study was published in 1983, it should be noted that Meersseman first made this claim in 1961 with the publication of his research in the French volume. Cf. *Dossier*, 37.

[190] Pompei presents an extensive study of the various designations of penitential groups in the thirteenth century. He concludes that the penitential groups with names which refer to Francis or to the Friars Minor, prior to 1289, would have been interpreted as indicating groups which had a simple relationship with Franciscan spirituality. Cf. Pompei, *Terminologia*, 19.

[191] Pompei, *Terminologia*, 21-22.

Minor. Originally, the only cleric with authority over the penitents was the local bishop[192].

These facts led Héribert Roggen to conclude that, juridically, it was Pope Nicholas IV, and not Francis, who founded the Franciscan Third Order[193]. But this judgment presumes too narrow a view of the meaning of "founder"[194]. Alfonso Pompei suggests that reflecting upon the analogous situation of developing legislation within the early Christian communities offers a broader and more adequate understanding of "founder". Given the need to keep alive the novelty and originality of the message of Jesus, the early New Testament communities adopted existing forms or institutions to give concrete expression to the newness given in Christ. As Pompei correctly reminds us, in the history of the Church the element of originality is almost always channeled into existing Church structures, but with a new interior dynamism, becoming a truly "new" institution in the Church. In Pompei's view, Francis' "founding" of the Order of Penitents is much more in line with the normal course of events for the "founding" of new institutes within the Church[195].

The development of penance within the Church, as discussed in *Chapter II*, offers an analogous situation. No formal institution for the forgiveness of sins other than Baptism existed within the earliest Christian communities. Only when presented with the dilemma of people having sinned after Baptism did the leaders of those communities consider the possibility of a "second" forgiveness of sin. Yet as the canonical Order of Penance developed and later the practice of "private penance", amidst all of their innovations and adaptations, the leaders of the community understood that the forgiveness of sin, as well as their own exercise of authority over the power of sin, had come in and through Christ. Thus, the Church claimed and continues to affirm that Christ instituted

---

192 H. Roggen, *Les relations du premier Ordre franciscain avec le Tiers-Ordre au XIIIe siècle*, in *CF* 43 (1973) 202-203.

193 *Ibid.*, 201.

194 Ciurana points out that both Meersseman and Roggen understand the concept of "founder" too narrowly, that is, primarily in a juridical sense. Cf. J. Ciurana, *La Orden de Penitencia de San Francisco: notas sobre sus orígenes y desarrollo en el s. XIII*, in *Selecciones de Franciscanismo* 8 (1979) 30.

195 Pompei, *Il movimento penitenziale*, 9-10.

the sacrament of penance, though quite obviously Jesus did not establish the later juridical norms of the sacrament.

Analogously, we can agree with Meersseman that Francis did not invent the Order of Penance. Francis' initiative and originality in rediscovering the true sense of Gospel *metanoia* became channeled within the existing canonical Order of Penance. But clearly, Francis' life and preaching greatly affected his hearers and brought many of them to embrace the life of penance. In this sense and not in a juridical sense, Francis did indeed found the Secular Franciscan Order, an Order which developed progressively and only gradually became more structured and organized.

Francis founded the Franciscan Order of Penitents in the sense that he engendered a new fervor, released new energies, and empowered the work of the Spirit, which then became channeled in the existent form of voluntary penance. Francis was, therefore, the "spiritual" founder of the Order; having spread the seed of the Gospel life he let it grow and develop along its way[196]. Within this understanding of founder, we can affirm that Francis founded not *the* penitential movement but *this* penitential movement, not *the* Order of Penance but *an* Order of Penance, that which was eventually to be designated the Secular Franciscan Order[197].

As we have already noted several times, Francis' own account in his *Testament* reveals that God began this work in him. The little poor man from Assisi did not seek to found any Order; he sought God in and through the Gospel. He lived and preached penance as the Way to God, but with such intensity that his life and words held a contagion. His life and words spoke to the deep-felt needs of the people and so they sought his wisdom and guidance.

The primitive Rule represents Francis' spiritual guidance for the penitents, not juridical norms for his followers; he exhorted them not to enter some "order" but to live the gospel[198]. But as the movement grew and even flourished, there grew also the need for more structure and so legislation developed[199]. Though the hierarchical Church gave the

---

[196] Schmucki, *Il T.O.F. nelle biografie*, 136.

[197] M. D'Alatri, *Il Terzo Ordine*, in *Francesco, il francescanesimo, e la cultura della nuova Europa*, edited by I. Baldelli and A. Romanini, Firenze 1986, 122.

[198] Manselli, *Francesco d'Assisi e i Laici*, 17.

[199] Pompei, *Il movimento penitenziale*, 10-11.

Franciscan Order of Penitents its institutional structure, Francis and the early friars originally spread the seed and encouraged its growth. Francis wanted the friars to be the "salt of the earth" and to encourage people to the life of the Gospel[200]. Thus, we might say, though not with explicit intention but implicitly by his life and example, Francis, and by extension the early friars, did indeed found this Order of Penitents.

This view of Francis as founder, as the charismatic or spiritual inspiration of the Order rather than its juridical legislator, does not diminish the achievement of Francis. In a world where the laity were often neglected and deprived of the Word of God, Francis appeared as if a "leaven" to announce anew the Good News and to encourage all people to an intimacy with God through a life of penance. Francis thus rightly remains the "founder" of this Order of Penance, the Secular Franciscan Order, since he remains the inspiration to a life of penance, to a response to God's love lived as a radical *metanoia*.

---

[200] Manselli, *Francesco d'Assisi e i Laici*, 18-19.

Chapter IV

THE DEVELOPMENT OF THE RULE TO 1978

From the Rule of 1289 to the Rule of 1883

The *Rule of 1289*, promulgated by Nicholas IV for the "Brothers and Sisters of the Order of Penance founded by Francis", remained in force until 1883 when Pope Leo XIII promulgated a new Rule for that same Order (which during the intervening centuries had come to be known as the Franciscan "Third Order"). After the *Rule of 1289* had been promulgated, the Rule itself was left intact and changes or additions were made in the form of statutes or constitutions[1]. Thus, with respect to the Rule itself we could proceed directly to a consideration of the new Rule given by Leo XIII. But the changes or amendments made by some of local communities of penitents reflected their own radically altered identity. Their emphases were so different, their statutes so altered the Rule, that their Constitutions eventually gave rise to new "rules"[2]. As a result, some of these groups of lay penitents gradually evolved into separate canonical religious Orders, that is, groups of penitents who took vows of poverty, chastity and obedience.

Two tendencies within the Order of Penitents fostered this development. The emphasis on conversion led many penitents to live the eremitical life; the emphasis on communal works of charity led others to live a communal life centered around their work in hospitals and hospices. Thus, from this lay Order of Penitents there emerged groups of hermits and also groups of penitents living the communal life in an established

---

[1] Iriarte, *Franciscan History*, 498.

[2] L. Temperini, *The Rule of the Third Order Regular of Saint Francis from its Origins to the Present Day*, in *Analecta TOR* XIII/123 (1974) 73-91; esp. 84-90.

house, rather than men and women living the penitential life in their own homes and working in diverse occupations[3]. The nature of the Order itself (with its profession, distinctive garb, and ecclesiastical privileges) allowed for a natural evolution towards the formation of the "regular life" for both men's groups and women's groups. These groups came to be known as the "Third Order Regular" (that is, living according to a rule) to distinguish them from the lay penitents who were then designated as the "Third Order Secular" (that is, living outside a conventual setting).

In 1447, Pope Nicholas V ordered all hermit communities in Italy to amalgamate into one "regular" Order. This resulted in one central community of men who elected its own central government. Then in 1521, Pope Leo X adapted the *Rule of 1289* for men and women penitents living in community (the Third Order Regular group of men formed in 1447 did not, however, follow this Rule). It required the women and men to take the three canonical vows of religious life, though it did not impose the cloister on the Franciscan women religious. In 1927, Pius XI promulgated a new Rule for all Franciscan women's and men's Third Order congregations. The *Rule of 1927* remained in effect until the promulgation of the new Rule for the Third Order Regular in 1982[4].

But the focus of our study is the Rule of the Secular Franciscan Order and since the *Rule of 1289* remained in effect for the "Third Order Secular" until the new Rule promulated by Leo XIII, we turn to a consideration of that Rule, the *Rule of 1883*.

The Rule of 1883

Leo XIII and the "Third Order"

Pope Leo XIII had a great devotion to Francis[5]. He himself was a member of the Third Order Secular and had served as the Cardinal-

[3] Though the documentation is scanty, a community at Monte Casale had formed for men by 1269 and the community of St. Clare of Montefalco for women by 1274. Cf. Pazzelli, *St. Francis and the Third Order*, 152-54.

[4] P. McMullen, *The Development of the New Third Order Regular Rule*, in *Analecta TOR* XIX/143 (1987) 365-410.

[5] Leo himself speaks of his great devotion to St. Francis in the encyclical *Auspicato*. For an English translation of the text, cf. Zaremba, *Franciscan Social Reform*, 14.

Protector of the First Order. Both as bishop and later as pope, he fostered the growth of the Franciscan Third Order. Three months before he became pope, the then Cardinal Pecci, bishop of Perugia, issued his second pastoral letter on the Third Order for his diocese. In that letter the Cardinal expressed his belief that, as in the thirteenth century so in their time, God willed to use the Third Order founded by Francis "to bring back among the faithful a perfect reformation of Christian life"[6].

As pope, Leo XIII continued to promote the Third Order. In 1882, on the seventh centenary of the birth of St. Francis, Pope Leo XIII sent the encyclical *Auspicato* to all bishops of the world[7]. This encyclical, written one year before his promulgation of the new Rule for the Secular Franciscan Order, requested that the bishops encourage all Catholics to enter the "Third Order". As Leo XIII himself explained, "We published the encyclical with the sole intent and purpose, that at Our invitation as many as possible might be promptly led to aspire after the glory of Christian sanctity"[8].

In his encyclical *Auspicato*, Leo claimed that the Way of Life proposed by Francis for the laity was indeed appropriate for all Catholics in the nineteenth century. To support this thesis, Leo first sketched the evils that beset society at the beginning of the thirteenth century and then moved to a discussion of how God worked through Francis to bring people back to the life of the Gospel. Leo described the evils in terms of an unbridled desire for wealth and luxury, the oppression of the poor, the decadence of the clergy, the spread of heresy, and the divisions and conflicts which led to war. He then presented Francis as a model of the gospel response to those evils. Leo described Francis in terms of his simplicity and poverty, emphasizing Francis' identification with Christ. Thus, Leo XIII concluded, given that Francis modeled the Gospel response to the evils of the thirteenth century, that "no one

---

[6] Zaremba, *Franciscan Social Reform*, 17.

[7] For the text of the encyclical and a commentary, cf. Zaremba, *Franciscan Social Reform*, 4-93.

[8] Leo XIII made this statement, reflecting back on the encyclical he had written one year prior, in the Introduction to the *Rule of 1883* given in the apostolic constitution *Misericors Dei Filius*. For the complete text of *Misericors Dei Filius*, including the Introduction as well as the *Rule of 1883*, cf. Poppy, *Survey of a Decade*, 758-65; or Zaremba, *Franciscan Social Reform*, 94-150.

can doubt that the Franciscan institutions will be exceedingly profitable in our own age, the more so as the nature of our times seems for many reasons to be like that of those days"[9].

Leo XIII believed that the evil and ills of society would be healed by a "restoration of Christian society based on the restoration of Christian culture and intelligence"[10]. To foster a return to Christian thought, Leo XIII championed a revival of Thomistic philosophy[11]. And to promote a return to the Christian life he encouraged all Catholics to become members of the "Third Order". Of course, Leo XIII did not consider the Third Order the only means of personal and social reform. He endorsed all associations which promoted the values of Christ and the Church within society and brought, therefore, a corrective influence to society. But Leo XIII proposed the Third Order as especially advantageous because by its very nature it called its members to live the Gospel within the world, to allow the Gospel to direct all of their activities within society[12].

To his credit, Leo XIII challenged the constitution of society to the exclusion of the supernatural order[13]. But, in his attempt to rekindle the gospel within the world, in his proposal of the Third Order as the solution to social problems, and in his promulgation of a new Rule in 1883, Leo actually presented *his* interpretation of that Way of Life. Leo XIII's "promotion" of the Third Order became a "transformation" of the Order. Let us examine Leo's understanding of the Third Order and how that understanding directed his reformulation of the Rule.

In the encyclical *Auspicato*, Leo described the founding of the Third Order:

> It is incredible beyond expression, with what great enthusiasm and nigh impetuosity the multitude thronged to Francis. Wherever he appeared, they followed him in the largest crowds; often the entire citizenry of

[9] *Auspicato*, 11. Cf. Zaremba, *Franciscan Social Reform*, 78.

[10] J. Hennesey, *Leo XIII's Thomistic Revival: A Political and Philosophical Event*, in *Journal of Religion* 58 (1978) 196.

[11] This study will not pursue this aspect of Leo XIII's program. For a discussion and further bibliography, cf. Hennesey, *Leo XIII's Thomistic Revival*, 185-97.

[12] Zaremba, *Franciscan Social Reform*, 100-101.

[13] Hennesey, *Leo XIII's Thomistic Revival*, 196.

> towns and more populous cities begged in a body that they wished to be duly received to his manner of living.
>
> Wherefore the most holy man conceived the reason why he ought to found the society of the Third Order, which was to comprehend every state of life, every age, and both sexes, without breaking family or household ties. To be sure he prudently moderated it, not so much with his own rules, as with those parts of the evangelical laws which certainly do not appear as more burdensome to any Christian. For instance, they were to obey the precepts of God and Church, to refrain from factions and quarrels, to take no goods of another, not to take up arms except for religion and country, to observe moderation in food and dress, to do away with luxury, and to avoid the dangerous lure of dances and plays[14].

Obviously, Leo's description of the Third Order depends heavily upon the text of the *Rule of 1289* given by Nicholas IV[15]. But even in this brief description of the Order, Leo provides an important insight into his own understanding of the identity of the Third Order. In his claim that Francis proposed a Way of Life based only on "those parts of the evangelical laws which certainly do not appear as more burdensome to any Christian", Leo has suggested an identity for the Third Order different from its identity in the thirteenth century. Let us consider the Rule itself to examine the identity that it gives to the Order and how Francis' exhortation to a life of conversion has been translated by Leo XIII.

The Rule of 1883

Leo XIII promulgated a new Rule for the Secular Franciscans in the papal constitution *Misericors Dei Filius*, dated May 30, 1883. The introduction presents the genesis of the new Rule. It explains briefly why a new Rule was necessary:

---

[14] *Auspicato*, 8. Cf. Zaremba, *Franciscan Social Reform*, 53.

[15] This text reasserts Nicholas IV's claim that Francis "founded" the Third Order. But more significantly, the instances cited by Leo come not from the primitive Rule or even the *Memoriale propositi*, but rather, from the *Rule of 1289*. For example, Leo includes the exceptions to bearing arms that were introduced in the *Rule of 1289* within his description of the ways that Francis "prudently moderated" the gospel way of life for his lay followers.

> it is a very special function of [the Church's] motherly kindness wisely to temper her laws, as far as may be, to the changes of times and manners... the Church contrives to unite the absolute and eternal immutability of her doctrine with a prudent alternation of her disciplinary measures...
>
> It has been Our pleasure to weigh by this standard that body of Franciscans known as the Third Order Secular, to determine whether it be not time to modify its laws to some extent, on account of changed conditions...
>
> Now, the order of Saint Francis is based entirely on the observance of the precepts of Jesus Christ. The holy founder had no other object in view than that the order should be a kind of training ground for a more intensive practice of the Christian rule of life...
>
> [F]rom many quarters comes the report of a growing devotion to Francis of Assisi and of a general increase in the number of those seeking admittance into the Third Order. Wherefore, like one giving additional inducements to the errants of a race, We determined to devote Our attention to whatever might in any way hinder or retard this salutary course of sentiments. We soon understood that the rule of the Third Order which Our predecessor Nicholas IV approved and confirmed by the apostolic constitution *Supra Montem* of August 18, 1289, is not in all things suited to modern times and customs. As the obligations undertaken can not be fulfilled without excessive trouble and difficulty, it has been necessary until now to dispense at the request of the members with many points of the rule. That this can not be done without detriment to general discipline, will be readily understood...[16]

Thus, Leo modified the Rule so that people would no longer experience obstacles in being members of the Secular Franciscan Order. Leo XIII greatly simplied the regulations of the *Rule of 1289* precisely in order to make it acceptable to the greatest possible number[17]. Let

---

[16] For the full text, cf. Poppy, *Survey of a Decade*, 758-60. The introduction also explained the need "to prescribe an entirely new list of indulgences for the order, revoking and abrogating all others". But the topic of "indulgences", that is, the history and development of the indulgences connected with the Order and how Leo XIII changed them, will not be treated within this work. Our study will focus only upon how the Rule of Life changed with the constitution *Misericors Dei Filius*. For a discussion of the history and development of these indulgences, cf. Zaremba, *Franciscan Social Reform*, 136-39; 146-50.

[17] Iriarte, *Franciscan History*, 504.

us therefore turn to a consideration of the text of the *Rule of 1883* itself and how it transformed the Way of Life of the penitents.

A Comparative Study of the Rule of 1289 and the Rule of 1883

The *Rule of 1883* eliminated or greatly abbreviated many of the prescriptions of the former Rule (resulting in a text one third its size). The text of the *Rule of 1883* reduced the twenty chapters of the *Rule of 1289* to three short chapters:

I: Reception, Novitiate, and Profession
II: Rule of Life
III: Offices, Visitation, and the Rule Itself.

But while the *Rule of 1883* greatly reduced the contents of the *Rule of 1289*, it retained the structure or outline of the former Rule. The ways in which the *Rule of 1883* differs from the *Rule of 1289* can be presented quite graphically, therefore, by a parallel arrangement of the two texts. This comparative analysis, which evidences all the deletions and modifications, makes obvious how the the *Rule of 1883* has shortened the former Rule. But more importantly, this comparative analysis convincingly demonstrates how the *Rule of 1883* has transformed the very nature of the Order by minimalizing many of the prescriptions or by removing the more difficult demands within the *Rule of 1289*. Let us therefore read the *Rule of 1883* in comparison with the *Rule of 1289* (the *Rule of 1883* being given in the right column on the following pages), and then consider the results of this redactional analysis.

Rule of 1289	*Rule of 1883*
I. On the Manner of Examining Those Desirous of Entering the Order[18]	*I. Reception, Novitiate, and Profession*
We, therefore, honoring this Order with fitting favors and very readily attending its growth, decree that	

[18] The original text of the Rule given in *Supra Montem* would not have had these subdivisions and chapter titles. Cf. Temperini, *Ai fratelli e alle sorelle dell'Ordine della penitenza*, 9. These titles were added later and are retained here (as given in Zaremba) to facilitate the location of material contained within the Rule. Cf. Zaremba, *Franciscan Social Reform*, 123, note 25.

Rule of 1289	*Rule of 1883*
1. All who may happen to take upon themselves the observance of this form of life, before the undertaking or their reception, be subjected to a diligent examination on the Catholic faith and their obedience to the aforesaid Church. And if they have firmly their faith and obedience and truly believe in them, they may safely be admitted or received to it.	1. Only those may be received as members who have completed their fourteenth year[19], and are of good character, peace-loving, and above all of tried fidelity in the practice of the Catholic Faith and in loyalty to the Roman Church and the Apostolic See.
[Cf. II, 5]	2. Married women may not be received without the husband's knowledge and consent unless their confessor judges otherwise.
2. Solicitous precautions must be taken, however, lest any heretic or one suspected of heresy, or even one of ill-repute be in any way admitted to the observance of this life.	
3. And if it happen that such a one was found to have been admitted, he should be turned over to the inquisitors as quickly as possible, to be punished for heretical depravity.	
II. On the Manner of Receiving into the Order	
1. When anyone, however, wishes to enter such a fraternity, let the ministers assigned for the reception of such, diligently investigate his office, state and condition, explaining to him very clearly the duties of this fraternity and especially the restitution of goods of others[20].	

[19] Pope Leo XIII set the age limit of fourteen both to prohibit parents from inscribing their infants in the Third Order (an abuse which occurred in some areas), and also to allow youths to join since their zeal and enthusiasm could encourage the growth of the Third Order. Cf. Zaremba, *Franciscan Social Reform*, 145.

[20] Pásztor notes that this provision for restitution should be understood as "reconciliation". Cf. Pásztor, *La "Supra montem" e la cancelleria pontificia*, 78.

Rule of 1289

After this, if he so wishes, he may be clothed after the manner of the fraternity,

and let him strive to make satisfaction for the goods of others, should any be in his possession, in money or by giving a pledge of security, and let him take no less care to reconcile himself with his neighbors.

2. A year after all these things had been done, he may, on the advice of some discreet brothers, if he shall appear fit to them, be received in this manner, namely,

   that he promise to keep
   all the divine precepts,
   and also to appear when summoned
   at the will of the visitor
   to make satisfaction, as it behooves,
   for all transgressions which he might commit against this manner of life.

3. After having been made, let this promise be set down in writing there by a notary public. Let no one be received by these ministers in any other manner unless it should

Rule of 1883

3. The members shall wear the small scapular and the cord as prescribed[21]; if they do not, they deprive themselves of the rights and privileges of the Order.

4. All who enter the Order
   must pass the first year in probation;

   then they shall duly
   make their profession
   upon the Rule of the Order,
   pledging themselves to observe the
   Commandments of God and of the Church,

   and to render satisfaction
   if they have failed
   against their profession.

[21] Originally the penitents wore a poor or simple tunic, a habit which clearly distinguished them as penitents. But because many members complained about the difficulties connected with the wearing of this tunic-habit, in 1508 Julius II established the *scapular* as a special form of habit for members of the Third Order. This scapular consisted of two large pieces of cloth covering the back and chest, and tied at the waist by a cord. The advantage for many was that this "scapular-habit" could be concealed under other clothing. Over time, especially after a concession made by Clement XI in 1704, the scapular greatly decreased in size. Its present form consists of two small pieces of material hanging on tapes which do not come into contact with the cord. Cf. Iriarte, *Franciscan History*, 493-94.

Rule of 1289	*Rule of 1883*
appear otherwise to them after having discussed with solicitous consideration the condition and dignity of the person.	
4. Moreover, We ordain and decree that after entering this fraternity, no one may leave it to return to the world; he may, however, freely transfer to another approved religious order.	
5. Married women may not be admitted to membership in this fraternity without the permission and consent of their husbands.	[Cf. I, 2]

III. On the Manner of Dress

1. Let the brothers of this fraternity be clothed alike in cloth of low price and of a color neither entirely white nor entirely black, unless, for a legitimate and apparent reason the visitors, upon the advice of their ministers, have temporarily dispensed someone with regard to the price. Let the above mentioned brothers also have cloaks and furred outer garments without an opening at the neck, divided or in one piece, and not open but fastened together as becomes modesty, and let the sleeves be closed.

2. Let the sisters also wear a cloak and tunic made of the same common cloth, or at least with the cloak let them have a black or white skirt or dress or an ample robe of hemp or linen, sewn without any pleats.

3. According to the condition of each of them and the local custom, a dispensation may be granted to the sisters concerning the quality of the cloth and the furred outer garments.

Rule of 1289

4. Let the brothers and sisters, however, not use ribbons or silk cords. Let them have furs only of lambskin, purses of leather and the thongs made without any silk, and none others shall they have. Other ornaments of the world are to be set aside according to the salutary counsel of St. Peter, Prince of the Apostles (1 Peter 3:3)[22].

IV. On Avoiding Immodest Gatherings

Let attendance at unseemly banquets, or shows or public festivals and dances be absolutely forbidden to them. They should give nothing to actors or for the sake of vanity, and let them take care to prohibit that anything be given by their own family.

V. On Abstinence and Fasting

1. Let all abstain from meat on Monday, Wednesday and Saturday, unless a condition of sickness or weakness would suggest otherwise. Let meat, however, be given on three successive days to those who have been bled, and it should not be denied to those making a journey.

Rule of 1883

II. Rule of Life

1. In all things let the members of the Third Order avoid extremes of cost and style, observing the golden mean suited to each one's station in life.

2. Let them with the utmost caution keep away from dances and shows which savor of license, as well as from all forms of dissipation.

---

[22] This biblical reference adds an important emphasis. The habit did serve to distinguish the penitents from the rest of society and to express the penitents' intent to live "humility and simplicity". But this reference to 1 *Pt* 3:3 clarifies the more profound motivation for these regulations concerning the manner of dress: *Your adornment should be not an exterior one, consisting of braided hair or gold jewellery or fine clothing, but the interior disposition of the heart, consisting in the imperishable quality of a gentle and peaceful spirit, so precious in the sight of God.* Cf. Pásztor, *La "Supra montem" e la cancelleria pontificia*, 79.

Rule of 1289	*Rule of 1883*
Let the eating of meat be lawful for all when a special solemnity occurs on which all other Christians, from ancient times, are wont to eat flesh foods;	
on other days, however, when fast is not observed, eggs and cheese should not be denied. When they are with other religious in their convents they may licitly eat what is placed before them.	
They should be content with dinner and supper, unless they are weak, sick or on a journey. Let the food and drink of the healthy be moderate, for the Gospel text has: *But take heed to yourselves, lest your hearts be overburdened with self-indulgence and drunkenness* (Luke 2:34).	3. Let them be temperate in eating and drinking,
Dinner or supper should not be eaten until the Lord's Prayer has been said once; after the meal it should be repeated together with "Thanks be to God". But if it is omitted, then let three Our Fathers be said.	and devoutly say grace before and after meals.
2. Let them fast on every Friday throughout the year unless the Feast of the Nativity of our Lord fall on that day; but from the Feast of All Saints until Easter they shall fast on Wednesdays and Fridays. No less shall they observe the other fasts prescribed by the Church or imposed by the Ordinaries for common cause.	4. They shall fast on the Vigil of the Immaculate Conception and on that of St. Francis; they are to be highly commended who, according to the original Rule of the Tertiaries, also either fast on Fridays or abstain from fleshmeats on Wednesdays.
During the Lent from the Feast of Blessed Martin until Christmas and from Quinquagesima Sunday until Easter, except Sundays, they should take care to fast every day, unless perhaps sickness or another necessity suggest otherwise.	

Rule of 1289	*Rule of 1883*
3. Pregnant sisters may abstain, if they wish, from all bodily mortification, except prayer, until the day of their purification.	
Workers, on account of the demands brought on by fatigue, may licitly take food three times a day on any day they are engaged in labor from Easter until the Feast of St. Francis.	
When it happens that they are engaged in labor for others, they are allowed every day to eat of all things placed before them except on Friday or a day on which it is known that a fast for all has been instituted by the Church.	
VI. On Confession and Holy Communion	
Let each of the brothers and sisters not neglect to confess their sins and devoutly receive the Eucharist three times a year, namely, on the Feasts of the Nativity of the Lord, the Resurrection of the Lord and Pentecost, reconciling themselves with their neighbors and restoring the goods of others.	5. They shall approach the Sacraments of Penance and of the Holy Eucharist every month[23].
VII. On not Bearing Arms	
Let the brothers not carry offensive weapons with themselves, unless in defense of the Roman Church, the Christian faith, or their country, or with the permission of their ministers.	

[23] To receive Eucharist three times a year was considered pious in the thirteenth century. That no longer being the case in 1883, Leo XIII mandated more frequent reception of Eucharist. Cf. Zaremba, *Franciscan Social Reform*, 145.

Rule of 1289	*Rule of 1883*
VIII. On Prayer	
Let all say the seven canonical hours daily, namely, Matins, Prime, Terce, Sext, None, Vespers, and Compline.	
The clerics, namely, knowing the psalter, should say for Prime (Psalm 53) *Deus in nomine tuo* and (Psalm 118, verses 1-32) *Beati immaculati* up to *Legem pone*, and also the other psalms of the hours with the Glorys according to the rite of clerics.	6. Tertiaries among the clergy, since they recite the Divine Office daily, shall be under no further obligation in this regard.
However, when they do not come to church, they should strive to say the psalms for Matins which are said by the clerics or the Cathedral Church, or at least, like the illiterate others,	Lay members who recite neither the Canonical Hours, nor the Little Office of
let them not neglect to say for Matins twelve Our Fathers and Glorys, and for each other hour, seven Our Fathers and Glorys. Those who know the minor Creed and the (Psalm 50) *Miserere mei, Deus* should add it for the hours of Prime and Compline. But if they have not said them at the appointed hours let them say three Our Fathers.	the Blessed Virgin Mary, shall say daily twelve Our Fathers, Hail Marys and Glorys,
The infirm, however, unless they wish to, shall not be obliged to say these hours.	unless they are prevented by ill health.
In the Lent of Blessed Martin and also during the Greater Lent, let them see to it that they be present in their parish churches for morning hours unless they are excused by a reasonable cause.	
IX. On Making A Will	
Besides, let all who have the right by law, draw up or make a testament, and arrange	7. Let those who are entitled to make a last will and testament, do so in good time.

Rule of 1289

and dispose of their goods within the three months immediately following their admission, lest any of them die intestate[24].

[Cf. XII, 3.]

Rule of 1883

8. In their daily life let them strive to lead others by good example and to promote practices of piety and good works. Let them not allow books or publications which are a menace to virtue, to be brought into their homes, or to be read by those under their care.

X. On Maintaining Peace

Let the peace which must be made among the brothers and sisters or even among outsiders who are in dissension, be brought about as it shall seem proper to the ministers, on the advice, if possible, of the diocesan bishop in this matter.

9. Let them earnestly maintain the spirit of charity among themselves and towards others. Let them strive to heal discord wherever they can.

XI. On Conduct During Persecution

If, contrary to law, the brothers or sisters or their privileges are assailed with molestations by those having authority or the magistrates of the places where they dwell, let the ministers try to have recourse to the bishops and other local ordinaries, and proceed according to their counsel and disposition in such matters.

---

[24] The obligation to make a testament must be understood within the context of reconciliation. The testament became a concrete expression of the penitent's intention to make restitution and to live in peace with everyone. Cf. Pásztor, *La "Supra montem" e la cancelleria pontificia*, 80.

Rule of 1289	*Rule of 1883*
XII. On Taking Oaths	
1. Let all abstain from solemn oaths unless forced by necessity in the cases excepted through the indulgence of the Apostolic See, namely, for peace, faith, calumny, and affirming a testimony, and also when it shall seem expedient in a contract of buying, selling, or giving.	10. Let them never take an oath except when necessary.
2. Furthermore, in their ordinary conversation, let them avoid oaths as much as they are able, and whoever on any day carelessly swears by a slip of the tongue, as it usually happens in much talking, that evening when he must reflect on what he had done, let him say the Lord's Prayer three times for having taken such oaths carelessly.	Let them never use indecent language or vulgar jokes. Let them examine their conscience every night whether they have offended in this regard; if they have, let them repent and correct their fault.
3. And let everyone remember to encourage his own family to serve God.	
XIII. On Hearing Mass and the Monthly Meetings	
1. Let all healthy brothers and sisters of every city or locality hear Mass daily if they conveniently are able to do so, and every month let them assemble at a Church or place which the ministers have been careful to announce in order to hear Mass there.	11. Let those who can do so, attend Mass every day. Let them attend the monthly meetings called by the Prefect.
2. Let each member give a piece of the usual money to the treasurer who shall collect such money and, on the advice of the ministers, suitably divide it among the brothers and sisters oppressed by poverty, and especially among the infirm and those who are known to lack the means for a funeral service, and finally among the other poor.	12. Let them contribute according to their means to a common fund, from which the poorer members may be aided, especially in time of sickness,

Rule of 1289	*Rule of 1883*
	or provision may be made for the dignity of Divine Worship.
3. Let them also offer some of this money to the aforesaid church.	
And then, if they can do so conveniently, they should have a religious, one ably instructed in the word of God, who will earnestly exhort, admonish and arouse them to penance and the exercise of the works of mercy.	
Let everyone strive to observe silence while the Mass is being celebrated and the sermon preached, and be intent upon the prayer and office, unless the common good of the fraternity impede.	
XIV. Of Sick and Departed Members	
1. When any of the brothers happens to take ill, the ministers either themselves or through another or others, are bound, if the sick person has notified them of the illness, to visit him once a week and earnestly urge him, as they shall judge it to be of greater advantage and profit, to receive penance, and provide for the necessities of the sick person from the common fund.	
2. If the aforementioned sick person should depart from the present life, it should be announced to the brethren and sisters then present in the city or locality where he happened to die, that they might be sure to attend personally the obsequies of the deceased from which let them not depart until after the Mass has been celebrated and the body placed in the grave. We wish that this be observed also with regard to sick and deceased sisters.	14. At the funeral of a deceased member the resident and visiting Tertiaries shall assemble and say in common five decades of the Rosary for the soul of the departed.

Rule of 1289

3. Moreover, during the eight days immediately following the death of the one interred, let each of the brothers and sisters say for his soul, namely: a priest, one Mass; one who knows the psalter, fifty psalms; and the illiterate, Our Father fifty times, and let them add at the end of each the Eternal rest.

And after this, during the year they should have three Masses celebrated for the welfare of the brothers and sisters, living and dead. Let those who know the psalter say it, and the rest should not fail to say the Our Father one hundred times, adding at the end of each the Eternal rest.

XV. Of Ministers

Also let everyone on whom the ministerial or other offices mentioned in the contents of this present document are imposed, undertake them devoutly and take care to exercise faithfully. Let each office be limited to a definite period of time and let no minister be installed for life, but let his ministry extend over a definite time.

XVI. Concerning the Visitation and Correction of Delinquents

1. For these things,

let the ministers, brothers and sisters of every city and locality convene for a visitation in common at some religious place, or in a church when it happens that a place of this kind is lacking, and they should have as visitor a priest who belongs to some approved religious order and who shall impose a salutary penance on those who have committed digressions.

Rule of 1883

Moreover, let the priests at the Holy Sacrifice and the lay members, if possible, having received Holy Communion, pray with fervent charity for the eternal rest of the deceased.

III. Offices, Visitation, and the Rule Itself

1. The offices shall be conferred at a meeting of the members. The term of these offices shall be three years. Let no one without good reason refuse an office tendered him, and let no one discharge his office negligently.

2. The Visitor, who is charged with the supervision of the Order, shall diligently investigate whether the Rule is properly observed. Therefore it shall be his duty to visit the Fraternities every year, or oftener if need be, and hold a meeting, to which all the officers and members shall be summoned.

Should the Visitor

recall a member to his duty by admonition or command, or impose a salutary penance,

Rule of 1289	*Rule of 1883*
	let such member meekly accept the correction and not refuse to perform the penance.
Nor may any other perform this office of visitation for them.	
2. Because this present form of life took its origin from the aforementioned Blessed Francis, We counsel that the visitors and instructors should be taken from the Order of Friars Minor, whom the custodes or guardians of the same Order shall appoint, when they have been requested in the matter. However, We do not want a congregation of this kind to be visited by a lay person.	3. The Visitors are to be chosen from the First Franciscan Order or from the Third Order Regular, and shall be appointed by the provincial or local superiors when requested. Laymen cannot hold the office of Visitor.
3. Let such an office of visitation be exercised once a year, unless some necessity urges that it be made more often. Let the incorrigible and disobedient be forewarned three times, and if they should not try to correct themselves, then, on the counsel of the discreets, let them be totally deprived of membership in this congregation.	4. Disobedient and harmful members shall be admonished of their duty a second and a third time; if they do not submit, let them be dismissed from the Order.

XVII. On Avoiding Lawsuits

Moreover, as far as they are able, let the brothers and sisters avoid quarrels among themselves, suppressing those which might happen to arise, otherwise, let them answer to the law before one vested with judicial power.

XVIII. Concerning Dispensations

Local ordinaries or the visitor may dispense all the brothers and sisters from abstinences, fasts and other austerities, when for a legitimate cause it shall seem expedient.

Rule of 1289

XIX. On Declaration of Faults

Let the ministers denounce the manifest faults of the brothers and sisters to the visitor that they may be punished.

And if any one might be incorrigible, after a third admonition, the ministers, on the advice of some of the discreet brothers should report him to the visitor that he deprive him of membership in the fraternity. Afterwards, this fact must be made known to the congregation.

XX. Concerning the Binding Force of the Rule

Finally, We wish that none of the brothers and sisters be obliged under pain of mortal sin to all the foregoing, except where they are bound by divine precepts and statutes of the Church. However, let them promptly and humbly receive the penance imposed upon them according to the gravity of the transgression, and effectively strive to fulfill it.

[Cf. XVIII.]

Rule of 1883

5. Those who offend against any provision of this Rule, do not incur the guilt of sin unless in so doing they also transgress the Commandments of God or of the Church.

6. Should a just and serious cause prevent a member from observing any provision of the Rule, such person may be dispensed therefrom, or the regulation may be prudently commuted. For this purpose the ordinary superiors of the First and Third Order Regular, as also the aforesaid Visitors, shall have full power.

[On Indulgences[25]]

Each and all the matters, as decreed, shall stand, abide, and hold for all times; notwith-

[25] The three chapters on Indulgences have been omitted since they will not be treated within this study. For the complete text of these chapters, cf. Poppy, *Survey of a Decade*, 763-65; Zaremba, *Franciscan Social Reform*, 146-50.

Rule of 1289	*Rule of 1883*
	standing constitutions, letters apostolic, statutes, customs, privileges and other rulings of Ours or of the apostolic chancery and all else to the contrary. Let no man, therefore, act in opposition to these Our letters in any manner or particular. Should any one dare any such infringement of these letters, let him know that he will incur the wrath of Almighty God and of his Apostles Blessed Peter and Paul[26].
Given at Rietti, on the sixteenth of the calends of September,	Given in Rome, at St. Peter's, on the third of the Kalends of June, in the year of the Incarnation of Our Lord 1883
and the second year of our pontificate. [August 17, 1289].	and in the sixth year of Our pontificate. [May 30, 1883]

An Appraisal of the Rule of 1883

Quite clearly the *Rule of 1883* has greatly reduced the *Rule of 1289* in size. The lengthy descriptions concerning the manner of dress and the numerous presciptions regulating fast and abstinence have been omitted in the later Rule. The paragraphs on prayer and the treatment of the sick and departed members have been greatly condensed. But the *Rule of 1883* has also greatly reduced the *Rule of 1289* in its demands.

The introduction to the *Rule of 1883* explained that the *Rule of 1289* contained many obligations which could "not be fulfilled without excessive trouble and difficulty". The *Rule of 1883* succeeded in removing these obstacles. In place of the rigorous regulations concerning the manner of dress, fasting and abstinence, prayer, and various prohibitions, the *Rule of 1883* prescribes that the members of the Third Order need:

[26] This conclusion is not specific to the constitution *Misericors Dei Filius*. Rather, it contains the normal solemn closing used in this type of papal document. Cf. Zaremba, *Franciscan Social Reform*, 150.

— wear a small concealed scapular as a habit
— observe the commandments
— avoid extremes of cost and style
— be temperate in eating and drinking
— fast on only two extra days each year
— and minimally say daily "twelve Our Fathers, Hail Marys and Glorys".

But by removing the "difficulties", by making minimal the obligations in the *Rule of 1289*, the *Rule of 1883* has transformed the identity of the Order of Penitents as given in the *Rule of 1289*.

Leo XIII did not intend to change the nature of the Order. In promulgating the new Rule for the Third Order, Leo wrote that it should "not be thought, however, that thereby the nature of the order has been altered; for We wish it to remain altogether unchanged and intact"[27]. In the introduction to the Rule Leo stated that "the order of Saint Francis is based entirely on the observance of the precepts of Jesus Christ. The holy founder had no other object in view than that the order should be a kind of training ground for a more intensive practice of the Christian rule of life"[28]. Pope Leo XIII attempted to express that intent within his own historical situation. Indeed, the Franciscan "Third Order" flourished after the promulgation of the *Rule of 1883*[29]. Initially, Leo's particular vision of the "Way of life" did inspire; the new Rule did attract many more Christians to a lived expression of their faith[30]. However, if the *Rule of 1883* did initially empower Franciscans to social action, with the passage of time that same Rule no longer was able to inspire and empower Secular Franciscans, as evidenced by the demands for revision of Rule and Constitutions after Vatican II.

The first chapter of the new Rule indirectly expressed the identity of the Order. Those suitable to be members "are of good character, peace-loving, and above all of tried fidelity in the practice of the Catholic

---

[27] Contained within the introduction to the new Rule in *Misericors Dei Filius*. Cf. Poppy, *Survey of a Decade*, 760; or Zaremba, *Franciscan Social Reform*, 140.

[28] Poppy, *Survey of a Decade*, 759.

[29] Iriarte, *Franciscan History*, 498-510.

[30] For example, cf. F. Calley, *The Third Order of St. Francis: A Historical Essay*, Pittsbourgh 1926, 63-66.

Faith and in loyalty to the Roman Church and the Apostolic See"[31]. This emphasis on fidelilty to the faith and loyalty to the Church appears to continue the "orthodox" identity given to the penitents by the *Rule of 1289*. The penitents' profession is described as their "pledging themselves to observe the Commandments of God and of the Church"[32]. This identity, the penitents as those who observe the commandments, could imply the original identity of the penitents, that is, as those who perform penance or those who radically respond to the gospel call to conversion. But the "Way of Life" presented in the second chapter of the *Rule of 1883*, at least from a post-Vatican II perspective, does not support this interpretation. The way of life outlined in the *Rule of 1883* at least as read from a twentieth century perspective with a heigtened sense of our social responsibility, bears little resemblance to the way of penance prescribed by Francis in the *Later Exhortation*.

For Francis, the life of penance entailed an absolute commitment to peace, reconciliation, and service:

> And let us love our neighbors as ourselves.
> And if there is anyone who does not wish to love them as himself,
> at least let him do no harm to them, but rather do good...
> We must not be wise and prudent according to the flesh;
> rather, we must be simple, humble, and pure.
> And let us hold ourselves in contempt and scorn,
> since through our own fault all of us are miserable and contemptible,
> vermin and worms, as the Lord says through the prophet: *I am a worm and no man, the scorn of men and the outcast of the people.*
> We must never desire to be over others; rather we must be servants
> and subject *to every human creature for God's sake*[33].

One of the ways that the *Memoriale propositi* translated this commitment to conversion through a life of penance was the prohibition against bearing arms: "Let them not take up lethal arms against anyone or carry them with themselves"[34]. The *Rule of 1289* mitigated the absolute nature of this demand by including exceptions: "Let the brothers not carry offensive weapons with themselves, unless in defense of the Roman Church,

---

[31] *Rule of 1883*, I: 1.
[32] *Rule of 1883*, I: 4.
[33] Later Exhortation, 26, 27, 45-47.
[34] *Memoriale propositi* VI, 4.

the Christian faith, or their country, or with the permission of their ministers"[35]. But the *Rule of 1883* completely omits this prescription. The exceptions introduced by the *Rule of 1289* reflected the Order's new role in service to orthodoxy attributed to it by Nicholas IV[36]. But the Order's identity changes even more radically in the *Rule of 1883*.

The Way of Penance proposed in the *Later Exhortation*, the exhortation to a radical conversion, becomes obvious by its absence in the *Rule of 1883*. In presenting the "discipline" of penance in Chapter II, the *Rule of 1883* places upon the members who must be "peace-loving" only the demands that they:

> strive to lead others by good example and
> to promote practices of piety and good works...
> maintain the spirit of charity among themselves and towards others...
> strive to heal discord wherever they can[37].

In the pope's zeal that the members of the Order "lead others by good example", he has diluted the original call to radical *metanoia* and transformed the "Rule of Life" to the simple praxis of the faith. Admittedly, the call of the Gospel or the praxis of that faith entails a radical conversion when truly and fully accepted and lived. However, the *Rule of 1883* appears reluctant to present the radical demands of the gospel. Whereas Francis challenged people to the true spirit of penance, whereas Francis exhorted his followers to a radically different wisdom, struggle, and sense of power in response to God's love, here the *Rule of 1883* merely exhorts these same followers to the simple and "not too burdensome" praxis of Catholicism.

The dilution of the demands of the earlier Rules has drained the *Rule of 1883* of the unique spirit or contribution of Francis. The gospel life that Francis had rediscovered in all of its radicality has not been translated well in the *Rule of 1883*. In attempting to remedy the evils of secular society by calling people to live their Catholic faith, Leo has reduced the radical demands of Gospel *metanoia* announced in the *Later Exhortation* to the "practices of piety and good works". While the Way of Life in the *Rule of 1883* might have initially inspired people

---

[35] *Rule of 1289*, VII.

[36] Cf. the discussion of the *Rule of 1289* in *Chapter III*, above p. 203-210.

[37] *Rule of 1883*, II, 8-9.

to follow Francis in living the gospel in all aspects of their lives, it allowed for a more privatized interpretation. Thus, rather than preserving the Way of Life preached by Francis "altogether unchanged and intact", the *Rule of 1883* allowed for the evolution from a Franciscan Order of Penitents to a Franciscan sodality.

But the Rule was again to be reformulated to meet the "changed conditions of the times". Let us turn then to a consideration of the *Rule of 1978*, beginning with an analysis of the process which led to the promulgation of the new Rule in 1978 by Paul VI.

THE "RULE PROJECT"
THE DEVELOPMENT OF THE NEW RULE OF 1978

1965: The Beginning of the "Rule Project"[38]

The process of *aggiornamento* for the Secular Franciscan Order, a process which included the revision of the *Rule of 1883*, began officially in November 1965. In a letter addressed to the four Ministers General[39],

---

[38] The first draft of the new Rule was referred to as the "Rule Project" ("*le Projet de Règle*"). But the term "Rule Project" was also used to refer, in a general sense, to the entire process of redacting the new Rule. Cf. *COURRIER de l'Assistance Spirituelle de la Fraternité Séculière de Saint François* 3 (1968) 2.

[39] "Minister General" is the title given to the head of each of the four canonical religious Orders of Franciscan men: the Order of Friars Minor (O.F.M.), the Order of Friars Minor Capuchin (O.F.M. Cap.), the Order of Friars Minor Conventual (O.F.M. Conv.), and the Third Order Regular (T.O.R.). The term "Minister General" dates back to the time of Francis. Francis wanted the brothers to be known as the Friars Minor and each to be servant to all the others, hence a superior was not to be called "Prior" but rather "minister", a servant to the others. Cf. the *Regula bullata* VIII, and the *Regula non bullata* IV-VI, in Armstrong, *Francis and Clare*, 142; 112-14.

the then four Commissaries General[40] for the Secular Franciscans proposed the reform or revision, "*servatis de iure servandis*", of the Rule, Constitutions, and Rituals of the Secular Franciscan Order[41].

Permission was granted to the four Commissaries General to begin the prepartory work of collecting worldwide suggestions and proposals for this renewal[42]. Thus, on March 9, 1966 the Commissaries General sent a circular letter to the "Minister Provincials, the Commissary Provincials, Directors and all Tertiaries" officially announcing and inaugurating this work of re-examining and accommodating the Rule, the Constitu-

---

[40] The term or title "Commissary General" designated the friar appointed by the Minster General of each of the four branches of the Order (that is, the O.F.M.; O.F.M. Cap.; O.F.M. Conv.; and the T.O.R.) as liaison with all of the Secular Franciscans throughout the world attached to that specific obedience. Analogously, the friars appointed at the national and provincial levels to be liaison with the respective groups of Secular Franciscans were designated as "National Commissary" and "Provincial Commissary". Later, around 1970, the term "Assistant" replaced "Commissary" to designate those friars working with the Secular Franciscans. The resultant titles ("Assistant General", "National Assistant", and "Provincial Assistant") are now used consistently throughout the world.

[41] This letter is contained in the Archives of Secular Franciscan Order (hereafter *SFO Archives*), document number 65 CRE 11.25. These archives are located at the General Curia of the Order of Friars Minor, via S. Maria Mediatrice 25, 00165 Roma, Italy. Wherever possible, this study will cite the identification number of the specific archival document referenced. Unfortunately, the archives of the Secular Franciscan Order have not been well organized and most of the documents remain unnumbered. Therefore, when referencing a document which does not contain a specific identification number, this study will cite the document as "unnumbered" and give some identifying title found on its first page. It should also be noted that the Archives of the Secular Franciscan Order contain documents in various languages. Most of the documents are in either Italian, French, or Spanish; very few of the archival documents are in English. The archives do contain some translations of documents (all of the Polish, most of the German and English, and some of the Portuguese documents have been translated), but those documents have been translated into either Italian or French. Hence, unless otherwise noted, all of the translations in this section are those of the author.

[42] Each of the four Ministers General wrote a letter of permission to his respective Commissary General. *SFO Archives*: 65 CRE 12.02; 65 CRE 12.27; 65 CRE 12.29; and 66 CRE 01.23.

tions, and the Ceremonials of the Secular Franciscan Order[43]. The letter stated clearly the reason and purpose of the work: the "changed conditions of the modern world" demanded renewal, and therefore, the purpose of the "re-examination" was to make the Rule "more positive, and more evangelical and Franciscan"[44].

The letter also outlined the process to be used in the formulation of a new Rule. The Commissaries General asked the recipients to collect "observations, suggestions, wishes and desires" with respect to the renewal of the Rule, beginning with local Fraternities, synthesizing the material at the provincial and national levels, and finally sending a summary report to their respective Commissary General in Rome. But in suggesting guidelines for this process, the letter presented contradictory instructions. Methodologically, the questions for reflection conflicted with the proposed point of departure.

The letter suggested that the discussions focus upon the elements which should be included in the text of the Rule and the sources from which those elements should be derived[45]. But the Commissaries General immediately limited any discussion with the restriction that "the re-examination of the actual legislation of the Third Order of St. Francis must be rightly and duly based on the very Rule which was promulgated by Pope Leo XIII on May 30, 1883"[46]. Thus, while the Commissaries

---

[43] The Latin text may be found in *Tertius Ordo* XXVII (1966) 29-32. The archives contain copies of the official English and Italian texts. *SFO Archives*: 66 CRE 03.09.

[44] The renewal included the Rule, the Constitutions, and the Ceremonials. Therefore, the purpose of the re-examination did include two other dimensions: b) to have the Constitutions reflect the spirit of both the Rule and the decrees of the Vatican II; c) to renovate the Ceremonials (Rituals) in accordance with the spirit of the Council's Constitution on the Sacred Liturgy. *SFO Archives*: 66 CRE 03.09, page 1, item number 3.

However, the focus or concern throughout this study is the *Rule*: the origin, development and renewal of the Rule of the Secular Franciscan Order. Thus, this study will not treat the related but separate topics of the revision of the Constitutions and the renovation of the Ceremonials.

[45] Two other less significant questions were also suggested: how these elements should be divided or presented in the Rule; and the specific terminology which should be recommended for the future legislation of the Third Order of St. Francis. *SFO Archives*: 66 CRE 03.09, page 1, item number 6.

[46] *SFO Archives*: 66 CRE 03.09, page 1, item number 4.

General invited an open discussion of the sources on which to base the new Rule, they effectively closed that discussion by predetermining the base to be the *Rule of 1883*. This restriction might well have short-circuited the process of renewal at its inception. One can only wonder what the responses and ensuing developments might have been had the base of the discussions not been restricted to the *Rule of 1883*. But at the beginning of the process, unfortunately, the central players in this work of renewal did not envision and did not empower others to envision a return to one or several thirteenth century documents from the origins of the Order as the "sources" on which "rightly and duly" to base this re-examination.

1967: The Initial Responses

The responses sent to Rome were assembled, ranked, and studied by Jean François Motte, O.F.M., the assistant to the Commissary General. Motte then compiled a summary report[47]. The majority of the responses called for a complete, radical reform of the *Rule of 1883* for the reason that it did not express the Franciscan charism. They called for a Rule which would present the members of the Third Order as followers of Francis, as those called to bring a new vigor to the renewal wrought by Francis in the church and in the world, but in

[47] The documents received from various countries thoughout the world (in response to the request of March 9, 1966) were ranked from 1 to 5 to indicate the weight or importance of each response based upon the number of opinions it represented: 1. a single individual or Commissary; 2. a provincial Commissariate; 3. an individual national Commissary; 4. a national Commissariate; 5. a national interobediential meeting. According to this ranking system, documents were received (in decreasing order of importance) from the following countries: 5. France, Austria, Spain, Brazil, Australia and New Zealand; 4. Netherlands, Germany, Italy; 3. Peru, Columbia, Poland, Yugoslavia, Japan, Philippines; 2. Belgium, Canada, United States, Mexico; 1. Rhodesia, England, Ireland, Austria, Canada, Mexico.

This summary document, written in French and dated 24 October 1967, has been preserved in the *SFO Archives* (unnumbered), along with the world-wide responses in various languages which it summarizes. The summary remarks given here, unless otherwise noted, are taken from that document containing Motte's summary analysis.

a manner truly adapted to the laity. Since the responses stressed that the Rule need express both the "Franciscan" and the "Secular" nature of the Order, Motte summarized the main ideas of the documents under those two foci. In order to reflect the Franciscan charism, the responses suggested that the Rule need express the following:

— the gospel as the Rule of Life
— an attachment to the humanity of Jesus, especially his passion
— the way to the Father through Christ
— being lead to Christ through the Spirit,
the "Minister General of the Order"
— loving Christ by absolute fidelity to the Church, his spouse
— relating to all people as servant, as their brother or sister
— living with a respect for the world, a joy and freedom,
and as servant to all
— living with a sense of the sacredness of human activity,
all things, and all creation.

For the Rule to reflect adequately the "secular" nature of the Order, the responses recommended that the new Rule:

— remove traces of the monastic life
— incorporate the decrees of Vatican II, especially
Lumen Gentium, *Gaudium et Spes*, and *Apostolicam Actuositatem*
— present "profession" not as an entrance into religious life,
but as an adult renewal and confirmation
of one's Baptismal commitment
— emphasize the personal nature of the secular vocation
and the need for community
— express the totality of one's involvement and commitment.

Motte had summarized the responses received at the OFM Curia, but responses had been received at the four different obediential curias at Rome. Therefore, to move forward with the process of renewal, an interobediential meeting was scheduled at Assisi in January 1968.

The Interobediential Meeting at Assisi

The meeting took place at Saint Mary of the Angels, but with no Secular Franciscans present![48] The twelve Franciscan male religious present did address this incredible incongruity. They noted the need to have Secular Franciscans involved throughout the process, however, in lieu of hastily selecting a few Secular Franciscans who would not necessarily be representative of the larger reality, the Commissaries General had decided to analyze among themselves the documents received from Secular Franciscans throughout the world. They resolved to proceed from those documents and to involve Seculars in all subsequent phases of the process[49].

The twelve studied the documents and attempted to synthesize what the Secular Franciscans had written concerning the nature of the Order. The discussion led to an agreement on the following points as essential elements of the Secular Franciscan Order:

— an evangelical life
— in intimate union with St. Francis
— in reciprocal union with all members of the Franciscan family
— in the midst of the world and in a secular way
— with the support of a fraternity
— to which one has been called personally
— to which one has made a promise acknowledged by the church
— putting one's self "at the dispostion" of the church and the world[50].

---

[48] Each of the four Commissaries General had been invited to bring two experts to the interobediential meeting. Thus, twelve Franciscan *men*, each a member of a canonical religious Order, met at Assisi to discuss the renovation of the Rule of the *Secular* Franciscans. The four Commissaries General were: Donatus d'Orange, O.F.M. Cap. (President of the Session); David Retana, O.F.M.; Alessando Zantvoort, O.F.M. Conv.; Giuseppe Marelić T.O.R.. The following six religious had been invited: Jean-François Motte, O.F.M.; Policarpo of Iraizoz, O.F.M. Cap.; Burchard of Wolfenschiessen, O.F.M. Cap.; Gaspare Fracassi, O.F.M. Conv.; Antonio Pedrelli, O.F.M. Conv.; Eléodor Mariani, O.F.M.; Jorge Perell Frontera, T.O.R.; and Hermes Peeters, O.F.M. (Secretary of the Session). *SFO Archives*: "Annexed Document III" offers a summary of the content of this interobediential session in *Courrier* 1 (Jan 1968) 7ff.

[49] *SFO Archives*: *Annexed Document III* offers a summary of the content of this interobediential session in *Courrier* 1 (Jan 1968) 8.

[50] *SFO Archives*: 1968 CRE 01.00, 2-3.

They agreed that the Rule should contain three parts (which parallel the three chapters in the *Rule of 1883*) and therefore formed three committees to work on the different sections:

I: Nature and Purpose of the Third Order
II: Norm of Life of the Secular Franciscans
III: Essential points of its organization[51].

Subsequent monthly meetings followed. The work of the three subcommittees was discussed and reworked by the whole committee. The resulting text, a "First Draft" of the new Rule for the Secular Franciscan Order, was sent in July 1968 to "Tertiaries and their Directors" throughout the world for consideration and comment[52].

The vast majority of the responses to this "First Draft" expressed negative views ranging from disappointment to complete rejection of the Project[53]. Since the responses also called for greater participation by

---

[51] Also, it was decided to create an Interobediential Secretariate where copies of all the documents sent to the four jurisdictions would be kept. Further, they agreed to broaden the respresentation on this Interobediential Secretariate by including two Secular Franciscans from each of the four jurisdictions. The hope was to chose eight Secular Franciscans from different nationalities residing at Rome to ensure broad representation as well as accessibillity for ongoing discussion at further meetings. The Secular Franciscans chosen were: Fausta Casolini, Anna Cesari, Lucia Mattei, Vincent McAloon, Augusto Natali, Lidia Pedroli, Riccardo Ricci, and Stefano Ricciardi. *SFO Archives*: 68 CRE 03.23.

[52] *Franciscan Herald* 47 (1968) 333. For the actual text of this "First Draft", cf. pp. 334-43.

[53] Among the numerous responses received, two representive critiques are presented here to demonstrate the negative reception of the 1968 draft. The response from an interobediential national French meeting reads in part: "Malgré ces aspects positifs, nous contestons le projet dans son ensemble, au point que une refonte complète nous apparaitrait nécessaire". *SFO Archives*: 68 CRE 07.21, page 1; for a summary statement of the French position, cf. P. Marquard, "The Draft of the New Rule", *Franciscan Herald* 48 (1969) 17-18. José Agustín Eleustondo, the National Commissary for Spain, unabashedly expresses his rejection of the project: "He terminado ahora mismo mi 'PASSIO': la traducción del Proyecto de la nueva Regla. Catastrofe! Estoy airado y muy triste. ESTO NO PUEDE SER. NO PUEDE SER. No somos unos niños, para que una Comisión MUNDIAL nos envíe este Proyecto de Regla. En la octava página de este PROYECTO CATASTROFICO falta una línea. Sería ésta ESCRITO EN EL ANO 1850. Antes de Léon XIII"! *SFO Archives*: 68 CRE 08.08, p. 1.

Secular Franciscans themselves in the whole project of renewal, the four Commissaries General decided to convoke an International Interobediential Congress of Secular Franciscans at Assisi the week of September 27 to October 3, 1969[54].

1969: The Assisi Congress

The Congress was to focus upon the revision of the Rule according to the responses received from around the world to the "First Draft". However, given the difficulty of working from the diverse documents, the Congress focused instead on developing guidelines for the future Rule, that is, on defining the essential elements of the Secular Franciscan life[55]. A president and two moderators were elected to serve, together with the general secretary, as the "Praesidium", or leaders of the Congress[56]. Three committees and five language groups were formed to facilitate the work of the Congress. The three committees were assigned different aspects of the project:

I: The Secular Franciscan Order and its characteristics in the world today
II: The essential elements of a Franciscan spirituality for the laity
III: The fundamental laws of government of the Order[57].

The individual committees concretized their ideas, suggestions, and recommendations in written statements which were then studied within each of the five language groups: English, French, German, Italian, and

---

[54] Archival letter with the title "Third Order Intercom", n. 2, 1969. *SFO Archives*: unnumbered document. The dates proposed in the original letter were October 5-11, however, in January 1969 the scheduled dates were moved to one week earlier.

[55] In a sixteen page document presented at the opening of the Congress, David Retana explained the difficulty of working from the responses and counter-Projects received and suggested an alternative method. *SFO Archives*: 69 CRE 09.27.

[56] President: Jan van der Putten (Holland); Moderators: Pomena Pefanis (Canada), and Abbot Pierre Souche (France); and General Secretary of the Congress: David Retana, O.F.M. (Mexico).

[57] *SFO Archives*: notes from the secretary of the Congress, unnumbered document.

Spanish. Finally, these statements were presented as "motions" to be discussed and voted upon by the entire assembly of delegates.

The International Congress at Assisi produced 25 motions[58]. Several of those motions, especially motion 9, guided the rest of the redactional process for the new Rule. Let us review the motions which played critically in the later development of the Rule. Two different motions defining the nature of the Order were passed by the delegates:

> 2. The Secular Franciscan Order is an institution formed by Christians who, by their vocation in the world and in the womb of the Church, are committed to living the gospel modeling themselves on the spirit of St. Francis. As the People of God on the way to the Father, [they live] in vital reciprocal exchange with all the Franciscan families, in community, according to a Rule approved by the Church[59].
>
> 3. The Secular Franciscan Order, a cell of the Church, the People of God on pilgrimage to the Father, is a community of brothers and sisters in a vital reciprocity with other branches of the Franciscan family. It brings together those Christians who are committed, by their vocation and according to a Rule approved by the Church, to live the Gospel in the secular world according to the spirit of St. Francis[60].

These two motions which defined the nature of the Order, briefly summarized, present the Secular Franciscan Order as:

(1) a community of brothers and sisters
(2) on pilgrimage to God
(3) committed to living the Gospel
(4) following the spirit of St. Francis
(5) according to a Rule and as seculars
(6) in communion with all Franciscans.

---

[58] The motions were presented and are recorded in the documentation in the original languages in which they were proposed. All 25 motions may be found in *Lettre aux Assistents* 1 (Oct 1969) 1-7; and also in *Tertius Ordo* (Dec 1969): 178ff.

[59] Commission I presented this motion.

[60] This motion was presented by the French language group.

The second commission, which dealt with the "Way of Life" of the Secular Franciscan Order, produced the famous "motion 9" which listed seventeen essential elements of the spirituality of the Order:

1. to live the gospel according to the spirit of St. Francis
2. to be converted continually (*metanoia*)
3. to live as a brother or sister of all people and of all creation
4. to live in communion with Christ
5. to follow the poor and crucified Christ
6. to share in the life and mission of the Church
7. to share in the love of the Father
8. to be instruments of peace
9. to have a life of prayer that is personal, communal and liturgical
10. to live in joy
11. to have a spirituality of a secular character
12. to be pilgrims on the way toward the Father
13. to participate in the Apostolate of the Laity
14. to be at the service of the less fortunate
15. to be loyal to the church in an attitude of dialogue and collaboration with her ministers
16. to be open to the action of the Spirit
17. to live in simplicity, humility, and minority[61].

These seventeen elements reaffirm and further specify the nature of the Order as defined in motions 2 and 3. In fact, the six defining characteristics of the Order (given above as the summary synthesis of the definitions contained in motions 2 and 3) offer a convenient way to summarize the seventeen points proposed as essential elements of the Secular Franciscans' Way of Life. The relatedness of those seventeen elements prohibits identifying each individual element with only one of the six defining characteristics of the Order, however, all seventeen are contained within those six[62]:

---

[61] For a discussion of these elements relative to the earlier Rules of the Secular Franciscan Order, cf. M. Habig, *Essential Elements of the Third Order Rule*, in *Franciscan Herald* 52 (1973) 42-48.

[62] The order of those six defining characteristics has been rearranged to provide a more logical presentation.

1. *To Live the Gospel* (1, 4, 5, 14)[63]
2. *Following Francis* (1, 3, 4, 5, 8, 10, 15, 17)
3. *Through Conversion / METANOIA* (2, 4, 5, 7, 9, 12, 16)
4. *In Community* (3, 4, 6, 7, 9, 13, 15)
5. *As Seculars* (3, 6, 8, 11, 13, 14)
6. *In Vital Reciprocity with All Franciscans* (3, 6,)

These six characteristics, which include the seventeen essential elements, will provide a more manageable tool for examining later redactions of the Rule since those redactions all depend upon these Assisi motions.

Commission III, which dealt with the government of the Secular Franciscan Order, produced, among others, the following motions:

13. There is only one Secular Franciscan Order. It must tend toward a unity of structures, but it must respect the concrete expressions in different times and places.

14. The Secular Franciscan Order is a fraternity and an institution which is regulated by its own government. It must assume full responsibility for its rights and obligations. This should be translated concretely into the structures and praxis of the Fraternity: substituting relationships of communion for those of hierarchical dependence as much as possible with the whole Franciscan family and according to the norms of the Church.

The Congress had accomplished the first part of its goal. The delegates had formulated guidelines, the "Assisi Motions", to direct future work on the new Rule. But since the Congress could not possibly produce a new Rule given the time constraints, the delegates voted that the work be continued by a commission consisting of the Praesidium, the Presidents of the Linguistic Groups[64], and the General Secretary

---

[63] The numbers given within parentheses indicate which of the 17 essential elements (as listed in Motion 9 of the Assisi Congress) correspond to each of the six characteristics of the nature of the Order.

[64] The presidents of the five language groups were, for English: Waldemar Roebuck (USA); French: Max Dravet (France); German: Annelies Kammenhuber (Germany); Italian: Augusto Natali (Italy); Spanish: Fernando de Trazegnies (Peru).

of the Congress, working in conjunction with the four Commissaries General[65].

1970-1975: From the Assisi Congress to a Rule

After the Congress Jan Van der Putten, the president of the Praesidium, outlined a procedure and schedule for completing the new schema of the Rule and for the constitution of an International Interobediential Council[66]. He projected the completion of the new draft of the Rule by October 1970 so that it could be sent before Christmas to all countries. Another international Congress would then follow on Pentecost 1971 when the Rule could be finalized and thus published on October 4, 1971. However, the work did not progress as rapidly as he had planned.

The Praesidium and not the entire commission worked on a new draft of the Rule. But the work progressed so slowly that by July 1972 the Praesidium and the Commission were restructured[67]. The Praesidi-

[65] Cf. motions 21 and 22. Besides commissioning this group to pursue the elaboration of the new Rule, the delegates also charged them with the task of inaugurating an International Interobediential Council for the Secular Franciscan Order. Cf. motion 19, developed by the Commissaries General. Further, the delegates voted that a common base text as a Rule for all countries be established in Latin, with each cultural area developing specific applications which would then be approved by their national interobediential authority. Cf. motion 24, developed by the French and Spanish Language Groups.

[66] *SFO Archives*: 69 CRE 12.13.

[67] It should be noted that the actual working committee changed through time. Leon Bédrune had replaced David Retana, the secretary of the Congress. Further, the Assistants General (the designation "Commissary General" had been changed to "Assistant General") had moved to enlarge the Rule Committee, however, this proposal was not accepted. Rather, the Praesidium, who had been commissioned by the Assisi Congress to direct the revision of the Rule, continued to direct the project. However, at the urging of the General Assistants, Manuela Mattioli (Venezuela), who was serving as interim head of the newly formed international interobediential Council, was added to the Rule Committee. *SFO Archives*: *Report on the Assisi Congresses, July 1972* by P. Pefanis, dated July 30, 1972, unnumbered document.

In order to make the Committee more efficient, it was suggested that competent members, one from each of the linguistic groups, should be added to

um had worked for two years to arrive at the "Basic Text". A third draft of that Basic Text was reviewed by the five member Praesidium in 1973[68], and finally in March 1974 a fourth draft was completed and sent to the International Commission[69].

The seventeen member International Commission then studied that draft and sent their comments to the committee at Rome[70]. They had been asked to indicate four things in their responses: elements which were lacking, points which should be emphasized, things which should be omitted, and the order in which the elements contained in the "Norm of Life" should be placed[71]. Based upon the suggestions made by members of the International Commission, the Praesidium once again redacted the text. They produced a new draft of the Rule and on April

---

the wider Commission. Several other members had already been added to make the Committee more representative: Bianca Maria Ventura (Italy), as youth representative; Simon Kafeschi (Zambia), as representative of the Conventual jurisdiction; and Nicolàs Dameto Squella (Spain), as representative of the T.O.R. jurisdiction. *SFO Archives*: Letter to all members of the Rule Commission, dated 29 May 1972, unnumbered document.

[68] This third draft, largely the work of Fr. Souche but with the cooperation of Bédrune and Van der Putten, was sent to Pefanis and Mattioli on April 18, 1973. This text was redacted based upon the critiques received from the latter two members. Cf. M. Mattioli, *Estado actual de los Trabajos de la Nueva Regla de la Tercera Orden Franciscana*, in *Tertius Ordo* 35 (1974) 129-34; and Pefanis' letter to P. Souche dated 29 October 1973, *SFO Archives*: unnumbered document.

[69] Since the Assisi Congress had passed a motion that the Rule be given in Latin, Bédrune explained in his cover letter that the final redaction of the Rule would be done in Latin. However, the working language of the Praesidium was French and therefore both the 1974 and 1975 Redactions were given in French. Bédrune's cover letter also contained a brief commentary on some of the passages. Relevant comments will therefore be added in footnotes to the text. Cf. *AG Archives*: 73 REI 08.31.

[70] At that time the international Commission was composed of 17 members (of whom only 3 were women), representing 11 different countries and including one representative for youth.

[71] These instructions were included within the cover letter sent by Léon Bédrune to all members of the International Commission. Cf. unnumbered letter contained within the archives of the *Italian National Commissariate*, viale delle Mura Aurelie, Roma.

30, 1975 sent that text to National Councils of the Secular Franciscan Order throughout the world for study and comment[72].

Our study of the redactional process will focus upon the resultant texts themselves. We will not attempt to analyze all of the observations received. The volume of comments and suggestions in response to the *1974 Basic Text* does not permit a brief synthesis[73]. An extensive summary (though of questionable value) would be possible, but no adequate synthesis can be offered given the diversity of those responses[74]. We will, therefore, analyze the texts themselves and only consider those specific observations which emerge as relevant to our analysis. Given that the *1974 Basic Text* provided the basis from which evolved all of the later redactions, we will first analyze that text to identify the spirituality it contains. We will then turn to an analysis of the *1975 Redaction*, and subsequently to an examination of later redactions, to determine how that spirituality evolved.

---

[72] Relevant explanatory notes from the cover letter by Bédrune will be included in footnotes to the *1975 Text*. Cf. *AG Archives*: 75 REI 04.30.

[73] The responses, when collated according to specific paragraphs of the Rule, resulted in eighty typewritten pages of commentary. These collated responses are contained within the document entitled *OBSERVATIONS GENERALES sur le Projet de Règle présenté par le Praesidium en Mars 1974*. Cf. *AG Archives*: 74 REI 03.20.

[74] For example, even with respect to an overall appraisal of the Rule, the responses include much diversity. Some of the positive assessments include: "Condividiamo il piano generale, il tono ispirazionale e lo stile". "[J]e n'ai rien à ajouter... Ce texte de base me semble parfait". "Circa il Prologo e la Forma Vitae dei Terziari, mi pare che ci sia poco o nulla da dire. Si tratta di elementi ed esortazioni di carattere spirituale, che riflettono abbastanza il carisma e lo spirito francescano". "La formulation spirituelle y a étée élaborée soigneusement. Certainement ce texte de base constituera un document précieux pour ceux qui voudrons enrichir les âmes des engagés à tous les niveaux..." Cf. *AG Archives*: 74 REI 03.20, pages 1, 2, 3, 5, respectively.

Some of the negative overall assessments include: "El contexto de este proyecto de REGLA es poco seglar". [Il texte] "reste désincarné et peu spécifique d'une règle pour un ordre ou une fraternité séculière. Il a encore souvent une tonalité piétiste". "Le commentaire universelle était que le texte est trop longue. Quelqu'un a remarqué que les tertiaires devront avoir un doctorate en Théologie pour comprendre ce texte". "Il decreto denuncia mentalità e stile clericale, piuttosto che apparire di Laici per Laici". Cf. *AG Archives*: 74 REI 03.20, pages 2, 6, 9, 12, respectively.

An Analysis of the 1974 Basic Text

The *1974 Basic Text* developed by the Praesidium contained three parts: the *Prologue*, the *Norms of Life*, and the *Fraternity*"[75]. In a cover letter sent with the text to the members of the International Commission, those who formulated the text offered a brief explanation of the purpose and content of these three parts[76]. In the Prologue, the redactors intended to set forth a Franciscan cristocentrism and to indicate the place of the Franciscan family within the Church as a whole and then the place of the Secular Franciscan Order within that Franciscan family. However, they attempted to limit the Prologue to the essentials, given that the Rule would eventually be promulgated within an "Apostolic Constitution" which would also provide the ecclesial context of the Rule.

In Chapter II, the redactors attempted to express the "Way of Life" given in the seventeen essential elements from the Assisi Congress (though they combined and rearranged some of the elements). In each of the nine paragraphs within Chapter II they chose to present a theological foundation for the "concrete but general attitude" it contained, leaving the specific application of each to the Constitutions.

Finally, in Chapter III the redactors sought to provide an "inspirational" base for the government of the Secular Franciscan Order. They intentionally avoided any specific mention of the Order's structure (for example, requirements for entry into the Order, profession, elections, offices, frequency of meetings), suggesting that these norms should be specified within the Constitutions rather than the Rule.

The Praesidium intended to follow the guidelines developed by the Assisi Congress. They attempted to write a Rule which reflected both the nature of Secular Franciscan Order and the essential elements of its "Way of Life" as expressed in the Assisi Motions. A cursory overview of the paragraphs contained within the *1974 Basic Text* confirms that the Rule presented by the Praesidium does indeed contain all of the elements listed by the Assisi Congress:

---

[75] The English translation of the *1974 Basic Text* is given below in the left column of the comparative analysis beginning on page 259. The original French text has been included in *Appendix III*, pp. 389-397.

[76] *AG Archives*: 73 REI 08.31.

I: Prologue

1. [God is Love]
2. In the Family of Saint Francis and the Fraternity

Chapter II: "Norm of life"

3. To live the Gospel of Christ
4. On the Path of Continual Conversion
5. With the Poor Christ
6. Brothers and Sisters to All
7. Living Members of the Church
8. Praying with Christ and the Church
9. With the Virgin Mary
10. Bearers of Peace
11. Living in the Father's Love

Chapter III: Fraternity

12. Cell of the Church
13. A Living organism
14. [Stages of Formation and Profession]
15. Fraternal Life Within the local Fraternity
16. [Communion with the Entire Franciscan Family]
17. To Live the Evangelical Life in Fraternal Unity

The Prologue presents the trinitarian expression of God's love: the Father so loved the world that he sent his Son through whom the Spirit is given. Through Christ and in the Spirit, God has called the Church to continue the work of Christ and, more particularly, God has called Secular Franciscans to that work in the spirit of Francis. Chapter II then specifies the manner of life for those followers of Francis: to translate the Gospel into life, to die to self and to embrace the cross, to participate in the mission of the Church by working for justice and peace for all people, and to embrace a life of community and prayer. Chapter III then briefly suggests the main elements which support that life of prayer, community, and service by describing the local Fraternity as a community within the Church and in "vital reciprocity" with other Franciscan groups.

The *1974 Basic Text* attempted to present the spirituality of the Secular Franciscans as outlined by the Assisi Congress:

1. To Live the Gospel
2. Following Francis
3. Through Conversion / *Metanoia*
4. In Community
5. As Seculars
6. In Life-giving Union with All Franciscans

The text does present the gospel life in the manner of Francis with a strong emphasis on conversion. The text articulates quite strongly and in concrete terms the role of the Secular Franciscan in the promotion of justice and the work of peace. But the *1974 Basic Text* does not consistently present a "secular" spirituality or emphasize the aspect of community. The text uses the term "secular" and speaks of the laity, their familial lives, and their concrete involvement in building up the Kingdom of God within society[77]. But other than the mention of "seculars" and the "laity", the *1974 Basic Text* contains little that would not also be appropriate within a rule for a canonical religious Franciscan group.

The 1975 Redaction

The members of the International Commission most strongly criticized the *1974 Basic Text* for its failure to present adequately a specifically "secular" spirituality. Thus, in the *1975 Redaction* (which, for the most part, followed the outline of the *1974 Basic Text*) a paragraph was added which addressed the nature of the Order as secular. Paragraph 9, "In the Midst of the World", reads in part:

> As seculars, we have our own vocation: living in the midst of the world, engaged in various duties and works of the world, it is our duty to enlighten and to direct all temporal realities to which we are closely united, in such a way that they may work and prosper constantly according to Christ and may be to the glory of the Creator and Redeemer... By our witness and our action, joined with that of other men and women, we will work in these different sectors towards the realization of the plan of God for the world.

---

[77] Cf. paragraphs 1, 2, 3, 5, 6, 8, and 10.

This later text does state more explicitly the Secular Franciscans' involvement in temporal realities. But the *1975 Redaction* appears to weaken that very involvement which it proclaims in the ways that it has redacted other paragraphs of the *1974 Basic Text.* For example, in speaking of the Secular Franciscans as "Bearers of Peace", the very strong and challenging demand for concrete action given within the earlier text has been changed to the choice of an "attitude" in the later version[78]. The *1974 Basic Text* reads:

> We always look for what unites,
> working with others to find solutions
> to conflicts which touch our neighbor,
> declaring ourselves against war in all its forms,
> refusing all participation in the arms race
> and in every antagonism
> between human beings and between peoples.

The *1975 Redaction* has changed this paragraph to read:

> Following the Church and with all people of good will,
> we chose an attitude of peace and of opposition
> to all that leads to violence and prepares for war.

Thus, while the *1975 Redaction* rightfully acknowledges and appropriately stresses the secular nature of the Secular Franciscans' vocation, it fails, at least in part, to present the concrete involvement in social and political spheres which it proclaims as the vocation of the Secular Franciscans. Let us turn to the texts themselves which are given below in parallel columns in order to provide a comparative analysis of the two versions. The left column contains an English translation of the *1974 Basic Text* and the right column contains the *1975 Redaction*[79]. The parallel arrangement evidences how the *1974 Basic Text* was redacted based upon the suggestions of the International Commission.

---

[78] For the full text, cf. paragraph 10 in both the *1974 Basic Text* and the *1975 Redaction*, given below in the comparative analysis, 271-272.

[79] The English translations by the author are intentionally somewhat literal in order to present more clearly the relationships between the two French texts. The original texts in French are given in *Appendix III*, pp. 389-406.

1974 Basic Text

I: Prologue

1. God so loved the world
that he gave his only Son:
the image of the Invisible God, the first born of all creation.

In Him and for him,
as all things, we have been created.
In Him
we have been chosen by the Father,
from before the creation of the world,
to be holy and blameless before him
in love.
It is in Him that,
after having heard the Word of truth,
the Good News of our salvation
and having believed it,
we have been stamped with
the seal of the Spirit of the Promise.

Thus, he is our way
to the Father.

In the Father, he wishes to gather us into the Church with all people, our brothers and sisters, to be his holy People, making us participate in his priestly, prophetic and royal functions. A new human being, he made us a new creature for the New Creation which he came to inaugurate by his birth and which he sealed in his death and his Resurrection.

1975 Redaction

Prologue

1. *God is love*: He so loved the world
that he sent his only Son

so that, led and gathered in the community of the Church by the Holy Spirit, we may participate in the very life of the Trinity.

In Him, through Him and for Him,
we have been chosen
from before the creation of the world
to be holy and blameless before him.

After having heard
the Good News of salvation
and having believed it,
we have received from Christ
the seal of the Spirit
by which God established an eternal alliance
with his People whom he calls to be
the witness of his love.
Christ is our way; it is by him alone
that we have access to the Father;
he is the light which illumines every person
on the way to the Father.

1974 Basic Text	*1975 Redaction*
	He is the truth, into which the Holy Spirit leads us ever more.
He is our eternal Life. Each day uniting us in his saving Love, he puts us in communion with all human beings and makes of each of us their brother or sister.	He is the life which he came to give in abundance to all human beings.
He invites us to continue his work of the Redemption and of the transformation of the world and of humanity	He calls us as Church to restore all things in Him, to help all human beings and creation to reach their fullness in Him, and so to continue his work of salvation,
which he himself will complete at the time of his triumphant Return.	which he himself will come to crown on the day of his triumphant return.
And so after him, we will rise as a new humanity for a new heavens and a new earth to the eternal glory of the Father.	
	Chapter I:
2. In the Family of St. Francis and the Fraternity:	*2. The Franciscan Family*:
So that we may participate better as Church in the loving design of the Father for the world,	To make the Church and her members participate better in this loving design of the Father for the world, and to represent all the richness of the person of Christ and of his Gospel,
Christ has gathered us into the Franciscan Family; as the other	the Spirit has raised up
spiritual Families, is a grace from the Lord to his People, and a manifestation of the diversity of the gifts of the Spirit. After St. Francis, Christ has called us to discover and to live the Gospel in his way and according to his spirit.	spiritual Families which are a grace of the Lord for his People and a manifestation of the diversity of his gifts. With respect to us, He calls us to become members of that [family] of Saint

1974 Basic Text	*1975 Redaction*
	Francis. The living image of Christ, Francis received the mission of restoring the Church by making the Gospel flourish again. The Lord gave him disciples and it was in communion with brothers that he was invited to live the Gospel; so it was together that they accomplished their salvation.
All those who gather in this way (priests, religious, laity) constitute his Family.	
At the heart of this unique Family, the different branches	And so, the three branches or orders, with the other institutes which form the Franciscan family, live the same charism, each with its own vocation,
are "in vital reciprocity".	and in vital reciprocity.
The Secular branch organized in FRATERNITY, gathers us as brothers and sisters so that we may walk together towards the Lord in living the Gospel.	The Order of Secular Franciscans (OSF or TOF), or the Secular Fraternity of St. Francis, is a community of fraternities, composed of christians who, impelled by the Spirit, commit themselves by a profession to live the Gospel *in and through their secular state*[80],
To guide our journey it gives us a "Form of life" inspired by that of brother Francis, approved by the Church, and which we take upon ourselves to live.	according to a "Form of life" (Rule) inspired by the spirit of St. Francis and approved by the Church.
	To this end it [the Secular Franciscan Order] benefits from the spiritual assistance and the duties of the First Order in its regard. *This "Form of life", with its organization and the involvement of its members in the world, consecrates its secular character.*

[80] Emphasis added by the author. This phrase and other parts of the *1975 Redaction* have been placed in *italics* in order to emphasize the additions within the text which attempt to express more specifically a *secular* spirituality.

1974 Basic Text	*1975 Redaction*
Day after day, through it and in it, we commit ourselves together in fraternal charity to follow Christ who is the Way, the Truth and the Life.	It is in Fraternity[81] and in mutual help that we live this Franciscan evangelical "Form of life".
	Indeed, it is not in isolation but in a gathering that the history of our salvation in the church is realized. It is to a people, a community, that God has given his Covenant. It is in community that the disciples of Jesus are called to live with Him and to witness as Church.
II: *Norm of life*	II: *Form of Life*[82]
3. *To live the Gospel of Christ*:	3. *To Live the Gospel*:
The Community of the Christ's Faithful has transmitted to us the Good News of the Lord Jesus.	The Gospel, transmitted
	by the living tradition of the Church, reveals the fullness of
It revealed to us the realization of the mystery hidden for centuries: the coming of the Word, the living Christ.	God's Word to us:
Such is still the message to announce in order to make all human beings perfect in Christ. Indeed, the Gospel entrusts to us the footprints	
of Christ whom we must follow. And the Lord himself revealed to Francis that he was lo live according to the form of the holy Gospel.	Christ Jesus whom we are called to follow. The Lord himself revealed to Francis that He was calling him "to live according to the form of the holy Gospel".

[81] The *1975 Redaction* placed this phrase, *c'est en Fraternité*, in the first chapter to emphasize the community aspect which St. Francis wished for all these groups. Cf. *AG Archives*: 75 REI 04.30.

[82] In both the *1974 Basic Text* and the *1975 Redaction*, each of the articles in *Chapter II* consists of two parts: first the "inspirational-doctrinal" aspects and then the life attitudes which follow from these. In the *1975 Redaction*, the future tense was chosen to indicate process, that is, *ongoing* renewal. Cf. *AG Archives*: 75 REI 04.30.

1974 Basic Text	*1975 Redaction*
He also tells us to hold on to the words, the life, the doctrine, and the holy Gospel of the One who had deigned to make known to us the name of the Father. We wish to draw the inspiration for our life from the Gospel and thus to become, as he asked us, witnesses of Christ.	And Francis taught his brothers to guard faithfully the words, the life, the doctrine and the holy Gospel of the One who had deigned to make known the name of the Father.
We will make it our foundational text in order to grow in knowledge of and intimacy with the Lord,	In the Gospel and in all of Scripture we seek first the living Person of Christ. Personally and in Fraternity, we meditate on it in order there to discover his Face.
to illumine our personal and familial lives and all our human relationships, confronting our concerns, our reactions, and our attitudes with the Gospel.	We draw inspiration from it for our attitudes, our judgments, and our actions in order to conform our life (familial, *social, civil*) to his. To live the Gospel today, is to actualize it under the inspiration of the Spirit, in a pursuit within the Church and in an attention to the signs of the times.
Untiringly, we will go from the Gospel to life and from life to the Gospel, thus we make Christ the center of our life.	And so, in all circumstances, we will go from the Gospel to life and from life to the Gospel.
4. *On the Path of Continual Conversion*:	4. *Conversion*:
The response to this evangelical life involves us on a path of continual conversion. It leads us to a total transformation, to a "new life" of which Baptism is the source: to die to ourselves in order to live for God in Christ. Like Francis, we hear the call which the crucified Jesus addresses to us	The response to this call involves us in a path of total transformation for a "new life", of which Baptism is the source: to die to sin in order to live for God in Christ. Francis responded generously to the call of Jesus crucified.

1974 Basic Text	*1975 Redaction*
and which he made the condition for following him: "If anyone wants to come after me, let him take up his cross", knowing well that the passage through the Cross issues, even here below, in the joy of the resurrection.	But he also experienced that the way of the Cross leads, even here below, to Easter joy.
We accept the radical exigencies of this work of death and resurrection daily:	We accept the radical exigencies of this daily work of death and life, the personal and communal
change of mentality, uprooting of egoism,	uprooting of egoism, the purification of our intentions, the involvement in an attitude of human solidarity,
of attention to others,	of attention to others, and of continual reorientation towards God. And with our brothers and sisters, mutually we will help each other to it.
In joy we travel this penitential way which, with the Liturgy, we punctuate by the celebration of the Mysteries of Christ.	In joy, we will travel this penitential way, with particular effort during those times recommended by the Church In spite of these efforts to welcome God and to open ourselves to our brothers and sisters, we experience our misery.
The Sacrament of Penance is the privileged sign of this continual conversion	The Sacrament of Penance is the means and the privileged sign of this continual striving for conversion and reconciliation.
and, for us, the Fraternity [is] a means.	
From the fatigues of our work, of our apostolic action, of our continual efforts at conversion, of our trials, of our disinterested service, as well as of our poverty, we choose [as] our preferred penance that which puts us in communion with the cross of Christ.	
We do not forget the practices which the tradition of the Church recommends to us at certain times, which St. Francis practiced so generously, and for which the Constitutions of the Fraternity will provide practical application.	

1974 Basic Text	*1975 Redaction*
5. *With the Poor Christ*:	5. *With the Poor and Crucified Christ*:
Christ and his Church call us to live the Beatitudes, the source of the fraternal life and in particular the first: poverty.	
Son of God, he receives everything from the Father.	Jesus, Son of God, receives everything from the Father.
"He whose state is divine has emptied himself, taking the form of a slave, becoming as human beings are".	In order to come to us, he empties himself, takes the condition of a slave, and choses to be poor in this world. In the Beatitudes, he blesses the poor and proclaims Poverty as the fundamental disposition of heart for entry into the kingdom.
"He placed his will in the will of his Father",	On the Cross he carries Poverty to its summit, and dies naked, "handing over" even his own spirit to the Father. Francis, the "little poor man", wants to know only Christ and Christ crucified,
and with his blessed Mother he chose poverty. Following his way	and he makes himself poor with him; he lives poverty with the poor, relying totally on the Father's generosity; he does not depend on wealth, knowledge or power. Effectively poor, in prosperity or even in abundance, our concern is to acquire the soul of the poor. To that end, not only will we avoid unnecessary things and luxury, but we will know how to accept a real poverty in order to involve ourselves in sharing with our brothers and sisters in need, and in a solidarity with the "little ones" of the world.
and being pilgrims here below, we recognize ourselves deprived of all and receiving all from the goodness of our Father.	Pilgrims here below, we recognize that "having nothing, we nevertheless possess all things" through the goodness of the Father.
We accept the obligation of emptying ourselves of ourselves (of our pride, of our satisfaction). More sensitive to being than to having, we will be on guard that our hearts never be captured by the desire for money and material goods so	

1974 Basic Text	*1975 Redaction*
as to be closer to our brothers and sisters, to break down the barriers and to bridge the gaps which separate human beings. We know how to make ourselves available in terms of ourselves and of our time, sharing and giving generously to those who are poorer than we. We share the battle of the unfortunate who fight for a more dignified life. In joy, by this self-emptying, we will live this rediscovered simplicity which nourishes Hope. Gratitude is the distinctive mark of this evangelical poverty.	Our attitude toward Him will be, therefore, one of gratitude.
	As his work of Redemption led Christ to accept persecution, suffering and death, we too are called to enter into this same way in order to communicate the fruits of salvation to women and men. In the work, difficulties, sickness, pains and sufferings of this life, we will accept walking with Christ on the royal road of the Cross as the means of completing what is lacking in his Passion and of cooperating in the Redemption of the world.
6. *Brothers and Sisters to All*:	6. *Brothers and Sisters to All*:
In every human being the Father sees the traits of his beloved Son.	In every human being the Father sees the traits of his Beloved Son, the first-born of a multitude of brothers and sisters. Through Him, he desired to reconcile all beings. Francis, brother to all, sees a brother or sister in every being, and not only in every human being. As we [are] sons and daughters of the same Father, in every human being,
In every human being we make every effort to see Jesus Christ who calls us to a universal community. We are all brothers and sisters, we have only one Father, the heavenly Father.	we make every effort to see Jesus Christ who calls us to a universal community.
Through his Son he desired to reconcile all beings. We wish to make our attitudes, our	

1974 Basic Text	*1975 Redaction*
judgments, our human relationships and our actions correspond to this call. Like Francis, we have confidence in each person and we make every effort to discover the good which is in each person and which God works through each person. In everyone that we meet we see a sister or brother to love, to respect, to serve.	
We make every effort to be more particularly attentive	We seek him especially in the poorest,
to the most disinherited, to the unloved, to the victims of unjust situations, and as far as possible,	the most disinherited, the unloved, the marginal, the victims of injustice.
to help them by concerted action to achieve their dignity as human beings and as children of God. We fight against the obstacles to universal community (racism, oppressions, injustices, violence).	Our attitudes, our judgments and our actions will lead us to become involved with them to fight against all the obstacles to universal community and to allow them to acquire their dignity as human beings and as children of God.
We make our work and our action a participation in the Redemption, the source of fraternity and, by the common human striving to build a just and fraternal world, the prefiguration of the city of God.	
7. *Living Members of the Church*:	7. *Living Members of the Church*:
In order to accomplish the will of the Father, Christ established the Church, born from his open side on the Cross,	Christ established the Church. Born from his open side on the Cross, ceaselessly brought to life by the Spirit, the new People of God,
in order to continue his work of salvation and reconciliation.	she continues his work.
The universal sacrament of salvation, the Church is the sign and means of union with God and of the unity of the whole human race.	The universal sacrament of salvation, she is the sign and means of union with God and of the unity of the whole human race.

1974 Basic Text	*1975 Redaction*
God has called all of those who look toward Jesus with faith; and God made of them the Church so that it might be the sacrament of this saving unity.	
By Baptism we have become living members, participating in her life and mission. And so we always desire to be in communion with her, responsible for her progress in history: open and attentive to her appeals as to the signs of the times.	Having become living members through Baptism, we participate in her life and mission. This is why we will always desire to be in communion with her, open and attentive to her appeals,
	consciously participating in the priestly, prophetic and royal roles of Christ. Entering into the Church's mission in heart and in action,
We consider all forms of the apostolate in conformity with the mission of the Church as a duty and a right.	we will consider forms of "service" and activities in conformity with that mission as a duty and a right.
Allowing ourselves to be guided by the Holy Spirt and in communion with our Fraternity, we commit ourselves concretely, knowing how to take daring initiatives as needed.	More profoundly involved in [the Church] by our profession of Franciscan life,
We remember the respect and love which animated Francis with regard to the "Lord Pope", the bishops and all those who have charge of the People of God. We wish to have toward the pastors of the Church an attitude of fidelity, of confident and loyal dialogue and of active obedience.	we will remember the respect and love which animated Francis with regard to the "Lord Pope", the bishops and those responsible for the People of God[83]. We also wish to have toward the pastors of the Church an attitude of fidelity, of confident and loyal dialogue, and of obedience conformed to the blessed freedom of the sons and daughters of God.

[83] The phrase "*des responsables du peuple de Dieu*" was used to indicate those who have an official mandate or function within the Church. The redactors intentionally left the language "vague" in order to include those parts of the Church where those "responsible" are lay leaders (for example, Africa and Latin America are cited). Cf. *GA Arch*: 75 REI 04.30.

1974 Basic Text

8. *Praying with Christ and the Church*:

In the Gospel,
Jesus gives us the example of frequent prayer
and shows us the necessity
of remaining in his love and
interceding for ourselves and others.

In this work the Holy Spirit comes to aid our weakness because we do not know how to pray as we should, but the Spirit himself prays for us. In the same way Francis, in the school of the Holy Spirit, became prayer made man.

Like Jesus,
we will know how
to find moments and days
to meet the Father, to listen to him,
to speak to him,
sometimes even in solitude.

We make the "Our Father" the nourishment
which will feed our praise of the Father,
our family life and work,
our temporal and apostolic action.

We will love to contemplate the Lord, his presence and his action in the history of the world and in human hearts, to discover his love there, and to hear better his calls.

1975 Redaction

8. *Praying with Christ and the Church*:
(The liturgical life of the Tertiary)

Jesus gives us the example of frequent prayer,
and shows us its necessity.

Francis, inhabited by the Spirit who alone "knows how to pray as one should", was "less a man praying than prayer made man". Like him, too poor to pray on our own, we will learn under the influence of the Spirit to make the prayer of our life and our action spring forth.
Like him [Francis],
we will know how
to take some time each day
to welcome the Father, to listen to him and
to speak to him in his Son;
sometimes even, in solitude, we will take several days for this encounter.
We assign a particular importance to this
privileged sign of the prayer of Christ:
the gathering in Church with our brothers and
sisters for the liturgical celebration.
We join there the prayer which Christ, with his
"Body", addressed to the Father.
According to the liturgical year, we will regulate
the rhythm of our personal and communal
prayer, as well as our life, by the celebration of
the mysteries of Christ.
We will make the "Our Father"
the source of our prayer, the nourishment

of our temporal and apostolic action.
We will take joy in praising the Lord with our
brothers and sisters in the Fraternity,
in contemplating [God's] presence and action
in human hearts and in the history of the
world, in marvelling at this [presence],
and in giving thanks.

1974 Basic Text

We love to receive the sacraments of the Church as a participation in the death and resurrection of Christ and as a source of our whole Christian life. In particular, with our hearts prepared and our wills committed, we celebrate the Eucharist. For us as for Francis, it is "the commemoration of the Passion and the death of Christ", redemption at work, and communion with his Person and with his People. It "makes the Church".

We are faithful to the prayer (Office) of the Fraternity by which we participate in the praise which the Church addresses to the Father for all men and women.

1975 Redaction

Every day we will unite ourselves by our prayer (Office) with that of the Fraternity.
Above all, with a heart prepared by the Word and with a will united with Christ, we will celebrate the Eucharist as often as possible: participation in his death and his resurrection, Redemption at work, communion with his Person and with his People. By so making all the aspects of our life spiritual offerings which are joined to the offering of the Body of the Lord, we will consecrate the world to God, rendering him everywhere a worship of adoration by the sanctity of our life.

9. In the Midst of the World:

Like all the members of the Franciscan Family, we are sent to the entire world. As seculars, we have our own vocation: living in the midst of the world, engaged in various duties and works of the world, it is our duty to enlighten and to direct all temporal realities to which we are closely united, in such a way that they may work and prosper constantly according to Christ and may be to the glory of the Creator and Redeemer. Also, as members of secular society, we will know how, according to the gifts given by the Lord, to take our share of responsibility, bringing to this management of temporal things the spirit of the Beatitudes. By our witness and our action, joined with that of other men and women, we will work in these different sectors towards the realization of the plan of God for the world. It is first of all in our family that we will live the Franciscan spirit, striving to make it a sign of the world already renewed in Christ. We will make our work a participation in the development of creation, in the redemption of men and women, and a service to

1974 Basic Text	*1975 Redaction*
	the whole human community. Finally, aware that it belongs to the whole Church to make people capable of building the temporal order well and of orienting it toward Christ, with a clear distinction of the rights and duties of ecclesial communities and those of human communities, the secular Fraternities will assume their apostolic and social responsibilities and commit themselves to concrete evangelical choices.
10. *Bearers of Peace*:	10. *Bearers of Peace and of Joy*:
	Acclaimed as "Prince of Peace" by the Prophets, greeted as Messenger of Peace by the Angels at Christmas, Christ invites us to peace: "Blessed are the peace-makers"!
Christ reconciled all beings, making peace by the Blood of his Cross; he calls us to enter into the mystery of his peace and to bring it about. The Church, the sign of this Fraternity which makes possible and strengthens a loyal dialogue, puts the Gospel of peace at the service of the whole human race. And having "condemned the barbarity of war, she launches an ardent appeal to Christians so that with the help of Christ, author of peace, they may work with all human beings to consolidate this peace among them, in justice and love, and to prepare the means for it".	
	In his turn, Francis, was a peacemaker in himself and in his institutions. If he was involved in disputes, it was by his life and in the name of the Gospel alone.
And so, messengers of the Good News as Francis was,	As Sons and daughters of Francis,
we make every effort, in all circumstances, to bring peace and joy to people, because	
we believe in the efficacy of dialogue and in the force of love.	we believe in the force of love, in the goodness of the human person, in the value of

1974 Basic Text	*1975 Redaction*
	dialogue, in the power of efforts at conciliation, and in the transforming wonders that forgiveness produces.
	Following the Church and with all people of good will,
We always look for what unites, working with others to find solutions to conflicts which touch our neighbor, declaring ourselves against war in all its forms, refusing all participation in the arms race and in every antagonism between human beings and between peoples.	we chose an attitude of peace and of opposition to all that leads to violence and prepares for war.
In order to be faithful to our Franciscan vocation, we seize opportunities to accomplish positive acts; in order to bring this about we participate in common actions, even taking positions of responsibility in bodies which favor peace.	
	In all the circumstances of our life (*familial, social*), we will make every effort to bring to others joy and hope, the fruit of the peace of the Resurrected One.
9. *With the Virgin Mary*[84]:	11. *With the Virgin Mary*:
	The Virgin Mary, predestined by a singular election to be the Mother of God and associated by a close and indissoluble bond with the mysteries of the Incarnation and the Redemption, became for us, in the order of grace, our Mother.
The Virgin wanted to be in solidarity with her people in waiting for the Messiah, a humble servant of the Lord, receptive to all his calls, always listening to his word, keeping it and meditating on it in her heart,	In solidarity with her people in waiting for the Messiah, humble servant of the Lord, receptive to all his calls, always listening to his word, she kept and meditated upon in her heart all the events to which she had been witness.
sharing the poor life of her Son,	

[84] Paragraph 9 of the *1974 Basic Text* has been placed here, out of sequence, in order to show parallels with paragraph number 11 of the *1975 Redaction*.

1974 Basic Text	*1975 Redaction*
praying with the Apostles gathered in awaiting the manifestation of the Spirit.	First disciple of her Son, she followed him all the way to the Cross, and offered herself with him. United to the prayer of the Apostles, she prayed for the gift of the Spirit on the Church. Now in heaven in glory, her role is uninterrupted: she ceaselessly intercedes to obtain for people the gifts which insure their salvation. Francis loved "with an inexpressible love the Mother of Christ Jesus" and always found in her the image of the poverty of her Son. Also he called her the "Poverella".
Like the Church and with her, we love to gaze upon her, to pray to her and to imitate her in all her attitudes.	With the Church and with Francis we love to gaze upon Mary, to call her to our aid, and to imitate her in all her attitudes.
11. *Living in the Father's Love*:	12. *Living in the Love of the Father and the Life of the Spirit*[85]
God has loved each of us with an eternal love. Our whole life is bathed in this love. All his works are acts of love. Christ, Image of the Father, is the manifestation of this; he loved us to the end.	Christ reveals to us the love with which the Father has loved us. In Jesus Christ,
	Francis discovered this love and sought it all his life. And so, in response to the promise of Jesus, he addressed this invitation to his brothers and sisters: "And so let us always make a home and dwelling place for Him Who is the Lord God Almighty, Father, Son, and Holy Spirit".
In imitation of Francis, we marvel at this continual tenderness of the Father; we seek his reflection in human goodness and intelligence.	Like Francis, we will marvel at this continual tenderness of the Father;
We praise the Lord for all his creation; we work with other human beings in order to free it and perfect it, thus hastening Christ's Return.	we will praise him for his entire creation;

[85] The *Prologue* began with "God is Love" and this article is given as the conclusion of the "Form of Life" to indicate that the entire life of the Secular Franciscan unfolds within the Love of God. Cf. *AG Archives*: 75 REI 04.30.

1974 Basic Text	*1975 Redaction*
	We will discover the presence of his love in every being and in all events; and especially we will give in him thanks for the infinite gift which he has given us in his Son Jesus Christ.
We make of our life praise and a song of gratitude.	Praise, thanksgiving, and the commitment of our life will be our response to the Father's love.
	The Spirit is the living expression of the life and the love of the Father and the Son. Francis wanted for his own "the Spirit of the Lord and his holy action", and he allowed himself to be led by the One whom he called "the Minister General of his Order". Receptive to [the Spirit's] call, we ask her to transform us by her Presence and gifts, in order to live more and more from Christ, becoming his witnesses, making of us an eternal offering to the glory of the Father.
And when our earthly Advent ends, as Francis we will celebrate our definitive Passover. Then our Sister Death will open her door to us and the mystery and the Face of the Father's love, which we have waited for and searched for all our life, will finally be revealed to us.	And when our earthly pilgrimage comes to an end, celebrating as Francis our final and definitive Passover, we will welcome with joy our "sister bodily death", to go at last to join the Father, the Son and the Spirit, whose love has accompanied us all our life.
III: Fraternity	*III: Fraternity*
12. *Cell of the Church*:	13. *Cell of the Church*:
	God chose Israel to be his People with whom he made a covenant, in order to prepare and prefigure the new and perfect Covenant which would be concluded in Christ.
The Spirit of the Lord has called us, therefore, to enter into the secular Fraternity of St. Francis, a new People whom the Lord gave to	This is why Christ called the multitudes to form a unity in the Spirit to become the new People of God[86].

[86] *Chapter III* begins with the call of the Church, the whole People of God, to emphasize that the Secular Franciscan Order is not itself "church" but rather has a place within the Church. Cf. *AG Archives*: 75 REI 04.30.

1974 Basic Text

Francis to restore his Church by living her life and her Gospel. The Fraternity welcomes us to help us
to live better the grace of the Father's design of love. To this end, in our turn, we welcome its teaching and its manner of communal living which the Church has authenticated.

We see in it
a true cell of the Church:
a community of prayer
which draws us to adoration and praise;
a privileged place
which develops our ecclesial sense;
a fraternal milieu which
gives us the experience of the evangelical life and tests our behaviors.

13. *A Living organism*:

The Fraternity, as every living human group, has its norms, its structure,
and individuals responsible at various levels (local, regional, national, international) determined by its Constitutions.
Loyally we accept them in order
to live in communion with the brothers and sisters of our Fraternity

and with those in the other Fraternities in the world.

14. Receptive to the inspiration of the Spirit
and to the leading of her grace,
and according to the various stages
of contact, information
and formation (novitiate)

1975 Redaction

The secular Fraternity is
a cell of this People of God;

as such
it tends to become a living and fraternal setting where, in the Spirit, the teaching of the Word
and fraternal communion are lived, where the breaking of the Bread and praise are celebrated, and where the missionary life is nourished.

14.

In order to attain this end,
the Fraternity, as every human group,
has its means, its norms, its structure,
and its ministers.

It is this Fraternity which welcomes us
to help us to live the call we have received and the project of the Father's love.

It proposes to us some stages:
their end is to help us experience its way of life, to know the Franciscan family, its spirituality and its history. Their duration

1974 Basic Text	*1975 Redaction*
established (by the Constitutions),	is fixed by the Constitutions, and they are preceded by a dialogue with the ministers. The preparatory stage leads toward entrance into the Fraternity. After formation (novitiate)
we commit ourselves to the "evangelical Form of Life" which it presents to us.	we make the Franciscan commitment to the evangelical life (profession), which renews and
We accept this commitment (profession) as a grace which strengthens in us the baptismal life, tightening our bond with the Church and	strengthens the grace of Baptism in us and
integrating us into the Franciscan family.	integrates us into the Family of St. Francis.
15. *Life within the local Fraternity*:	15.
Committed to the Fraternity, we make it our duty to participate in its life, its gatherings,	Committed to the Fraternity we journey with our brothers and sisters in the evangelical "Form of life". In the meetings to which [the Fraternity] calls us, we share prayer, the Word, the life of our brothers and sisters, and our goods to the degree that this is possible for us.
its initiatives, and in the appeals which it receives from the Lord, from the Church, and from men and women.	We participate in its life, its initiatives, in the appeals which it receives from the Lord, from the Church, and from men and women.
Not content to receive, we will take part in exchanges, in the work of striving to improve it, and in study sessions.	
In order to progress together better, we welcome with humility and gratitude the observations of our brothers and sisters (fraternal correction).	In order to progress, we welcome with humility and gratitude the observations of our brothers and sisters (fraternal correction).
Being a Fraternity, we are co-responsible for its life and its progress. We attentively follow the efforts of the ministers and the Council, even giving our advice.	
We make it our duty to participate in the elections established by the Constitutions for the government of the Fraternity.	

1974 Basic Text	*1975 Redaction*
In the Franciscan spirit of service, we will accept the responsibilities which our brothers and sisters might entrust to us.	In the spirit of service, we will accept the responsibilities in the Fraternity which our brothers and sisters might entrust to us by elections determined by the Constitutions.
16. The Franciscan Family received us at the time of profession; we wish to remain in communion with it, to know its history, to feel ourselves in solidarity with its vitality, to plum the depths of its spirituality, in order better to live it, to witness to it, and so to transmit its message.	[Cf. 14]
	16. While mutually aiding our brothers and sisters by these different means,
In very special communion with the brothers of the First Order who assure spiritual assistance to our Fraternity,	we are also helped by our brothers of the First Order. Spiritual assistance, which is entrusted by the Church to the latter, commits them to bring support and devotion [to the Fraternity],
we will make with them, according to what is provided in legislation, the review of our personal Franciscan life and the progress of the Fraternity (canonical visit), so as to advance together with greater generosity in the work of the Kingdom and in our path to the Father.	to examine with us, in due course, the Franciscan quality of our personal life and that of the Fraternity (Canonical Visit). Living with them in life-giving union, we will take care to pray for them, mutually to comfort and to enrich each other by the witness and the sharing of an authentic Franciscan life.
	16b. Forming a world-wide Order, the local Fraternities collaborate among themselves at various levels: diocesan, provincial, national, world-wide. And so, fraternally united in one family, living together the same message, we will make every effort to be for our sisters and brothers, witnesses to the Gospel.

17. *To Live the Evangelical Life in Fraternal Unity*:

"I urge you, therefore, in the Lord, to lead a life worthy of the vocation to which you were

1974 Basic Text	*1975 Redaction*
called. With all humility and gentleness, and with patience, support each other in love. Take every care to preserve the unity of the Spirit by the peace that binds you together. There is one Body, one Spirit, just as one hope is the goal of your calling by God... one God and Father of all, over all, through all and within all" (Eph 4:1-6).	
Blessing of St. Francis:	*Blessing of St. Francis*:
"May whoever observes these things, be filled in heaven with the blessing of the most high Father, and on earth with the blessing of His beloved Son together with the Holy Spirit, the Comforter".	"May whoever observes these things, be filled in heaven with the blessing of the most high Father, and on earth with the blessing of His beloved Son together with the Holy Spirit, the Comforter".

Some Conclusions based upon the Comparative Analysis

To summarize the results of the comparative analysis of the *1974 Basic Text* and the *1975 Redaction*, let us return to the six characteristics of the Secular Franciscan Order:

1. To Live the Gospel
2. Following Francis
3. Through Conversion / *Metanoia*
4. In Community
5. As Seculars
6. In Life-giving Union with All Franciscans

The *1974 Basic Text* outlined well the gospel life in the manner of Francis by emphasizing conversion. However, it failed to articulate the community aspect and the secular nature of that spirituality. The *1975 Redaction*, therefore, attempted to stress those two points (points 4 and 5) but lost some of the strength of the earlier text's presentation of conversion and the articulation of the gospel life in terms of the Secular Franciscan's commitment to the work of peace and social justice.

The *1975 Redaction* was sent to Secular Franciscans worldwide for their evaluation. Based upon their responses the text was again redacted.

In fact, several new texts emerged. We turn, therefore, to that next phase in the Rule Project and how the text of the Rule evolved.

1976-1977: The Emergence of Three Additional Texts

The responses received from National councils of the Secular Franciscan Order throughout the world (as well as responses from individuals) varied greatly and so, once again, defy an adequate synthesis. In fact, some countries even submitted alternative texts which they had developed as experimental rules. Instead of attempting to summarize those responses, we will look, therefore, to the later redactions, the text of the rule itself as it developed from 1976 through 1978.

In September 1976, after the Assistants General had analyzed the various nations' responses to the *1975 Redaction*, the Presidential Council of the International Interobediental Council decided to form a "Local Commission" to whom they entrusted the task of redacting the Rule[87]. This Local Commission, which consisted of five lay people and two religious, presented a new "Rule Project" (referred to here as the "text of the *Local Commission*"). This text was then submitted to a group of four experts for their response from the perspectives of canon law, history, theology, and Franciscan spirituality[88]. The Assistants General then further redacted the text of the *Local Commission* according to the suggestions made by these experts which resulted in yet another text (referred to here as the "text of the *Assistants General*").

In April 1977, these texts were studied and further redacted by the International Commission at a meeting held at Saints Cosmas and Damien in Rome. Through their discussions at that meeting, the group arrived at a consensus text (referred to here as the "*April 1977 Redaction*")[89]. They commissioned those members who lived in Italy with the task of refining the text into a "polished" Italian version, and gave

---

[87] *SFO Archives*: 77 CRE 06.27, 2. Unfortunately, the members of this "Local Commission" are not identified in the documents.

[88] This group of experts included Ludovico Cava, O.F.M. Conv.; Lázaro Iriarte, O.F.M. Cap.; Atanasio Matanić, O.F.M.; and Francesco Provenzano, T.O.R.

[89] A document contains the minutes of this meeting. Cf. *AG Archives*: 77 REI 04.04.

to the Assistants General the responsibility of presenting the final text for approval to the Ministers General, who would then submit the text to the Sacred Congregation for Religious and Secular Institutes for final approbation.

The Text of the Local Commission

As delegated, the Local Commission attempted to reformulate the *1975 Redaction* according to the responses received from National Councils throughout the world. They intended to present a text which would be "normative, practical, easily understood, and not simply a spiritual message"[90]. They explained that they considered the text of a "Rule" to be "absolute" and therefore they included only essential elements without specifying details that would have their proper place within the Constitutions. Further, they opted for the use of the subjunctive, as both imperative and exhortative (which, unfortunately, cannot easily be conveyed in English)[91].

With respect to the *1975 Redaction*, they omitted the *Introduction*, explaining that it would more appropriately be included within the decree of promulgation and not within the Rule itself. In place of the Introduction they substituted an excerpt from the *Later Exhortation* (the *Letter to All the Faithful*) as more appropriate to the content of the Rule[92]. Within the first chapter they sought to present the role of the Franciscan family within the Church, inscribing within that family the secular branch of the Order. They attempted to make the second chapter more cristocentric and the third chapter more specific about the structure

[90] The Local Commission presented two explanatory documents along with their text. The first, four pages, outlined the criteria they followed in formulating the new text. *AG Archives*: unnumbered document entitled *Criteri seguiti nella redazione della Regola del TOF*, hereafter referenced as *Criteri*. The second, eight pages, offered notes on specific paragraphs within the text which, for the most part, presented the sources on which the text depended (for example: the writings of Francis, the early biographies of Francis, the documents of Vatican II, and other earlier versions of the Rule). *AG Archives*: unnumbered document entitled *Alcune note illustrative al testo della Regola*, hereafter, *Alcune note*.

[91] *AG Archives*: *Criteri*, 1.

[92] *AG Archives*: *Criteri*, 1; *Alcune note*, 2.

of the Order. Finally, they moved the single paragraph on Mary in the *1975 Redaction* and made it a separate fourth chapter to emphasize the role of Mary and to avoid making devotion to Mary simply a practice of piety[93].

The text of the *Local Commission* greatly abbreviated many of the paragraphs in the second chapter of the *1975 Redaction*:

3. on the Gospel as the Rule of life
4. on Conversion
5. on following the poor and crucified Christ
6. on being brothers and sisters to all
7. on being members of the Church
8. on praying with Christ and the Church
9. on being "In the Midst of the World"
10. on being Bearers of Peace.

But it was the additions made by the Local Commission that added a pious or "monastic" tone to the text. The Local Commission added a mention of chastity, the obligation to make a testament, an authentic veneration of the clergy and acceptance of their teachings, adoration of the Eucharist, frequent recourse to the sacrament of reconciliation, praying the liturgy of the hours, and the fostering of religious vocations.

The text of the *Local Commission* also presented many of the elements of the *1975 Redaction* in a more juridical fashion. It greatly expanded the third chapter on the government of the Order. The four sentences in the *1975 Redaction* on "formation" were expanded to three full paragraphs concerning admission, formation, and permanence in the Order. The role of the Minister was emphasized over that of the Council as the director of the Fraternity. The text became not only more juridical but also less "secular" and more "monastic".

The Text of the Assistants General

The four experts reviewed both the text of the *Local Commission* and the *1975 Redaction* and submitted written responses[94]. They then

---

[93] *AG Archives*: *Criteri*, 2-3.

[94] The archives contain only three of these written responses: L. Cava, *AG Archives*: 77 REI 03.07; L. Iriarte, *AG Archives*: 77 REI 03.10; A. Matanić, *AG Archives*: 77 REI 03.12. The fourth expert, F. Provenzano, was present and contributed his reactions to the texts at the subsequent meeting. However, if he did submit a written response, it is not preserved within the archives.

met with the Assistants General to discuss the results of their analysis[95]. The experts concurred in their judgment of the texts. They did not recommend either text in its entirety but listed the strengths and weaknesses of each text as a "Rule". They criticized the content of the text of the *Local Commission* for being "too monastic", but commended its style as more suitable for a "Rule" given that its juridical presentation of various elements more closely reflected the traditional style of a Rule. Conversely, they criticized the style of the *1975 Redaction* as non-juridical but applauded its content and theological presentation as "profoundly Franciscan, more faithful to the mentality of Vatican II, and more incisive concerning the aspect of secularity"[96].

They therefore suggested that the Assistants General recast the text of the *Local Commission*, preserving its juridical style while incorporating some of the content of the *1975 Redaction*. They also offered some more specific recommendations:

— that the text speak of "purity of heart" rather than "chastity"
— that the text present, in addition to devotion to the Eucharist, the dimension of Eucharist which demands the commitment of the total person
— that paragraph 9 of the *1975 Redaction* ("In the Midst of the World") be abbreviated and reinserted
— that the "ancient custom of the Our Father" be omitted
— that certain paragraphs be transposed (for example, to move paragraphs 20 and 21 of the text of the *Local Commission* to Chapter I to introduce the constitutive elements of the Fraternity within the description of the Order)
— that the Third Order Regular be mentioned in conjunction with the First Order
— that mention be made within the Rule of the Constitutions, and
— that the Blessing of Francis be taken from the *Testament* rather than from the *Letter to All the Faithful*[97].

The experts also discussed the appropriateness of an Introduction or Prologue within a Rule, however, they remained somewhat ambivalent

[95] The archives contain minutes from that meeting. *AG Archives*: 77 REI 03.19.
[96] *AG Archives*: 77 REI 03.19.
[97] *AG Archives*: 77 REI 03.19.

concerning the inclusion of a Prologue. They applauded the content of the Introduction given in the *1975 Redaction*, but they felt it should be contained within the document of approbation rather than within the Rule itself. They therefore suggested the inclusion of a Prologue or Introduction only if the more general theological framework were not included within the decree in which the Rule would be promulgated. But over against this reservation, they did nonetheless affirm that "as a spiritual document introducing the Rule, it would be useful to quote the *Letter to All the Faithful*"[98].

Subsequently, the Assistants General did formulate a new text reflecting the input received from the experts. They redacted the text of the *Local Commission* by incorporating some material from the *1975 Redaction*. The Assistants General omitted both the Introduction of the *1975 Redaction* and the Prologue contained in the text of the *Local Commission*. Apparently, the Assistants General understood the experts' hestitation to include any Introduction to be stronger than their affirmation of the appropriateness of Francis' *Letter to All the Faithful*. The newly formulated text was presented to the seventeen members of the International Commission at their April meeting.

The April 1977 Redaction

Although the Assistants General had already reformulated the text of the *Local Commission* according to the suggestions made by the "experts", at the April 1977 meeting the participants decided to study *not* the text of the *Assistants General* but the text of the *Local Commission* in comparison with the other texts[99]. In their discussions, therefore, they worked from the text of the *Local Commission*, substituting paragraphs or adding phrases from the text of the *Assistants General* where the latter were judged to be preferable. Although the members opted to work from the text of the *Local Commission*, they did accept many of the modifications made by the Assistants General. Let us turn, then, to a comparative analysis of the texts. The text of the *April 1977 Redaction*, when viewed against the text of the *Local Commission* and the text of the *Assistants General*, graphically presents the actual

[98] *AG Archives*: 77 REI 03.07; and 77 REI 03.19.
[99] *AG Archives*: 77 REI 04.04, 6.

process of redaction. Unfortunately, the minutes of that April meeting record the choice of specific paragraphs or alternative wording within the text but, for the most part, omit the reasons for these choices[100]. Therefore, we will study the Commission's redactional work through a comparative analysis of these three redactions. The three texts (the text of the *Local Commission*, the text of the *Assistants General*, and the *April 1977 Redaction*) have been placed parallel to one another to demonstrate clearly the relationship between them.

Local Commission	*Assistants General*	*April 1977 Redaction*
Introduction[101]:		
How happy and blessed are those who love God and do as the Lord Himself says in the Gospel: *You shall love the Lord you God will all your heart and all your mind, and your neighbor as yourself.* Let us love God, therefore, and adore Him with a pure heart and a pure mind... let us praise Him and pray to Him *day and night*... confess all our sins to a priest, and receive from him the Body and Blood of our Lord Jesus Christ... Moreover, let us perform *worthy fruits of penance*. And upon all men and women, if they have done these things and have persevered to the end, *the Spirit of the Lord will rest* and He will make His home and *dwelling among them*. They will be children of the heavenly Fa-		

[100] *AG Archives*: 77 REI 04.04. For the original texts in Italian, cf. *Appendix III*, pp. 407-423.

[101] These specific sentences from the *Letter to All the Faithful* (18-22, 25, and 48-50) were chosen as "most pertinent to and summing up the content expressed in the Rule". Cf. *AG Archives*: *Alcune note*, 2.

Local Commission	*Assistants General*	*April 1977 Redaction*
ther whose works they do. And they are spouses, brothers, and mothers of our Lord Jesus Christ.		
(from St. Francis' *Letter to All the Faithful*)		
	I: The Secular Franciscan Fraternity	*I: The Secular Franciscan Order*
Among the numerous spiritual families which gladden	1. Among the many spiritual families	1. Among the many spiritual families
the Church of Christ, the Holy Spirit has also raised up	raised up by the Holy Spirit in the Church,	raised up by the Holy Spirit in the Church,
that of St. Francis of Assisi in order to offer men and women an ulterior way to live in union with the heavenly Father. The Poverello, called by the Crucified to restore his "house", received God's revelation of the need to live within the Church "according to the form of the holy Gospel" together with the brothers that the Lord himself had given him. With the council and guidance of Francis, Clare of Assisi also established an Order of sisters desirous of following the same way of Gospel perfection. Still many other men and women[102],		

[102] This phrase was chosen to avoid all of the questions concerning the origin of the "Third Order". Cf. *AG Archives*: *Alcune note*, 2.

Local Commission	*Assistants General*	*April 1977 Redaction*
attracted by the example of life and Franciscan preaching, felt called to a life of evangelical penance, but without leaving their own homes and occupations. Thus by means of the various families originated by Saint Francis of Assisi, image of the living Christ, the heavenly Father has willed that the "newness of life" brought by His Son be renewed in the Church and in the world. Even today the Franciscans, attentive to the call of the Crucified, offer their own contribution of presence and work within the Church and in society, observing the Gospel according to the example of their Seraphic Father.		
I: The Secular Franciscan Order		
The Franciscan family in the Church		
1. The Franciscan family unites all members of the people of God - laity, religious, and priests - who recognize that they are called to follow Christ, poor and crucified, following the example of Saint Francis of Assisi.	the Franciscan [family] unites the laity, religious, and priests called to follow Christ in the footsteps of Saint Francis of Assisi.	the Franciscan [family] unites all members of the people of God - laity, religious, and priests - who recognize that they are called to follow Christ in the footsteps of Saint Francis of Assisi.

Local Commission	*Assistants General*	*April 1977 Redaction*
In various ways and forms but in life-giving union[103] with each other, they make present the charism of the Poverello in the life and mission of the Church.	In various ways and forms but in life-giving union with each other, they make present the charism of the Poverello in the life and mission of the Church.	In various ways and forms but in life-giving union with each other, they make present the charism of the Poverello in the life and mission of the Church.
The Secular Franciscan Order		
2. Within this spiritual family, the Secular Franciscan Order (also called the Franciscan Third Order or the Secular Franciscan Fraternity)	2. Within this spiritual family, the Secular Franciscan Order (S.F.O., T.O.F.)	2. Within this family, the Secular Franciscan Order (S.F.O., T.O.F.)
	has a particular place.	has a particular place.
is that "community of all members and groups of	It is a community of the fraternities scattered throughout the world and open to every group of	It is a community of the fraternities scattered throughout the world and open to every group of
the faithful who, moved by the Spirit of God,	the faithful who, led by the Spirit, strive for perfect charity in their own secular state.	the faithful who, led by the Spirit, strive for perfect charity in their own secular state.
commit themselves, by profession of a Rule approved by the Church,	By their profession they pledge themselves	By their profession they pledge themselves
to live the Gospel of our Lord Jesus Christ in their own secular state	to live the gospel	to live the Gospel
following the example and teaching of Saint Francis of Assisi".	in the manner of Saint Francis	in the manner of Saint Francis

[103] The French phrase "*en réciprocité vitale*" used in both the *1974 Basic Text* and the *1975 Redaction* (literally, in vital reciprocity) has been changed to "*in communione vitale reciproca*" (literally, in vital reciprocal communion). This Italian phrase remains throughout all of the later redactions, including the *Rule of 1978*. The official English translation of the approved Rule translates the phrase as "in life-giving union", and therefore, that translation has been used here to indicate the genesis of the phrase which appears within officially approved *Rule of 1978*.

Local Commission	*Assistants General*	*April 1977 Redaction*
	by means of a Rule approved by the Church.	by means of a Rule approved by the Church,
Those striving for perfection in the Christian life are grouped together in fraternities under the direction of their respective ministers who govern them in that state (married, celibate, or priestly) in which each person's secular vocation has placed them.		grouped together in fraternities under the direction of their respective ministers.
II. The Way of Life	*II. The Way of Life*	*II. The Way of Life*
The Gospel as Life		
3. The Rule and life of the Secular Franciscans is to observe the gospel of our Lord Jesus Christ.		3. The Rule and life of the Secular Franciscans is to observe the gospel of our Lord Jesus Christ.
	4. Christ, the gift of the Father's love, is our way to Him, the truth into which the Holy Spirit leads us. and the life which he has come to give us in abundance[104]. Thus, Francis of Assisi made Christ the inspiration and the center of his life with God and people[105].	Christ, the gift of the Father's love, is our way to him, the truth into which the Holy Spirit lead us, and the life which he has come to give us in abundance. Thus, Francis of Assisi made Christ the inspiration and the center of his life with God and people.
In the Gospel and in all of Sacred Scripture handed on by the Church, let them first seek	5. Let us, therefore, seek	4. Let us, therefore, seek

[104] This sentence, though a very brief summary, reflects the content of the *Prologue* of the *1975 Redaction*, cf. above pp. 259-260.

[105] Paraphrase of paragraph 12 of the *1975 Redaction*, cf. above pp. 273-274.

Local Commission	*Assistants General*	*April 1977 Redaction*
	in the Gospel	in the Gospel
the living person of Jesus,	the living person of Jesus Christ, conforming ourselves to	the living person of Jesus Christ, conforming ourselves to
the teacher, model and strength of their existence.	Him, the model and strenght of our existence.	Him, the model and strength of our existence.
Attentive to the "signs of the times", let them put to the test both individually and as a group, the salvific power of the "Good News" to the point of becoming its joyful and faithful bearers among people.	And let us become joyous and faithful bearers of Him among people.	And let us become joyous and faithful bearers of Him among people.
	Let us commit ourselves to a continual reading of the Gospel, in full harmony with our Franciscan charism, going from the Gospel to life and from life to the Gospel[106].	
4. The Gospel commitment demands that the "brothers and sisters of penance"	6. Let the brothers and sisters of penance, precisely	5. Let the "brothers and sisters of penance",
	in virtue of their vocation, motivated by the dynamic power of the gospel to a continuous and radical conversion or metanoia, participate in a new life in Christ.	in virtue of their vocation, and motivated by the dynamic power of the gospel,
conform their way of thinking and acting to that of Christ by means of a total interior change which the gospel itself designates with the name "conversion", which		conform their way of thinking and acting to that of Christ by means of a radical interior change which the gospel itself calls "conversion", which

[106] See the last sentence in paragraph 3 of the *1975 Redaction*, above p. 263. Although this sentence was omitted in the *April 1977 Redaction*, it was later reinserted. This sentence appears within paragraph 5 of the *Final Redaction* sent to the Ministers General and is also contained within paragraph 4 of the *Rule of 1978*. Cf. *Appendix IV*, p. 438.

Local Commission	*Assistants General*	*April 1977 Redaction*
because of human frailty must be renewed daily.		because of human frailty must be renewed daily.
On this penitential way, let them take advantage of meditation, revision of life, retreats, and "spiritual exercises", but above all, frequent recourse to the	For this conversion, the	On this way of conversion the
sacrament of reconciliation, the privileged sign of the Father's mercy and the source of new grace.	sacrament of reconciliation is the privileged means and reality.	sacrament of reconciliation is the privileged sign of the Father's mercy and the source of new grace.
With Christ Poor and Crucified		
5. Following the example of Christ	7. In obedience to the will of the Father and as true disciples of Christ, the Son of God and truly human,	6. Following the example of Christ,
who chose for Himself and His mother a poor and humble life, let them make sure to simplify their own material needs to the advantage of the needy.		who trusting in the Father chose for Himself and His mother a poor and humble life, let them make sure to simplify their own material needs to the advantage of the needy, conscious of the gospel sense of goods.
Let them strive, in the spirit of "the Beatitudes", and as pilgrims and strangers on their way to the home of the Father, to purify their hearts from every yearning for possession and power,		Let them strive, in the spirit of "the Beatitudes" and as pilgrims and strangers on their way to the home of the Father, to purify their hearts from every yearning for possession and power.
and dispose of their goods in time by a testament[107].		

[107] The obligation to make a testament was added by the Local Commission because of the "ancient custom" within the Order, that is, because it

Local Commission	*Assistants General*	*April 1977 Redaction*
	we will be quick to give testimony to him among people by the fulfillment of our commitments in all circumstances.	**
6. Uniting themselves to the redemptive obedience of Jesus,		7. Uniting themselves to the redemptive obedience of Jesus,
who from Bethlehem to Calvary placed his will in that of the Father, let them accept	And we will be ready	who placed his will in that of the Father, let them faithfully fulfill the duties proper to their various circumstances of life.
	* *	
	to follow him, poor and crucified, in the way of the cross amidst difficulties and persecutions.	And let them follow the poor and crucified Christ, witnessing to him even amidst difficulties and persecutions.
the difficulties of life as children [of God]. With the same feelings as the "Suffering Servant", let them dispose themselves to welcome as a sister even death, comforted by the hope of sharing in the glory of the Resurrection.		
7. While they await with living faith the completion of their being in the fullness of that future life, let them cultivate Christian chastity, according to their own state, as a concrete sign of [their] search for the only All-Good.		
	8. Following the example of St. Francis, lover of poverty, we will detach ourselves from every form	

was contained in the *Memoriale propositi*, the *Rule of 1289*, and also within the *Rule of 1883*. Cf. *AG Archives: Alcune note,* 4.

Local Commission	*Assistants General*	*April 1977 Redaction*
	of egoism and greed. Thus free and conscious of the Gospel sense of goods, we will be ready, according to the gift received, to place our- selves and our [goods] at the ser- vice of others, especially the most poor and disinherited[108].	
Moreover, they will strive to acquire a purity of heart which, freeing them from the cares of this world, will help them to open themselves in generosity	Witnesses of the good yet to come, we will commit ourselves to acquiring a purity of heart which will make us free amidst the cares of this world and available	8. Witnesses of the good yet to come, we will commit ourselves to acquiring a purity of heart which will make us free amidst the cares of this world and available
to the inspirations of the Lord	for the love of God and	for the love of God
and the appeal of their brothers and sisters.	of our brothers and sisters.	and of our brothers and sisters.
With Christ, "firstborn of many brothers and sisters"		
8. In order to imitate Christ	9.	9.
  who became our brother,	As the Father sees in every person the features of his Son, the first- born of many brothers and sisters, we too will make every effort to see Christ in others[109], where- by they will become for us	As the Father sees in every person the features of his Son, the first- born of many brothers and sisters, we too will make every effort to see Christ in others, where- by they will become for us
let them be and show themselves as authentic brothers and sisters of all.	authentic brothers and sisters, transcending every barrier.	authentic brothers and sisters.
Therefore, with a humble and gentle spirit, let them accept every person, welcoming each as a gift from the Lord		Therefore, with a humble and gentle spirit, we will accept all people as a gift of the Lord.

[108] Cf. paragraphs 4, 5, and 6 of the *1975 Redaction*, above pp. 263-267.
[109] A paraphrase of the first half of paragraph 6 in the *1975 Redaction*, p. 266.

Local Commission	*Assistants General*	*April 1977 Redaction*
without regard for the person's condition, politics or faith. And let them avoid judging anyone.		
Likewise, let them show respect towards other creatures, animate and inanimate, which "bear the imprint of the Most High".		Likewise, let them show respect towards other creatures, animate and inanimate, which "bear the imprint of the Most High".
9. In the spirit of "minority" and service which should distinguish them, let them be involved in the various works of Christian charity.		
Let them try above all to place themselves on an equal basis with all people, especially the weak, the suffering, those under whatever form of oppression And uniting themselves with people of good will,	This sense of community will make us happy to place ourselves among the lowliest	The sense of community will make us happy to place ourselves on an equal basis with all people, especially with the lowliest,
let them give concrete aid to them so that they might live with the dignity of creatures redeemed by Christ.	and at their defense,	helping them to live with the dignity of creatures redeemed by Christ;
	and it will lead us to promote justice and to work with others to eliminate every obstacle to a truly universal community[110].	and it will lead us to promote justice and peace and to work with others to eliminate every obstacle to a truly universal community.
In the Church, the "Body of Christ"		
10. Members of the Church through Baptism,	11. Through Baptism we are members of the Church	10. Members of the Church through baptism,

[110] Cf. the last sentence of paragraph 6 of the *1975 Redaction*, p. 267.

Local Commission	*Assistants General*	*April 1977 Redaction*
	which Christ willed as	
	an instrument of salvation,	
and more perfectly	and through profession	and more strongly
bound to her	we are more strictly	bound to her
by profession,	committed to her.	by profession,
let them be	Let us strive to become	let them be
witnesses and instruments	witnesses and participants	witnesses and instruments
of her mission among the	in her mission.	of her mission among the
people, proclaiming Christ by		people, proclaiming Christ by
[their] life and words.		[their] life and words.
As humble Francis,	Inspired by St. Francis,	Inspired by St. Francis
		and with him called to rebuild
let them have		the Church, let us live
an authentic veneration of		
	in full communion with	in full communion with
the pope, bishops, and priests.	the pope, bishops, and priests,	the pope, bishops, and priests,
	let us feel united with them	
Let them welcome	in a trusting and open dialogue	in a trusting and open dialogue
	of apostolic creativity.	of apostolic creativity.
their teachings		
with a filial trust, being certain		
to offer them fraternal charity in		
an obedient and creative love.		
11. In union with all true	12. As Jesus was the true	11. As Jesus was the true
worshippers of the Father,	worshipper of the Father,	worshipper of the Father,
let them make	so we will make	so we will make
prayer	prayer	prayer and contemplation
	the sustenance of our life.	
	Following the example of the	
with the Church	primitive Church and	
	in order to become ever more	
the heart	of one heart and one mind	the heart
of their being and acting.		of our being and acting.
In living the mysteries of		
Redemption through the		
liturgical year, let them nurture	we will participate in prayer,	We will participate in the
a life of union with God		
through his Word and		
the Sacraments.		sacramental life of the Church,

Local Commission	*Assistants General*	*April 1977 Redaction*
Let them be particularly devoted to the celebration of the Eucharist, attentive to adoring the body and blood of Christ present among us.	in the breaking of the bread or Eucharist,	above all the Eucharist;
	and in listening to the Word, thus reliving the mysteries of the life of Christ.	**
With joy let them join the people of God	We will participate in the liturgical prayer of the Church using one of the approved forms.	and we will join in liturgical prayer in one of the forms proposed by [the Church] thus reliving the mysteries of the life of Christ.
	**	
in the liturgy of the Hours or in a sincere recitation of the Our Father following the ancient custom. In their charity before God, let them embrace all men and women and in particular their [Franciscan] brothers and sisters both living and dead. And let them give thanks to the Lord for his presence in the human heart, in the events of history, and in the marvels of creation.		
IV: With Mary, the Mother of Jesus		
	10. The Virgin Mary, united with her people in awaiting the Messiah,	12. The Virgin Mary,
	humble servant of the Lord, open to his word	humble servant of the Lord, open to his word

Local Commission	*Assistants General*	*April 1977 Redaction*
	and to all his calls[112],	and to all his calls,
25[111] As sons and daughters of		
Saint Francis who embraced	was embraced by Francis	was embraced by Francis
the Mother of Jesus		
with indescribable love;	with indescribable love;	with indescribable love
and designated her	and he designated her	and designated
the protectress and advocate	the Protectress and Advocate	the protectres and advocate
of his spiritual family,	of his family.	of his family.
let the Secular Franciscans	The brothers and sisters	The brothers and sisters
be inspired by her as a "most		
excellent model of faith, charity,		
and perfect union with Christ".	will witness to her	will witness to her
	their ardent love	their ardent love
Let them venerate her		
and call upon her with the		
recitation of her praise,		
and above all, let them imitate	by imitation of	by imitation of
her in self-giving	her unconditional self-giving	her unconditional self-giving
	and by an out-pouring of faithful	and by an out-pouring of faithful
	and conscious prayer.	and conscious prayer.
to the Father		
and in their attitudes by learning		
from her how to be, they too,		
"spouses, brothers, [sisters], and		
mothers of the Lord Jesus".		

[111] Paragraph 25, which by itself constitutes a separate fourth chapter in the Rule of the *Local Commission*, has been placed out of sequence. Some of the paragraphs within the text of the *Local Commission*, and the text of the *Assistants General* have been moved from their original place within these two texts in order to show their parallels with the text of the *April 1977 Redaction* which, while incorporating content from both the Rule of the *Local Commission* and the Rule of the *Assistants General*, has rearranged the order of some of the material. The numbers of the paragraphs (which remain unchanged from the original Italian texts) indicate their original placement within the respective text. The original Italian texts may be found in *Appendix III*, pp. 407-423.

[112] See the second sentence in paragraph 11 of the *1975 Redaction*, p. 272.

Local Commission	*Assistants General*	*April 1977 Redaction*
With Christ the Perfect *human being*		
12. Having been called, together with all people of good will, to build from within a more loving and evangelical world,	*13*[a]. By our vocation	13. Called, together with all people of good will, to build from within a more loving and evangelical world for the realization of the Kingdom of God
let them zealously translate into practice in their own lives their profession as "seculars".	as seculars, involved in temporal society,	
Mindful that anyone "who follows Christ, the perfect human, becomes more human," let them competently exercise their own responsibilities (personal, familial, professional, civic, religious, and political) in the Christian spirit of service.	we will assume our responsibilities at whatever level and according to [our] gifts from God.	and mindful that anyone "who follows Christ, the perfect human, becomes more human," let the Secular Franciscans competently exercise their own responsibilities in the Christian spirit of service.
Let them be active, even with courageous individual and communal initiatives, in the field of social justice and of public life, committing themselves through concrete choices in harmony with their faith.		Let them be active, even with courageous individual and communal initiatives, in the field of social justice and of public life, committing themselves through concrete choices in harmony with their faith.
	[13b] Aware that in living the Beatitudes one is as leaven in the world, we will commit ourselves with all people of good will to constructing from within a more fraternal and evangelical world towards the realization of	[cf., beginning of 13]

Local Commission	*Assistants General*	*April 1977 Redaction*
	the Kingdom of God,[113] attentive always to the "signs of the times"[114].	
	[14b] We will esteem work both as a gift and as a sharing in the creation, redemption, and service of the human community[115].	We will esteem work both as a gift and as a sharing in the creation, redemption, and service of the human community.
	[14a] Above all in our family we will live the Franciscan spirit, striving to make it a sign of a world already renewed in Christ[117].	14. In our family we will live the Franciscan spirit, striving to make it a sign of a world already renewed in Christ.
13. Aided by the community,		Aided by the community and living the grace of matrimony,
let those who are married[116] live the sacramental grace of matrimony,	The married members will live the sacramental graces of marriage	the married members
Let them witness to the "mystery"	and will be the first witnesses to the Christian faith	will bear witness in the world to the love of Christ for his Church.
above all in an instructive relationship with their children, accompanying them on their journey of Christian initiation.	for their children.	They will accompany their children on their spiritual journey with a simple and open upbringing, being attentive to the vocation of each [child].
And let them foster the growth of religious vocations.		

---

[113] Taken from paragraph 9, "In the Midst of the World", of the *1975 Redaction*, p. 270.

[114] Cf. paragraph 3 of the *1975 Redaction*, above pp. 262-263.

[115] Taken from paragraph 9 of the *1975 Redaction*, above p. 270.

[116] The Local Commission introduced a specific mention of married members given that the Order began, for the most part, for them. Cf.: *AG Archives*; "*Alcune note*", 7.

[117] Taken verbatim from paragraph 9 of the *1975 Redaction*, above p. 270.

Local Commission	*Assistants General*	*April 1977 Redaction*
With Christ, our peace *and the joy of our hearts*		
14. As "bearers of peace,"	[13c] Bearers of peace and mindful that this [peace] must be built up,	15. Bearers of peace and mindful that this [peace] must be built up unceasingly,
let them bring to all of their endeavors a heart which knows no violence.		
Thus, let them seek unity and loving understanding	we will seek ways to a loving understanding and union	let them seek out ways of unity and loving understanding
through dialogue,	with people through dialogue and action.	through dialogue,
evidencing trust in the presence of the divine seed in everyone and mainly in the transforming power of pardon which Christ, the author of peace, has obtained for us.		trusting in the presence of the divine seed in everyone and in the transforming power of pardon.
Let the certitude that God loves, redeems and guides the human person and the events of the world towards salvation,		
even amidst apparent contradictions and difficult times,	15. Messengers of perfect joy in every circumstance,	Messengers of perfect joy in every circumstance,
make them strong and faithful in the manifestation and diffusion of perfect joy,	we will make every effort to bring to others joy and hope,	we will make every effort to bring to others joy and hope,
the first fruit of Christian hope.	fruits of the peace of resurrection, which gives true meaning to Sister Death, as the ultimate encounter with the Father.	fruits of the resurrection of Christ, which gives true meaning to Sister Death as the ultimate encounter with the Father.

Local Commission	*Assistants General*	*April 1977 Redaction*
III: Life in Fraternity	*III: Life in Fraternity*	*III: Life in Fraternity*
Structure and Government of the Order[118]		
15. The Secular Franciscan Order is divided into groups or fraternities at various levels- local, regional, national, and international. These fraternities, each one having its own moral personality in the Church, are coordinated among themselves at the same level but dependent upon those at a higher level.	16. The Secular Franciscan Fra- ternity is divided into groups or fraternities at various levels- local, regional, national, and international. These fraternities, each one having its own moral personality in the Church, are coordinated among themselves.	16. The Secular Franciscan Order is divided into groups or fraternities at various levels- local, regional, national, and international. These fraternities, each one having its own moral personality in the Church, are coordinated among themselves and united with those at a higher level.
16. The government of the fraternities at the various levels is exercised by the respective Minister or President, aided by some brothers and sisters who constitute the Council. Let all of these be designated at the appropriate levels by the professed members by means of an election.	Each Fraternity, at various levels, is animated and guided by its respective Council and minister, who are elected based upon the norms in force.	17. Each Fraternity, at various levels, is animated and guided by its respective Council and minister (or president) who are elected based upon appropriate approved norms.
Their service, which is temporary, is a commitment of availability and responsibility towards the individual members and the groups.		Their service, which is temporary, is a commitment of availability and responsibility to each member and to the community.

[118] The Local Commission attemped to present the "lay government" of the Secular Franciscan Order, without legal dependence upon the "First Order". Cf. *AG Archives: Alcune note*, 8. However, the text does not fully manifest their intent.

Local Commission	*Assistants General*	*April 1977 Redaction*
	Within themselves, the fraternities are structured in different ways according to the various needs of their members and their regions, and under the guidance of the Council.	Within themselves, the fraternities are structured in different ways according to the various needs of their members and their regions, and under the guidance of their respective Council.
The Local Fraternity		
17. The local Fraternity is the basic nucleus of the whole Order and a visible sign of the Church, the community of love. Its erection occurs in the ways prescribed by ecclesiastical norms, but its development is entrusted in a particular way to those charged with its animation, with the contribution and experience of the brothers and sisters who comprise it.	17. The local Fraternity is the prime nucleus of the whole Order.	18. The local Fraternity, established canonically, is the basic unit of the whole Order and a visible sign of the Church, the community of love.
	It is the privileged place for developing a sense of Church and the Franciscan vocation and for enlivening the apostolic life of its members. Let the so-called isolated brothers and sisters, who because of changing circumstances are not able to participate in the life of their Fraternity, strive to be united with some Fraternity in order to receive and an support.	It is the privileged place for developing a sense of Church and the Franciscan vocation and for enlivening the apostolic life of its members.

Local Commission	*Assistants General*	*April 1977 Redaction*
Admission to the Order		
20. In order to be admitted to the Secular Franciscan Order, the petitioner must profess the Catholic faith, evidence the desire to respond to their vocation, possess the capacity to share the life of the Fraternity and have reached the age of maturity.	3. The request to enter a local Fraternity is made	19. The request for admission to the local Fraternity is made
It is the responsibility of the Council to decide upon the admission and profession of new brothers and sisters.	to the respective Council, which has responsibility for the Fraternity.	to the respective Council, which has responsibility for the Fraternity.
21. Membership in the Fraternity occurs in three successive phases:	One becomes a member	One is admitted [to the Fraternity]
- a time of preparation, whose duration is left to the judgment of the Council	through a time of initiation,	through a time of initiation,
- a time of formation for at least a year, but which can be prolonged by the decision of the same Council or at the request of the interested party	a period of formation of at least one year,	a period of formation of at least one year,
- the Profession of the Rule which, renewing and deepening the grace of Baptism, establishes the fully-fledged members of the entire Franciscan family. During the first two phases the new brother or sister must acquire the formation adequate to the life commitment that awaits them. He or she is aided and supported in this by an	and profession of the Rule.	and profession of the Rule.

Local Commission	*Assistants General*	*April 1977 Redaction*
appropriatly designated Director and also by the teaching, example and prayer of the whole Fraternity.	The entire community is committed to this process of growth even by its manner of living.	The entire community is involved in this process of growth even by its manner of living. For admission one must be legally of age.
Permanence in the Order		
22. Profession of the Rule is by its nature a permanent commitment.	This profession of the life is by its nature a permanent commitment. Members who find themselves in particular difficulties will deal with them in fraternal dialogue with the Council.	This profession of the life is by its nature a permanent commitment. Members who find themselves in particular difficulties will deal with them in fraternal dialogue with the Council.
However, the Council can suspend from the life of the Fraternity for a given period of time (preserving their right of recourse to superiors) those brothers and sisters who have not observed their assumed commitment, have been insubordinate, or have given scandal and who, though fraternally admonished, have not amended [their ways].		
Permanent dismissal from the Order is the competence of the ministers at a higher level and is decided only for grave reasons. But whoever might spontaneously ask to be dismissed from the Order		If it happens to come to a permanent dismissal from the Order, such an act is the competence of the ministers at a higher level.

Local Commission	*Assistants General*	*April 1977 Redaction*
is by that itself released from every assumed commitment.		
18. To facilitate the members' spiritual growth in a vocation responding to each person's condition of life, let the leaders be concerned to form particular groups in an atmosphere of community, while preserving the unified familial character of the Order itself.	18. To facilitate	
To foster then a		20. To foster
sharing of the life and purpose of all the brothers and sisters who compose [the Fraternity],	communion among the members,	communion among members,
let all [the members], at the invitation of the Minister,	the Council	the Council, with the aid of individual [members],
join together periodically.	will provide for frequent assemblies,	organizes regular assemblies and frequent meetings,
In these encounters or meetings, let the hearing of the Word, the celebration of Prayer and Eucharist,	adopting the most appropriate means	adopting the most appropriate means
and fraternal correction itself, in addition to being an aid to the Gospel life, be a special stimulus for reflecting upon the appeals coming from the Church and from the human community in order to be able to offer them concrete responses through joint efforts in harmony with the overall pastoral [mission].	for growth in Franciscan and ecclesial life, and with the contribution of individuals,	for growth in Franciscan and ecclesial life
	encouraging everyone to participate in the life of fraternity, and to share spiritual and material goods as brothers and sisters.	and encouraging everyone to the life of fraternity.
		This communion continues with deceased brothers and sisters offering prayer for them.

Local Commission	*Assistants General*	*April 1977 Redaction*
19. Regarding expenses necessary for the life of the Fraternity and those necessary for worship, the apostolate, and charity, let all the brothers and sisters offer a contribution according to their means. Let it be a concern of the local fraternities participate in the higher level fraternities.		21. Regarding expenses necessary for the life of the Fraternity and those necessary for worship, the apostolate, and charity, let all the brothers and sisters offer a contribution according to their means. Furthermore, let it be a concern of the local fraternities to participate in the higher level fraternities.
The Spiritual Assistant		
23. As a concrete sign of spiritual communion		22. As a concrete sign of communion and responsibility,
and in compliance with ecclesiastical norms, the Ministers of the First Order, in accord with the Ministers of the respective secular Fraternities,		
		let the Councils on various levels,
will designate suitable and prepared religious		ask for
[to offer] spiritual assistance		spiritual assistance from the First Order and the Third Order Regular.
to [the Fraternities] at the various levels. Besides that of representing the hierarchy within the [Fraternities], the task of the Assistant (who by right is part of the Council of the respective Fraternity) is to see to the religious and moral life of the brothers and sisters, as well as that of the groups, to be present at		

Local Commission	*Assistants General*	*April 1977 Redaction*
prayer and study meetings, and to preside at liturgies.		
24. To ensure growth in the observance of the Rule,		To ensure growth in the observance of the Rule and to promote the life of the Fraternity,
let the ministers of the Fraternities, with the consent of their own Council,	19. Let the respective Councils at the various levels	let the minister or president, with the consent of the Council,
take care to request of Superiors	request ordinary assistance	take care to ask the concerned religious superiors periodically
a pastoral visitation	and, in due course, a pastoral visitation from the First Order and the Third Order Regular, to whom the Church has entrusted the care of the fraternities and who will provide Spiritual Assistants.	for a pastoral visitation,
and a fraternal [visitation], in the general manners prescribed by law and according to the ancient custom of the Order.		and the lay ministers for a fraternal visitation.
	20. What is not provided for here [in the Rule], will have its suitable place in the General Constitions.	
"I, Brother Francis, your little servant, ask and implore you in the love which is God and with the desire to kiss your feet, to receive these words and others of our Lord Jesus Christ with humility and love, and observe them and put them into practice.		

Local Commission	*Assistants General*	*April 1977 Redaction*
And to all men and women who will receive them kindly and understand their meaning and pass them on to others by their example: *If they have persevered in them to the end, may the Father and the Son and the Holy Spirit bless them. Amen.*"	"And may whoever observes all this be filled in heaven with the blessing of the most high Father, and on earth with that of his beloved Son, together with the Holy Spirit, the Comforter."	"And may whoever observes all this be filled in heaven with the blessing of the most high Father, and on earth with that of his beloved Son, together with the Holy Spirit, the Comforter."
(from St. Francis' *Letter to All the Faithful*)	(Blessing of St. Francis from the *Testament*)	(Blessing of St. Francis from the *Testament*)

An Analysis of the April 1977 Text

While the International Commission began with the text of the *Local Commission*, they did incorporate most of the changes suggested by the text of the *Assistants General*. That is, most of the paragraphs reinserted by the Assistants General, paragraphs taken from the *1975 Redaction* emphasizing the "secular" nature of the Order, were incorporated into the *April 1977 Redaction*. Also, the text omitted the somewhat pious or monastic aspects contained within the text of the *Local Commission*: adoration of the Eucharist, frequent recourse to the sacrament of reconciliation, praying the Office, fostering religious vocations, and the authoritative role of the Minister. Thus, the *April 1977 Redaction* did more adequately present the spirituality of the Secular Franciscan, at least as it had been defined within the Rule Project:

1. To Live the Gospel
2. Following Francis
3. Through Conversion / *Metanoia*
4. In Community
5. As Seculars
6. In Life-giving Union with All Franciscans

Since the *April 1977 Redaction* very closely parallels the *Rule of 1978*, let us consider the changes within the text in the final year of the Rule Project and then examine more closely the spirituality of the Rule.

The Redaction of the Rule from April 1977 through June 1978

For the most part, the text of the Rule did not change significantly from the *April 1977 Redaction* through to the officially approved text of the *Rule of 1978*. Thus, rather than analyzing individually each of the texts which were developed during the final year of the Rule Project, we will focus upon the changes introduced into the *April 1977 Redaction* or how the Rule itself evolved during those final months. Our study will focus upon three further redactions of the April 1977 text: the "*Final Redaction*" sent by the Assistants General to the Ministers General, the "*Text sent to the Curia*" by the Ministers General, and the offically approved *Rule of 1978*[119]. Let us consider how the Rule changed within each of these texts.

The local members of the International Commission, those who were charged with refining the Italian text produced at the April 1977 meeting, introduced only minor changes within the text. They made the verb forms consistent throughout the text[120]. They added and deleted a few sentences or phrases to emphasize further the *secular* vocation

---

[119] *Appendix IV* contains a comparative analysis of these four texts: the *April 1977 Redaction*, the *Final Redaction* sent by the Assistants General to the Ministers General, the *Text sent to the Curia* by the Ministers General, and the final version of the *Rule of 1978*. That analysis graphically presents the evolution of the Rule during the final year of the Rule Project. The four texts have been arranged in parallel columns to indicate how the text was redacted at each stage leading to the officially approved *Rule of 1978*. Within this chapter we will analyze the changes evidenced by the comparative analysis given in *Appendix IV*, below pp. 435-453.

[120] Basically, they decided to use the third person plural present subjunctive form of the verb and, therefore, substituted that form of the verb wherever the *April 1977 Redaction* had switched to the first person plural future indicative form.

of Secular Franciscans[121]. Finally, they added some clarifications within *Chapter III*: that one is admitted to the Secular Franciscan *Order* rather than to the Fraternity, that the local Fraternities not only participate in the higher level fraternities but also *contribute financially* to their Councils, and that the request for a fraternal visitation be made to the ministers *at a higher level* rather than at the local level. The text of the *April 1977 Redaction* remained essentially intact, therefore, in the *Final Redaction* sent to the Ministers General.

The four Ministers General further amended the text before submitting it to the Sacred Congregation for Religious and Secular Institutes for formal approval. In several places they simply added the phrase "according to the norm of the Constitutions". They also added some clarifications: that communion be fostered "especially with youth groups", that the Councils ask for "suitable and well prepared religious" for spiritual assistance, and that within their own families the members live the Franciscan spirit "of peace, fidelity, and respect for life"[122]. Curiously, while they specified the Franciscan spirit in terms of peace and respect for life, they omitted the sentence which read: "Thus, they will be quick to commit themselves in service to the promotion of the human person and to work with all people of good will to realize peace and to eliminate every obstacle to a truly universal community"[123]. While this omission did weaken the text with respect to the Secular Franciscans' commitment to the work of justice and peace, their changes did not essentially alter the text.

---

[121] For example, the text "Let them be active... in the field of social justice and public life" has become "Let them be active *by the testimony of their own human life... in the promotion of justice and in particular* in the field of public life". The full text of the *Final Redaction* submitted by the Assistants General to the Ministers General has been given in *Appendix IV*, column two. The changes made to the *April 1977 Redaction* have been *italicized* within the text in order to indicate more clearly how the local members changed the text prior to sending it to the Ministers General. Cf. below, pp. 435-453.

[122] This last "clarification" could well reflect a reaction against the liberalization of abortion laws in Europe as well as the increased rate of divorce among Catholics. It could therefore be understood as a call to "orthodoxy" in the sense of "listening" to the teaching of the Church.

[123] The last sentence of paragraph 9 in the *Final Redaction*, is omitted from paragraph 13 of the *Text sent to the Curia* by the Ministers General. Cf. below, p. 444.

However, the Ministers General did introduce one very significant change in the text, a change which profoundly altered the Rule. They included as a "Prologue" to the Rule the entire text of the *Earlier Exhortation* (the Earlier version of Francis' *Letter to All the Faithful*). The archives contain no documentation which explains or even notes this addition. The Prologue simply appears in the text sent by the Ministers General to the Curia. The text that had been submitted for approval to the Minsiters General by the Assistants General contained no Prologue. The Assistants General had, in fact, suggested that an Introduction be included, but that it be included within the decree of promulgation *not* within the Rule itself. Further, they recommended the inclusion of the Introduction given in the *1975 Redaction* and not the Prologue contained within the text of the *Local Commission*[124]. That is, they recommended that the Introduction present a theological or ecclesial context for the Rule; they did not recommend the inclusion of one of Francis' writings.

Although the Ministers General did not offer an explanation for their inclusion of Francis' *Earlier Exhortation*, their decision to include that text as a Prologue probably was based upon Esser's analysis of that early document[125]. Esser had claimed that the *Earlier Exhortation* "*could* be" the original Rule given by Francis to the penitents[126]. Only in their later correspondence with the Sacred Congregation do the Ministers General indicate the influence of Esser's research in their decision.

After the Sacred Congregation had completed its review of the Rule, the secretary of the Congregation sent a report to the Ministers General with some specific objections and recommendations. In the name of the Congregation, he objected to the text chosen by the Ministers General

---

[124] *AG Archives*: 77 CRE 06.27, 2.

[125] Esser's original article, written in 1974, was first published as *Ein Vorläufer der "Epistola ad Fideles" des hl. Franziskus von Assisi (Cod. 225 de Biblioteca Guarnacci zu Volterra)*, in *CF* 45 (1975) 5-37. It was later translated and published in both English and Italian: *A Forerunner of the "Epistola ad Fideles" of St. Francis of Assisi*, and *Un (Documento) precursore della "Epistola ad Fidelis" di San Francesco d'Assisi (Il Codice 225 della Biblioteca Guarnacci di Volterra)*, in *Anal TOR* 129 (1978) 11-47.

[126] Esser, *A Forerunner of the "Epistola ad Fideles"*, 39. For a discussion of Esser's research, cf. *Chapter I*, above pp. 83-86.

for the Prologue. The secretary applauded the insertion of one of Francis' writings as a Prologue to the Rule as "worthy of praise". However, he recommended that Francis' "Exhortation to the Brothers and Sisters of Penance" be replaced with his "Letter to the Faithful", contending that the latter presents "a dogmatic, ascetical and mystical synthesis which constitutes a complete program of life for the Christian who wishes to live the Gospel in the world according to the Franciscan spirit"[127]. While earlier the Ministers General had not offered an explanation for the insertion of the text in question, when challenged by the Sacred Congregation they defended their choice with an implicit reference to Esser's research. They argued that the "Exhortation to the Brothers and Sisters of Penance" was preferable because it had been accepted as the earlier version of the *Epistola ad Fideles*. Further, the Ministers General claimed that the *Earlier Exhortation* was preferable above all because it was "more concise and more adapted to the needs of today"[128]. Subsequently, the Sacred Congregation accepted the decision of the Ministers General and the officially approved *Rule of 1978* contains this Prologue. Thus, the *Earlier Exhortation* remains the lens through which the *Rule of 1978* must be understood and interpreted and this change made by the Ministers General did, therefore, profoundly alter the text of the Rule.

Several other changes recommended by the Sacred Congregation were incorporated into the text before it was promulgated[129]. In a few places it added some specification (for example: to observe the gospel of our Lord Jesus Christ "by following the example of Saint Francis of Assisi"). In the paragraph which speaks about Christ having chosen a poor and humble life, it adds "even though he valued created things attentively and lovingly" to emphasize the positive assessment of reality within a spirituality for the laity[130]. But the significant change was the Congregation's insertion of the paragraph which reads:

---

[127] Letter from B. Heiser, undersecretary of the Sacred Congregation for Religious and Secular Institutes, to C. Koser, O.F.M., Minister General. Cf. *OFM Archives*: 049786 30.1.78.

[128] *OFM Archives*: 050055 26.2.78.

[129] These changes have been *italicized* to make them more readily apparent within the comparative overview given in *Appendix IV*, below pp. 435-453.

[130] *OFM Archives*: 049786 30.1.78.

> The present rule, succeeding the "Memoriale Propositi" (1221) and the rules approved by the Supreme Pontiffs Nicholas IV and Leo XIII, adapts the Secular Franciscan Order to the needs and expectations of the Holy Church in the changed conditions of the times.
>
> Its interpretation belongs to the Holy See and its application will be made by the General Constitutions and particular statutes[131].

The Sacred Congregation inserted this paragraph so that the Rule would be clearly presented both as in continuity with the preceding Rules and as the definitive end of the project of renewal. Their explanation also stated that "if the Rule receives approbation by the Holy See, then the interpretation of the Rule also belongs to the Holy See"[132].

But even if the final interpretation of the Rule remains under the auspices of the Holy See, Secular Franciscans must also interpret the Rule. The translation of the text into life demands a process of interpretation, a process we will consider in *Chapter V*. But since we have now arrived at the final text of the Rule, let us summarize the Way of Life presented within the *Rule of 1978* and then consider the task of interpretation.

The Rule of 1978[133]

As the preceding analysis of the Rule Project has shown, the *Rule of 1978* followed the guidelines initially set by the Assisi Congress in 1969. Essentially, the *Rule of 1978* represents the result of several years of refining, organizing, and integrating the seventeen essential points of Franciscan spirituality outlined by that Congress. The only exception within the process was the insertion by the Ministers General of Francis' *Earlier Exhortation* as a Prologue to the Rule. This incorporation of

---

131 Paragraph 3 of the *Rule of 1978*.

132 *OFM Archives*: 049786 30.1.78.

133 The full text of the *Rule of 1978*, which will not be repeated here, appears in column four of the comparative analysis contained in *Appendix IV*. The officially approved English version of the *Rule of 1978* (a somewhat less literal translation) was included at the beginning of this study, pp. 31-38.

the primitive Rule within the new Rule represents, at least in this author's opinion, the most critical decision in the whole redactional process and provides the key for all future interpretations of the Rule, for the renewal of the Order. But before focusing upon the Prologue and how that affects the interpretation of the Rule, which will be the central focus of *Chapter V*, let us consider the "body" of the text.

Throughout most of the Rule Project the text of the rule did not include the *Earlier Exhortation*. Throughout the redactional process the "rule" was understood to be the three chapters which presented the identity, discipline, and government of the Order. Unfortunately, this connotation persists. In most discussions concerning the *Rule of 1978*, the term "Rule" connotes those three chapters or the body of the text; the Prologue itself receives little attention. Thus, let us examine what commonly is understood as the "text" of the Rule, the three chapters of the *Rule of 1978*.

Those three chapters of the new Rule followed the guidelines set by the Assisi Congress. An overview of the paragraphs of the *Rule of 1978* shows how the text specified those seventeen elements:

I: The Secular Franciscan Order

1. the vocation of all Franciscans:
   to make present within the Church the charism of Francis (6)[134]

---

[134] The numbers given within parentheses indicate which of the seventeen essential elements (as listed in Motion 9 of the Assisi Congress) correspond to each of the paragraphs in the *Rule of 1978*:

1. to live the gospel according to the spirit of St. Francis
2. to be converted continually (*metanoia*)
3. to live as a brother or sister of all people and of all creation
4. to live in communion with Christ
5. to follow the poor and crucified Christ
6. to share in the life and mission of the Church
7. to share in the love of the Father
8. to be instruments of peace
9. to have a life of prayer that is personal, communal and liturgical
10. to live in joy
11. to have a spirituality of a secular character
12. to be pilgrims on the way toward the Father
13. to participate in the Apostolate of the Laity
14. to be at the service of the less fortunate
15. to be loyal to the church in an attitude of dialogue and collaboration with her ministers
16. to be open to the action of the Spirit
17. to live in simplicity, humility, and minority

2. the vocation of Secular Franciscans:
   to live the Gospel within their secular state (11)
3. the interpretation of the Rule is reserved to the Holy See

II: The Way of Life

4. to observe the Gospel
   by following the example of Francis (1, 7)
5. to seek Christ (4)
6. to participate in the life and mission of the Church (13, 15)
7. to conform themselves to Christ through conversion (2)
8. to participate in the prayer of the Church, especially Eucharist (9)
9. to imitate Mary
10. to witness to Christ in the circumstances of their own lives (11, 15)
11. to live a simple life, sharing the goods of creation,
    and avoiding greed and power (12, 17)
12. to acquire purity of heart (17)
13. to be humble and gentle, serving the lowliest (14, 17)
14. to build a more fraternal and evangelical world (3, 8, 11, 16)
15. to promote justice, especially "in the field of public life" (8, 14, 16)
16. to see their work as redemptive for humanity (11)
17. to make their family life a sign of God's love (11)
18. to respect all of creation (3)
19. to seek out ways of unity and understanding (3, 8, 16)

III: Life in Fraternity

20. the Secular Franciscan Order is divided into Fraternities
21. the Fraternity is guided by a Minister and a Council
22. the local Fraternity must be a community of love (3, 4)
23. admission involves a time of initiation, a period of formation,
    and the Profession of the Rule
24. the Council organizes meetings to foster the community life
25. the members should contribute for expenses
26. each Fraternity should ask for spiritual assistance, a canonical
    visit, and a fraternal visit (15)

By comparing the contents of the *Rule of 1978* with the seventeen essential elements, it can easily be demonstrated that the *Rule of 1978* does indeed express the nature of the Secular Franciscan Order as defined by the Assisi Congress. Clearly, the *Rule of 1978* has included all six of the defining characteristics of the Order contained within motions 2 and 3 of that same Congress:

1. To Live the Gospel
2. Following Francis
3. Through Conversion / *Metanoia*
4. In Community
5. As Seculars
6. In Life-giving Union with All Franciscans

Thus, if the criteria for evaluating the *Rule of 1978* are the guidelines given by the Assisi Congress, then the *Rule of 1978* can be judged quite adequate. But are those criteria adequate? Should we not judge the *Rule of 1978* over against the primitive Rule? Should not the criteria for evaluating the *Rule of 1978* be the guidelines given by Francis to the early penitents?

Even a cursory comparison between the primitive Rule and the new Rule evidences a stark contrast. The ecstatic exultation and dramatic exhortation concerning penance find little echo in the new Rule. Admittedly, the difference in style between the two documents, the new Rule being more formal and juridical according to the genre of a rule, does explain the difference in tone. But the new Rule has changed not only the tone but also the content and spirit of the primitive Rule. The call to radical conversion which remains the heart of the *Earlier Exhortation* finds little echo within the new Rule.

But as we have seen, the *Rule of 1978* followed the Assisi guidelines; it did not attempt a translation of the primitive Rule. The initial seventeen essential elements of the Assisi Congress have been so refined that the resultant text, with its comfortable and appealing style, lacks vigor. The second chapter on the Way of Life (paragraphs 4 through 19) presents the demands of the Gospel: to seek God by following Christ crucified, to promote justice and work for peace, to build the kingdom, and even to live a life of "conversion". But these demands — which do present the gospel call to radical conversion — somehow lose their vitality and their radical nature amidst the Rule's more pious (or seemingly pious) exhortations that the Secular Franciscans should:

- devote themselves to a careful reading of the gospel (4)
- devote themselves to living in full communion with the clergy (6)
- conform their thoughts and deeds to those of Christ (7)
- imitate Mary's complete self-giving (9)
- faithfully fulfill their duties (10)
- seek a proper spirit of detachment (11)

- acquire a purity of heart (12)
- accept all people as a gift from God (13)
- cultivate a spirit of peace, fidelity, and respect for life in their families (17)
- strive to bring joy and hope to others (19).

Admittedly, these demands are gospel demands. But the radical response of Francis to the gospel, the radical conversion at the heart of the *Later Exhortation*, appears to have been lost in the refinement. As we have seen, the *1974 Basic Text* presented a strongly worded challenge to work for peace:

> And so, messengers of the Good News as Francis was, we make every effort, in all circumstances, to bring peace and joy to people, because we believe in the efficacy of dialogue and in the force of love. We always look for what unites, working with others to find solutions to conflicts which touch our neighbor, declaring ourselves against war in all its forms, refusing all participation in the arms race and in every antagonism between human beings and between peoples.
>
> In order to be faithful to our Franciscan vocation, we seize opportunities to accomplish positive acts; in order to bring this about we participate in common actions, even taking positions of responsibility in bodies which favor peace[135].

This challenge to work for peace in the process of "refinement" has been weakened. The *Rule of 1978* reads:

> Mindful that they are bearers of peace which must be built up unceasingly, they should seek out ways of unity and fraternal harmony through dialogue, trusting in the presence of the divine seed in everyone and in the transforming power of love and pardon[136].

Similarly, the *1974 Basic Text* presents the gospel challenge to work for justice with more force and vigor:

> We make every effort to be more particularly attentive to the most disinherited, to the unloved, to the victims of unjust situations and, as far as possible, to help them by concerted action to achieve their dignity as human beings and as children of God.

---

[135] The *1974 Basic Text*, paragraph 10.

[136] The *Rule of 1978*, paragraph 19.

> We fight against the obstacles to universal community (racism, oppression, injustice, violence)[137]

The *Rule of 1978*, by becoming more global and less concrete in its presentation of the various elements, drains much of the strength from the earlier text. It presents this challenge to work for justice much more blandly:

> Let them individually and collectively be in the forefront in promoting justice by the testimony of their human lives and their courageous initiatives. Especially in the field of public life, they should make definite choices in harmony with their faith[138].

Thus, while the *Rule of 1978* includes an exhortation to promote justice and peace, the overall language and tone could encourage a privatization of the various demands of conversion. Let us reexamine that process of "refinement", the methodology of the Rule Project, for further insight into the *Rule of 1978*.

The "Rule Project" in Retrospect

The new *Rule of 1978* was promulgated so that the Secular Franciscan Order might "gain a new impetus" and "flourish vigorously"[139]. But the new Rule has not, in general, engendered a new impetus within the Order. This failure suggests that the Rule might well be flawed or that it might not as yet have been correctly understood. I would suggest that both are true: on one level, the Rule (at least, as the "Rule" is commonly understood) is flawed; from a different perspective the Rule has not yet been understood. I will try to explain how both are true.

The flaw or basic inadequacy of the Rule results from the methodology used for formulating the new Rule. At the beginning of the process

---

[137] The *1974 Basic Text*, paragraph 6.

[138] The *Rule of 1978*, paragraph 15.

[139] Pope Paul VI made the statement in his Apostolic Letter, *Seraphicus Patriarcha*, with which he approved the new Rule of the Secular Franciscan Order. Cf. *Tertius Ordo* XXXIX (1978) 108; or Z. Grant, ed., *The Rule of the Secular Franciscan Order*, 12.

the Commissaries General, in their March 1966 letter, suggested that the renewal of the Rule be based upon the *Rule of 1883*. The 1967 responses, however, called for a complete reformulation of the Rule which would be both Franciscan and secular. Those responses also called for a real autonomy for the Secular Franciscan Order. Nonetheless, the "First Draft" of 1968 was formulated by clerics and, not surprisingly, rejected by the Secular Franciscans. The Rule Project then properly involved Secular Franciscans through the Assisi Congress of 1969. Unfortunately, however, guidelines for the new Rule were developed without any conscious return to the primitive sources of the Order, and those guidelines effectively determined all of the subsequent redactions. The one instance where not the Assisi motions but rather the primitive documents of the Order directly influenced the redactional process was the insertion of the *Earlier Exhortation* as a Prologue to the Rule in October 1977.

In retrospect, the failure to return to the origins of the Order and to the primitive documents looms large. But viewed from within the historical context of the Rule Project, the magnitude of this "failure" disappears in the then-pervading uncertainty concerning the origins of the Order. Though volumes, quite literally, have emerged concerning the origins of the Secular Franciscan Order, unfortunately, this historical research emerged only toward the end of or even subsequent to the Rule Project. In fact, five major historical congresses which focused specifically upon the Franciscan Order of Penitents were held in 1972, 1976, 1979, 1981, and 1987; and the proceedings of these congresses were subsequently published[140]. But as the dates clearly show, much

---

[140] The research presented at those five congresses has been published in five separate volumes: *L'Ordine della Penitenza di san Francesco d'Assisi nel secolo XIII. Atti del [1°] Convegno di Studi Francescani (Assisi, 3-5 luglio 1972)*, edited by O. Schmucki, Roma 1973; *I Frati Penitenti di San Francesco nella società del Due e Trecento. Atti del 2° Convegno di Studi Francescani (Roma, 12-14 ottobre 1976)*, edited by M. D'Alatri, Roma 1977; *Il movimento francescano della penitenza nella società medioevale. Atti del 3° Convegno di Studi Francescani (Padova, 25-27 settembre 1979)*, edited by M. D'Alatri, Roma 1980; *Prime manifestazioni di vita comunitaria, maschile e femminile, nel movimento francescano della Penitenza (1215-1447). Atti del [4°] Convegno di Studi Francescani (Assisi, 30 giugno - 2 luglio 1981)*, edited by R. Pazzelli and L. Temperini, Roma 1982; *La "Supra Montem" di Niccolò IV (1289): genesi e diffusione di una regola. Atti del 5° Convegno di Studi Francescani (Ascoli Piceno, 26-27 Ottobre 1987)*, edited by R. Pazzelli and L. Temperini, Roma 1988.

of the work on the new Rule had already been done. The Assisi Congress which set the guidelines for the future work on the Rule was held in 1969.

Of all the research which emerged, probably the study most critical to the development of the new Rule was Esser's analysis of the Volterra document. His study first appeared in German only in 1975. His conclusion — that the Volterra text could well represent the "norm of life" given by Francis to the penitents, as described by Thomas of Celano — undoubtedly influenced the decision of the Ministers General to insert that text as a Prologue to the Rule. But, unfortunately, the widespread popular recognition of the centrality of that text for the Secular Franciscan Order emerged too late for the text itself to have influenced or directed the entire Rule Project.

Thus, the *Rule of 1978* took shape against the background of the Assisi Congress' motions. In retrospect we can critique the methodology of the Rule Project. The process of renewal began not with the primitive documents but with suggestions from contemporary Secular Franciscans. While the experience of contemporary Secular Franciscans is of vital importance, their horizon (their own context, experience, and understanding) must be brought into dialogue with the tradition. The process somewhat precluded that dialogue. The method followed did not include a conscious return to the origins of the Order and, therefore, it is not surprising that the resultant Rule (the three main chapters separate from the Prologue) bears little resemblance to the primitive Rule.

Had the process of formulating a new Rule begun but ten years later, given the advantage of much historical research and the example of other Orders who had grounded their renewal in their primitive documents, undoubtedly the Rule Project would have evolved very differently. Most probably the redactors would have begun with the *Earlier Exhortation*, the primitive Rule, and sought a way to interpret that Rule in contemporary form. The process of renewal, the *aggiornamento* of the Secular Franciscan Order, would then truly have been a bringing up to date of the primitive Rule.

The letter inaugurating the Rule Project asked what elements should be included in the new Rule and from what sources those elements should be taken. Had that question been posed ten years later, the respondents would probably have suggested that the *Earlier Exhortation* be used as the source for the new Rule. Certainly today there remains no question that the new Rule would have to take as its source the primitive documents of the Order. There remains only the question of how to interpret those documents. But the *Earlier Exhortation* was, in fact, included within the *Rule of 1978* as a Prologue. Thus, while the redactional process for the new Rule did not return to the primitive Rule as a source, nonetheless the primitive Rule *is* contained within the new Rule. So even if the Rule Project never addressed the question of how to interpret the primitive Rule today, the basis for our asking that question has been provided by the inclusion of the primitive Rule within the *Rule of 1978*. The question which should have controlled the entire Rule Project is presented by the text of the Prologue itself: how do we interpret the primitive Rule or what does the text mean? In the *Introduction* I suggested that quite possibly the Rule has not yet been adequately understood. I would suggest that it has not been adequately understood, that it has not yet truly been appropriated, precisely because the question of its meaning has yet to be raised critically.

That question affords no easy answer but allows no escape if *radical* renewal of the Order is sought. The following chapter focuses specifically on the task of interpretation, the meaning of the primitive Rule today. But the question of meaning must be asked and answered not once and not by me but by each of the readers who seeks to know what the text means. Each Secular Franciscan must interpret the text. Each person must ask what the text means in his or her life. Thus, *Chapter V* will focus upon the question without pretending to give any definitive answer. It will instead present a method which suggests a direction towards an answer. Let us, then, turn to *Chapter V* and move towards an interpretation of the primitive Rule.

Chapter V

TOWARDS AN INTERPRETATION OF THE RULE OF 1978

The analysis of the Rule Project presented in the preceding chapter revealed two moments within that process of renewal as particularly critical. The first, which occurred toward the beginning of the process, was the articulation or definition of the Secular Franciscan "Way of Life" in terms of seventeen essential elements by the members of the Assisi Congress. Those seventeen elements given in Motion 9 served as the guidelines for all the future redactions of the Rule. The moment inscribed in those seventeen elements was critical precisely because it was so determinative. That "moment" determined both the content and the process for the new Rule. The content of all future redactions was determined quite explicitly by the seventeen essential elements. But the process of redacting the new Rule was also determined by those seventeen elements. Motion 9 had, in effect, answered the question of the source of the new Rule. It took the rightful source for the Rule's content to be the statements of the Secular Franciscans themselves and effectively closed any future discussion concerning the sources on which to base the new Rule. Motion 9 was, therefore, the first critical moment because essentially it determined the entire course of the Rule Project.

The second critical moment, resulting from a decision made by the Ministers General toward the end of the Rule Project, was the inclusion of the *Earlier Exhortation* as a Prologue to the Rule. Whereas the first moment was critical for directing the life of the Rule Project, this second "moment" was and is critical for directing the life of the Rule beyond the Rule Project. Whereas the first moment was critical for determining a process of renewal which omitted a return to the primitive sources of the Order, the second moment was critical for determining that all future interpretations of the Rule do, in fact, begin with the primitive Rule. The papally approved *Rule of 1978* begins with Francis' *Earlier Exhortation*, it presents the primitive Rule as the interpretative lens through which to read the paragraphs that follow.

The Rule Project's methodology was tragically flawed, no less flawed than an attempt to articulate a contemporary Christology without recourse to the Gospels. It is precisely because of this initial failure to base the new Rule upon the primitive Rule that the later decision of the Ministers General becomes so significant. Their decision to include the *Earlier Exhortation* as a Prologue to the Rule not only gave attention to the primitive Rule but presented it as the interpretive lens of the new Rule.

Our review of the "Rule Project" in *Chapter IV* brought us to a critical question: what form would the new Rule have taken had the process of renewal been based upon the primitive Rule? The inclusion of the primitive Rule as the Prologue to the new Rule, though of critical importance, has not yet answered that question. The task of interpreting the primitive Rule, the task of deciphering what the text meant and what the text means, remains to be done. It is to that task and in particular to the question of what the text *means* that we turn our attention.

Beginning with a "Text"

How we understand a "text" will determine how we interpret that text. For many interpreters a text is simply "talk writ down". The text then is understood as a semantic container which holds the original conversation and so contains the original meaning intended by the author. To understand a text we have to find out what the text meant. Therefore, the most appropriate methods for interpreting any text are those of historical criticism.

Unfortunately, most biblical scholars and Franciscan scholars accept this understanding of a text and therefore confine themselves to the role of "exegete". That is, they employ historical critical methods to explain what the text meant and go no further. An unspoken presupposition is that what the text *means* is given in what the text *meant*. Seldom do they give attention to the process of appropriation, that is, the way in which the contemporary hearer translates the meaning of the text into his or her own life.

The philosopher Paul Ricoeur challenges the basic presupposition that a text is a semantic container. Ricoeur analyzes the nature of text and then proposes a theory of interpretation which takes into account the very nature of a text as different from "talk writ down". He addresses quite specifically the problem of "appropriating" a text, that is, the process by which the reader arrives at an understanding of the meaning of the text. Ricoeur's insights into the nature of text and the process of interpretation provide a productive approach for interpreting texts[1]. Thus, we will consider Ricoeur's hermeneutical approach to texts and then proceed to a specific application of that approach: the interpretation of the primitive Rule for Secular Franciscans today.

Ricoeur's Hermeneutical Approach

Ricoeur, in his reflection upon linguistic experience, has analyzed the nature of a text as a particular instance of language. Probably Ricoeur's most important insight concerning the nature of texts is that a text is not just "talk writ down", that is, written discourse is not simply the transcription of oral discourse. Writing differs from speaking in its structures and dynamics. Therefore, dialogue as the appropriate model for speaking is *not* the appropriate model for interpreting texts. An adequate approach to interpreting texts must take into account the differences between oral and written discourse and approach a text *qua* text.

Ricoeur's approach does just that. He developed a theory of interpretation based upon the nature of a text. But since Ricoeur understands the uniqueness of a text in contrast to oral discourse, we will first look at Ricoeur's analysis of discourse and then proceed to his theory of interpretation. This brief overview of the central points in

[1] For a good summary of Ricoeur's hermeneutical presuppositions and an inspiring application to a biblical text, cf. S. Schneiders, *The Foot Washing (John 13:1-20): An Experiment in Hermeneutics*, in *The Catholic Biblical Quarterly* 43 (1981) 76-92. For a discussion of the implications of Ricoeur's work for the understanding of liturgical texts, cf. R. K. Seasoltz, *The Sacred Liturgy: Development and Directions*, in *Remembering the Future: Vatican II and Tomorrow's Liturgical Agenda*, edited by C. Last, New York 1983, 48-79.

Ricoeur's approach to texts does not pretend to summarize Ricoeur's analysis of text, much less his numerous and complex hermeneutical studies. Rather, this outline attempts only to present the main lines of Ricoeur's argument:

- language as discourse
  (how language is structured dialectically)

- text as written discourse
  (how the dialectics change from speaking to writing)

- the effects of the resultant distanciation
  (how the text projects a "world")

- and the implications for interpreting texts
  (how the reader appropriates the meaning of the text).

Language as Discourse

In order to question some of the operative hermeneutical assumptions concerning texts and to arrive at a correct definition of the hermeneutical task, Ricoeur begins with an analysis of language as discourse[2]. According to Ricoeur, discourse is structured dialectically. That is, there are a series of matched poles which create certain tensions within discourse itself. He identifies three distinct dialectics within discourse which can be presented schematically as follows[3]:

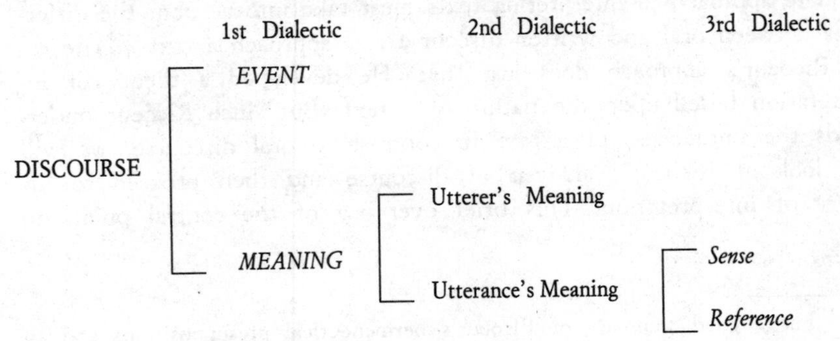

[2] P. Ricoeur, *Interpretation Theory: Discourse and the Surplus of Meaning*, Fort Worth 1976, 1-23.

[3] Sandra Schneiders presented this quite helpful schematic summary in a seminar on hermeneutics.

Let us consider each of these three dialectics.

Discourse is structured dialectically primarily in terms of *event* and *meaning*. Discourse is first of all an event. Something happens when someone speaks. Discourse is not language as a pure atemporal system but language *used*, that is, language in the present which refers both to the speaker and to the "world" it attempts to describe, express, or represent. But the speaker communicates this world to the hearer and so discourse is an event because it is a temporal phenomenon of exchange[4].

But "if all discourse is actualized as an event, it is understood as meaning"[5]. Discourse does not just happen, it is about something. Discourse intends meaning. Speaking is an event, but the speaker uses words to convey a message or meaning.

> Just as language, by being actualised in discourse, surpasses itself as system and realises itself as event, so too discourse, by entering the process of understanding, surpasses itself as event and becomes meaning. The surpassing of the event by the meaning is characteristic of discourse as such[6].

Thus, discourse is structured dialectically in terms of *event* and *meaning* (the first dialectic). And although the event character of discourse passes away, its meaning can be preserved. What is said becomes separate or distant from the saying, the event. Thus, as Ricoeur points out, even in oral form discourse displays a primitive form of distanciation which gives rise to the characteristics of text[7]. But before we consider distanciation let us examine the other two dialectics.

The meaning which is distinct from the event character of discourse itself involves a dialectic. This second dialectic involves the relationship between the *utterer's meaning* and the *utterance's meaning*, between what the speaker means and what the speaker says[8]. Questions within our

[4] P. Ricoeur, *The Hermeneutical Function of Distanciation*, in *Hermeneutics and the Human Sciences*, edited by J. Thompson, Cambridge/New York 1981, 133-34.

[5] Ricoeur, *Interpretation Theory*, 12.

[6] Ricoeur, *The Hermeneutical Function of Distanciation*, 134.

[7] *Ibid.*, 132.

[8] Ricoeur, *Interpretation Theory*, 12-19.

everyday conversation reveal this dialectic: "Did you mean what you just said"? or "What did you mean by that"? Normally or ideally these two would coincide in oral discourse. But what is said might mean more than what the speaker intended. The meaning is no longer controlled by the speaker but exists within the sentence as separate from the speaker.

Further, the utterance's meaning or the meaning within the sentence is structured dialectically in terms of its *sense* and *reference*, "what" is said and "about what" it is said (the third dialectic)[9]. This dialectic results from the very nature of language as fundamentally referential[10]. That is, language not only points towards ideal meanings but it also refers to what *is*. For example, if this were a conversation and not a written text, I could ask you, "is the last word in the previous sentence dialectic"? My words have an immediate *reference* which you could verify. In oral discourse the *sense* and *reference* normally coincide, that is, what is said and about what it is said are immediately related.

Since writing is a form of discourse these dialectics obtain in a text as well. But, as Ricoeur clearly demonstrates, writing is not just written conversation. The dynamics change when discourse changes from speaking to writing. Let us move to Ricoeur's analysis of those changes.

Text as Written Discourse

According to Ricoeur, a text is discourse under the condition of inscription[11]. But in written discourse *event* and *meaning* are separated and the meaning becomes fixed. This fixing of meaning gives to the text a semantic autonomy — which is precisely what makes a text unique. This "semantic autonomy" of the text is still governed by the dialectic of event and meaning. The move from speaking to writing does not destroy the dialectic of event and meaning which exists in oral discourse. Rather this dialectic is made more obvious. Ricoeur insists

---

[9] *Ibid.*, 19-22.

[10] *Ibid.*, 21.

[11] P. Ricoeur, *What is a Text? Explanation and Understanding*, in *Hermeneutics and the Human Sciences*, edited by J. Thompson, Cambridge/New York 1981, 145-64.

that "[w]riting is the full manifestation of discourse"[12]. A text originates as an event (the event of composition) but its meaning exists beyond the event. The meaning becomes liberated from the original event but can be actualized subsequently as event (though a different event) when it is read.

But while both written and oral discourse share the same dialectical structure, writing does exhibit several characteristics different from those of speaking. The first and most obvious change is that in writing the meaning or message of the discourse is fixed. It is not just that the medium of the message is different. The meaning, as separate from the original event and fixed in the text, is no longer determined by the intention of the author, by the mind of the original audience, or by the original situation. That is, the fixing of meaning significantly changes relations between different components of the communicative process.

First, the relation between the *message* and the *speaker* is altered radically. In oral discourse the intention of the speaker and the meaning of the discourse coincide such that to understand what the speaker means is to understand what the discourse means. But with written discourse the intention of the author and the meaning of the text no longer coincide and, therefore, to understand what the text means is *not* equivalent to understanding what the author meant. The meaning of the text is relatively independent of the intent of the author. Discourse as written explodes this relationship between the author and the text. "The text's career escapes the finite horizon lived by its author. What the text means now matters more than what the author meant when he wrote it"[13]. Thus, the meaning of the text cannot be equated with the intention of the author (the "intentional fallacy"). But Ricoeur cautions that we must avoid the other extreme which denies any relevance to the author's intention (the 'fallacy of the absolute text'). The author's intent is neither irrelevant nor totally determinative.

Secondly, the relation between the *message* and the *hearer* is changed. Whereas oral discourse is addressed to specific hearers, written discourse cannot predetermine its audience. A written text is addressed potentially to whomever can read. But the very nature of a text as open to various readers makes the text open to various interpretations.

---

[12] Ricoeur, *Interpretation Theory*, 25-26.

[13] *Ibid.*, 30.

Whereas oral discourse presupposes a relatively uniform context for its hearers, a text is read from within very different contexts. In oral discourse the speaker has control over the meaning of the discourse and the speaker and hearers in some way share a common horizon. But with a text, not only does the speaker no longer have control over the meaning of the discourse, the "hearers" attempt to understand a text from within their own situations, within different contexts. But this new relation between author and "hearer", between text and reader, produces the need for interpretation. In the dialogic situation, the hearer can ask the speaker to clarify what has not been understood. But where discourse no longer exists as event, no questions can be directed to the speaker. Consider, for example, the sentence: "this page should be red". In oral discourse the hearer can ask the speaker if "red" means "read" or "red", the verb or the color. However, given the written sentence, "this page should be red", you the reader need to determine what the text means: did the author intend to indicate the color of the page or was there a typographical error? A "hearer" of a *text* who encounters problems understanding the text has no recourse to the author. The reader must interpret the text. "Hermeneutics begins where dialogue ends"[14].

Thirdly, writing makes the relation between the *message* and the *code* more complex. The literary genre of a text is not merely a convenient classification device. Rather, it is part of the code of the text; it helps to express the meaning. Different genres speak differently to the reader both cognitively and intuitively. In this sense, texts must be approached as works rather than objects, that is, as analogous to works of art rather than objects of science. The literary genre shapes and forms; it helps give expression. For example, poetry, law, narrative, and fiction shape meaning differently. Analogous to the artist's expression in sculpture, the author "sculpts" meaning in genre. We do not just read words. We read words embodied in a particular genre. The literary genre and the style of the author together produce a *work*, that is, "discourse both as inscribed and wrought"[15].

Finally, the relation between the *sense* and *reference* changes once oral discourse ends and with it the situation of the ostensive reference. In oral discourse there is a one-to-one relationship between the sense

---

[14] *Ibid.*, 32.
[15] *Ibid.*, 33.

and reference. The reference can be identified or indicated because the speaker and hearers share the same situation. But a text cannot point to its reference because it is situationless. But the text's loss of a specific situation does not debilitate the reference but instead frees it. In the same way that the text frees the meaning from the intent of the author, it frees the reference from the limits of a specific situation. There is no longer a one-to-one relationship between sense and reference. The reader is not confined, therefore, to one particular situation but can enter a world created by all of the different references opened up by texts. Thus by the very nature of writing "the 'world' of the *text* may explode the world of the *author*"[16].

A very clear and powerful example of what Ricoeur describes abstractly is given by Sandra Schneiders. Concretizing Ricoeur's reflections concerning the "world of the text", she writes:

> the American Declaration of Independence was written in the patriarchal slave culture of 18th-century America by adult, white, property-owning, free males who did not question the divinely ordained rightness of their own superior social status. When they wrote that "all men are created equal" they certainly did not intend to affirm the equal dignity and rights of children, non-whites, the landless, slaves, or females. Indeed, if they had been asked, they would have denied the very possibility that social order could be sustained in a situation of universal equality. However, as the document they authored has been read in successive periods of American history it has been decontextualized in the struggle for the emancipation of slaves, suffrage for women, civil rights for blacks, and the inviolability of children. The world of the text, namely, that of equality for all, has literally exploded the patriarchal world of its authors[17].

But this projecting of a world is, according to Ricoeur, the very "destination of discourse"[18]. Thus, let us look more closely at how the text projects a world.

---

[16] Ricoeur, *The Hermeneutical Function of Distanciation*, 139.

[17] S. Schneiders, *Feminist Ideology Criticism and Biblical Hermeneutics*, in *Biblical Theology Bulletin* 19 (1989) 7.

[18] Ricoeur, *Interpretation Theory*, 37.

The Text as Projecting a World

Prior to the work of Ricoeur and others in contemporary hermeneutics, historical distance was considered a disadvantage to accurate understanding. But as Ricoeur has shown, distanciation does not impoverish but enriches. Distanciation becomes an advantage to understanding a text[19]. Providing that the world of the interpreter has been enriched in the intervening time, the reader can appropriate *more* meaning. The "more" within a text results from its nature as a "work"[20].

> An essential characteristic of a literary work, and of a work of art in general, is that it transcends its own psycho-sociological conditions of production and thereby opens itself to an unlimited series of readings, themselves situated in different socio-cultural conditions. In short, the text must be able, from the sociological as well as the psychological point of view, to "decontextualise" itself in such a way that it can be "recontextualised" in a new situation - as accomplished, precisely, by the act of reading[21].

Ricoeur emphasizes that a text as a *work* operates at a level beyond signs and even sentences[22]. Writing is not just a re-producing but a transforming of the discourse. Writing, like art, does not merely reproduce a reality but creates something in which the reality comes to stand by itself in a new way. Writing projects a world, a world which readers are invited to enter.

> Iconicity is the re-writing of reality. Writing, in the limited sense of the word, is a particular case of iconicity. The inscription of discourse is the transcription of the world, and transcription is not reduplication, but metamorphosis[23].

Writing liberates discourse from its particularity, releasing the universal which is at the heart of the reality. Because of distanciation a text operates as an icon. Distanciation is, therefore, quite productive.

---

[19] Ricoeur, *The Hermeneutical Function of Distanciation*, 131-44.

[20] P. Ricoeur, *Metaphor and the Central Problem of Hermeneutics*, in *Hermeneutics and the Human Sciences*, edited by J. Thompson, Cambridge/New York 1981, 165-81.

[21] Ricoeur, *The Hermeneutical Function of Distanciation*, 139.

[22] *Ibid.*, 175.

[23] Ricoeur, *Interpretation Theory*, 42.

Les Misérables offers a concrete example of the iconicity of a text. I mentioned to a friend with whom I had seen the show that it spoke powerfully to me about the struggle of the people in El Salvador. My friend, who works in a parish in the South East Bronx, responded that the show had been for him about the struggle of the blacks. On one level, *Les Misérables* is about the struggle of the poor in early 19th century France. On another level, the play is about the timeless struggle of the oppressed for freedom. *Les Misérables* spoke to me and my friend about different things; it spoke powerfully to both of us about the same reality. A text, as a play or any other work of art, as icon, releases the universal because distanciation has freed it from being tied to only one particular situation or reference.

But while distanciation can be rich and productive, it does present a problem when the text is read. This distanciation which grounds the possibility of the text projecting a world must be overcome if the reader is to enter that world. That is, the text which is distant or alien to the reader must somehow be made close and intimate to the reader. Thus, between the two poles of *writing* and *reading* emerges the dialectic of *distanciation* and *appropriation*. The distance or alienation between the reader and the text demands a process by which the reader can overcome the otherness of the text and make the text his or her own. Ricoeur's hermeneutical theory focuses upon that struggle between "otherness" and "ownness". In fact, according to Ricoeur, "[i]nterpretation, philosophically understood, is nothing else than an attempt to make estrangement and distanciation productive"[24]. Let us turn to the process of making that distanciation productive, the process of interpreting a text.

The Interpretation of a Text

According to Ricoeur, a text is both an *object* and a *work*. It is both an object of nature and a work of art. Therefore, both of these aspects of a text must be held in dialectic relationship to interpret a text. Interpretation of a text involves both *explanation* and *understanding*[25]. For Ricoeur, interpretation is not a third term alongside explanation and understanding, nor is it the name of the dialectic

[24] *Ibid.*, 44.

[25] Ricoeur, *What is a Text? Explanation and Understanding*, 145-64.

between these last two terms. Interpretation is "the whole process that encompasses explanation and understanding"[26].

Interpretation involves a process which moves from understanding to explanation and then from explanation to a new understanding or comprehension. The reader's first understanding or general sense of the text represents a first naïveté. But often what at first appeared to make sense becomes confusing under closer examination. Where the sense of the text presents problems for understanding explanation becomes necessary. For example, at the level of a first naïveté *Genesis* reveals how the world was created. However, closer observation reveals that there are two differing accounts of creation in *Genesis* which cannot be reconciled as accounts of how the world was created[27]. By a process of explanation, properly the work of historical criticism, we can discover many things about the world from which the text emerged and explain why two separate accounts were included within *Genesis*.

By going through an explanatory or interpretive process the reader comes to a second naïveté, what Ricoeur calls "comprehension". At this second level of understanding, the level of comprehension, real appropriation is possible. Thus, for Ricoeur, explanation mediates between two levels of understanding: the original understanding and comprehension. To return to the example of *Genesis*, explanation can reveal that the Israelites' creation accounts were the work of different authors expressing a monotheistic faith in the face of a polytheistic culture. Through the process of explanation we can move to a different understanding of the text. *Genesis* is about God creating the world, but not *how* God created the world. Explanation shows us that *Genesis* must be read through the lens of "exodus". The God who saves and frees is also the God who creates and gives life. Where we first understood the text to be about how God created the world, we come to comprehend that the text is about faith in a God who gives life.

Ricoeur suggests that the first act of understanding takes the form of a "guess". A guess becomes necessary because the dialogical situation present in oral discourse no longer exists. The text is mute and can be construed in different ways. But to construe the meaning of the text as a whole *is* to venture a guess. Unfortunately, there are no rules

[26] Ricoeur, *Interpretation Theory*, 74.

[27] The first creation account begins with *Genesis* 1:1. The second account follows right after the first, beginning at *Genesis* 2:4.

for making good guesses, but there are methods for validating those guesses. Thus, while there are different ways to construe a text, not all interpretations are equivalent. Each text presents a limited field of possible constructions and so an interpretation need be not only probable but more probable than other interpretations. And the process of demonstrating the probability of an interpretation is the process of validation. Thus, the process of interpretation encompasses understanding which involves guessing and explanation which involves validation. Only after we have made an initial guess and validated that understanding through explanation can we authentically appropriate the meaning of the text.

Music provides a good example of the possibility of different interpretations and how not all interpretations are equivalent[28]. We have all heard very different interpretations of the National Anthem. The talent of the singer or of the musician affects the interpretation. Not all interpretations are equivalent. Yet to be valid interpretations they must follow the musical score as written. The "interpretation" can so change the words or musical score that it is no longer recognizable as the National Anthem. But following the text of the music does not mean slavishly imitating the original intent of the composer. Few would argue that the only correct interpretation of *Silent Night* is a version in German with guitar accompaniment. Yet Franz Gruber wrote *Silent Night* in German in the nineteenth century for the guitar because the Church's organ was broken. We have all heard many different interpretations of *Silent Night.* Not all interpretations of *Silent Night* are equivalent; the ability of the performer in large part determines the adequacy of the interpretation. Some renditions of *Silent Night* are truly inspired. But as the talent of the musician enhances the interpretation, so too the "talent" or holiness of the Christian enhances his or her interpretation of the Gospel. The more studied musician can deliver a richer interpretation of a musical text; the more committed and Christ-like disciple can more authentically interpret the Gospel today; and as we will see, the more authentically converted Secular Franciscan can more authentically interpret the primitive Rule.

We have described this process of interpretation in terms of the dialectic between distanciation and appropriation. It could also be described in terms of the dialectic between *sense* and *reference*. Ricoeur speaks

---

[28] Ricoeur, *Interpretation Theory*, 75; S. Schneiders, *Faith, Hermeneutics, and the Literal Sense of Scripture*, in *Theological Studies* 39 (1978) 735.

of the non-ostensive reference of written discourse as a "world". That is, the text projects a reality, not what was, or even what is, but what can be. The process of interpretation involves the discerning of that world (understanding and explanation) and responding to the invitation to enter it (appropriation). What we appropriate or "make our own" is not some past world but the projection of a world[29]. The meaning of a text "lies not behind the text but in front of it"[30]. The meaning of a text is disclosed to us, discovered by us.

Since the reference of the text is no longer ostensively obvious, the reference is disclosed in and through the sense of the text.

> To understand a text is to follow its movement from sense to reference: from what it says, to what it talks about...
>
> The text speaks of a possible world and of a possible way of orientating oneself within it. The dimensions of the world are properly opened up by and disclosed by the text[31].

Our task then in interpreting the primitive Rule, in appropriating the meaning of Francis' *Earlier Exhortation*, is to follow the text from what it says to what it is about. By a process of understanding and explanation we must attempt to discern the world projected by the text. Only then can we authentically respond to that world. Only then can we truly appropriate the meaning of the text. Only then will we have adequately interpreted the primitive Rule.

The Primitive Rule as "Text"

As a "text", the primitive Rule projects a world. Our goal, therefore, is not to determine Francis' intent or the response of the original hearers but to discern the meaning of the text for us as readers. To enter the world of the text, to see the possibilities for living that it

---

[29] P. Ricoeur, *Appropriation*, in *Hermeneutics and the Human Sciences*, edited by J. Thompson, Cambridge/New York 1981, 192.

[30] Ricoeur, *Metaphor and the Central Problem of Hermeneutics*, 177.

[31] Ricoeur, *Interpretation Theory*, 87-88.

projects, we will begin with the *sense* of the text, with what the text says. We will go through the *sense* of the text to get to the *reference* of the text, what the text is about.

The "Sense" of the Primitive Rule

Scholars have ventured guesses with respect to the meaning of the text as a whole and then attempted to validate those guesses. In *Chapter I* we reviewed how Sabatier's original proposal was eventually verified through careful historical and literary criticism: that the Volterra text was an earlier version of the *Letter to All the Faithful* and *could* be the primitive Rule of the brothers and sisters of penance. Esser's title for the text, "An Exhortation to the Brothers and Sisters of Penance", suggested the sense of the text as a whole: an exhortation to penance.

The first part of the text proclaims the blessedness of those who do penance, of those who:

> love the Lord *with their whole heart, with their whole soul and mind, with their whole strength* and love their neighbors as themselves,
> and hate their bodies with their vices and sins,
> and receive the Body and Blood of our Lord Jesus Christ,
> and produce worthy fruits of penance[32].

Upon those who persevere in these things the Spirit of God will come to rest and they are the "spouses, brothers, and mothers of our Lord Jesus Christ"[33]. The second part of the text then warns of damnation for those who do not do penance. Thus, briefly put, the text says that doing penance brings a person to salvation and not doing penance leads a person to damnation.

Chapter II and *Chapter III* both focused on what the text meant, on what the text was about. Both chapters attempted to explain what "penance" and "doing penance" meant. In *Chapter II* we reviewed the development of penance within the Church and then examined the "penitential climate" of thirteenth century Assisi. In *Chapter III* we attempted to study the text itself within that historical context. We reviewed

---

[32] *Earlier Exhortation*, 1-4.

[33] *Earlier Exhortation*, 6-7.

the exegetical studies which help to explain what the text meant. Esser's historical critical analysis indicated that the primitive Rule exhorted the hearers to embrace voluntarily the practice of penance as it had evolved in the thirteenth century. Flood's socio-historical analysis clarified the radical nature of those practices with respect to the existent social structures of Assisi. Finally, Lehmann's structural analysis highlighted the text's proclamation of the salvific effects wrought by those practices.

Using historical critical analysis to explain some of the ambiguity of the text, we arrived at the understanding that "to do penance" meant to enter the Order of Penitents and to embrace a life of rigorous penitential practices. This life of penance meant a conversion, a turning from a former way of life and the beginning of a new life. To do penance was "to leave the world", to die to sin and live in Christ. The conversion involved was indeed dramatic. The penance required was decidedly severe. Many therefore avoided becoming penitents until they were dying, and yet, great numbers of men and women did become voluntary penitents, apparently with the expectation that penitential practices did facilitate contact with the divine.

At the level of *sense*, the text claims that doing penance brings us to an intimate union with God, and conversely, not doing penance destroys our relationship with God. But we need to go from the *sense* to the *reference*, from what the text says to what the text is about, from what the text *meant* to what the text *means*.

The "Reference" of the Primitive Rule

Through a long process of explanation, which included the study of some other writings of Francis, we have seen that doing penance meant choosing a life of conversion. The primitive Rule is not about hating our bodies, or wearing a habit, or working with lepers in any literal sense. The primitive Rule is *about* conversion, radical conversion. It is about people choosing to respond in faith to the God revealed by Jesus.

The text proclaims the blessedness of a life of conversion; the text exults in the visitation of God which results from conversion. The question behind the text might well be expressed as "how are we to experience this intimacy with God". The primitive Rule proclaims that by doing penance we *are* the "spouses, brothers and mothers of our Lord Jesus Christ". That is, by undergoing radical conversion we *are* close to God; we live in holiness.

But can the text really mean that radical conversion brings us close to God and transforms our lives to holiness? Where do we find hints of this reality? Our ordinary experience would contradict rather than support that claim. Unfortunately, many of those who claim to have undergone a radical conversion evidence little holiness. Too often "born-again" Christians who proclaim loudly the radical nature of their conversion evidence little knowledge of the God of compassion. If radical conversion makes us the "spouses, brothers, and mothers of our Lord Jesus Christ", then we can expect the radically converted to follow the way of the Gospel. We can expect the radically converted to live the Beatitudes: to be poor and humble, to work for justice, to be merciful, to be peacemakers. But often the "radically converted" of our world (not all, but certainly some of the born-again Christian fundamentalist types) are rich, proud, and evidence little mercy in their oppressive moral positions.

On the other hand, some Christians who do appear "close to God", who clearly evidence a holiness, have not undergone any "radical conversion". They often have been Christians all their lives and have not experienced any dramatic "turn about" or conversion. Where then do we find evidence for the claim that radical conversion brings holiness? Can the primitive Rule really be about "conversion"?

The conflict between the claim of the text and our experience of conversion suggests that we might not have an adequate understanding of "conversion". What does conversion mean? What does radical conversion mean? If the primitive Rule *is* about conversion, then we must try to understand as fully as possible what conversion means.

The Meaning of "Conversion"

Unfortunately, "conversion" is generally understood today in one of two ways. Often it connotes a dramatic reversal in a person's life, usually as the result of a significant crisis. In this sense it may or may not be a "religious" conversion. When conversion does deal with faith it often connotes the adult choice to become a member of a specific religious tradition and the person is referred to as a "convert". In this second sense, conversion is often less dramatic. But both of these connotations of conversion restrict the experience to a small number of people. The majority of people do not experience an extremely dramatic "turn-about" in their lives. Similarly, the majority of people do not become "converts" as adults, entering a specific religious tradition as an adult.

We could expand this second understanding of conversion. We could by extension speak of all members of a religious tradition, not only those who chose the tradition as adults, as "converts". We could speak of the ongoing embrace of a specific religious tradition as "conversion". But while this broadens the experience of conversion, it does not help to explain the primitive Rule's claim that conversion brings holiness. The examples of good "practicing" religious people who propagate violence and oppression are legion.

So how then can the primitive Rule be proclaiming conversion as the way to intimacy with God? The text cannot mean conversion in the general connotation of religious conversion, unless perhaps, our understanding of conversion is inadequate. But if the text is about conversion, then we must search for an adequate understanding of conversion. Thus, in order to move forward in our interpretation of the primitive Rule, we will turn to an examination of the nature, structure, and dynamics of conversion. With a more informed understanding of conversion we will then return to our task, the interpretation of the primitive Rule.

An Analysis of Conversion

The Work of Bernard Lonergan

Bernard Lonergan has presented an analysis of conversion that is "not only strikingly original but deeply rooted in the best of traditional and modern philosophical and theological thought"[34]. Lonergan's work brought him to distinguish different types of conversion. His understanding of conversion derived from his analysis of human consciousness and the dynamism of the human spirit. Lonergan distinguished four different levels of human consciousness:

---

[34] W. Conn, *Bernard Lonergan's Analysis of Conversion*, in *Angelicum* 53 (1976) 362.

> There is the *empirical level* on which we sense, perceive, imagine, feel, speak, move. There is an *intellectual level* on which we inquire, come to understand, express what we have understood, work out the presupppositions and implications of our expression. There is the *rational level* on which we reflect, marshal the evidence, pass judgment on the truth or falsity, certainty or probability, of a statement. There is the *responsible level* on which we are concerned with ourselves, our own operations, our goals, and so deliberate about possible courses of action, evaluate them, decide, and carry out our decisions[35].

According to Lonergan, our consciousness unfolds from experiencing to understanding to judging to deciding. Further, he suggests that this pattern operates in all of our decisions and activities, from the most mundane to the most profound. Human consciousness does not end with sensing data. We intuitively seek to understand the data, to verify the truth of our understanding, and to determine the worth of our insight. At each level of consciousness there is a natural dynamism which moves us to the next level. These dynamic exigencies or *transcendental notions* move us through the successive stages of consciousness which are really "the unfolding of a single thrust, the eros of the human spirit"[36].

This unfolding is a process of self-creation. In our understanding, deciding, and acting we create ourselves. At each level more of who we are is involved, as verified by the increasing responsibility we feel when we acknowledge failure at a particular level:

> To acknowledge that we haven't noticed something that others have noticed is generally an easy admission to make; to acknowledge we haven't understood something that others have understood hits closer to home; to acknowledge that our judgment has been wrong is an even more personal admission of some failure in ourselves; and to acknowledge that one has chosen, embraced, or done what was evil addresses the core of who one is[37].

Thus, as we move through the different levels of consciousness, not only are our operations different, but *we* are different. "On all

[35] Lonergan, *Method in Theology*, 9 (emphasis added).
[36] *Ibid.*, 13.
[37] V. Gregson, *The Desire to Know: Intellectual Conversion*, in *The Desires of the Human Heart: An Introduction to the Theology of Bernard Lonergan*, edited by V. Gregson, New York 1988, 20.

four levels, we are aware of ourselves but, as we mount from level to level, it is a fuller self of which we are aware and the awareness itself is different"[38].

We all have experienced responsibility for failure at some level of consciousness. We can subvert the self-transcending dynamism of the human spirit for meaning, truth, value, and love. The transcendental notions constitute our capacity for self-transcendence[39]. But we choose, however consciously or unconsciously, fidelity or infidelity to these transcendental notions, to the most basic dynamisms of our human spirit. Lonergan is inviting his readers to fidelity, to human authenticity. His purpose in describing the levels of human consciousness is to make us more aware of our consciousness, to make us more conscious of our experiencing, understanding, judging, and deciding - precisely so that we might be more faithful to the dynamic exigencies of our human spirit.

Lonergan himself states that his later work "takes its stand on discovering what human authenticity is and showing how to appeal to it"[40]. But this appeal to human authenticity is a call to conversion which is the gradual process of "finding out for oneself and in oneself what it is to be intelligent, to be reasonable, to be responsible, to love"[41]. Thus, the *heart of the matter* is, at least for later Lonergan, "the events that constitute intellectual, moral, and religious conversion"[42].

As we have seen, the *heart of the matter* for the primitive Rule is conversion. In our continuing quest to understand the primitive Rule, we turn therefore to an analysis of conversion suggested by Lonergan. We will consider both Lonergan's basic reflections on conversion as well as some other authors' extensive development of Lonergan's initial insights.

---

[38] Lonergan, *Method in Theology*, 9.

[39] *Ibid.*, 104-105.

[40] *Ibid.*, 254.

[41] *Ibid.*, 253.

[42] R. Doran, *Introduction - Lonergan: An Appreciation*, in *The Desires of the Human Heart*, 1. For a treatment of how the notion of conversion developed within Lonergan's thought, cf. M. Rende, *The Development and the Unity of Lonergan's Notion of Conversion*, in *Method* 1 (1983) 158-73; and K. Colleran, *Bernard Lonergan on Conversion*, in *Dunwoodie Review* 11 (1971) 3-23.

A Methodological Note

Lonergan's analysis of human authenticity and the movement to authenticity or "conversion" has been much studied. Two authors in particular, Walter Conn and Donald Gelpi, have offered extensive treatments of conversion in which they not only explicate Lonergan's theory of conversion but further develop that theory by their own additions and nuances[43]. Conn brings Lonergan's theory of conversion into dialogue with various psychological theories of development to situate the various types of conversion within a pattern of personal development[44]. Gelpi, whose concerns are more philosophical and theological, attempts to ground Lonergan's theory of conversion within a North American philosophical tradition of experience[45].

Our present and much less ambitious concern is to describe the reality of conversion critically, that is, to make more explicit the nature and dynamics of conversion. This analysis will follow a somewhat eclectic approach in its attempt to present a Lonerganian theory of conversion. Our primary concern is to present a critical analysis of conversion, an analysis based upon Lonergan's original insights but not restricted solely

---

[43] W. Conn, *Bernard Lonergan's Analysis of Conversion*, in *Angelicum* 53 (1976) 362-404; *Conscience: Development and Self-Transcendence*, Birmingham 1981; *Moral Development: Is Conversion Necessary?*, in *Creativity and Method*, 307-324; *Passionate Commitment: The Dynamics of Affective Conversion*, in *Cross Currents* 34 (1984) 329-36; *Christian Conversion: A Developmental Interpretation of Autonomy and Surrender*, New York 1986; *The Desire for Authenticity: Conscience and Moral Conversion*, in *The Desires of the Human Heart*, 36-56.

D. Gelpi, *Charism and Sacrament: A Theology of Christian Conversion*, New York 1976; *Experiencing God: A Theology of Human Emergence*, New York 1978; *The Converting Jesuit*, in *Studies in the Spirituality of Jesuits* XVIII (1986) 1-38; *Religious Conversion: A New Way of Being*, in *The Human Experience of Conversion*, 175-202; *Inculturating North American Theology: An Experiment in Foundational Method*, Atlanta 1988; *Conversion: Beyond the Impasses of Individualism*, in *Beyond Individualism: Toward a Retrieval of Moral Discourse in America*, edited by D. Gelpi, Notre Dame 1989, 1-30; *Committed Worship: A Sacramental Theology for Converting Christians* (unpublished manuscript), copyright 1990.

[44] Conn situates Lonergan's theory of conversion principally within the developmental theories of Piaget, Kohlberg, Erikson, Fowler, and Kegan. Cf. Conn, *Christian Conversion*.

[45] Cf. Gelpi, *Inculturating North American Theology*.

to his articulation of the phenomenon. The insights of other authors who have built upon Lonergan's insights, who have developed extensive "Lonergan-inspired" theories of conversion, will also be incorporated.

Our analysis will, in fact, lean heavily on the work of both Conn and Gelpi[46]. Conn offers a fuller description and treatment of affective, intellectual, moral, and religious conversion[47]. Gelpi, for his part, not only advances Lonergan's thought in terms of the types of conversion but reflects extensively on the dynamics of conversion, that is, on the ways in which the various types of conversion affect or mutually condition one another. Let us, then, eclectically proceed.

The Meaning of "Conversion"

According to Lonergan, conversion "is not merely a change or even a development; rather, it is a radical transformation on which follows, on all levels of living, an interlocked series of changes and developments"[48]. These changes and developments occur in different ways and to varying degrees, but Lonergan insists that conversion is *ontic*. The person who has undergone a conversion "apprehends differently, values differently, relates differently because he has become different"[49].

Lonergan derives his basic notion of conversion from Joseph de Finance's distinction between a horizontal and a vertical exercise of human freedom[50]. A *horizontal* exercise of freedom describes a choice made within a person's given horizon or world. In contrast, a *vertical* exercise of freedom designates the type of decision by which a person

---

[46] For Gelpi's comment on how he and Conn differ, cf. Gelpi, *Inculturating North American Theology*, page 47, note 9.

[47] In his earlier work Conn used the term "intellectual conversion". For example, cf. Conn, *Conscience*, 156. However, in his later work he uses the term "cognitive conversion" rather than "intellectual conversion" to describe the same reality since he feels that "intellectual" has too narrow a connotation and therefore can suggest a misleading view of this type of conversion. Cf. Conn, *Christian Conversion*, 116-27. For consistency, we will use the term "intellectual conversion".

[48] Lonergan, *Theology in Its New Context*, 13.

[49] *Ibid.*, 13.

[50] Lonergan, *Method in Theology*, 40.

moves into a different horizon or a new world[51]. Based upon this distinction, Lonergan describes conversion as a vertical exercise of freedom, a movement to a new horizon, which involves an "about-face", that is, a repudiation of the past and a choice of something new.

Gelpi, who derives his approach to conversion from an analysis of responsibility[52], defines conversion more concretely as "the decision to pass from irresponsible to responible behavior in some distinguishable realm of human experience"[53]. As Gelpi points out, conversion is not simply a once-and-for-all decision. Conversion involves both an *initial* and an *ongoing* decision. That is, beyond the initial decision to change there is the continuing affirmation of the initial decision and acceptance of the consequences of that decision[54].

According to Lonergan, these decisions or conversions occur on four different levels of experience: affective, intellectual, moral, and religious[55]. Gelpi describes these four types of conversion as *personal*

---

[51] *Ibid.*, 237.

[52] Gelpi's approach to conversion derives from H. Richard Niebuhr's *The Responsible Self*. Cf. Gelpi, *Committed Worship*, 27, note 2. According to Gelpi, Lonergan's approach makes conversion into a transformation of subjectivity and is, therefore, inadequate. Gelpi's approach includes the transformation of subjectivity but insists explicitly on the social character of conversion from the start by defining "responsibility" as accountability. Gelpi calls into question the methodological adequacy of Lonergan's presupposition that the turn to the subject alone provides adequate grounds for a theory of conversion. Gelpi, therefore, attempts to ground his theory of conversion in the North American philosophical tradition with a much broadened understanding of "experience". Cf. Gelpi, *Inculturating North American Theology*, 1-47.

[53] Gelpi, *Committed Worship*, 24. Gelpi's earlier definition of conversion more emphasized Lonergan's stress on conversion as an "about-face", that is, as a repudiation of the past and start of a new beginning: "the double decision to repudiate irresponsible behavior and to take responsibillity for the subsequent development of some aspect of my experience". Cf. Gelpi, *The Converting Jesuit*, 4-5. But both formulations are essentially equivalent.

[54] Gelpi, *The Converting Jesuit*, 6-7.

[55] Originally Lonergan described only three types of conversion: intellectual, moral, and religious. Cf. *Method in Theology*, 237-44; and *Theology in Its New Context*, 15-21. But in his later work he acknowledged the existence of a fourth type of conversion, affective conversion. Cf. *Natural Right and Historical Mindedness*, in *A Third Collection: Papers by Bernard J. F. Lonergan, S.J.*, edited by F. Crowe, New York 1985, 169-83, esp. 179.

because in each of these conversions the person assumes responsibility for his or her own decisions[56]. Gelpi originally identified only four types of conversion: affective, intellectual, moral, and religious[57]. Later, however, he became convinced that there was a distinct type of conversion over against "personal" conversion which he identified as socio-political conversion[58]. Let us consider each of these five types of conversion.

Affective Conversion

Lonergan acknowledged but never developed the notion of affective conversion[59]. Others have, however, reflected extensively on affective conversion as a distinct type of conversion[60]. Affective conversion involves a recognition and integration of our feelings and attitudes. This

---

[56] Gelpi, *The Converting Jesuit*, 5.

[57] For example, cf. Gelpi, *Charism and Sacrament*, 17-25; *Experiencing God*, 178-88.

[58] Initially I resisted this distinction, believing that socio-political conversion would or *should* be included within moral conversion, especially when trans-valued by religious conversion. But I believe that Gelpi argues convincingly that socio-political conversion, though a moment within the process of moral conversion, is sufficiently distinct that it need be identified as a conversion in its own right. Cf. Gelpi, *Religious Conversion*, 180-83.

[59] For a discussion of the development of the term "affective conversion", cf. B. Tyrrell, *Affective Conversion: A New Way of Feeling*, in *The Human Experience of Conversion: Persons and Structures in Transformation*, edited by F. Eigo, Villanova 1987, 110-11.

[60] Whereas Lonergan, Conn, and Gelpi all speak of "affective conversion", other authors use different terms to designate this experience of conversion. Bernard Tyrrell prefers to designate this experience of conversion as "psychological conversion". Cf. Tyrrell, *Affective Conversion*, 109-142, esp. 110-11. Robert Doran, on the other hand, develops a theory of "psychic conversion". Cf. R. Doran, *Subject and Psyche: Ricoeur, Jung and the Search for Foundations*, Washington D.C. 1977, 240ff.

Although the three terms (and quite obviously, the various theories of conversion) cannot simply be equated, nevertheless, both Tyrrell and Doran, speaking respectively of "psychological conversion" and "psychic conversion", do essentially describe the same experience that we here designate "affective conversion".

cultivation of a healthy affective life generally progresses gradually and involves a conscious ongoing commitment to recognizing, understanding, and judging our affective responses[61].

Affective conversion is a radical transformation of our affective life. Falling-in-love offers an example of how our affective life can be transformed[62]. Falling-in-love turns us from ourselves, shifts our focus of attention to the other, and changes how we perceive reality. But, as Conn cautions, the description of affective conversion as "falling-in-love", given the term's sentimental connotations, can be misleading. Affective conversion is not strictly passive. Rather, it involves both passion and commitment[63]. Affective conversion is a reorientation of the whole person. While it does primarily reorient our prereflective desires, it also involves conscious decisions, choices, and loving commitments which are supported by those transformed desires[64].

Gelpi captures the commitment aspect of affective conversion. He defines affective conversion as "the decision to turn from an irresponsible resistance to facing one's disordered affectivity to the responsible cultivation of a healthy, balanced, aesthetically sensitive emotional life"[65]. Gelpi's definition should not be construed to mean that affective conversion is a completely rational matter because it entails a decision. All conversions entail a decision to move from irresponsible to responsible behavior in some realm of experience. But a decision can be more or less conscious, more or less rational, and more or less emotionally motivated.

Conn stresses that affective conversion involves *both* passion and commitment; Gelpi defines it in terms of our decision. But while their descriptions might appear to differ, both understand and explain affective conversion in the same way. Our commitment or decision follows upon the radical reorientation of our passionate desires. This transformation is not merely a matter of our will but depends upon the "prereflective influence of powerfully imaginative symbols of self-transcendence"[66].

---

[61] Gelpi, *Experiencing God*, 180-81.

[62] Lonergan described religious conversion as an "other-worldly falling-in-love". Cf. Lonergan, *Method in Theology*, 240.

[63] Conn, *Passionate Commitment*, 336.

[64] Conn, *Christian Conversion*, 149.

[65] Gelpi, *Committed Worship*, 24.

[66] Conn, *Christian Conversion*, 152.

Intellectual Conversion[67]

For Lonergan, intellectual conversion consists in the recognition and affirmation that knowing involves not just seeing but a series of operations: experiencing, understanding, judging, and deciding.

> Intellectual conversion is a radical clarification and, consequently, the elimination of an exceedingly stubborn and misleading myth concerning reality, objectivity, and human knowledge. The myth is that knowing is like looking, that objectivity is seeing what is there to be seen and not seeing what is not there, and that the real is what is out there now to be looked at[68].

Lonergan speaks of this changed perception as a "conversion" precisely because it is so decisive a break with the pervasive misconception that knowing is seeing. When we have experienced an intellectual conversion we no longer confuse the world of immediacy and the world mediated by meaning because we have then realized that knowing "is not just seeing; it is experiencing, understanding, judging, and believing"[69].

The example of viewing an x-ray presents the difference quite graphically[70]. I and an orthopedic surgeon see an x-ray of my hand differently. My untrained eye sees various light and dark images which I can identify as the skeletal outline of the bones in my hand (which itself requires understanding and is more than just "looking"). But a trained orthopedic surgeon sees the same reality differently. The doctor not only looks more attentively at the visual presentation, she is able to understand or interpret what she sees. The doctor recognizes the barely perceptible line as a fracture which will take several weeks to heal. The doctor *knows* not just by "looking" but by a type of "seeing" which involves a set of operations: experiencing, understanding, and judging.

---

[67] For an alluring treatment of intellectual conversion, especially as transvalued by religious conversion, cf. D. Carmody, *Cognitive Conversion: A New Way of Understanding*, in *The Human Experience of Conversion*, 75-108. Also cf. Gregson, *The Desire to Know: Intellectual Conversion*, 16-35.

[68] Lonergan, *Method in Theology*, 238.

[69] *Ibid.*, 238.

[70] Gregson, *The Desire to Know: Intellectual Conversion*, 26.

This changed perception has important implications. If knowing is looking, then values such as love and friendship are merely "subjective" and not real. But objectivity does not mean disinterested passive looking. Rather, true objectivity involves our experiencing, understanding, judging, and deciding critically. As Lonergan quite pointedly states, "[g]enuine objectivity is the fruit of authentic subjectivity"[71].

Intellectual conversion is obviously critical for clarifying philosophical issues, but more importantly, on a personal existential level it is the recognition that our own self-transcending judgments constitute the criterion of the real[72]. Gelpi sums up this reality of intellectual conversion as "the decision to turn from an irresponsible and supine acquiescence in accepted beliefs to a commitment to validating one's personal beliefs within adequate frames of reference and in ongoing dialogue with other truth seekers"[73]. Intellectual conversion involves both inferential judgments and judgments of feeling, both intuitive and inferential perceptions of reality[74].

Moral Conversion[75]

According to Lonergan, moral conversion involves shifting the criterion of our decisions and choices from satisfactions to values[76]. Gelpi divides moral conversion into personal moral conversion and socio-political conversion. He defines *personal* moral conversion as "the decision to turn from irresponsible selfishness to a commitment to measure the motives and consequences of personal choices against ethical norms and ideals that both lure the conscience to selfless choices and judge its relapses into irresponsible selfishness"[77].

---

[71] Lonergan, *Method in Theology*, 292.

[72] Conn, *Christian Conversion*, 127.

[73] Gelpi, *Committed Worship*, 24.

[74] According to Gelpi, this emphasis on both types of judgments makes an important qualification on Lonergan's position. Cf. Gelpi, *Inculturating North American Theology*, 49-97.

[75] Cf. Conn, *The Desire for Authenticity: Conscience and Moral Conversion*, 36-56; and R. Marstin, *Moral Conversion: Being Neighbor by Transforming Structures*, in *The Human Experience of Conversion*, 143-74.

[76] Lonergan, *Method in Theology*, 240.

[77] Gelpi, *Committed Worship*, 24.

Moral conversion, at least according to Conn, can be either critical or uncritical[78]. In *critical* moral conversion we accept the responsibility of recognizing and affirming our own personal values (in dialogue with the community). In contrast, if our moral conversion is *uncritical* then we have made the shift from satisfaction to values but we have accepted uncritically some given set of values presented by an external source[79].

Critical moral conversion, which presupposes some level of intellectual conversion, has increasingly become a necessity in our complex world of competing moral values. As Conn graphically captures it, "the person without critical self-appropriation is like most of us simple folks in the hands of the proverbial used-car salesman - going around kicking the tires with no more purpose than the desperate hope that they might secretly tell us what to do"[80]!

Religious Conversion[81]

Religious conversion, for Lonergan, does not mean a change from one religious tradition to another but rather a shift of focus from finite to transcendent realities. "Religious conversion is being grasped by ultimate concern. It is other-worldly falling in love"[82]. But as we said with respect to affective conversion, this "being-in-love" transforms our consciousness. When we fall in love, our love is embodied not in a single act or even a series of acts but in a dynamic state of "being-in-love". Religious conversion transforms our experiencing, understanding, judging, and deciding in terms of unrestricted love.

Gelpi defines religious conversion as "the decision to turn from either ignorance of or opposition to God to acceptance in faith of some

---

[78] Gelpi would deny that an uncritical conversion has the degree of responsibility that genuine conversion requires. For Gelpi, a conversion without critical self-appropriation is not a conversion at all.

[79] W. Conn, *Conscience: Development and Self-Transcendence*, Birmingham 1981, 190-94.

[80] Conn, *Christian Conversion*, 126-27.

[81] Cf. D. Carmody, *The Desire for Transcendence: Religious Conversion*, in *The Desires of the Human Heart*, 57-73; and Gelpi, *Religious Conversion: A New Way of Being*, 175-202.

[82] Lonergan, *Method in Theology*, 240.

historical, revelatory self-communication of God and its consequences"[83]. There are, therefore, different forms of religious conversion. However, our concern will be to examine only *Christian* conversion, the decision to accept the revelation of God given in Jesus and the consequences of that decision to follow Jesus.

The various types of conversion are analogous, not equivalent. Religious conversion differs from the other four types of conversion in at least two significant ways. First, religious conversion requires divine initiative; it does not occur "naturally". Affective, intellectual, moral, and socio-political conversion can all occur *naturally*, that is, apart from any specific recognition of God's presence and action in human history. Religious conversion as a response to God's love presupposes God's initiative. It is a commitment in faith to God's self-revelation. This commitment demands that we reexamine our natural habits and decisions, which suggests a second way that religious conversion differs. The other four types of conversion each change a distinguishable realm of experience: affectivity, thought, conscience, and society. Religious conversion does not change some fifth distinct realm of experience, rather, it calls us to reexamine our values and habits in these four realms of experience. Religious conversion *transvalues* or interpenetrates each of these other realms[84].

Socio-political Conversion

Of the various theorists, only Gelpi specifies socio-political conversion as a distinct fifth type of conversion. Conn does insist that moral conversion must include a social commitment and must extend to action or it is not moral conversion[85]. But Conn does not go so far as to distinguish it as a separate type of conversion. As we mentioned above, Gelpi himself had originally held this position but later became convinced that the socio-political dimension of moral conversion

[83] Gelpi, *Committed Worship*, 24.

[84] Moral conversion can also endow experience with a broad and vague religious character to the extent that it engages concern with questions of ultimacy. Natural moral conversion fails, however, to discover in God the ultimate ground of ultimacy.

[85] Conn, *Christian Conversion*, 153-57.

was so distinct that it needed to be identified as a separate type of conversion.

Personal moral conversion involves a concern for others. As morally converted people we make decisions in interpersonal relationships based upon norms like the "golden rule". Our motivation shifts from self-satisfaction to value, to concerns which involve others. But as Gelpi points out, questions of the public good invoke a different set of norms, specifically those that address the common good. In attempting to make decisions which affect the public good, we are then dealing with a distinct moral frame of reference, capable of grounding a distinct kind of conversion[86].

The countless people, good *morally* converted people, who resist any type of political involvement or who are blind to institutional oppression offer great support for Gelpi's argument. We have Christians who support apartheid and a Roman Catholic hierarchy that excludes women from ministry. It would appear that moral conversion often exists separate from socio-political conversion. We could say that most people are not morally converted, but I think that Gelpi's insistence upon socio-political conversion as a separate type of conversion offers an important corrective, especially within our specific culture with its pervasive myth of individualism. Gelpi speaks boldly of the need for socio-political conversion:

> the failure to advance beyond personal conversion to sociopolitical conversion subverts all four types of personal conversion and renders them inauthentic. The absence of sociopolitical conversion leaves one vulnerable to the institutionalized injustice that distorts human passion, blinds the human mind with lies and half-truths, perverts the conscience by teaching it to degrade and dehumanize other persons, and transforms the religious person into a pious hypocrite[87].

Gelpi defines socio-political conversion as "the decision to turn from unreflective acceptance of the institutional violations of human rights to a commitment to collaborate with others in the reform of unjust

---

[86] Gelpi's distinction and approach to socio-political conversion roots itself in Josiah Royce's *The Philosophy of Loyalty*. Cf. Gelpi, *Conversion: Beyond the Impasses of Individualism*, 2-3.

[87] Gelpi, *Committed Worship*, 51.

social, economic, and political structures"[88]. Socio-political conversion differs from personal moral conversion and the other types of conversion precisely in terms of the area of responsibility chosen. In personal conversion, we choose to be responsible in some specific area or our own lives. In socio-political conversion, we choose to be responsible in a much broader area of concern; we choose to influence the decisions of those who shape the large impersonal social structures of our world.

The large, impersonal nature of the socio-political realm and the enormity of the challenge to influence those structures often breeds passivity. Morally converted people often refrain from socio-political involvement. The ease with which people in this country isolate the socio-political realm from religious and other areas of their experience suggests that each of us needs to examine critically our need for socio-political conversion. To be socio-politically converted does not mean that we are necessarily full-time political activists. As there are many different gifts within the Church there are different ways in which socio-political converts express their conversion. Gelpi distinguishes four different levels of political involvement, naming each in terms of the person's involvement:

1. *civic minimalists* exercise their right to vote responsibly. However, they prescind from any further decision with respect to the impact that large institutions have upon them and others and are not, therefore, socio-politically converted.

2. *teaching activists* study specific instances of institutional injustice and attempt to educate themselves and others about the moral issues raised by situations of oppression. By educating others and by their commitment to social reform, teaching activists evidence at least an initial socio-political conversion. However, ongoing socio-political conversion will almost certainly require more involvement.

3. *participatory activists* support in concrete ways public leaders and professional activists who work for the reform of unjust social institutions. This involvement evidences an ongoing socio-political conversion.

4. *professional activists* undertake institutional reform as a career. This involvement would include, for example, politicians, lobbyists, and industrial leaders who are motivated by a concern for economic justice and actively support the cause of the poor, the oppressed, and victims of injustice[89].

---

[88] *Ibid.*, 24.

[89] Gelpi, *Committed Workship*, 49.

The exact nature of our involvement depends upon our talents and gifts and call. The nature of our involvement matters less than the fact that we *are* involved, that we do accept responsibility on a socio-political level. If we are to be socio-politically converted, if we are to be fully authentic, then we must commit ourselves to influencing those whose decisions will shape the social structures of our world. Our work for justice cannot remain on an interpersonal level.

Dynamics of Conversion

We can be converted in one or several of these areas without being converted in all five. Each of the five conversions is distinct. Yet, the various types of conversion are not unrelated. Each type of conversion has specific effects on the other forms of conversion. Gelpi has identified seven specific "dynamics" of conversion which flow from the esthetic, organic construct of experience that he endorses. There are seven ways in which the different types of conversion affect or mutually condition one another:

1. Affective conversion animates intellectual, moral, religious, and socio-political conversion
2. Intellectual conversion informs affective, moral, religious, and socio-political conversion
3. Moral conversion helps orient affective, intellectual, religious, and socio-political conversion to realities and values that make ultimate and absolute claims on human behavior
4. Religious conversion mediates between affective and moral conversion
5. Affective, intellectual, moral, and religious conversion authenticate socio-political conversion by supplying it with personal norms that help measure institutional responsibility
6. Socio-political conversion authenticates affective, intellectual, moral, and religious conversion by deprivatizing them
7. Religious conversion transvalues affective, intellectual, moral, and socio-political conversion[90].

Each of the various types of conversion changes radically one aspect of our experience. But changes in the way we perceive, sense, feel,

[90] *Ibid.*, 37; cf. also Gelpi, *The Converting Jesuit*, 14, 25.

think, image, or judge have effects in other realms of experience. Thus, to undergo a specific type of conversion does affect other realms of experience; it does condition other types of conversion. Let us consider each of these dynamics of conversion briefly.

The First Dynamic: Affective conversion animates intellectual, moral, religious, and socio-political conversion[91]. Affective conversion *animates* the other forms of conversion precisely by healing the distortion caused by disordered affectivity, by providing enthusiasm, and by encouraging creativity. When affectively converted, we no longer repress but rather deal honestly with our negative feelings which frees our imagination and our perception of ourselves and our world. In dealing honestly with guilt, fear, anger, and other negative emotions we are free to accept ourselves and our world, and to respond sympathetically to incarnate beauty. This freedom for love, appreciation, and affection breeds enthusiasm and animates our very being. This enthusiasm and freedom penetrates our other levels of experience.

Affective conversion animates intellectual conversion by allowing the mind to dream dreams but also to deal realistically with the intellectual problems. The mind needs some freedom to "play" if it is to solve problems creatively. This flexibililty also animates moral and socio-political conversion by allowing freedom in dealing with complex ethical dilemmas. Further, affective conversion, by freeing our hearts from crippling neuroses and psychoses, allows true Christian hope to take root in us. In this way affective conversion animates not only religious conversion, but the other forms of conversion as well.

The Second Dynamic: Intellectual conversion informs affective, moral, religious, and socio-political conversion[92]. Intellectual conversion *informs* the other types of conversion by enabling critical reflection within each of these different types, by bringing a critical awareness to each of the different conversions. Intellectual conversion involves a love of truth, a love of truth at both an intuitive and an inferential level. This love of truth brings to affective conversion a fascination with human psychological development, to moral conversion a concern to understand the workings of human conscience, to religious conversion a passion for the-

[91] Gelpi, *The Converting Jesuit*, 18-20; *Committed Worship*, 37-39.
[92] Gelpi, *The Converting Jesuit*, 20; *Committed Worship*, 39-40.

ology, and to socio-political conversion a drive to understand social ethics and the social sciences.

The Third Dynamic: Personal moral conversion helps orient affective, intellectual, religious, and socio-political conversion to realities and values that make ultimate and absolute claims on human behavior[93]. Personal moral conversion *orients* the other forms of conversion by bringing each into dialogue with those values. Confronting complex moral dilemmas demands such dialogue. Some ethical questions require that we use our reason to sort through the complexities. Other ethical problems (for example, questions concerning human sexuality) engage our affectivity. Some raise religious questions for which revelation gives no specific answers; and still others demand insight into the working of conscience but on the level of social institutions.

When, as morally converted people we engage our other areas of experience to deal with these types of dilemmas, they in turn are confronted with our operative ethical values. For example, personal moral conversion offers insights into personal human rights and responsibilities that social structures violate. Critical moral conversion requires that we take into account the moral consequences of our affective, intellectual, and religious options. But because of this "dialogue", each of the other types of conversion is in turn oriented to the personally discerned and chosen values which place ultimate claim upon us.

The Fourth Dynamic: Religious conversion mediates between affective and moral conversion[94]. Religious conversion *mediates* between these two types of conversion by bringing them into a relationship they would not otherwise enjoy. *Christian* conversion mediates between affective and moral conversion because it expresses a heart-felt, intuitive response to God which culminates in a faith response of commitment which directly affects our moral reasoning.

Christian conversion begins in the heart. It transforms affective conversion into repentance and so sensitizes the human heart to the beauty of God incarnate in Jesus and in others in the world who resemble him. But that faith response brings specific moral demands of Christian discipleship. As affectively converted Christians, we accept in faith Jesus'

---

[93] Gelpi, *The Converting Jesuit*, 21; *Committed Worship*, 40-42.

[94] Gelpi, *The Converting Jesuit*, 14-18; *Committed Worship*, 42-44.

moral teachings which operate both as lure and constraint on our conscience. Thus, affective conversion no longer merely animates moral conversion. It now discerns religious value in faith, with a conscience informed by a commitment to discipleship. An affectively motivated commitment to Jesus changes the values which guide our moral decisions. Transformed by a commitment in faith to Jesus, affective conversion animates the morally converted to an enthusiastic commitment to imitate Christ, to embrace his values and teaching[95].

The Fifth Dynamic: Affective, intellectual, moral, and religious conversion authenticate socio-political conversion by supplying it with personal norms that help measure institutional responsibility[96]. One form of conversion *authenticates* another form of conversion when it enables the latter to develop responsibly. Since injustice can result from disordered emotions, since evil can hide behind false ideological or even religious justifications, socio-political conversion needs to be authenticated by the different forms of personal conversion. To develop responsibly, socio-political conversion requires ordered affectivity, critical reasoning, operative personally chosen values, and transvaluation by faith.

Affective conversion helps us to unmask emotional disorders and prejudice operative within social systems. It also empowers our imagination to envision a world free from oppression and injustice. Intellectual conversion enables us to diagnose the causes of institutional injustice in order to deal effectively with its consequences. It enables us to distinguish the truth from false ideology and to design viable alternatives or policies that ensure justice. Moral conversion supplies us with insight into the personal rights and duties that unjust institutions violate. Finally, Christian conversion transvalues all of the socio-political situtations by bringing the demands of the Gospel to bear upon each decision. Therefore, we need all four forms of personal conversion to authenticate socio-political conversion. If we are lacking in any one area of personal conversion then our socio-political conversion cannot develop responsibly; inevitably, we act irresponsibly in the management or reform of social institutions.

---

[95] Gelpi explains this dynamic most clearly in *Religious Conversion*, 184-89.
[96] Gelpi, *The Converting Jesuit*, 26-28; *Committed Worship*, 44-47.

The Sixth Dynamic: Socio-political conversion authenticates affective, intellectual, moral, and religious conversion by deprivatizing them[97]. That is, socio-political conversion enables the four forms of personal conversion to develop responsibly precisely by deprivatizing them. It deprivatizes personal conversion in two ways: by demanding dedication to some concrete cause of universal moral import, and by bringing us into contact with people different from ourselves which necessarily confronts us with new issues. Both a commitment to a specific social or political cause and an involvement with others help reveal to us the other areas in which we need to be converted.

Unfortunately, most Christians in the United States do not connect socio-political conversion with religious conversion. They strenuously defend the separation of religion and politics. But the gospel call to justice must direct the decisions of the Christian in both the personal and socio-political realms. Our personal conversion develops responsibly *only* when it is deprivatized. Gelpi speaks forcefully of the demand for socio-political conversion and the inauthenticity of a conversion which remains merely personal:

> Only when we actively confront institutional corruption and injustice do we come to understand the extent to which they have consciously and unconsciously shaped and used us as individual persons to tainted and exploitative ends. Only in dealing with the members of a less advantaged social class do we come to recognize fully our own classist conditioning. Only by dealing with the members of a different race do we learn fully to confront our own racial prejudices. Only by facing the members of other nations we have wronged, can we transcend mindless nationalism. In other words, not only does sociopolitical conversion enable the personally converted to act responsibly in their interpersonal dealings with others; but it also resists the corrupting influence of institutional injustice that betrays the personally converted into treating other persons irresponsibly whether for distorted affective, cognitive, pseudo-ethical, or religiously hypocritical motives[98].

The Seventh Dynamic: Religious conversion transvalues affective, intellectual, moral, and socio-political conversion[99]. A response is *trans-*

---

[97] Gelpi, *The Converting Jesuit*, 28-30; *Committed Worship*, 47-51.
[98] Gelpi, *Committed Worship*, 51.
[99] Gelpi, *The Converting Jesuit*, 21-24; *Committed Worship*, 51-54.

valued when having been used in one frame of reference we move it to another where it acquires new meaning and connotations. For example, within the framework of business and the importance of a given meeting, our initial response to an interruption might be anger or resentment. However, the information that our spouse was just rushed to the hospital changes our understanding of the interruption and hence our response to it.

Since each of the other conversions can occur naturally, religious conversion *transvalues* them precisely by changing the frame of reference. Whereas the other four conversions can occur with no explicit recognition of God, religious conversion brings to each a faith perspective which entails a profoundly different view of ourselves and our world.

Natural affective conversion involves the healing of negative feelings and the subsequent release of positive feelings. Religious conversion transforms these two movements to repentance followed by hope. Through intellectual conversion we can develop conceptions of God. Religious conversion transforms these by bringing God's self-revelation to our discussions. Further, the heartfelt consent to God, which brings fidelity to the teachings of Jesus for the Christian convert, also transforms natural moral and socio-political conversion by introducing Gospel values as *the* frame of reference. The Christian convert's commitment to the cause of Christ, a cause which encompasses every aspect of human living, transvalues or relativizes all other causes.

Some Summary Remarks on Conversion

Conversion, properly understood, involves all dimensions of the human person. Authentic conversion includes affective, intellectual, moral, socio-political, and religious conversion. It must be both personal and socio-political, not only natural but transvalued by faith, not only an initial experience but an ongoing commitment. In sum, authentic conversion entails being in a state of ongoing affective, intellectual, moral, socio-political, and religious conversion.

As Christians, our ongoing conversion on all levels is transvalued by our faith response to Christ. Our ongoing decision to live responsibly in the various realms of our experience is a commitment to the demands of Christian discipleship given in the Gospel. Conversely, authentic discipleship requires authentic conversion, that is, conversion in all its dimensions. With this more adequate understanding of conversion let us turn again to our principle concern: the interpretation of the primitive Rule.

Towards an Interpretation of the Rule

Our examination of the primitive Rule as a "text" led us to conclude that it is "about" conversion, about radical conversion. The primitive Rule proclaims the blessing of conversion, that is, it promises the experience of intimacy with God for those who choose conversion. The apparent incongruity of that statement and our lived experience brought us to reexamine our understanding of conversion. With a more adequate understanding of conversion we now return to the task of interpreting the rule, of discovering what the text *means*.

The Reference of the Text: Radical Conversion

The primitive Rule is about conversion, but conversion understood as living in a state of ongoing affective, intellectual, moral, socio-political, and religious conversion. If conversion is understood as ongoing fivefold conversion then the claims of the text make sense. Going through the *sense* that doing penance makes us spouses, brothers and mothers of the Lord, we arrived at the *reference* that radical conversion is the way to authentic human fulfillment.

The proclamation that doing penance draws us into an intimate relationship with God begins to make sense when we grasp the radical nature of fully authentic conversion. "Oh how blessed are those who do penance". Oh how blessed are those who:

- responsibly face their own disordered affectivity
  and strive to cultivate a healthy emotional life
- commit themselves to examining critically
  their values and beliefs in dialogue with others
- commit themselves to living by ethical norms and ideals
  that make an ultimate claim upon them
- accept God's self-revelation of love given in Jesus
  and the consequences of following Jesus' teaching

- commit themselves to collaborate with others
  in the reform of unjust social institutions.

We can sense the palpable holiness of those who have fallen in love with God and allow God's love and revelation to transvalue all the other areas of their lives. We can understand the closeness to God of those who in their repentance have experienced God's healing of their prejudices, fears, and guilt. We can affirm the blessedness of those who live not for their own satisfaction but according to gospel values.

The Exhortation to Penance / The Call to Conversion

By beginning its presentation of the Secular Franciscans' Way of Life with the primitive Rule, the *Rule of 1978* presents that Way of Life as a call to radical conversion. The entire text must be understood as a call to live in an ongoing state of affective, intellectual, moral, socio-political, and religious conversion. As we have already mentioned, the *Rule of 1978* was promulgated with the hope that the Order might gain a new impetus, and yet that hope has not, in general, been realized. In proposing a reason for this failed hope, I suggested two possibilities: that the Rule itself was flawed, or the Rule was not as yet understood. Given that the primitive Rule was eventually inserted into the text and is contained within the officially approved *Rule of 1978*, I would suggest that the problem is that the Rule has not been adequately understood. Further, I would suggest that the Rule has not been adequately understood and the individual Secular Franciscan Fraternities have not been revitalized because the reality of conversion, and therefore the call of the Rule, has not been adequately understood.

The early sources record the incredible growth and vitality of the Franciscan penitents in the thirteenth century. The life of Francis and the early penitents held a great attraction for others. Radically lived penance brought a holiness that was palpable and "many converted to penitence"[100]. Radically lived conversion will bring a holiness that is palpable and many will be converted. Secular Franciscans, individually and collectively as fraternities, who embody radically lived conversion, who commit themselves to an ongoing affective, intellectual, moral, socio-

[100] *LP* 34, in Brooke, *Scripta Leonis*, 149.

political, and religious conversion, will speak a holiness that attracts others.

There are many socio-politically converted people who are not religiously converted. They lack the faith experience which could transvalue and empower their work to change unjust social structures. Would not some of these "peace-makers" and "builders of the Kingdom" find attractive the holiness of a Secular Franciscan Fraternity which as a group was engaged in an ongoing fivefold conversion? Would not the holiness incarnate in the love among the members, in their service to the needy, in their commitment to the work of justice, proclaim the blessing of penance? Would not the groups "gain a new impetus" and "flourish vigorously" as others were attracted to the reality of lived authentic conversion?

But the Rule must be understood and appropriated as the call to radical conversion, as the call to live in a state of ongoing affective, intellectual, moral, socio-political, and religious conversion. When the Rule is interpreted in this light, the paragraphs of the *Rule of 1978* which follow that Prologue take on a different meaning. Amidst *Chapter IV*'s analysis of the Rule Project, I criticized the *Rule of 1978* (that is, the *body* of the new Rule) as lacking in vigor. However, we could read some of those same passages now in a very different light. For example, the challenge to work for justice rings very differently when received by "authentically converted ears":

> Let them individually and collectively be in the forefront in promoting justice by the testimony of their human lives and their courageous initiatives. Especially in the field of public life, they should make definite choices in harmony with their faith[101]

The different challenges in the *Rule of 1978*, if read through the lens of the primitive Rule, if read as demands for an ongoing fivefold conversion, can be inspiring. But the interpretation of the Rule involves an appropriation of the text's meaning. To enter the world of the text is to be confronted by the call to radical conversion, to be opened to a new understanding of conversion, to be drawn into the possibility of a truly authentic conversion in all realms of our experience. To appropriate the meaning of the text is to respond to that call, to commit ourselves to an ongoing affective, intellectual, moral, socio-political and religious conversion.

---

[101] The *Rule of 1978*, paragraph 15.

But we might well then ask how an initial conversion might be facilitated and how ongoing conversion might be nurtured. The Rule as a call to conversion is a call to the individual and to the group. Each person individually and each Fraternity as a group must be involved in the process of ongoing conversion. But how then do we empower both an individual and a communal response?

The Way of Penance / Conversion

Conversion is a process, not a program. There is not any specific or defined "way" to conversion. Sadly, fully authentic conversion in all realms of experience appears to be a rare phenomenon. But if radical conversion is not simple and commonplace, all the more reason that some guidance would be helpful in an attempt to appropriate the primitive Rule. No specific answer but some directions for an answer can be found both in the analysis of conversion and in the Rite of Christian Initiation of Adults (RCIA). Gelpi's reflections on the dynamics of conversion, the ways one type of conversion affects and mutually conditions other forms of conversion, offer some insight into how conversion might be nurtured. The RCIA also offers suggestions since it is the process developed by the Church to facilitate conversion in a person's life. We will consider both of these sources together since they are complementary.

The RCIA is structured as a gradual process which takes place within a community of believers and is varied according to the different people and circumstances[102]. At the second stage, the Catechumenate, it suggests four ways to help facilitate conversion:

1. catechesis
2. involvement in the community's prayer and way of life
3. participation in liturgy
4. apostolic involvement with others[103]

But these suggested ways presuppose that the process of conversion occurs *in community*. The catechumen learns about conversion, about a faith response to the God of love, by experiencing that conversion

---

[102] *The Rite of Christian Initiation of Adults: Study Edition* [hereafter, *RCIA*], Washington, D.C. 1988, paragraph 4-5.

[103] *RCIA*, paragraph 75.

lived by others. Analogously, a Secular Franciscan learns about the Franciscan way of radical conversion by experiencing that reality lived by the members of a Fraternity. A community of faith which is open and hospitable, committed to ongoing conversion, attentive to God's Word, involved in ministry, and empowered by prayer and worship invites individuals to conversion.

Within such a community members can be led through catechesis to the knowledge and appropriation of God's Word. This teaching component can encourage intellectual conversion, especially if done within a community of affectively converted Christians. Affective conversion animates intellectual conversion but it also frees people to raise questions and entertain challenges without being threatened. So the community offers a loving environment in which each of the members can examine his or her own thoughts, feelings, beliefs, and practices. Honest dialogue with others can reveal our own unconverted areas: prejudice, illogic, false values, privatization. Secular Franciscans searching together honestly for the meaning of God's Word or for an interpretation of Francis' writings can discover areas of blindness within themselves and be invited to further conversion.

The involvement in prayer and moral discernment with the community, as well as participation in liturgy, heightens the possibility for affective, moral, and religious conversion. Prayer and liturgy can speak symbolically to our unconverted affect and draw us to repentance. Spiritual direction can help us explore the various dimensions of our experience from the perspective of faith. A group discernment of responsible moral action as informed by Gospel values can challenge our own values and encourage our own moral conversion. Our participation in prayer and liturgy, our being confronted by God's Word, can deepen our own religious conversion and thereby transvalue our other experience.

The participation with others in apostolic activity will nurture socio-political conversion. Socio-political conversion authenticates personal conversion by helping to deprivatize our experience. Ministering with others and reflecting with them on that ministry can help us to discern our own gifts and calling, but it also helps us avoid a privatization of values or conversion. Involvement in ministry raises our consciousness of the suffering and the needs of others and therefore confronts us with questions of social justice.

Thus, the experience of community and its teaching, prayer, liturgy, discernment, and ministry, all help to facilitate and nurture conversion. But the RCIA presuppposes a community of converted Christians. Our description of Secular Franciscan Fraternities presupposes that the members are indeed committed to an ongoing conversion in all areas of their lives. But fully authentic conversion appears to be somewhat rare even in individuals much less groups. Do these fraternities exist? Can the process be realized?

The task of the Secular Franciscan is not to find the perfect community; the task is to take up the challenge. The challenge of the Gospel holds the promise of life. The call in the primitive Rule contains the promise of blessing. Francis preached the Gospel as the *only* way. The primitive Rule calls each hearer to a radical conversion. That conversion, both initially and as ongoing, will be nurtured and facilitated if Secular Franciscans struggle together with other committed Secular Franciscans who, though stumbling, are committed to the journey, are committed to a life of ongoing conversion.

The specific ways in which each Secular Franciscan appropriates the Rule will differ, yet every authentic appropriation of the Rule will be a commitment to a life of ongoing radical conversion. The expression of each person's conversion will be different. That expression depends upon the person's gifts, call, and depth of authenticity. Socio-political conversion can be expressed in response to many different forms of injustice. Some will be called to work for nuclear disarmament, others for an end to racism and sexism, still others for more just economic systems. Violence and oppression take many forms within our world. No Secular Franciscan can work for the reform of every oppressive system; yet every Secular Franciscan must be involved somehow in the work of justice if they are authentically converted, if they truly appropriate the Rule. Each response to the Rule will be unique; each person must interpret what that call to radical conversion means in his or her life. But to all those who do respond authentically will come the blessing of penance.

The Blessing of Penance / Conversion

The primitive Rule proclaims the blessing of penance, the fruit of conversion. Those who persevere in an ongoing state of affective, intellectual, moral, socio-political, and religious conversion *are* "the spouses, brothers, and mothers of our Lord Jesus Christ". But the blessing of penance, the blessing of this way of conversion goes beyond the individual.

The Church needs to be renewed in each age. Not all baptized Christians, not all members of the hierarchy, and not all Secular Franciscans are converted in all areas of their lives. Where the members of Secular Franciscan Fraternities fully commit themselves individually and collectively to ongoing conversion in all areas of their lives, a blessing will be given to the Church. The example of committed Christians working together as equals on institutional forms of injustice can call the official Church to reflect on the ways in which she is not fully converted. That example can challenge members of the Franciscan First Order to examine the lack of conversion which prohibits a true "vital reciprocity" between the orders. The palpable holiness of authentically lived conversion cannot but be grace in the Church.

As we have seen, Francis lived in a world that knew great injustice and suffering. Francis' consciousness did not permit the question of socio-political involvement, of the changing of social and political structures. Our contemporary historical consciousness allows a dialogue with the primitive Rule to open new horizons with respect to the meaning of conversion. The call, the response, and the blessing of penance remain. The Secular Franciscan Order will gain a "new impetus" when the challenge of the primitive Rule becomes event again, when the radical conversion envisioned is lived individually and communally by the members such that the fraternities themselves become living sacraments, become palpable expressions of God's love and presence in our world.

And so may all who read the words of the primitive Rule appropriate the meaning of those words, for "*they are spirit and life*"[104].

---

[104] *Earlier Exhortation*, II, 21.

Appendix I

INNOCENT III'S BULL OF APPROBATION OF THE WAY OF LIFE FOR THE HUMILIATI

Innocent, etc., to the beloved sons G(uido) of Porta Orentali, C. Modeciensi, A. Cumano, N. Papiensi, G. Brixiensi, I. Bergamensi, I. Placentino, I. Laudensi, R. Cremonsensi, and the other ministers of the same order and their brothers and sisters, etc.

From the duty of our pastoral office it is incumbent on us both to plant holy religion and to nourish what is planted, and as fas[t] as we can, to confirm all and each in what they have religiously proposed lest, if they should be deprived of the apostolic favor, they make no progress but fall back even or return to their own vomit or grow lukewarm in the good they have begun. Hence, when your proposed way of life had been presented to Us, we had it read aloud and diligently heard it together with our brothers, and after some things were corrected we have taken care to approve it in your favor; for greater precaution we have considered that it ought to be inserted word for word in the present page.

1. With the Lord aiding you, you have proposed to keep humility of heart and meekness in manners. So, the Lord in the gospel: "*Learn from Me, because I am meek and humble of heart, and you will find rest for your souls*" (Mt 11:29). Also, to observe obedience to the prelates of the church. Hence the apostle: "*Obey those put in charge of you and be subject to them, for they keep watch as men who must render an account for your souls*" (Hb 13:17). Indeed, there is no true humility, when its companion obedience is abandoned. Patience also in adversities is very neces-

sary (Hb 10:34), by tolerating with equanimity evils inflicted on oneself by others. Hence, the Lord in the Gospel: "*It has been said of old, An eye for an eye, a tooth for a tooth. But I tell you not to resist evil, but if someone should strike you on the right cheek, give him your left cheek also*", and "*If anyone should force you to go one mile, go another two with him*", and "*If someone would want to go to court and take away your tunic, give him your cloak too*" (Mt 5:39-41). Likewise the Apostle, "*Not defending yourselves, dearly beloved, but give place to wrath, for it is written: Vengeance is mine, and I will pay back, says the Lord*" (Rm 12:19). The same Apostle says: "*Now there is plainly a fault among you, that you have lawsuits one with another. Why not rather accept the wrong, why not let yourselves be cheated?*" (1 Cor 6:7). Furthermore, the Lord in the Gospel: "*In patience you will possess your souls*" (Lk 21:19). And, "*Forgive, and you will receive forgiveness*" (Lk 6:37). The fervor of charity must be joined to this too; as contained in the two commandments, viz., in the love of God and of neighbor, as it is written, "*You shall love the Lord your God with your whole heart, and with your whole soul, and with all your mind, and all your powers, and your neighbor as yourself*" (Lk 10:27). Charity must also be shown to enemies, for the Lord says: "*Do good to those who lie about you, so that you may be children of your father in heaven, who makes the sun to rise overjthe just and the unjust, and sends rain upon both good and bad*" (Mt 5:44-5). The Apostle says: "*If your enemy is hungry, feed him, and if he asks for drink, give it to him*" (Rm 12:20).

2. Furthermore, "*above all, brothers, do not swear, neither by heaven, nor by earth, nor by any manner of oath. But let your speech be, Yes, yes, No, no, so that you do not incur condemnation*", as the blessed Apostle James says (Jm 5:12). Do not allow any indiscreet or spontaneous affection induce you to take an oath, but if sometimes it must be done, let it be some great and urgent instance of necessity that compels you. Not only does James in the Epistle prohibit indiscreet and spontaneous swearing, but also Christ in the gospel says: "*It has been said of old: You shall not swear, but you shall perform your oaths to the Lord. But I tell you not to swear at all, neither by heaven, for it is God's throne; nor by earth, for it is His footstool; and*

neither by Jerusalem for it is the city of the great king; nor by your head, because you cannot make one hair white or black" (Mt 5:33-36). Likewise, "*Above all, brothers of mine, do not swear, neither by heaven nor by earth, nor by any manner of oath*" (Jn 5:12). When he says, "*do not swear*", he prohibits spontaneous swearing, for we must not swear because we want to, but if necessity requires it. When he adds, "*neither by heaven, nor by earth*", he prohibits indiscreet swearing; for one must not swear by creation but rather by the Creator. Let your speech be Yes, yes, No, no; that is, the affirmation or denial, you make with your mouth should express what you have in your heart. This is not referring to simple statements of affirmation or denial, but rather to one that is asserted as truthful, as when Christ, according to John, frequently asserts "*Amen, amen, I am telling you*". But what is over and above these, is of evil; and the evil is not so much of the moral order as of the penal order; and it is not so much of the one making the oath as of the one who demands the oath. This demanding an oath comes from some kind of weakness of unbelief, and it always pertains to the penal order even if not always to the moral order. But that it is licit to swear when necessity demands is taught by the Apostle when he says, "*For men swear by one greater than themselves; and an end for all their controversy is an oath for confirmation*" (Hb 6:16). Also, the Angel which John saw in the Apocalypse "*standing upon the sea and the earth, lifted up his hand to heaven, and he swore by Him who lives for ever and ever*" (Apoc 10:5). Jeremiah, too, prophesying about those who were to be in the time of grace, testifies: "*And they will swear, As the Lord lives, in truth and in judgment and in justice, and all the nations will bless Him and praise Him*" (Jer 4:2). It is read that Paul frequently swore: "*God is my witness*", he says (Rm 1:9), and "*By your glory, brethren, which I have in Christ Jesus*" (1 Cor 15:31).

3. Next, as the Lord says: "*All things whatever you wish, that men should do to you, do the same to them. Strive to enter through the narrow gate, because strait is the way and narrow the gate which leads to life, and there are few who discover it. On the other hand, wide and broad is the gate which leads to perdition, and there are many who go in through it*" (Mt 7:12-15). "*Repent, therefore*", (Mt 3:3) and "*do not sin*" (1 Cor 15:34). "*Have peace with men*" (Rm 12:18).

4. Give back interest monies and all ill-gotten things; for the sin is not remitted unless the restitution is made. And make satisfaction for other wrongs. So the Lord in the gospel: "*If you are offering your gift at the altar and remember that your brother has anything against you, leave your gift before the altar and go first to be reconciled to your brother, and then come offer your gift*" (Mt 5:24).

5. Tithes, too you must not keep, for in no way is it licit for laity to possess them. *Hence Gregory VII: "Tithes which the canonical authority demonstrates to have been granted for charitable use, by apostolic authority we prohibit to be kept by laymen. For whether they receive them from bishops, religious, or any other kind of persons, unless they return them to the church, let them know that they commit the crime of sacrilege and incur the danger of eternal damnation*"[1]. Let your tithes and first fruits be paid to the clerics for distribution; do this canonically according to the arrangement of the diocesan bishop. For in the gospel the Lord shows that tithes ought to be given: "*Woe to you scribes and pharisees, hypocrites, who tithe mint and anise and cummin and leave behind the weightier things of the Law: judgment and mercy and faith. These things you ought to have done, and not to leave those undone*" (Mt 23:23). But concerning those fruits and crops which you have left over among you, use them for giving alms; and the whole sum that is over and above your just and necessary expenses distribute to the poor; but do it in such a way, as the Apostle says, "*not that others should be relieved, and you burdened or impoverished*" (2 Cor 8:13). Wherefore, also, the Lord says in the gospel: "*But yet what is left over, give alms, and behold all things are clean to you*" (Lk 11:41). Moreover, "*do not lay up treasures for yourselves on earth, where moth and rust eat away and thieves break in and steal. Lay up treasure for yourselves in heaven, where neither rust nor moth consume, and where thieves do not break in and steal*" (Mt 8:19-20).

6. "*Do not love the world, brethren, nor those things which are in the world; for if anyone loves the world the charity of the Father*

[1] *Gratian* II, C. 16, q. 7, c. 1. Cf. Meerssemann, *Dossier*, 279, note 5.

is not in him. Because everything that is in the world is concupiscence of the flesh, concupiscence of the eyes, and pride of life, which is not of the Father, but is of the world. And the world will pass away, and its concupiscence; but the one who does the will of God abides forever", as John the Apostle testifies (1 Jn 2:15-17). The same is declared by James the Apostle, saying: "*O you unfaithful ones, are you not aware that love of the world is enmity to God. Whoever chooses to be a friend of this world is marked out as an enemy of God*" (Jm 4:4). To those joined by matrimony the Lord commands a husband not to divorce his wife, excepted is the cause of lewd conduct (Mt 19:9), but as the Apostle says, "*the husband should fulfill his conjugal obligations to his wife, the wife hers toward her husband, unless perhaps by mutual consent they might abstain*" (1 Cor 7:3-5).

7. Unless prevented by sickness, debility, or labor, each one should fast on Wednesdays and Fridays, excepting the days of Pentecost, and from Christmas to Epiphany, and other solemn days.

8. On those days on which they do not fast, they should be content with lunch and dinner, and food and drink should be moderate and temperate. Hence, the Lord in the gospel: "*Be on guard lest our spirits become bloated with indulgence and drunkenness and worldly cares*" (Lk 21:34).

9. When you come for meals, before you eat say the Lord's Prayer, and do the same after your meal.

10. You ought to observe the seven canonical hours, namely, matins, prime, terce, sext, none, vespers, and compline so that you may praise the Lord seven times a day, as the Prophet said (Ps 118:164). At each of the hours you should say the Lord's Prayer seven times on account of the seven gifts of the Holy Spirit. At prime and compline, however, you should say the Symbol, that is, *Credo in Deum*.

11. Your clothes ought to be neither too elegant nor too shabby, but of a kind that have no irreligious note about them, for neither affected dirtiness nor shabbiness nor exquisite neatness and elegance are suitable for a Christian.

12. Because it is your custom, you should know how to come to the aid of any member of your fellowship who is in need of temporal things or is laid up with sickness; help them in their temporal need or in taking the necessary care of them.

13. If any of your members shall have died, announce this to the brethren and let each one come to the funeral, and let each say twelve times the Lord's Prayer and *Miserere mei, Deus* for the soul of the deceased, seeing that you intend and arrange, with the help of the Lord, to remain and persevere in the order and your way of life.

14. But in order that your way of life may be supported by the prayers of your brethren, each one of you ought to say every day the *Pater Noster* three times for the living and three times for the dead members of this fraternity of yours; and say it once for the peace of the Church and of the whole Christian people.

15. As for the rest, it will also be your custom to come together every Sunday in a suitable place to hear the word of God, where one or several of the brethren of proven faith and religious experience who are powerful in work and speech (Lk 24:19) will, with the permission of the diocesan bishop, propose a word of exhortation to those who have gathered to hear the word of God. The speakers should admonish [and] lead them to an upright life and works of piety, and do this in such a manner that they should not speak about the articles of faith and the sacraments of the Church.

16. Moreover, we prohibit any bishop, contrary to the form we have prescribed, to prevent such brethren from proposing the word of exhortation since, according to the Apostle, "*the spirit must not be extinguished*" (1 Th 5:19).

17. Therefore, beloved sons and daughters in the Lord, "*with pure heart and good conscience and sincere faith*" (1 Tm 1:5) may you observe the form of living which we have taken care diligently to examine, prudently to correct, and beneficially to ap-

prove, so that you may return home to receive the everlasting reward from him who is the rewarder of merits and the searcher of hearts.

Let no one therefore... etc. But if anyone... etc.

Given at the Lateran on the 7th day of June in the fourth year of our pontificate.

Appendix II

A COMPARISON OF THE MEMORIALE PROPOSITI AND THE RULE OF 1289

Memoriale propositi

The Rule and Life of the Brothers and Sisters of Penance begins

In the name of the Father, the Son, and the Holy Ghost. Amen.

Memorial of the manner of life of the Brothers and Sisters of Penance living in their own homes, begun in the year of our Lord 1221. In the time of the lord Pope Gregory IX, 13th day of June, the first indication is such.

The Rule of 1289

Nicholas, Bishop, Servant of the Servants of God. To our beloved sons and our beloved daughters in Jesus Christ, the Brothers and Sisters of the Order of Penance, present and to come, Health and Apostolic benediction:

Not to be shaken by any storms or shattered by any waves of tempests, the solid foundation of the Christian religion is known to be placed on the rock of the Catholic faith which the sincere devotion, glowing with the fire of charity, of the disciples of Christ taught by solicitous preaching to the nations walking in darkness, and which the

Memoriale propositi	*The Rule of 1289*
	Roman Church holds and preserves. For, this is the right and true faith without which no one is rendered acceptable, no one appears pleasing in the eyes of the Most High. It is this faith which prepares the way to salvation and promises the rewards and joys of an eternal happiness.
	Wherefore the glorious Confessor of Christ, Blessed Francis, the founder of this Order, showing by words as well as by example the way leading to God, instructed his children in the sincerity of the same faith, and wished them to confess it boldly, retain it firmly and fulfill it in deed, so that as they profitably advanced along its path, they might merit, after the imprisonment of the present life, to be made possessors of eternal beatitude.
	I. On the Manner of Examining Those Desirous of Entering the Order.
	We, therefore, honoring this Order with fitting favors and very readily attending its growth, decree that
	1. All who may happen to take upon themselves the observance of this form of life, before the undertaking or their reception, be subjected to a diligent examination on the Catholic faith and their obedience to the aforesaid Church. And if they have firmly their faith and obedience and truly believe in them, they may safely be admitted or received to it.
[Cf. XI, 1]	2. Solicitous precautions must be taken, however, lest any heretic or one suspected of heresy, or even one of ill-repute be in any way admitted to the observance of this life.

Memoriale propositi	*The Rule of 1289*
	3. And if it happen that such a one was found to have been admitted, he should be turned over to the inquisitors as quickly as possible, to be punished for heretical depravity.
	II. On the Manner of Receiving into the Order
[Cf. X, 5-6; XIII, 11]	1. When anyone, however, wishes to enter such a fraternity, let the ministers assigned for the reception of such, diligently investigate his office, state and condition, explaining to him very clearly the duties of this fraternity and especially the restitution of goods of others. After this, if he so wishes, he may be clothed after the manner of the fraternity, and let him strive to make satisfaction for the goods of others, should any be in his possession, in money or by giving a pledge of security, and let him take no less care to reconcile himself with his neighbors.
[Cf. X, 7-9]	2. A year after all these things had been done, he may, on the advice of some discreet brothers, if he shall appear fit to them, be received in this manner, namely, that he promise to keep all the divine precepts, and also to appear when summoned at the will of the visitor to make satisfaction, as it behooves, for all transgressions which he might commit against this manner of life.
[Cf. X, 10-11]	3. After having been made, let this promise be set down in writing there by a notary public. Let no one be received by these ministers in any other manner unless it should appear otherwise to them after having discussed with solicitous consideration the condition and dignity of the person.

Memoriale propositi	*The Rule of 1289*
[Cf. X, 12]	4. Moreover, We ordain and decree that after entering this fraternity, no one may leave it to return to the world; he may, however, freely transfer to another approved religious order.
[Cf. XI, 2]	5. Married women may not be admitted to membership in this fraternity without the permission and consent of their husbands.
I. On the Manner of Dress	*III. On the Manner of Dress*
1. Let the men of this fraternity wear garments of ordinary colorless cloth the price of which shall not exceed six soldi of Ravenna money per yard, unless from this they shall be dispensed for a time because of an evident and necessary cause. The width and length of the cloth shall be included in the said price.	1. Let the brothers of this fraternity be clothed alike in cloth of low price and of a color neither entirely white nor entirely black, unless, for a legitimate and apparent reason the visitors, upon the advice of their ministers, have temporarily dispensed someone with regard to the price.
2. Let them have cloaks and furred outer garments without any opening at the neck, fastened or in one piece, and not buckled as the seculars wear, and with closed sleeves.	Let the above mentioned brothers also have cloaks and furred outer garments without an opening at the neck, divided or in one piece, and not open but fastened together as becomes modesty, and let the sleeves be closed.
3. Let the sisters wear cloaks and tunics of ordinary cloth of the same price, or at least with the cloak let them have black or white skirts or dresses or a roomy linen robe without plaits whose cost is not more than 12 denarii of Ravenna money per yard.	2. Let the sisters also wear a cloak and tunic made of the same common cloth, or at least with the cloak let them have a black or white skirt or dress or an ample robe of hemp or linen, sewn without any pleats.
4. According to the state of each woman and the local custom they may be dispensed from the price and manner of outer garments.	3. According to the condition of each of them and the local custom, a dispensation may be granted to the sisters concerning the quality of the cloth and the furred outer garments.

Memoriale propositi	*The Rule of 1289*
5. Let them not wear silk or colored ribbons or cords, and let the brothers as well as the sisters have furs of lambskin only.	4. Let the brothers and sisters, however, not use ribbons or silk cords. Let them have furs only of lambskin,
6. It is unlawful to have other than leather purses and the thongs sewn without silk. Other ornaments let them put away at the judgment of the visitor.	purses of leather and the thongs made without any silk, and none others shall they have. Other ornaments of the world are to be set aside according to the salutary counsel of St. Peter, Prince of the Apostles (1 Peter 3:3).
	IV. On Avoiding Immodest Gatherings
7. Let them not attend shameful entertainments, theatres, or dances, and let them give nothing to actors and prohibit that anything be given by their family.	Let attendance at unseemly banquets, or shows or public festivals and dances be absolutely forbidden to them. They should give nothing to actors or for the sake of vanity, and let them take care to prohibit that anything be given by their own family.
II. On Abstinence	*V. On Abstinence and Fasting*
1. Let all abstain from meat except on Sundays, Tuesdays, and Thursdays, unless because they are ill, weak, been bled (in which case they are excused) for three days, or in journey, or	1. Let all abstain from meat on Monday, Wednesday and Saturday, unless a condition of sickness or weakness would suggest otherwise. Let meat, however, be given on three successive days to those who have been bled, and it should not be denied to those making a journey.
2. because of a special solemnity occurring, namely, for three days at the Nativity of our Lord, the new year, Epiphany, for three days at Easter, the apostles Peter and Paul, the nativity of John the Baptist, the glorious Assumption of the Virgin Mary, the feast of All Saints and St. Martin.	Let the eating of meat be lawful for all when a special solemnity occurs on which all other Christians, from ancient times, are wont to eat flesh foods;

Memoriale propositi	*The Rule of 1289*
3. On the other days of non-fasting it is lawful to eat cheese and eggs. But when with the religious in their convents it shall be lawful for them to eat what is set before them.	on other days, however, when fast is not observed, eggs and cheese should not be denied. When they are with other religious in their convents they may licitly eat what is placed before them.
4. And let them be content with dinner and supper, excepting the sick, weak and those travelling. Let the healthy be moderate in food and drink.	They should be content with dinner and supper, unless they are weak, sick or on a journey. Let the food and drink of the healthy be moderate, for the Gospel text has: *But take heed to yourselves, lest your hearts be overburdened with self-indulgence and drunkenness* (Luke 2:34).
5. Before dinner and supper let them say once the Our Father and after eating, one Our Father and give thanks to the Lord. Other times let them say three Our Fathers.	Dinner or supper should not be eaten until the Lord's Prayer has been said once; after the meal it should be repeated together with "Thanks be to God". But if it is omitted, then let three Our Fathers be said.
6. From Easter to All Saints let them fast on Fridays. From All Saints to Easter they shall fast on Wednesdays and Fridays, observing notwithstanding other fasts which may be indicated by the Church in general observance.	2. Let them fast on ever Friday throughout the year unless the Feast of the Nativity of our Lord fall on that day; but from the Feast of All Saints until Easter they shall fast on Wednesdays and Fridays. No less shall they observe the other fasts prescribed by the Church or imposed by the Ordinaries for common cause.
III. Concerning Fasts	
1. During the Lent from the feast of St. Martin to Christmas and during the greater Lent from Sunday of Carnival to Easter let them fast continually unless dispensed because of illness or some other necessity.	During the Lent from the Feast of Blessed Martin until Christmas and from Quinquagesima Sunday until Easter, except Sundays, they should take care to fast every day, unless perhaps sickness or another necessity suggest otherwise.
2. Until their purification pregnant sisters may abstain from all bodily mortifications except those pertaining to dress and prayer.	3. Pregnant sisters may abstain, if they wish, from all bodily mortification, except prayer, until the day of their purification.

Memoriale propositi	*The Rule of 1289*
3. It is lawful for those who perform hard work to eat three times a day from Easter to the feast of St. Michael.	Workers, on account of the demands brought on by fatigue, may licitly take food three times a day on any day they are engaged in labor from Easter until the Feast of St. Francis.
4. It shall be lawful for those who work for others to eat of all things set before them except on Fridays and fast days generally appointed by the Church.	When it happens that they are engaged in labor for others, they are allowed every day to eat of all things placed before them except on Friday or a day on which it is known that a fast for all has been instituted by the Church.
	VI. On Confession and Holy Communion:
[Cf. VI, 1; XIII, 3]	Let each of the brothers and sisters not neglect to confess their sins and devoutly receive the Eucharist three times a year, namely, on the Feasts of the Nativity of the Lord, the Resurrection of the Lord and Pentecost, reconciling themselves with their neighbors and restoring the goods of others.
	VII. On not Bearing Arms
[Cf. VI, 3]	Let the brothers not carry offensive weapons with themselves, unless in defense of the Roman Church, the Christian faith, or their country, or with the permission of their ministers.
IV. On Prayers	*VIII. On Prayer*
1. Daily let all say the seven canonical hours, that is Matins, Prime, Terce, Sext, None, Vespers, and Compline.	Let all say the seven canonical hours daily, namely, Matins, Prime, Terce, Sext, None, Vespers, and Compline.

Memoriale propositi	*The Rule of 1289*
2. The clerics according to the order of the clerics; let those who know the psalter say for prime (Psalm 53) *Deus in nomine tuo* and (Psalm 118, verses 1-32) *Beati immaculati* as far as *Legem pone*, and the other psalms of the hours with the Glorys.	The clerics, namely, knowing the psalter, should say for Prime (Psalm 53) *Deus in nomine tuo* and (Psalm 118, verses 1-32) *Beati immaculati* up to *Legem pone*, and also the other psalms of the hours with the Glorys according to the rite of clerics.
3. But when they do not go to church, let them say for Matins the psalms said by the Church, or at least some other 18 psalms or at least the Our Fathers, just as the illiterate.	However, when they do not come to church, they should strive to say the psalms for Matins which are said by the clerics or the Cathedral Church, or at least, like the illiterate others,
4. All the others must say for the hours: 12 Our Fathers for Matins, and 7 Our Fathers for each of the other hours together with the Glory after each one.	let them not neglect to say for Matins twelve Our Fathers and Glorys, and for each other hour, seven Our Fathers and Glorys.
5. Let those who know the Creed and (Psalm 50) *Miserere mei Deus*, say them at Prime and Compline. If they have not said them at the constituted hours, let them say the Our Father. Let the infirm not say the hours unless they wish to.	Those who know the minor Creed and the (Psalm 50) *Miserere mei, Deus* should add it for the hours of Prime and Compline. But if they have not said them at the appointed hours let them say three Our Fathers. The infirm, however, unless they wish to, shall not be obliged to say these hours.
V. When They Must Go for Matins	
1. Let all go for Matins during the Lent of St. Martin and the greater Lent, unless an inconvenience of persons or things would result.	In the Lent of Blessed Martin and also during the Greater Lent, let them see to it that they be present in their parish churches for morning hours unless they are excused by a reasonable cause.
	IX. On Making A Will
[Cf. X, 1]	Besides, let all who have the right by law, draw up or make a testament, and arrange and dispose of their goods within the three months immediately following their admission, lest any of them die intestate.

Memoriale propositi	*The Rule of 1289*
	X. On Maintaining Peace
[Cf. X, 2]	Let the peace which must be made among the brothers and sisters or even among outsiders who are in dissension, be brought about as it shall seem proper to the ministers, on the advice, if possible, of the diocesan bishop in this matter.
	XI. On Conduct During Persecution
[Cf. X, 3]	If, contrary to law, the brothers or sisters or their privileges are assailed with molestations by those having authority or the magistrates of the places where they dwell, let the ministers try to have recourse to the bishops and other local ordinaries, and proceed according to their counsel and disposition in such matters.
VI. On Confession, Communion, Restitution, Not Bearing Arms and Not taking Oaths	*XII. On Taking Oaths*
1. Let them confess their sins three times a year and receive Communion on the Nativity of the Lord, Resurrection Sunday and Pentecost.	[Cf. VI]
2. Let them make satisfaction for past tithes and make ready for the future.	[Cf. VI]
3. Let them not take up lethal arms against anyone or carry them with themselves.	[Cf. VII]
4. Let all refrain from solemn oaths unless forced by necessity in the cases excepted by the Sovereign Pontiff in his indulgence, namely, for peace, faith, calumny and testimony.	1. Let all abstain from solemn oaths unless forced by necessity in the cases excepted through the indulgence of the Apostolic See, namely, for peace, faith, calumny, and affirming a testimony, and also when it shall seem expedient in a contract of buying, selling, or giving.

Memoriale propositi

5. And in their speech as much as possible let them avoid oaths. Those who by a slip of the tongue shall unwarily have taken oath, as it happens in much talking, that same day at evening when they must recall what they did, let them say three Our Fathers for such oaths.

6. Let everyone encourage his family in serving God.

VII. Concerning the Monthly Mass and Meeting

1. Let all the brothers and sisters in every city and locality gather each month whenever it shall appear expedient in a church announced by the ministers and there hear the divine word.

2. And let each one give to the treasurer one of the usual denari which he shall collect and on the advice of the ministers distribute among the poor brothers and sisters, and mostly to the infirm and those who would not have funeral services. Finally let him offer of that money to the other poor

and to that church.

3. And then, if they conveniently can, let them have one religious, instructed in the word of God, who would admonish and encourage them to penance, perseverance and the performance of works of mercy.

The Rule of 1289

2. Furthermore, in their ordinary conversation, let them avoid oaths as much as they are able, and whoever on any day carelessly swears by a slip of the tongue, as it usually happens in much talking, that evening when he must reflect on what he had done, let him say the Lord's Prayer three times for having taken such oaths carelessly.

3. And let everyone remember to encourage his own family to serve God.

XIII. On Hearing Mass and the Monthly Meetings

1. Let all healthy brothers and sisters of every city or locality here Mass daily if they conveniently are able to do so, and every month let them assemble at a Church or place which the ministers have been careful to announce in order to hear Mass there.

2. Let each member give a piece of the usual money to the treasurer who shall collect such money and, on the advice of the ministers, suitably divide it among the brothers and sisters oppressed by poverty, and especially among the infirm and those who are known to lack the means for a funeral service, and finally among the other poor.

3. Let them also offer some of this money to the aforesaid church.

And then, if they can do so conveniently, they should have a religious, one ably instructed in the word of God, who will earnestly exhort, admonish and arouse them to penance and the exercise of the works of mercy.

Memoriale propositi

4. And, except the officials, let them be silent during the Mass and preaching, attentive to the Office, prayer, and sermon.

The Rule of 1289

Let everyone strive to observe silence while the Mass is being celebrated and the sermon preached, and be intent upon the prayer and office, unless the common good of the fraternity impede.

VIII. Concerning the Works of Mercy, Wills, and the Settling of Discords

1. When any of the Brothers or sisters might happen to take ill, let the ministers, if informed of this by the sick one, either themselves or through others visit the sick, excite him to penance and provide from the common fund for his bodily needs as they shall see fit.

XIV. Of Sick and Departed Members

1. When any of the brothers happens to take ill, the ministers either themselves or through another or others, are bound, if the sick person has notified them of the illness, to visit him once a week and earnestly urge him, as they shall judge it to be of greater advantage and profit, to receive penance, and provide for the necessities of the sick person from the common fund.

IX. Concerning the Dead Brothers

1. And if any sick brother or sister shall depart from this life, let it be announced to the brothers and sisters who are present in the city or locality, so that they gather at his funeral and let them not depart until Mass has been celebrated and the body given burial.

2. If the aforementioned sick person should depart from the present life, it should be announced to the brethren and sisters then present in the city or locality where he happened to die, that they might be sure to attend personally the obsequies of the deceased from which let them not depart until after the Mass has been celebrated and the body placed in the grave. We wish that this be observed also with regard to sick and deceased sisters.

2. And after that let each one, within eight days of the death itself, say for the soul of the departed, the priest a Mass, those who know how, fifty psalms; and the others fifty Our Fathers together with the Eternal rest after each.

3. Moreover, during the eight days immediately following the death of the one interred, let each of the brothers and sisters say for his soul, namely: a priest, one Mass; one who knows the psalter, fifty psalms; and the illiterate, Our Father fifty times, and let them add at the end of each the Eternal rest.

Memoriale propositi	*The Rule of 1289*
3. Besides this during the year let a priest say three Masses for the welfare of the brothers and sisters, living and dead; he who knows the psalter let him say it, and let the rest say a hundred Our Fathers together with the Eternal rest at the end of each. Otherwise let them duplicate.	And after this, during the year they should have three Masses celebrated for the welfare of the brothers and sisters, living and dead. Let those who know the psalter say it, and the rest should not fail to say the Our Father one hundred times, adding at the end of each the Eternal rest.
X. On Making a Will	
1. Let all who by right can do so, make a testament and dispose of their things within three months after their profession so that none of them die intestate.	[Cf. IX]
2. Let it be as it shall appear to the ministers concerning peace among the brothers and sisters or outsiders causing discord; counsel also may be had of the diocesan bishop if it appears necessary.	[Cf. X]
3. If the right or privileges of the brothers and sisters are molested by the authorities or governors of the places in which they live, let the local ministers, with the counsel of the lord Bishop do what shall appear necessary.	[Cf. IX]
	XV. Of Ministers
4. Let everyone on whom the office of minister or the other offices here mentioned fall, accept and faithfully perform them, though anyone may vacate an office after a year.	Also let everyone on whom the ministerial or other offices mentioned in the contents of this present document are imposed, undertake them devoutly and take care to exercise faithfully. Let each office be limited to a definite period of time and let no minister be installed for life, but let his ministry extend over a definite time.
5. When anyone shall petition to enter this fraternity, let the ministers inquire into	[Cf. I,1]

Memoriale propositi	*The Rule of 1289*
his condition and office and let them explain to him the duties of this fraternity and most of all the restitution of the goods of others.	
6. And if he shall be pleased with the aforementioned rule, let him be vested, and let him satisfy his creditors either by money or by a given security. Let him be reconciled with his neighbors and pay his tithes.	[Cf. II, 1]
7. A year after this is fulfilled, he may, on the advice of some discreet brother, if he shall appear fit to them, be received in this manner:	
8. that he promise to observe all that is here written or should be written or taken away, according to the Council of the brothers, all the time of his life, unless some time it should occur by the permission of the minister.	[Cf. II, 2]
	XVI. Concerning the Visitation and Correction of Delinquents
9. And that if he do anything against this manner of life, questioned by the minister he shall make satisfaction according to the will of the visitor.	1. For these things, let the ministers, brothers and sisters of every city and locality convene for a visitation in common at some religious place, or in a church when it happens that a place of this kind is lacking, and they should have as visitor a priest who belongs to some approved religious order and who shall impose a salutary penance on those who have committed digressions. Nor may any other perform this office of visitation for them.
	2. Because this present form of life took its origin from the aforementioned Blessed Francis, We counsel that the visitors and

Memoriale propositi	*The Rule of 1289*
	instructors should be taken from the Order of Friars Minor, whom the custodes or guardians of the same Order shall appoint, when they have been requested in the matter. However, We do not want a congregation of this kind to be visited by a lay person.
[Cf. XII, 2]	3. Let such an office of visitation be exercised once a year, unless some necessity urges that it be made more often. Let the incorrigible and disobedient be forewarned three times, and if they should not try to correct themselves, then, on the counsel of the discreets, let them be totally deprived of membership in this congregation.
10. And let him make a public promise in writing thereto.	[Cf. II, 3]
11. Let no one be receive in any other way, unless it shall appear otherwise to them, considering the condition and dignity of the person.	
12. Let no one depart from this fraternity or from what is here contained unless to enter into religion.	[Cf. II, 4]
XI. Concerning Contempt and Distrust of Heretics	
1. Let no heretic or one accused of heresy be received. If, however, he was only suspected of it, he may be admitted if, cleared before the bishop, he is fit in other respects.	[Cf. I, 2 and 3]
2. Women having husbands shall not be received unless with the consent and permission of their spouses.	[Cf. II, 5]

Memoriale propositi	*The Rule of 1289*
3. Incorrigible brothers and sisters expelled from the fraternity shall in no wise be again received, unless it should so please the more prudent part of the brothers.	[Cf. XVI, 3]
	XVII. On Avoiding Lawsuits
[Cf. XIII, 13-14]	Moreover, as far as they are able, let the brothers and sisters avoid quarrels among themselves, suppressing those which might happen to arise, otherwise, let them answer to the law before one vested with judicial power.
	XVIII. Concerning Dispensations
[Cf. XII, 5]	Local ordinaries or the visitor may dispense all the brothers and sisters from abstinences, fasts and other austerities, when for a legitimate cause it shall seem expedient.
XII. Concerning the Declaration of Faults	*XIX. On Declaration of Faults*
1. Let the ministers of each city and place declare the manifest faults of the brothers and sisters to the visitor for punishment.	Let the ministers denounce the manifest faults of the brothers and sisters to the visitor that they may be punished.
2. And if anyone show himself incorrigible, let the visitor be informed of him through the ministers on the advice of some discreet brothers and expel him from the fraternity and let it be announced in the congregation.	And if any one might be incorrigible, after a third admonition, the ministers, on the advice of come of the discreet brothers should report him to the visitor that he deprive him of membership in the fraternity. Afterwards, this fact must be made known to the congregation. [Cf. XVI, 3]
3. Furthermore, if it is a brother, let him be denounced to the local authority or governor.	

Memoriale propositi

4. If one should know of some scandal concerning the brothers or sisters let him make it known to the ministers and he ought to inform the visitor, but they are not bound to denounce anything between husband and wife.

5. The visitor has the power to dispense all the brothers in all these things when he shall see fit.

6. Let the ministers with the counsel of their brothers after a year elect two other ministers, and a faithful treasurer who would provide for the necessities of the brothers and sisters and the other poor, and messengers who, at their bidding, should announce the things said and done by the fraternity.

7. In all the aforesaid let none be obliged under sin but to the punishment, so that if twice admonished by the minister he neglects to perform the imposed punishment or that which must be imposed, let him be obliged under sin as one who is contumacious.

The Rule of 1289

[Cf. XVIII]

XX. Concerning the Binding Force of the Rule

Finally, We wish that none of the brothers and sisters be obliged under pain of mortal sin to all the foregoing, except where they are bound by divine precepts and statutes of the Church. However, let them promptly and humbly receive the penance imposed upon them according to the gravity of the transgression, and effectively strive to fulfill it.

To no one, therefore, be it allowed to infringe on this page of Our statute and confirmation or to oppose it with rash temerity. But if anyone shall have presumed to attempt this, let him know that he will incur the wrath of Almighty God and of His holy Apostles Peter and Paul. Given at Rietti, on the sixteenth of the calends of September, and the second year of our pontificate. (17th of August, 1289)

Appendix III

ARCHIVAL DOCUMENTS

The Original Texts From The "Projet de Règle"

THE 1974 BASIC TEXT

Texte de base établi par le Presidium de la Commission de la Règle pour inspirer un Projet de Règle à travailler par la Commission et être ensuite soumis aux Conseils nationaux

I: *Prologue - Appel*

1. Dieu a tellement aimé le monde qu'il lui a donné son Fils unique: Image du Dieu Invisible, Premier-Né de toute créature. En lui et pour Lui, comme toutes choses, nous avons été crées. En Lui, nous avons été élus par le Père, dès avant la création du monde, pour être saints et immaculés en sa présence dans l'amour. C'est en Lui que, après avoir entendu la Parole de vérité, la Bonne Nouvelle de notre salut et y avoir cru, nous avons été marqués d'un sceau par l'Esprit de la Promesse. Il est ainsi notre chemin vers le Père.

Dans le Père il veut nous rassembler en Église avec tous les hommes nos frères pour être son Peuple saint, nous faisant participer à sa fonction sacerdotale, prophétique et royale. Homme nouveau, il fait de nous une créature nouvelle pour la Nouvelle Création qu'il est venu inaugurer par sa naissance et qu'il a scellée dans sa mort et sa Résurrection.

Il est notre Vie éternelle. Chaque jour nous unissant dans son Amour sauveur, il nous fait communier avec tous les hommes et fait de chacun de nous leur frère. Il nous invite à continuer son œuvre de Rédemption et de transformation du monde et de l'humanité, que lui-même viendra parachever lors de son Retour triomphant. Ainsi à sa suite, nous surgirons humanité nouvelle pour de nouveaux cieux et une nouvelle terre à la gloire éternelle du Père.

2. *Dans la famille de St-François et la fraternité*

Pour mieux nous faire participer en Église au dessein d'amour du Père sur le monde, le Christ nous a rassemblés dans la Famille Franciscaine; comme les autres Familles spirituelles, elle est une grâce du Seigneur à son Peuple, et une manifestation de la diversité des dons de l'Esprit.

A la suite de saint François, le Christ nous y a appelés pour découvrir et vivre l'Évangile à sa manière et selon son esprit. Tous ceux que rassemble cette volonté: prêtres, religieux, laïcs constituent sa Famille.

Au sein de cette unique Famille, les différentes branches sont "en réciprocité vitale". La branche Séculière organisée en FRATERNITÉ (T.O.F.S.), nous regroupe en frères pour marcher ensemble vers le Seigneur en vivant l'Évangile. Elle nous donne, pour éclairer notre marche, une "Forme de vie" inspirée de celle de frère François, authentifiée par l'Église et que nous nous engagerons à vivre.

Jour après jour, par elle et en elle, nous nous entraînons ensemble dans la charité fraternelle à suivre Celui qui est la Voie, la Vérité et la Vie.

II: "*Norme de Vie*"

3. *Vivre l'Évangile du Christ*

La Communauté des Fidèles du Christ nous a transmis la Bonne Nouvelle du Seigneur Jésus. Elle nous révèle la réalisation du mystère caché depuis des siècles: l'avènement de la Parole, le Christ vivant. Tel est encore le message à annoncer afin de rendre tout homme parfait en Christ. En effet, l'Évangile nous livre les traces du Christ que nous devons suivre. Et le Seigneur lui-même révéla à François qu'il devait vivre selon la forme du saint Évangile. Aussi, il nous dit de tenir les paroles, la vie, la doctrine et le saint Évangile de Celui qui a daigné nous manifester le nom du Père.

Dans l'Évangile nous voulons puiser l'inspiration de notre vie et devenir ainsi, comme il nous est demandé, des témoins du Christ. Nous en faisons notre livre de base pour avancer dans la connaissance et l'intimité du Seigneur, pour éclairer notre vie personnelle, familiale et toutes nos relations humaines, confrontant notre regard, nos réactions, nos attitudes avec l'Évangile. Inlassablement nous irons de l'Évangile à la vie et de la vie à l'Évangile: ainsi nous ferons du Christ le centre de notre vie.

4. *Sur le chemin d'une conversion continue*

La réponse à cette vie évangélique nous engage sur le chemin d'une conversion continue. Elle nous conduit à une transformation totale pour une "vie nouvelle" dont le Baptême est la source: mourir à nous-mêmes afin de vivre pour Dieu dans le Christ.

Comme François, nous entendons l'appel que Jésus crucifié nous adresse et dont il fait la condition pour marcher à sa suite: "Si quelqu'un veut venir après mois, qu'il prenne sa croix", sachant bien que le passage par la crois débouche, même ici-bas, dans la joie de la résurrection.

De cette œuvre de mort et de résurrection quotidiennes nous acceptons les exigences radicales: changement de mentalité, arrachement à l'égoïsme, attention aux autres. Dans la joie nous parcourons cette route pénitentielle que, avec la Liturgie, nous rythmons par la célébration des Mystères du Christ.

De cette conversion continue le Sacrement de Pénitence est le signe privilégié et, pour nous, la Fraternité un moyen. Des fatigues de notre travail, de notre action apostolique, de notre effort continu de conversion, de nos épreuves, de notre service désintéresse ainsi que de notre pauvreté nous ferons notre pénitence préférée qui nous fait communier à la croix du Christ.

Nous n'oublions pas les pratiques que la tradition de l'Église nous recommande en certains temps, que saint François a si généreusement pratiquées et dont les Constitutions de la Fraternité prévoieront l'application.

5. *Avec le Christ pauvre*

Le Christ et son Église nous appellent à vivre les Béatitudes, source de vie fraternelle, et en particulier la 1ère: la pauvreté. Fils de Dieu, il reçoit tout du Père. "Lui qui est de condition divine s'est dépouillé lui-même, prenant la condition de serviteur, devenant semblable aux hommes". "Il mit sa volonté dans la volonté de son Père" — et avec sa bienheureuse Mêre il choisit la pauvreté.

Suivant sa route et pélerins ici-bas, nous nous reconnaissons démunis de tout et recevant tout de la bonté de notre Père. Nous nous obligeons à nous dépouiller de nous-mêmes (de notre orgueil, de notre satisfaction); plus sensibles à l'être qu'à l'avoir, nous veillerons à ce que notre cœur ne se laisse point prendre par la recherche de l'argent et des biens matériels, afin d'être plus proches de nos frères, de briser les barrières et combler les fossés qui séparent les hommes. Nous saurons nous rendre disponibles de nous-mêmes et de notre temps, partageant et donnant largement à plus pauvre de nous. Nous partagerons le combat des malheureux qui luttent pour une vie plus digne.

Dans la joie, par ce dépouillement, nous vivrons cette simplicité retrouvée qui nourrit l'Espérance. De cette pauvreté évangélique, la reconnais[s]ance est la marque distinctive.

6. *Frères de tous les hommes*

En tout homme le Père voit les traits de son Fils Bien-aimé. En tout homme nous nous efforçons de voir Jésus-Christ qui nous appelle à une fraternité universelle. Nous sommes tous frères, nous n'avons qu'un Père, le Père des cieux. Par son Fils il a voulu réconcilier tous les êtres. A cet appel nous voulons faire correspondre nos attitudes, nos jugements, nos relations humaines, notre action.

Comme François, nous faisons confiance en chacun, en chacun nous nous efforçons de découvrir le bien qui est en lui et que Dieu opère par lui. En tout homme rencontré, nous voyons une frère à aimer, à respecter, à servir. Nous nous efforçons d'être plus particulièrement attentifs aux plus déshérités, aux mal-aimés, aux victimes de situations injustes et, autant qu'il est possible, nous les aidons, à travers une action concertée, à acquérir leur dignité d'homme et de fils de Dieu.

Nous luttons contre les obstacles à la fraternité universelle (racisme, oppressions, injustices, violences). Nous faisons de notre travail et de notre action une participation à la Rédemption, source de fraternité, et à l'effort commun des hommes pour bâtir un monde juste et fraternel, préfiguration de la cité de Dieu.

7. *Membres vivants de l'Église*

Pour accomplir la volonté du Père, le Christ a fondé l'Église, née de son côté ouvert sur la Croix, pour continuer son œuvre de salut et de réconciliation. Sacrement universel de salut, elle est signe et moyen d'union avec Dieu et d'unité de tout le genre humain. L'ensemble de ceux qui regardent avec la foi vers Jésus, Dieu les a appelés, il en fait l'Église pour qu'elle soit le sacrement de cette unité salutaire.

Par le baptême nous sommes devenus des membres vivants, participant de sa vie et de sa mission. Aussi, nous nous voulons toujours en communion avec elle, responsables de son avancée dans l'histoire: ouverts et attentifs à ses appels comme aux signes des temps. Nous regardons toute forme d'apostolat conforme à la mission de l'Église comme un devoir et un droit. Nous laissant guider par l'Esprit-Saint et en communion avec notre fraternité, nous nous engageons concrètement, sachant prendre des initiatives audacieuses, si besoin est.

Nous souvenant du respect et de l'amour qui animaient François à l'égard du "Seigneur Pape", des évêques et de tous ceux qui ont la charge du Peuple de Dieu, nous voulons avoir envers les Pasteurs de l'Église une attitude de fidélité, de dialogue confiant et loyal et d'obéissance active.

8. *Priant avec le Christ et l'Église*

Dans l'Évangile Jésus nous donne l'exemple d'une prière fréquente et nous en montre la nécessité pour rester dans son amour et supplier pour nous et pour les autres. Dans cette œuvre, l'Esprit-Saint vient en aide à notre faiblesse, car nous ne savons pas prier comme il faut, mais l'Esprit lui-même prie pour nous. C'est ainsi que François, à l'école de l'Esprit-Saint, était devenu la prière faite homme.

Comme Jésus, nous saurons trouver des moments, des jours, pour rencontrer le Père, l'écouter, lui parler, parfois même dans la solitude. Nous faisons du "Notre Père" la nourriture qui alimentera notre louange du Père, notre vie de famille et de travail, notre action temporelle et apostolique. Nous aimerons contempler le Seigneur, sa présence et son action dans l'histoire du monde et le cœur des hommes, pour y découvrir son amour et mieux entendre ses appels.

Nous aimons recevoir les sacrements de l'Église comme participation à la mort et à la résurrection du Christ, et comme source de toute notre vie chrétienne. En particulier, avec un cœur préparé et une volonté engagée, nous célébrons l'Eucharistie: pour nous, comme pour François, elle est "commémoration de la Passion et de la mort du Christ", rédemption à l'œuvre, communion à sa Personne et à son Peuple. Elle "fait l'Église".

Nous sommes fidèles à la prière (Office) de la Fraternité, qui nous fait participer à la louange que l'Église adresse au Père pour les hommes.

9. *Avec la Vierge Marie*

La Vierge se voulut solidaire de son peuple en attente du Messie, humble servante du Seigneur, disponible à tous ses appels, toujours à l'écoute de sa parole, la gardant et la méditant en son cœur, partageant la vie pauvre de son Fils, priant avec les Apôtres réunis dans l'attente de la manifestation de l'Esprit.

Comme l'Église et avec elle, nous aimerons la regarder, la prier, et l'imiter dans toutes ses attitudes.

10. *Porteurs de paix*

Le Christ a réconcilié tous les êtres en faisant la paix par le Sang de sa Croix; il nous appelle à entrer dans le mystère de sa paix et à la faire advenir.

L'Église, signe de cette fraternité qui rend possible un dialogue loyal et le renforce, met au service de tout le genre humain l'Évangile de paix. Et ayant "condamné la barbarie de la guerre, elle lance un appel ardent aux chrétiens pour qu'avec l'aide du Christ, auteur de la paix, ils travaillent avec tous les hommes à consolider cette paix entre eux, dans la justice et l'amour, et à en préparer les moyens".

Aussi, messagers de la Bonne Nouvelle, comme François nous nous efforçons, en toute circonstance, de porter aux hommes la paix et la joie, car nous croyons à l'efficacité du dialogue et à la force de l'amour. Nous cherchons toujours ce qui unit, travaillant avec les autres à trouver des solutions aux conflits qui atteignent notre prochain, nous déclarant contre la guerre sous toutes ses formes, nous refusant à toute participation à la course aux armements et à tout antagonisme entre les homme et les Peuples.

Pour être fidèles à notre vocation franciscaine, nous saisissons les occasions pour accomplir des actes positifs; pour la faire arriver, nous participons à des actions communes, prenant même des responsabilités dans les organismes en faveur de la paix.

11. *Vivant dans l'amour du Père*

D'un amour éternal Dieu a aimé chacun de nous. Toute notre vie baigne dans cet amour. Toutes ses œuvres sont des actes d'amour: le Christ, image du Père, en est la manifestation, il nous a aimés jusqu'à la fin.

A l'exemple de François, nous nous émerveillons de cette continuelle tendresses du Père; nous cherchons son reflet dans la bonté et l'intelligence des hommes. Nous louons le Seigneur pour toute sa création; pour la libérer et la parfaire, nous travaillons avec les autres hommes, hâtant ainsi le Retour du Christ.

Nous faisons de notre vie une louange et un chant de reconnaissance. Et lorsque notre Avent terrestre se terminera, comme François nous célébrerons notre Pâque définitive; alors notre Sœur la Mort nous ouvrira la porte, et nous seront enfin révélés le mystère et le Visage d'amour du Père, que nous avons attendus et cherchés toute notre vie.

III: *Fraternité*

12. *Cellule d'Église*

L'Esprit du Seigneur nous a donc appelés à entrer dans la Fraternité séculière de St-François, Peuple nouveau que le Seigneur a donné à François pour restaurer son Église en vivant de sa vie et de son Évangile.

La Fraternité nous accueille pour nous aider à mieux vivre la grâce du projet d'amour du Père. Dans ce but, à notre tour, nous accueillons sa pédagogie et sa manière de vivre communautaire que l'Église a authentifiée.

Nous voyons en elle une vrai cellule d'Église:

- communauté de prière qui nous entraîne à l'adoration et à la louange,
- lieu privilégié qui développe notre sens ecclésial,

- milieu fraternel qui nous fait expérimenter la vie évangélique et éprouver nos comportements.

13. *Organisme vivant*

La Fraternité, comme tout groupe humain vivant, a ses normes, son cadre, et ses responsable aux divers niveaux (local, régional, national, international) déterminés par ses Constitutions: loyalement nous les acceptons pour vivre en communion avec les frères de notre fraternité, et avec ceux des autres fraternités du monde.

14. Dociles à l'inspiration de l'Esprit et au cheminement de sa grâce, et selon les diverses étapes de contacts, d'information et de formation (noviciat) établies (par les Constitutions), nous nous engageons dans la "Forme de Vie évangélique" qu'elle nous présente. Nous regardons cet engagement (profession) comme une grâce qui fortifie en nous la vie baptismale, resserre notre lien avec l'Église, et nous intègre dans la famille franciscaine.

15. *Vie fraternelle* (*avec la fraternité locale*)

Engagés dans la fraternité, nous nous faisons un devoir de participer à sa vie, à ses réunions, à ses initiatives, aux appels qu'elle reçoit du Seigneur, de l'Église et des hommes. Ne nous contentant pas de recevoir, nous prendrons part aux échanges, au travail de recherche pour l'améliorer, aux sessions d'études.

Pour mieux progresser ensemble, nous accueillons avec humilité et reconnaissance les remarques de nos frères (correction fraternelle).

Etant une fraternité, nous sommes corresponsables de sa vie et de son progrès, nous suivons attentivement les efforts des responsables et du Conseil, donnant même nos avis. Nous nous faisons un devoir de participer aux élections prévues dans les Constitutions pour le gouvernement de la fraternité. En esprit franciscaine de service, nous accepterons les responsabilités que nous confieraient nos frères.

16. *La Famille franciscaine* nous a reçus au moment de la profession, nous voulons rester en communion avec elle, connaître son histoire, nous

sentir solidaires de sa vitalité, approfondir sa spiritualité, pour mieux en vivre, en témoigner et transmettre ainsi son message.

En communion plus particulière avec les frères du 1er Ordre qui assurent l'assistance spirituelle de notre fraternité, nous en ferons avec eux, selon ce qui est prévu dans la législation, la révision de notre vie franciscaine personnelle et de la marche de la fraternité (visite canonique), afin d'avancer ensemble et avec plus de générosité dans l'œuvre du Royaume et dans notre chemin vers le Père.

17. *Vivre la vie évangelique dans une unité fraternelle*

"Je vous exhorte donc dans le Seigneur: accordez votre vie à l'appel que vous avez reçu; en toute humilité et douceur, avec patience, supportez-vous les uns les autres dans l'amour. Rassemblés dans la paix, ayez à cœur de garder l'unité dans un même esprit. Comme votre vocation vous a tous appelés à une seule espérance, de même, il n'y a qu'un seul Corps et un seul Esprit, ...un seul Dieu et Père de tous, qui est au-dessus de tous, parmi tous, et en tous".

Bénédiction de S. François: "Quiconque observera ces choses, qu'il soit béni dans le ciel de la bénédiction du Père très Haut, qu'il soit rempli sur la terre de la bénédiction de son Fils bien-aimé, avec celle du Très Saint Esprit Paraclet".

THE 1975 REDACTION

PROJET DE REGLE

Prologue (Appel)

1. *Dieu est amour*

Il a tant aimé le monde qu'il lui a envoyé son Fils unique, pour que, conduits et rassemblés en communauté d'Église par l'Esprit Saint, nous participions à la vie même de la Trinité. En Lui, par Lui, et pour Lui, nous avons été élus dès avant la création du monde pour être saints et immaculés en sa présence.

Après avoir entendu la Bonne Nouvelle du Salut et y avoir cru, nous avons reçu du Christ le sceau de l'Esprit, par lequel Dieu établit une alliance éternelle avec son Peuple qu'il appelle a être le témoin de son amour.

Le Christ est notre chemin: c'est par Lui seul que nous avons accès auprès du Père; il est la lumière qui éclaire tout homme en marche vers le Père. Il est la vérité, dans laquelle l'Esprit Saint nous introduit de plus en plus. Il est la vie, qu'il est venue donner en abondance à tous les hommes.

Il nous appelle en Église à restaurer en Lui toutes choses, aider les hommes et la création à atteindre en Lui leur plénitude, et ainsi à continuer son œuvre de salut, que Lui-même viendra couronner au jour de son retour triomphant.

Chapitre I

2. *La famille franciscaine*

Pour mieux faire participer son Église et ses membres à ce dessein d'amour du Père sur le monde, et représenter toute la richesse de la Personne du Christ et de son Évangile, l'Esprit a suscité des familles spirituelles qui sont une grâce du Seigneur pour son Peuple et une manifestation de la diversité de ses dons. Pour nous, Il nous appelle à faire partie de celle de saint François.

Vivante image du Christ, François reçut la mission de restaurer l'Église en faisant refleurir l'Évangile; le Seigneur lui donna des disciples, et c'est en communion avec des frères qu'il qu'il [*sic*] fut invité à vivre l'Évangile, comme c'est ensemble que ceux-ci accomplissaient leur salut.

Ainsi, les trois branches ou Ordres, avec les autres Instituts qui forment la Famille franciscaine, vivent du même charisme, chacun dans sa vocation propre, et en réciprocité vitale.

L'Ordre Séculier franciscain, OSF, ou TOF, ou Fraternité Séculière de St-François, est une communauté de fraternités, groupant des chrétiens qui, poussés par l'Esprit, s'engagent par une profession à vivre l'Évangile dans et par leur condition séculière, selon une "Forme de vie" (Règle) inspirée de l'esprit de S. François et authentifiée par l'Église; elle bénéficie pour cela de l'Assistance spirituelle et des devoirs du 1er Ordre à son égard.

Cette "Forme de vie", avec son organisation et l'engagement de ses membres dans le monde consacrent son caractère séculier.

C'est en Fraternité et nous aidant mutuellement que nous vivons cette 'Forme de vie" évangélique franciscaine. En effet ce n'est pas isolément, mais dans un rassemblement que se réalise l'histoire de notre salut en Église. C'est à un peuple communauté que Dieu avait donné son Alliance. C'est en communauté que les disciples de Jésus sont appelés à vivre avec Lui et à témoigner en Église.

Chapitre II: Forme de Vie

3. *Vivre l'Évangile*

L'Évangile, transmis par la tradition vivante de l'Église nous révèle en plénitude la Parole de Dieu: Le Christ Jésus qui nous appelle à le suivre.

Le Seigneur lui-même révéla à François qu'il l'appelait à "vivre selon la forme du Saint Évangile". Et François enseigna à ses frères de garder fidèlement les paroles, la vie, la doctrine et le Saint Évangile de Celui qui a daigné manifester le nom du Père.

Dans l'Évangile et dans toute l'Écriture nous chercherons d'abord la Personne vivante du Christ. Personnellement et en Fraternité, nous le méditerons pour y découvrir son Visage; nous y puiserons l'inspiration de nos attitudes, de nos jugements, de nos actions pour conformer à la sienne notre vie (familiale, sociale, civique).

Vivre l'Évangile aujourd'hui, c'est l'actualiser sous la motion de l'Esprit, dans une recherche en Église et une attention aux signes des temps. Ainsi, en toute circonstance, nous irons de l'Évangile à la vie et de la vie à l'Évangile.

4. *Conversion*

La réponse à cet appel nous engage sur la voie d'une transformation totale pour une "vie nouvelle", dont le Baptême est la source: mourir au péché, afin de vivre pour Dieu dans le Christ. François a répondu généreusement à l'appel de Jésus crucifié. Mais il a expérimenté aussi que le passage par la Croix conduit, même dès ici-bas, à la joie de Pâques.

De cette œuvre quotidienne de mort et de vie, nous acceptons les exigences radicales: arrachement à l'égoïsme personnel et collectif, purification de nos intentions, engagement dans une attitude de solidarité humaine, attention aux autres, réorientation continuelle vers Dieu. Et avec nos fr[è]res, nous nous y aiderons mutuellement.

Dans la joie, nous parcourons cette route pénitentielle, avec un effort particulier pendant les temps recommandés par l'Église. Malgré des efforts pour accueillir Dieu et nous ouvrir à nos frères, nous faisons l'expérience de notre misère. De cet effort continu de conversion et de réconciliation, le Sacrement de Pénitence est le moyen et le signe privilégie.

5. *Avec le Christ pauvre et crucifié*

Fils de Dieu, Jésus reçoit tout du Père. Pour venir à nous, il se dépouille, prend la condition du serviteur, et choisit d'être pauvre en ce monde. Dans les Béatitudes, il béatifie le pauvre et proclame la Pauvreté comme disposition fondamentale du cœur pour entrer dans le Royaume. Sur la Croix, il porte la pauvreté à son sommet, et meurt nu, en "remettant" au Père même son esprit.

François, le "petit pauvre", ne veut connaître que le Christ et le Christ crucifié, et il se fait pauvre avec lui; il vit pauvre avec les pauvres, s'appuyant totalement sur la libéralité du Père; il ne compte pas sur la richesse, la science et le pouvoir.

Effectivement pauvres, dans l'aisance ou même dans l'abondance, notre souci sera d'acquérir une âme de pauvre. Pour cela, non seulement nous éviterons le superflu et le luxe, mais nous saurons accepter une pauvreté assez r[é]aliste pour nous engager dans un partage avec nos frères dans le besoin, et dans la solidarité avec les "petits" de ce monde. Pèlerins ici-bas, nous reconnaissons que "n'ayant rien, nous possédons cependant tout" par la bonté du Père. Notre attitude envers lui sera donc de reconnaissance.

Comme son œuvre de Rédemption a conduit le Christ à accepter la persécution, la souffrance et la mort, nous somme appelés, nous aussi, à entrer dans cette même voie pour communiquer aux hommes les fruits du salut.

Dans le travail, les difficultés, la maladie, les peines et les souffrances de cette vie, nous accepterons de marcher avec le Christ sur la voie royale de la Croix comme moyen de compléter ce qui manque à sa Passion et de coopérer à la Rédemption du monde.

6. *Frères de tous les hommes*

En tout homme, le Père voit les traits de son Fils bien-aimé, premier-né d'une multitude de frères. Par Lui, il a voulu réconcilier tous les êtres.

François, frère universel, voit un frère en tout être, et pas seulement en tout homme. En tout homme, comme nous fils du même Père, nous nous efforcerons de voir Jésus-Christ qui nous appelle à une fraternité universelle. Nous le chercherons particulièrement dans les plus pauvres, les plus déshérités, les mal-aimés, les marginaux, les victimes de situations injustes.

Nos attitudes, nos jugements, notre action nous conduiront à nous engager avec eux, pour lutter contre tous les obstacles à la fraternité universelle, et leur permettre d'acquérir leur dignité d'hommes et de fils de Dieu.

7. *Membres vivants de l'Église*

Le Christ a fondé l'Église. Née de son côté ouvert sur la Croix, vivifiée sans cesse par l'Esprit, nouveau Peuple de Dieu, elle continue son œuvre. Sacrement universel de salut, elle est signe et moyen d'union à Dieu et d'unité de tout le genre humain.

Par le Baptême devenus ses membres vivants, nous participons à sa vie et à sa mission. C'est pourquoi nous nous voudrons toujours en communion avec elle, ouverts et attentifs à ses appels, participants conscients de la fonction sacerdotale, prophétique et royale du Christ. De cœur et d'action entrant dans la mission de l'Église, nous regarderons formes de "service" et d'activités conformes à cette mission comme un devoir et un droit.

Plus profondément engagés envers elle par notre profession de vie franciscaine, nous nous souviendrons du respect et de l'amour qui animaient François à l'égard du "Seigneur Pape", des évêques et des responsables du Peuple de Dieu.

Aussi nous voulons avoir envers tous les pasteurs de l'Église une attitude de fidélité, de dialogue confiant et loyal, et d'obéissance conformejà la bienheureuse liberté des fils de Dieu.

8. *Priant avec le Christ et l'Église*

Jésus nous donne l'exemple d'une prière fréquente, et nous en montre la nécessité. François, habité par l'Esprit qui seul "sait prier comme il faut", était "moins un homme priant que la prière faite homme".

Comme lui, trop pauvres pour prier de nous-mêmes, nous apprendrons sous la motion de l'Esprit à faire surgir la prière de notre vie et de notre action.

Comme lui, nous saurons prendre des moments chaque jour pour accueillir le Père, l'écouter et lui parler dans son Fils; parfois même, dans la solitude, nous prendrons des jours pour cette rencontre.

Nous attacherons une importance particulière à ce signe privilégié de la prière du Christ: le rassemblement en Église avec nos frères pour la célébration liturgique. Nous y rejoignons la prière que le Christ, avec son "Corps", adresse au Père. Avec les étapes de la Liturgie, nous rythmerons notre prière personnelle et communautaire ainsi que notre vie, par la célébration des mystères du Christ.

Nous ferons du "Notre Père" la source de notre louange, la nourriture de notre action temporelle et apostolique. Nous nous ferons une joie de louer le Seigneur avec nos frères en Fraternité, de contempler sa présence et son action dans le cœur des hommes et dans l'histoire du monde, de nous en émerveiller, d'en rendre grâces.

Dans chacune de nos journées, nous nous unirons par notre prière (Office) à celle de la Fraternité. Par dessus tout, avec un cœur préparé par la Parole et avec une volonté engagée dans l'union au Christ, aussi souvent que possible nous célébrerons l'Eucharistie: participation à sa mort et à sa résurrection, Rédemption à l'œuvre, communion à sa Personne et à son Peuple.

En faisant ainsi de tous les aspects de notre vie des offrandes spirituelles qui rejoignent l'offrande du Corps du Seigneur, nous consacrerons le monde à Dieu, lui rendant partout, dans la sainteté de notre vie, un culte d'adoration.

9. *En plein monde*

Comme tous les membres de la Famille franciscaine, nous sommes envoyés dans le monde entier. Comme séculiers, nous y avons une vocation propre: vivant au milieu du siècle, engagés dans les divers devoirs et ouvrages du monde, il nous revient d'éclairer et d'orienter toutes les réalités temporelles auxquelles nous sommes étroitement unis, de telle sorte qu'elles se fassent et prospèrent constamment selon le Christ et soient à la gloire du Créateur et du Rédempteur.

Aussi, comme membres de la société temporelle, nous saurons, selon les dons accordés par le Seigneur, prendre notre part de responsabilité, apportant dans cette gérance des choses temporelles l'esprit des Béatitudes. Par notre témoignage et notre action associée à celle des autres hommes, nous travaillerons dans ces différents domaines à la réalisation du plan de Dieu sur le monde.

C'est d'abord dans notre famille que nous vivrons l'esprit franciscain, nous efforçant d'en faire le signe d'un monde déjà rénové dans le Christ. De notre travail nous ferons une participation au développement de la création, à la rédemption des hommes et un service de toute la communauté humaine.

Enfin, conscients qu'il appartient à toute l'Église de rendre les hommes capables de bien construire l'ordre temporel et de l'orienter vers le Christ, dans la distinction des droits et des devoirs des communautés ecclésiastiques et des communautés humaines, les Fraternités séculières prendront leurs responsabilités apostoliques et sociales et s'engageront dans des options évangéliques et concrètes.

10. *Porteurs de paix et de joie*

Acclamé "Prince de la Paix" par les Prophètes, salué Messager de la Paix par les Anges à Noël, le Christ nous invite à la paix: "Bienheureux les artisans de paix"!

A sa suite, François a été pacificateur par lui-même et par ses institutions. S'il a contesté, c'est par sa vie, et au nom du seul Évangile. Fils de François, nous croyons à la force de l'amour, à la bonté de l'homme, à la valeur du dialogue, à la puissance des efforts de conciliation, aux merveilles de transformation que produit le pardon.

A la suite de l'Église et avec tous les hommes de bonne volonté, nous prenons parti pour une attitude de paix et d'opposition à tout ce qui aboutit à la violence et prépare la guerre. Dans toutes les circonstances de notre vie (familiale, sociale), nous nous efforcerons de porter aux autres la joie et l'espérance, fruit de la paix du Resuscité.

11. *Avec la Vierge Marie*

La Vierge Marie prédestinée par une élection singulière pour être la Mère de Dieu, et associée par un lien étroit et indissoluble aux mystères de l'Incarnation et de la Rédemption, est devenue pour nous, dans l'ordre de la grâce, notre Mère.

Solidaire de son peuple en attente du Messie, humble servante du Seigneur, disponible à tous ses appels, toujours à l'écoute de sa parole, elle gardait et méditait dans son cœur tous les évènements dont elle était le témoin. Première disciple de son Fils, elle le suivit jusqu'à la croix, et s'offrit avec lui. Unie à la prière des Apôtres, elle appela sur l'Église le don de l'Esprit. Maintenant au ciel dans la gloire, son rôle ne s'interrompt pas: elle intercède sans cesse pour obtenir aux hommes les dons qui assurent leur salut.

François "aimait d'un amour indicible la Mère du Christ Jésus" et retrouvait toujours en elle l'image de la pauvreté de son Fils. Aussi l'appelait-il la "Poverella". Avec l'Église et avec François nous aimerons regarder Marie, l'appeler à notre aide, l'imiter dans toutes ses attitudes.

12. *Vivant dans l'amour du Père et la vie de l'Esprit*

Le Christ nous révèle de quel amour le Père nous a aimés. En Jésus-Christ, François a découvert cet amour et l'a cherché toute sa vie. Aussi, en réponse à la promesse de Jésus, il adresse cette invitation à ses frères: "Faisons-lui donc toujours, en nous, un temple et une demeure: pour lui, le Seigneur Dieu tout-puissant, Père, Fils et Saint Esprit"!

Comme François, nous nous émerveillerons de cette continuelle tendresse du Père; nous le louerons pour sa création entière; nous découvrirons en tout être et en tout évènement une présence de son amour; et surtout nous lui rendrons grâce pour le don infini qu'il nous fait en son Fils Jésus-Christ. Louange, action de grâce et engagement de notre vie seront notre réponse à l'amour du Père.

L'Esprit est l'expression vivante de la Vie et de l'Amour du Père et du Fils. François voulait pour les siens "l'Esprit du Seigneur et sa sainte activité", et lui-même se laissait conduire par Celui qu'il appelait "le Ministre général de son Ordre".

Dociles à son appel, nous lui demandons de nous transformer par sa Présence et par ses dons, pour vivre de plus en plus du Christ, devenir ses témoins, faire de nous une éternelle offrande à la gloire du Père.

Et lorsque notre pèlerinage terrestre se terminera, célébrant comme François notre Pâque dernière et définitive, nous accueillerons avec joie notre "sœur la mort corporelle", pour aller enfin rejoindre le Père, le Fils et l'Esprit, dont l'amour nous a accompagnés toute notre vie.

Chapitre III: Fraternité - Cellule d'Église

13. Dieu s'est choisi Israël pour être son Peuple avec qui il fait alliance, pour préparer et figurer l'Alliance nouvelle et parfaite qui serait conclue dans le Christ. C'est pourquoi le Christ appelle la foule des hommes pour former un tout dans l'Esprit et devenir le nouveau Peuple de Dieu.

La Fraternité séculière est une cellule de ce Peuple de Dieu: comme telle, elle tend à devenir un milieu vivant et fraternel, où dans l'Esprit se vivent l'enseignement de la Parole et la communion fraternelle, où se célèbrent la fraction du Pain et la louange, et où s'alimente la vie missionnaire.

14. Pour atteindre ce but, la fraternité comme tout groupe humain a ses moyens, ses normes, son cadre, ses responsables. C'est cette Fraternité qui nous accueille pour nous aider à vivre l'appel reçu et le projet d'amour du Père.

Elle nous propose des *étapes*: leur but est de nous aider à expérimenter son mode de vie, à connaître la Famille franciscaine, sa spiritualité, son histoire. Leur durée est fixée par les Constitutions, et elles sont précédées d'un dialogue avec les responsables.

L'étape de préparation nous achemine à l'entrée dans la Fraternité. Après l'étape de formation (noviciat), nous prenons l'engagement franciscain de vie évangélique (profession), qui renouvelle en nous et fortifie la grâce du Baptême et nous intègre à la Famille de S. François.

15. *Engagés dans la Fraternité*, nous cheminons avec nos frères dans la "Forme de vie" évangélique. Dans les réunions où elle nous convoque, nous partageons la prière, la Parole, la vie de nos frères, et nos biens dans la mesure de nos possibilités. Nous participons à sa vie, à ses initiatives, aux appels qu'elle reçoit du Seigneur, de l'Église et des hommes.

Pour progresser, nous accueillons avec humilité et reconnaissance les observations de nos frères (correction fraternelle).

En esprit de service, nous accepterons les responsabilités dans la Fraternité que nos frères nous confieraient par les élections, déterminées par les Constitutions.

16. Nous aidant mutuellement avec nos frères par ces différents moyens, nous nous aidons aussi avec nos frères du 1er Ordre: *l'Assistance spirituelle*, qui par l'Église est confiée à ses derniers, les engage à lui apporter appui et dévouement, à vérifier avec nous, au temps marqué, la qualité franciscaine de notre vie personnelle et de celle de la Fraternité (Visite Canonique).

Vivant avec eux en *réciprocité vitale*, nous aurons à cœur de prier pour eux, de nous conforter et nous enrichir mutuellement par le témoignage et le partage d'une vie authentiquement franciscaine.

16-b. Formant un *Ordre mondial*, les Fraternités locales collaborent entre elles aux divers niveaux: diocésain, provincial, national, mondial.

Ainsi, fraternellement unis dans une même famille, vivant ensemble le même message, nous nous efforcerons d'être pour nos frères les hommes des témoins de l'Évangile.

Bénédiction de S. François: "Quiconque observera ces choses, qu'il soit béni dans le ciel de la bénédiction du Père très Haut, qu'il soit rempli sur la terre de la Bénédiction de son Fils bien-aimé, avec celle du très Saint Esprit Paraclet"!

THE TEXT OF THE LOCAL COMMISSION

REGOLA DELL'ORDINE FRANCESCANO SECOLARE (TOF)

Introduzione

"Quanto beati e benedetti sono quelli che amano il Signore e fanno come lui dice nel Vangelo: 'Amerai il Signore Dio tuo con tutto il tuo cuore e con tutta la tua anima, e il prossimo tuo come te stesso'. Amiamo perciò Dio e adoriamolo con puro cuore e pura anima... lodiamolo e preghiamolo giorno e notte... confessiamo al sacerdote tutti i nostri peccati e riceviamo da lui il corpo e sangue del nostro Signore Gesú Cristo... e facciamo frutti degni di penitenza.

E su tutti coloro che avranno fatto queste cose e perseverato fino alla fine riposerà lo Spirito del Signore, ed Egli ne farà la sua dimora, e saranno figli del Padre celeste del quale compiono le opere, e sono sposi, fratelli e madri del Signore nostro Gesú Cristo". (Dalla *Lettera a Tutti i Fedeli* di san Francesco)

Tra le numerose famiglie spirituali che allietano la Chiesa di Cristo, lo Spirito Santo ha suscitato anche quella di san Francesco d'Assisi per offrire agli uomini un'ulteriore via a partecipare alla vita d'unione col Padre celeste.

Il poverello, chiamato dal Crocefisso a restaurare la sua "casa", ebbe la rivelazione, da parte di Dio, di dover vivere nella Chiesa "secondo la forma del santo Vangelo" insieme con i fratelli che il Signore stesso gli aveva dato.

Con il consiglio e la guida di Francesco, Chiara d'Assisi istituí anche lei un Ordine di sorelle, desiderose di seguire l'identica via di perfezione evangelica.

Molti altri ancora, uomini e donne, attratti dagli esempi di vita e dalla predicazione francescana, si sentirono chiamati alla vita di penitenza evangelica, ma senza lasciare le proprie case e occupazioni.

In tal modo il Padre dei cieli, a mezzo della molteplice Famiglia originata da san Francesco d'Assisi, immagine vivente di Cristo, ha voluto che si rinnovasse nella Chiesa e nel mondo la "novità di vita" portata dal Figlio suo.

Anche oggi i francescani, attenti all'invito del Crocefisso, offrono il proprio contributo di presenza e di operosità nella chiesa e in mezzo alla società, osservando il Vangelo dietro l'esempio del loro Padre serafico.

Capitolo primo: L'Ordine Francescano Secolare

La famiglia francescana nella Chiesa

1. La famiglia francescana riunisce tutti quei membri del Popolo di Dio, laici religiosi sacerdoti, che si riconoscono chiamati alla sequela di Cristo povero e crocefisso, seguendo l'esempio di san Francesco d'Assisi. In modi e forme diverse, ma in comunione vitale reciproca, essi rendono presente il carisma del Poverello nella vita e nella missione della Chiesa.

L'Ordine francescano secolare

2. In seno a questa famiglia spirituale, l'Ordine Francescano Secolare, chiamato anche Terz'Ordine Francescano o Fraternità Francescana Secolare, si configura quale "comunità di tutti i gruppi di fedeli che, mossi dallo Spirito di Dio, s'impegnano, mediante la Professione di una Regola autenticata dalla Chiesa, a vivere nel proprio stato secolare il Vangelo di nostro Signore Gesú Cristo, seguendo l'esempio e gl'insegnamenti di san Francesco d'Assisi".

Costoro tendono alla perfezione della vita cristiana raggruppati in fraternità sotto la guida dei rispettivi responsabili che li governano, in quello stato — coniugale o celibatario o sacerdotale — in cui la vocazione secolare di ciascuno li ha posti.

Capitolo secondo: La Forma di Vita

Il Vangelo come vita

3. La regola e vita dei francescani secolari è osservare il Vangelo di nostro Sigonore Gesú Cristo. Nel Vangelo e in tutta la S. Scrittura, trasmessi dalla Chiesa, essi ricerchino in primo luogo la Persona vivente di Gesú, maestro modello e forza della loro esistenza.

Attenti poi ai "segni dei tempi", sperimentino nella propria vita, individuale e di gruppo, la potenza salvifica della "buona novella" al punto da divenirne lieti e fedeli portatori tra gli uomini.

4. L'impegno evangelico esige che, quali "fratelli e sorelle della penitenza", conformino il loro modo di pensare e di agire a quello di Cristo

mediante un totale capovolgimento interiore che lo stesso Vangelo designa col nome di "conversione", la quale, per la fragilità umana, dev'essere rinnovata ogni giorno.

In questo cammino penitenziale si giovino della meditazione, della revisione di vita, dei "ritiri" ed "esercizi spirituali", ma soprattutto del frequente ricorso al Sacramento della Riconciliazione, segno privilegiato della misericordia del Padre e sorgente di nuova grazia.

Con Cristo povero e crocefisso

5. Sull'esempio di Cristo che per sé e per la madre sua scelse una vita povera ed umile, procurino di semplificare le proprie materiali esigenze a vantaggio dei bisognosi; s'adoperino, nello spirito delle "Beatitudini", a purificare il cuore da ogni cupidigia di possesso e di dominio; e, quali "pellegrini e forestieri" in cammino verso la casa del Padre, dispongano per tempo con testamento del loro beni.

6. Unendosi all'obbedienza redentrice di Gesú, che da Betlemme al Calvario depose la sua volontà in quella del Padre, accettino con animo di figli le difficoltà della vita. Con gli stessi sentimenti del "Servo sofferente" si dispongano a salutare come sorella anche la morte, confortati dalla speranza di trovare posto nella gloria della resurrezione.

7. Mentre attendono con viva fede il compimento del loro essere nella pienezza della vita futura, coltivino la cristiana castità secondo il proprio stato, come segno concreto della ricerca dell'unico sommo Bene. Pongano inoltre ogni impegno nell'acquistare la purità di cuore che, liberandoli dalle sollecitudini di questo mondo, li aiuta ad aprirsi con generosità alle ispirazioni del Signore e al richiamo dei fratelli.

Con Cristo "primogenito di molti fratelli"

8. Per imitare Gesú che si è fatto nostro fratello, siano e si dimostrino autentici fratelli di tutti. Accettino perciò con animo umile e cortese ogni uomo, accogliendolo come dono del Signore, al di là di ogni sua sua [*sic*] condizione e fede politica e religiosa, ed evitino di giudicare chiunque. Altrettanto rispetto usino verso le altre creature, animate e inanimate, che dell' "Altissimo portano significazione".

9. Nello spirito di "minorità" e di servizio che deve contraddistinguerli, siano solleciti nelle varie opere di cristiana misericordia. Studino soprattutto di porsi "alla pari" di tutti, specie dei deboli, dei sofferenti, dei colpiti da qualsivoglia forma di oppressione, e, unendosi agli uomini di buona volontà, porgano loro concreto aiuto perché vivano nella dignità di creature redente da Cristo.

Nella Chiesa "Corpo di Cristo"

10. Membri della Chiesa per il Battesimo e ad essa piú perfettamente vincolati per la Professione, si rendano testimoni e strumenti della sua missione tra gli uomini, annunciando Cristo con la vita e con la parola. Come l'umile Francesco, abbiano in autentica venerazione il Papa, i vescovi, i sacerdoti; ne accolgano con filiale fiducia gl'insegnamenti, certi di rendere loro, nell'amore obbediente e creativo, un servizio di fraterna carità.

11. In unione con tutti i veri adoratori del Padre, facciano della preghiera con la Chiesa l'anima del loro essere e del loro operare.

Nel vivere i misteri della Redenzione durante l'anno liturgico, alimentino la comunione di vita con Dio alle fonti della sua Parola e dei Sacramenti. Siano particolarmente assidui alla celebrazione dell'Eucarestia, premurosi nell'adorare il corpo e sangue di Cristo presente in mezzo a noi. Si associno con gioia al Popolo di Dio nella liturgia delle Ore o nella recita devoto [*sic*] del "Padre nostro" secondo l'antica consuetudine.

Nella loro carità innanzi a Dio abbraccino tutti gli uomini, in modo particolare i fratelli e le sorelle di vocazione tanto vivi che defunti; e siano grati al Signore per la sua presenza nel cuore degli uomini, negli evanti [*sic*] della storia e nelle meraviglie del creato.

Con Cristo uomo perfetto

12. Con ogni diligenza traducano nella pratica della propria vita la Professione di "secolari" chiamati, insieme con tutti i battezzati, a costruire dal di dentro un mondo piú fraterno ed evangelico.

Consapevoli che "chiunque segue Cristo, uomo perfetto, si fa lui pure piú uomo", esercitino con competenza le proprie responsabilità

— personali familiari professionali civiche religiose e politiche — nello spirito cristiano di "servizio".

Siano presenti, anche con iniziative coraggiose tanto individuali che comunitarie, nel campo della giustizia sociale e della vita pubblica, impegnandosi in scelte concrete ma coerenti alla loro fede.

13. Quelli che sono coniugati, aiutati dalla Fraternità, vivano le grazie sacramentali del matrimonio; ne testimonino il "ministero" soprattutto nel rapporto educativo con i figli, camminando con essi nell'itinerario della iniziazione cristiana; favoriscano il crescere delle vocazioni di speciale consacrazione.

Con Cristo nostra pace e gioia dei cuori

14. Quali "operatori di pace", portino in tutti gl'impegni un cuore disarmato; ricerchino pertanto l'unità e le fraterne intese attraverso il dialogo, dimostrando fiducia nella presenza del germe divino che è nell'uomo e, maggiormente, nella potenza tr[a]sformatrice del perdono che ci ha ottenuto Cristo, autore della pace.

La certezza che Dio ama, redime, guida l'uomo e gli eventi del mondo verso la salvezza, anche nell'apparente contraddizione delle ore oscure, li renda forti e costanti nella manifestazione e nella diffusione della perfetta letizia, primo fiore della speranza cristiana.

Capitolo terzo: La Vita in Fraternità

Articolazione e governo dell'Ordine

15. L'Ordine Francescano Secolare si articola in gruppi o Fraternità a vari livelli: locale, regionale, nazionale, internazionale. Queste fraternità, aventi ciascuna la sua personalità morale nella Chiesa, sono tra loro coordinate sullo stesso piano, ma dipendenti da quelle di grado superiore.

16. Il governo delle Fraternità ai vari livelli è esercitato dal rispettivo Ministro o Presidente, coadiuvato da alcuni fratelli e sorelle che ne costituiscono il Consiglio.

Tutti costoro vengono designati, sempre ai vari gradi, dai relativi fratelli professi, mediante elezioni. Il loro servizio, che è temporaneo, è un impegno di disponibilità e di responsabilità verso i singoli e verso i gruppi.

La fraternità locale

17. La fratenità locale è il nucleo primo di tutto l'Ordine e il segno visibile della Chiesa, comunità di amore. La sua erezione avviene nei modi previsti dalle norme ecclesiastiche; ma il suo sviluppo è affidato in modo particolare all'animazione dei responsabili con il contributo e l'esperienza dei fratelli e delle sorelle che la compongono.

18. Per agevolare la crescita spirituale dei membri nella vocazione rispondente alla condizione di vita di ciascuno dei membri, i responsabili abbiano cura di formare nell'ambito della Fraternità gruppi particolari, salvo il carattere unitario di famiglia proprio dell'Ordine.

Per incrementare poi la comunione di vita e d'intenti di tutti i fratelli e le sorelle che la compongono, questi, su invito del Ministro, si ritrovino periodicamente tutti insieme.

In questi incontri o riunioni l'ascolto della Parola, la celebrazione dell'Eucarestia e della Lode, la stessa correzione fraterna, oltre che aiuto a vivere l'esperienza evangelica, siano particolare stimolo a riflettere sugli appelli provenienti dalla Chiesa e dalla comunità umana per poter offrire ad essi, attraverso comuni iniziative armonizzate nella pastorale d'insieme, concrete risposte.

19. Per le spese occorrenti alla vita della Fraternità e per quelle necessarie alle opere di culto, di apostolato e di carità, tutti i fratelli e le sorelle offrano un contributo commisurato alle proprie possibilità. Sia poi cura della Fraternità locale farne partecipi le Fraternità di grado superiore.

Ammissione all'Ordine

20. Per essere ammessi all'Ordine Francesco Secolare, il richiedente deve professare la fede cattolica, manifestare la volontà di rispondere alla vocazione, possedere la capacità di condividere la vita della Fraterni-

tà e aver raggiunto la maggiore età. Spetta al Consiglio decidere circa l'ammissione e la professione dei nuovi fratelli.

21. L'inserimento nella Fraternità avviene in tre fasi successive:
- tempo di preparazione, la cui durata è lasciata al giudizio del Consiglio;
- tempo di formazione, della durata di almeno un anno, ma che può essere protratta a giudizio dello stesso Consiglio o dietro richiesta dell'interessato;
- emissione della Professione della Regola che, rinnovando e accrescendo la grazia del Battesimo, costituisce membri a pieno diritto di tutta la famiglia francescana.

Durante le prime due fasi, il nuovo fratello deve acquisire la formazione adeguata all'impegno di vita che lo attende. In ciò venga aiutato e sostenuto, oltre che da un maestro appositamente designato, dall'insegnamento, dall'esempio e dalla preghiera di tutta la Fraternità.

Permanenza nell'Ordine

22. La Professione della Regola è per sé impegno perpetuo. Tuttavia il Consiglio può sospendere per un dato periodo di tempo dalla vita della Fraternità, salvo il diritto di ricorso ai superiori, quei fratelli che non osservassero l'impegno assunto o che fossero insubordinati o che dessero scandalo e che, fraternamente ammoniti, non si fossero emendati.

La dimissione definitiva dall'Ordine è di competenza dei responsabili di grado superiore, e viene decisa soltanto per motivi gravi. Chi però spontaneamente richiedesse di essere dimesso dall'Ordine con ciò stesso viene sciolto da ogni impegno assunto.

Assistenza spirituale

23. In segno concreto di spirituale comunione e in ottemperanza alle norme ecclesiastiche [*sic*] i Ministri del Primo Ordine, in accordo con i responsabili delle Fraternità secolari rispettive, designeranno ai vari livelli religiosi idonei e preparati per l'assistenza spirituale alle stesse.

Compito dell'Assistente, che fa parte di diritto del Consiglio della relativa Fraternità, oltre quello di rappresentare la Gerarchia in seno ad esse, è di curare la vita religiosa e morale dei fratelli e delle sorelle nonchè dei gruppi, presenziare agl'incontri di preghiera e di studio, presiedere alle azioni liturgiche.

24. Per assicurare la crescita nella osservanza della Regola i responsabili delle Fraternità, d'accordo con il proprio Consiglio, siano solleciti nel richiedere ai Superiori la visita pastorale e quella fraterna nei modi previsti dal Diritto comune e secondo l'antica consuetudine dell'Ordine.

Capitolo quarto: Con Maria Madre di Gesú

25. Figli di san Francesco che circondò di indicibile amore la Madre di Gesú e la designò Protettrice ed Avvocata della sua spirituale famiglia, i francescani secolari si ispirino a lei come ad "eccellentissimo modello nella fede, nella carità, nella perfetta unione con Cristo". La venerino e la invochino con la recita delle sue lodi, soprattutto la imitino nella disponibilità verso il Padre e nei suoi atteggiamenti per apprendere da lei ad essere essi pure "sposi, fratelli e madri del Signore Gesú".

"Io, frate Francesco, minimo vostro servo, prego e scongiuro tutti voi, nella carità che è Dio e con il desiderio di baciarvi i piedi, che vogliate ricevere con umiltà e carità e benevolmente praticare e perfettamente adempiere queste odorifere parole del Signore nostro Gesú Cristo. E tutti, uomini e donne, che le riceveranno benevolmente e le capiranno, se persevereranno in esse sino alla fine, li benedica il Padre e il Figlio e lo Spirito Santo. Amen". (S. Francesco, dalla *Lettera a tutti i fedeli*)

THE TEXT OF THE ASSISTANTS GENERAL

REGOLA DELLA FRATERNITÀ SECOLARE DI SAN FRANCESCO

Testo Assistenti Generali

Cap. I: Fraternità Francescana Secolare (T.O.F.)

1. Tra le famiglie spirituali, suscitate dallo Spirito Santo nella Chiesa, quella Francescana raggruppa laici, religiosi, sacerdoti chiamati alla sequela di Cristo sulle orme di s. Francesco di Assisi. In modi e forme diverse, ma in comunione vitale reciproca, essi rendono presente il carisma del Poverello nella vita e nella missione della Chiesa.

2. In seno a questa famiglia spirituale, ha una sua specifica collocazione la Fraternità Francescana Secolare (O.F.S., T.O.F.); si configura come comunità delle fraternità sparse nel mondo e aperte ad ogni ceto di fedeli, i quali, spinti dallo Spirito a raggiungere la perfezione della carità nel proprio stato secolare, s'impegnano a vivere il Vangelo alla maniera di s. Francesco e mediante una Regola autenticata dalla Chiesa.

3. La domanda, per entrare in tale fraternità locale, viene fatta al Consiglio rispettivo, al quale spetta la responsabilità della fraternità. Ci si inserisce mediante un tempo di iniziazione, un tempo di formazione e la Professione della Regola; a tale sequenza di sviluppi è impegnata tutta la fraternità anche nel suo modo di vivere. Questa professione di vita è di per sé un impegno perpetuo. I membri, che si trovino in particolare difficoltà, ne tratteranno in dialogo fraterno con il Consiglio.

Cap. II: "Forma di Vita"

4. Cristo, dono dell'amore del Padre, è la nostra via a Lui, è la verità nella quale lo Spirito Santo ci introduce, è la vita che Egli è venuto a darci in sovrabbondanza. Per cui, Francesco d'Assisi fece del Cristo l'ispiratore e centro della sua vita con Dio e con gli uomini.

5. Ricerchiamo, quindi, nel Vangelo la persona vivente di Gesú Cristo, conformandosi a Lui modello e forza della nostra esistenza; e diventiamone lieti e fedeli portatori tra gli uomini. Ci impegniamo ad una assidua lettura del Vangelo, passando dal Vangelo alla vita e dalla vita al Vangelo, in piena sintonia con il nostro carisma francescano.

6. I fratelli e le sorelle della Penitenza, in virtú proprio di questa loro vocazione, sospinti dalla dinamica del Vangelo ad una perenne e radicale conversione, o metanoia, partecipano alla vita nuova in Cristo. Di questa conversione il Sacramento della Riconciliazione è mezzo privilegiato e realtà.

7. Come veri discepoli di Cristo, Figlio di Dio e vero uomo, saremo pronti a confessarlo davanti agli uomini, in obbedienza alla volontà del Padre con l'adempimento dei nostri impegni e in ogni circostanza, ed anche a seguirLo, povero, e crocifisso, per la via della Croce tra le difficoltà e le persecuzioni.

8. Sull'esempio di s. Francesco, amatore della povertà, ci distaccheremo da ogni forma di egoismo e di cupidigia: liberi cosí e consci del senso evangelico dei beni, saremo pronti, secondo il dono ricevuto, a mettere noi ed essi a servizio degli altri, specialmente dei piú poveri e diseredati.

Testimoni dei beni futuri, ci impegneremo all'acquisto della purità di cuore, la quale ci farà liberi tra le sollecitudini di questo mondo e disponibili all'amore di Dio e dei fratelli.

9. Come il Padre vede in ogni uomo i lineamenti del suo Figlio, primogenito di una moltitudine di fratelli, anche noi di sforzeremo di vedere Cristo negli altri, che cosí ci diventeranno autentici fratelli, al di là di ogni barriera. Questo senso di fraternità ci renderà lieti di trovarci tra i piú piccoli a loro difesa e ci spingerà a promuovere la giustizia ed a lavorare con gli altri per eliminare ogni ostacolo alla fraternità universale.

10. La Vergine Maria, solidale col suo popolo nell'attesa del Messia, umile serva del Signore, disponibile alla sua parola e a tutti i suoi appelli, fu circondata da Francesco di indicibile amore e la designò Protettrice e Avvocata della sua famiglia. I fratelli e le sorelle testimonieranno a

Lei il loro ardente amore, con l'imitazione della sua incondizionata disponibilità e nell'effusione di una fiduciosa e cosciente preghiera.

11. Per il Battesimo, siamo membri della Chiesa voluta da Cristo come istrumento di salvezza, e con essa piú strettamente impegnati per la Professione. Intendiamo farci testimoni e partecipi della sua missione.

Ispirati da s. Francesco, in piena comunione con il Papa, i vescovi, e i sacerdoti, ci sentiamo ad essi uniti in un fiducioso e aperto dialogo di creatività apostolica.

12. Come Gesú fu il vero adoratore del Padre, cosí noi faremo della preghiera la sostanza della nostra vita.

Sull'esempio della Chiesa primitiva e per divenire sempre piú un cuor solo e un'anima sola, parteciperemo alla preghiera, alla frazione del pane o Eucaristia, e all'ascolto della parola, rivivendo cosí i misteri della vita di Cristo.

Parteciperemo alla Preghiera liturgica della Chiesa con una delle forme approvate.

13. Per vocazione propria di secolari, coinvolti nella società temporale, assumeremo la nostra parte delle responsabilità a qualunque livello e secondo i doni di Dio. Consapevoli che, nel vivere le Beatitudini, si è fermento, ci impegneremo con gli uomini di buona volontà a costruire dal di dentro un mondo piú fraterno ed evangelico per la realizzazione del Regno di Dio, attenti sempre ai "segni dei tempi".

Quali operatori di pace e memori che essa va costruita, ricercheremo nel dialogo e nell'azione le vie ad una fraterna intesa e all'unione con gli uomini.

14. Innanzitutto nella nostra famiglia vivremo lo spirito francescano, sforzandoci di farne il segno di un mondo già rinnovato in Cristo. I coniugi vivranno le grazie sacramentali del matrimonio e saranno i primi testimoni della fede cristiana per i loro figli.

Riputeremo il lavoro come dono e come partecipazione alla creazione, redenzione e servizio della comunità umana.

15. Messaggeri di perfetta letizia, in ogni circostanza, ci sforzeremo di portare agli altri la gioia e la speranza, frutti della pace del Risorto, che dà il vero significato a sorella morte, come al punto d'incontro con il Padre.

Cap. III: Organizzazione della Fraternità Secolare

16. La Fraternità Francescana Secolare si articola in gruppi o fraternità a vari livelli: locale, regionale, nazionale, internazionale.

Queste fraternità, aventi ciascuna la sua personalità morale nella Chiesa, sono tra loro coordinate.

Ogni fraternità a diversi livelli è animata e guidata dal rispettivo Consiglio e Ministro, che vengono eletti in base alle norme vigenti.

Le fraternità al loro interno si strutturano diversamente secondo i vari bisogni dei loro membri e delle regioni, sotto la guida del Consiglio.

17. La fraternità locale è il nucleo primo di tutto l'Ordine.

Essa è l'ambiente privilegiato per sviluppare il senso ecclesiale, la vocazione francescana e per animare la vita apostolica dei suoi membri.

I cosiddetti fratelli e sorelle isolati, che, per alterne circostanze, non possono partecipare alla vita della loro fraternità, cerchino di tenersi collegati con una fraternità, per riceverne aiuti e impulsi.

18. Per agevolare la comunione tra i membri, il Consiglio provveda frequenti adunanze, adottando i mezzi piú appropriati, per una crescità con l'apporto anche dei singoli, nella vita francescana e ecclesiale, stimolando ognuno a partecipare alla vita di fraternità, a condividere i beni spirituali e materiali come fratelli.

19. I Consigli rispettivi ai diversi livelli chiedano l'assistenza ordinaria e, a suo tempo, la visita pastorale, al Primo Ordine ed al T.O.R., ai quali dalla Chiesa è affidata la cura delle fraternità, e che provvederanno queste di capaci Assistenti spirituali.

20. Quanto non è previsto qui, avrà il suo posto adatto nelle Costituzioni generali.

Benedizione di S. Francesco: "E chiunque osserverà queste cose, sia colmato in cielo della benedizione dell'altissimo Padre e in terra sia colmato della benedizione del Figlio suo diletto con il santissimo Spirito Paraclito".

THE APRIL 1977 REDACTION

REGOLA DELL'ORDINE FRANCESCANO SECOLARE

Cap. I: Ordine Francescano Secolare (T.O.F.)

1. Tra le famiglie spirituali, suscitate dallo Spirito Santo nella Chiesa, quella Francescana riunisce tutti quei membri del Popolo di Dio, laici, religiosi, e sacerdoti, che si riconoscono chiamati alla sequela di Cristo, sulle orme di S. Francesco di Assisi. In modi e forme diverse, ma in comunione vitale reciproca, essi rendono presente il carisma del Poverello nella vita e nella missione della Chiesa.

2. In seno a questa famiglia, ha una sua specifica collocazione la Fraternità Francescana Secolare (O.F.S., T.O.F.); si configura come comunità delle fraternità sparse nel mondo e aperte ad ogni ceto di fedeli, i quali, spinti dallo Spirito a raggiungere la perfezione della carità nel proprio stato secolare, si impegnano a vivere il Vangelo alla maniera di s. Francesco e mediante una Regola autenticata dalla Chiesa, raggruppati in fraternità sotto la guida dei rispettivi respons[a]bili.

Cap. II: "La Forma di Vita"

3. La regola e vita dei francescani secolari è osservare il Vangelo di Nostro Signore Gesú Cristo.

Cristo, dono dell'amore del Padre, è la nostra via a Lui, è la verità nella quale lo Spirito Santo ci introduce, è la vita che Egli è venuto a darci in sovrabbondanza. Per cui, Francesco d'Assisi fece del Cristo l'ispiratore e centro della sua vita con Dio e con gli uomini.

4. Ricerchiamo, quindi, nel Vangelo la persona vivente di Gesú Cristo, conformandoci a Lui, modello e forza della nostra esistenza; e diventiamone lieti e fedeli portatori tra gli uomini.

5. Quali "fratelli e sorelle della penitenza", in virtú della loro vocazione, sospinti dalla dinamica del Vangelo, conformino il loro modo di pensare e di agire a quello di Cristo mediante un radicale capovolgimento

interiore che lo stesso Vangelo designa con il nome di "conversione", la quale, per la umana fragilità, deve essere rinnovata ogni giorno.

In questo cammino di conversione il Sacramento della Riconciliazione è segno privilegiato della misericordia del Padre, e sorgente di nuova grazia.

6. Sull'esempio di Cristo, fiducioso nel Padre, che per Sé o per la Madre sua scelse una vita povera ed umile, procurino di semplificare le proprie materiali esigenze a vantaggio dei bisognosi, consci del senso evangelico dei beni; s'adoperino, nello spirito delle "Beatitudini", a purificare il cuore da ogni cupidigia di possesso e di dominio, quali "pellegrini e forestieri" in cammino verso la casa del Padre.

7. Unendosi all'obbedienza redentrice di Gesú, che depose la sua volontà in quella del Padre, adempiano fedelmente agli impegni propri della condizione di ciascuno nelle diverse circostanze della vita, e seguano Cristo, povero e crocifisso, testimoniandolo anche fra le difficoltà e le persecuzioni.

8. Testimoni dei beni futuri, ci impegneremo all'acquisto della purità di cuore, la quale ci farà liberi tra le sollecitudini di questo mondo e disponibili all'amore di Dio e dei fratelli.

9. Come il Padre vede in ogni uomo i lineamenti del suo figlio, primogenito di una moltitudine di fratelli, anche noi ci sforzeremo di vedere Cristo negli altri che cosí ci diventeranno autentici fratelli; perciò accoglieremo tutti gli uomini con animo umile e cortese come dono del Signore.

Altrettanto rispetto usino verso le altre creature, animate e inanimate, che "dell'Altissimo portano significazione".

Il senso di fraternità ci renderà lieti di metterci alla pari di tutti gli uomini, specialmente dei piú piccoli, aiutandoli perchè vivano nella dignità di creature redente da Cristo, e ci spingerà a promuovere la giustizia e la pace e a lavorare con gli altri per eliminare ogni ostacolo alla fraternità universale.

10. Membri della Chiesa per il Battesimo e ad essa piú fortemente vincolati per la Professione si rendano testimoni e strumenti dalla sua missione tra gli uomini, annunciando Cristo con la vita e con la parola.

Ispirati da s. Francesco e con lui chiamati a ricostruire la Chiesa, vogliamo vivere in piena comunione con il Papa, i Vescovi e i Sacerdoti in un fiducioso e aperto dialogo di creatività apostolica.

11. Come Gesú fu il vero adoratore del Padre, cosí noi faremo della preghiera e della contemplazione l'anima del nostro essere e del nostro operare.

Parteciperemo alla vita sacramentale della Chiesa, soprattutto alla Eucarestia, e ci associeremo alla preghiera liturgica in una delle forme da essa proposta, rivivendo cosí i misteri della vita del Cristo.

12. La Vergine Maria, umile serva del Signore, disponibile alla sua parola e a tutti i suoi appelli, fu circondata da Francesco di indicibile amore e fu designata Protettrice e Avvocata della sua famiglia. I fratelli e le sorelle testimonieranno a Lei il loro ardente amore, con l'imitazione della sua incondizionata disponibilità e nella effusione di una fiduciosa e cosciente preghiera.

13. Chiamati, insieme con tutti gli uomini di buona volontà, a costruire dal di dentro un mondo piú fraterno ed evangelico per la realizzazione del Regno di Dio; consapevoli che "chiunque segue Cristo, Uomo Perfetto, si fa lui pure piú uomo", i francescani secolari esercitino con competenza le proprie responsabilità nello spirito cristiano di servizio.

Siano presenti, anche con iniziative coraggiose tanto individuali che comunitarie, nel campo della giustizia sociale e della vita pubblica, impegnandosi in scelte concrete e coerenti alla loro fede. Reputeremo il lavoro come dono e come partecipazione alla creazione, redenzione e servizio della comunità umana.

14. Nella nostra famiglia vivremo lo spirito francescano, sforzandoci di farne il segno di un mondo già rinnovato in Cristo.

I coniugati poi, aiutati dalla Fraternità, vivendo le grazie del matrimonio, testimonieranno nel mondo l'amore di Cristo per la sua Chiesa. Con una educazione semplice ed aperta cammineranno con i loro figli nel loro itinerario spirituale, attenti alla vocazione di ciascuno.

15. Quali portatori di pace e memori che essa va costruita continuamente, ricerchino le vie dell'unità e delle fraterne intese, attraverso il dialogo, fiduciosi nella presenza del germe divino che è nell'uomo e nella potenza trasformatrice del perdono.

Messaggeri di perfetta letizia, in ogni circostanza, ci sforzeremo di portare agli altri la gioia e la speranza, frutti della Resurrezione di Cristo, che dà il vero significato a Sorella Morte, come al punto di incontro con il Padre.

Cap. III: "La Vita in Fraternità"

16. L'Ordine Francescano Secolare si articola in gruppi o Fraternità a vari livelli: locale, regionale, nazionale, internazionale.

Queste fraternità, aventi ciascuna la sua personalità morale nella Chiesa, sono coordinate tra loro e collegate con quelle di livello superiore.

17. Ogni fraternità a diversi livelli è animata e guidata dal rispettivo Consiglio e Ministro (o Presidente), che vengono eletti in base ad apposite norme approvate.

Il loro servizio, che è temporaneo, è un impegno di disponib[il]ità e di responsabilità verso i singoli e verso i gruppi.

Le Fraternità al loro interno si strutturano diversamente secondo i vari bisogni dei loro membri e delle loro regioni, sotto la guida del Consiglio rispettivo.

18. La fraternità locale, canonicamente eretta, è la cellula prima di tutto l'Ordine e un segno visibile della Chiesa, comunità di amore. Essa è l'ambiente privilegiato per sviluppare il senso ecclesiale e la vocazione francescana e per animare la vita apostolica dei suoi membri.

19. La domanda di ammissione alla fraternità locale viene fatta al Consiglio rispettivo, al quale spetta la responsabilità della fraternità.

Ciò si inserisce mediante un tempo di iniziazione, un tempo di formazione di almeno un anno e la Professione della Regola; a tale sequenza di sviluppi è impegnata tutta la fraternità anche nel suo modo di vivere. L'età per l'ammissione è la maggiore età.

Questa professione di vita è di per sè un impegno perpetuo. I membri che si trovino in particolare difficoltà, ne tratteranno in fraterno dialogo con il Consiglio. Se occorre poi addivenire ad una definitiva dimissione dall'Ordine, tale atto è di competenza dei responsabili di grado superiore.

20. Per incrementare la comunione tra i membri, il Consiglio organizza adunanze periodiche ed incontri frequenti, adottando i mezzi piú appropriati per una crescita, con l'apporto anche dei singoli, nella vita francescana ed ecclesiale, stimolando ognuno alla vita di fraternità.

Tale comunione continua anche con i confratelli defunti suffragando le loro anime.

21. Per le spese occorrenti alla vita della Fraternità e per quelle necessarie alle opere di culto, di apostolato e di carità, tutti i fratelli e le sorelle offrano un contributo commisurato alle proprie possibilità.

Sia poi cura delle fraternità locali farne partecipi le fraternità di grado superiori.

22. In segno concreto di comunione e di responsabilità, i Consigli ai diversi livelli chiedano la assistenza spirituale al primo Ordine e al TOR.

Per assicurare la crescita nella osservanza della regola e per favorire la vita di fraternità, il Ministro o il Presidente, d'accordo con il suo Consiglio, sia sollecito nel chiedere periodicamente ai competenti Superiori religiosi la visita pastorale e ai responsabili laici la visita fraterna.

Benedizione di San Francesco: "E chiunque osserverà queste cose, sia colmato in cielo della benedizione dell'Altissimo Padre e in terra sia colmato della benedizione del Figlio suo diletto con il santissimo Spirito Paraclito".

THE FINAL REDACTION SENT TO THE MINISTERS GENERAL

REGOLA DELL'ORDINE FRANCESCANO SECOLARE

Cap. I: Ordine Francescano Secolare (O.F.S.)

1. Tra le famiglie spirituali, suscitate dallo Spirito Santo nella Chiesa, quella Francescana riunisce tutti quei membri del Popolo di Dio, laici, religiosi, e sacerdoti, che si riconoscono chiamati alla sequela di Cristo, sulle orme di s. Francesco di Assisi. In modi e forme diverse, ma in comunione vitale reciproca, essi rendono presente il carisma del Poverello nella vita e nella missione della Chiesa.

2. In seno a detta famiglia, ha una sua specifica collocazione la Fraternità Francescana Secolare. Questa si configura come comunità di gruppi o fraternità sparse nel mondo e aperte ad ogni ceto di fedeli, i quali, spinti dallo Spirito a raggiungere la perfezione della carità nel proprio stato secolare, si impegnano a vivere il Vangelo alla maniera di s. Francesco e mediante una regola autenticata dalla Chiesa.

Cap. II: "La Forma di Vita"

3. La regola e vita dei francescani secolari è osservare il Vangelo di Nostro Signore Gesú Cristo. Cristo, dono dell'amore del Padre, è la nostra via a Lui, è la verità nella quale lo Spirito Santo ci introduce, è la vita che Egli è venuto a darci in sovrabbondanza. Francesco d'Assisi fece del Cristo l'ispiratore e centro della sua vita con Dio e con gli uomini.

4. I francescani secolari, quindi, ricerchino nel Vangelo la persona vivente di Gesú Cristo, conformandosi a Lui, modello e forza della nostra esistenza, e diventandone lieti e fedeli portatori tra gli uomini. Essi si impegnino ad una assidua lettura del Vangelo, passando dal Vangelo alla vita e dalla vita al Vangelo.

5. Quali "fratelli e sorelle della penitenza", in virtú della loro vocazione, sospinti dalla dinamica del Vangelo, conformino il loro modo di

pensare e di agire a quello di Cristo mediante un radicale mutamento interiore che lo stesso Vangelo designa con il nome di "conversione", la quale, per la umana fragilità, deve essere attuata ogni giorno. In questo cammino di rinnovamento il Sacramento della Riconciliazione è segno privilegiato della misericordia del Padre, e sorgente di grazia.

6. Unendosi all'obbedienza redentrice di Gesú, che depose la sua volontà in quella del Padre, adempiano fedelmente agli impegni propri della condizione di ciascuno nelle diverse circostanze della vita, e seguano Cristo, povero e crocifisso, testimoniandolo anche fra le difficoltà e le persecuzioni.

7. Sull'esempio di Cristo, fiducioso nel Padre, che per Sé o per la Madre Sua scelse una vita povera ed umile, cerchino di distaccarsi dai beni terreni, semplificando le proprie materiali esigenze; siano consapevoli, poi, del senso evangelico dei beni e dell'invito a disporre di essi a vantaggio dei bisognosi, secondo le loro possibilità. Cosí, nello spirito delle "Beatitudini" s'adoperino a purificare il cuore da ogni cupidigia di possesso e di dominio, quali "pellegrini e forestieri" in cammino verso la Casa del Padre.

8. Testimoni dei beni futuri, e impegnati all'acquisto della purità di cuore, si renderanno liberi e saranno cosí disponibili all'amore di Dio e dei fratelli.

9. Come il Padre vede in ogni uomo i lineamenti del Suo Figlio, Primogenito di una moltitudine di fratelli, i francescani secolari si sforzino di vedere Cristo negli altri, i quali per loro diventeranno autentici fratelli. In tale modo tutti gli uomini saranno accolti con animo umile e cortese come dono del Signore.

Essi inoltre abbiano rispetto verso le altre creature, animate e inanimate, che "dell'Altissimo portano significazione". Il senso di fraternità li renderà lieti di mettersi alla pari di tutti gli uomini, specialmente dei piú piccoli, per i quali si sforzeranno di creare condizioni di vita degne di creature redente da Cristo.

Cosí si sentiranno sollecitati ad impegnarsi nel servizio della promozione umana e a lavorare con tutti gli uomini di buona volontà per realizzare la pace e per eliminare ogni ostacolo alla fraternità universale.

10. Sepolti e risuscitati con Cristo nel Battesimo che li rende membri vivi della Chiesa, e ad essa piú fortemente vincolati per la Professione, si facciano testimoni e strumenti della sua missione tra gli uomini, annunciando Cristo con la vita e con la parola.

Ispirati da S. Francesco e con lui chiamati a ricostruire la Chiesa, si impegnino a vivere in piena comunione con il Papa, i Vescovi e i Sacerdoti in un fiducioso e aperto dialogo di creatività apostolica.

11. Come Gesú fu il vero adoratore del Padre, cosi facciano della preghiera e della contemplazione l'anima del proprio essere e del proprio operare. Partecipino alla vita sacramentale della Chiesa curando di avere per la Eucarestia una devozione del tutto speciale, e si associno alla preghiera liturgica in una delle forme dalla Chiesa stessa proposta, rivivendo cosí i misteri della vita di Cristo.

12. La Vergine Maria, umile serva del Signore, disponibile alla sua parola e a tutti i suoi appelli, fu circondata da Francesco di indicibile amore e fu designata Protettrice e Avvocata della sua famiglia. I francescani secolari testimonino a Lei il loro ardente amore, con l'imitazione della sua incondizionata disponibilità e nella effusione di una fiduciosa e cosciente preghiera.

13. Chiamati, insieme con tutti gli uomini di buona volontà, a costruire dal di dentro un mondo piú fraterno ed evangelico per la realizzazione del Regno di Dio, consapevoli che "chiunque segue Cristo, Uomo Perfetto, si fa lui pure piú uomo", esercitino con competenza le proprie responsabilità nello spirito cristiano di servizio.

Siano presenti con la testimonianza della propria vita umana ed anche con iniziative coraggiose tanto individuali che comunitarie, nella promozione della giustizia, ed in particolare nel campo della vita pubblica, impegnandosi in scelte concrete e coerenti alla loro fede. Reputino il lavoro come dono e come partecipazione alla creazione, redenzione e servizio della comunità umana.

14. Nella loro famiglia vivano lo spirito francescano, sforzandosi di farne il segno di un mondo già rinnovato in Cristo. I coniugati in particolare, vivendo le grazie del matrimonio, testimonino nel mondo l'amore di Cristo per la sua Chiesa. Con una educazione semplice ed aperta camminino con i propri figli nel loro itinerario spirituale, attenti alla vocazione di ciascuno.

15. Quali portatori di pace e memori che essa va costruita continuamente, ricerchino le vie dell'unità e delle fraterne intese, attraverso il dialogo, fiduciosi nella presenza del germe divino che è nell'uomo e nella potenza trasformatrice dell'amore e del perdono. Messaggeri di perfetta letizia, in ogni circostanza, si sforzino di portare agli altri la gioia e la speranza, frutti della Resurrezione di Cristo, che dà il vero significato a Sorella Morte, come al punto di incontro con il Padre.

Cap. III: "La Vita in Fraternità"

16. L'Ordine Francescano Secolare si articola in gruppi o Fraternità a vari livelli: locale, regionale, nazionale, internazionale. Queste fraternità, coordinate tra loro in ciascun livello, sono collegate con quelle di livello superiore. Esse hanno singolarmente la propria personalità morale nella Chiesa.

17. Nei diversi livelli, ogni fraternità è animata e guidata da un Consiglio e Ministro (o Presidente), che vengono eletti in base ad apposite norme approvate. Il loro servizio, che è temporaneo, è un impegno di disponibilità e di responsabilità verso i singoli e verso i gruppi. Le fraternità al loro interno si strutturano diversamente secondo i vari bisogni dei loro membri e delle loro regioni, sotto la guida del Consiglio rispettivo.

18. La fraternità locale, canonicamente eretta, è la cellula prima di tutto l'Ordine e un segno visibile della Chiesa, comunità di amore. Essa è l'ambiente privilegiato per sviluppare il senso ecclesiale e la vocazione francescana, nonché per animare la vita apostolica dei suoi membri.

19. Le domande di ammissione all'Ordine Francescano Secolare vengono presentate ad una fraternità locale, il cui Consiglio decide l'accettazione dei nuovi fratelli. L'inserimento si realizza mediante un tempo di iniziazione, un tempo di formazione di almeno un anno e la professione della Regola. A tale sequenza di sviluppi è impegnata tutta la fraternità anche nel suo modo di vivere. Possono professare i fedeli che hanno la maggiore età.

Questa professione di vita è di per sé un impegno perpetuo. I membri che si trovino in particolari difficoltà, cureranno di trattare i loro problemi con il Consiglio in fraterno dialogo. La definitiva dimissione dall'Ordine, se proprio necessario, è atto di competenza dei responsabili di grado superiore.

20. Per incrementare la comunione tra i membri, il Consiglio organizza adunanze periodiche ed incontri frequenti, adottando i mezzi piú appropriati per una crescita, con l'apporto anche dei singoli, nella vita francescana ed ecclesiale, stimolando ognuno alla vita di fraternità. Una tale comunione prosegue con i fratelli defunti con l'offerta di suffragi alle loro anime.

21. Per le spese occorrenti alla vita della Fraternità e per quelle necessarie alle opere di culto, di apostolato e di carità, tutti i fratelli e le sorelle offrano un contributo commisurato alle proprie possibilità. Sia poi cura delle fraternità locali di contribuire alle spese dei Consigli delle fraternità di grado superiore.

22. In segno concreto di comunione e di corresponsabilità, i Consigli ai diversi livelli chiedano la assistenza spirituale ai Superiori delle quattro famiglie religiose francescane, alle quali è stata affidata dalla Santa Sede la cura spirituale della Fraternità Secolare.

Per favorire la fedeltà al carisma e la osservanza alla regola e per avere maggiori aiuti nella vita di fraternità, il Ministro o il Presidente, d'accordo con il suo Consiglio, sia sollecito nel chiedere periodicamente la visita pastorale ai competenti Superiori religiosi e la visita fraterna ai responsabili laici di livello superiore.

"E chiunque osserverà queste cose, sia colmato in cielo della benedizione dell'Altissimo Padre e in terra sia colmato della benedizione del Figlio suo diletto con il santissimo Spirito Paraclito" (*Benedizione di San Francesco*).

THE TEXT SENT TO THE CURIA BY THE MINISTERS GENERAL

REGOLA DELL'ORDINE FRANCESCANO SECOLARE

Prologo: Esortazione di S. Francesco ai Fratelli ed alle Sorelle della Penitenza[1].

Cap. I: Ordine Francescano Secolare (O.F.S.)

1. Tra le famiglie spirituali, suscitate dallo Spirito Santo nella Chiesa, quella Francescana riunisce tutti quei membri del Popolo di Dio, laici, religiosi, e sacerdoti, che si riconoscono chiamati alla sequela di Cristo, sulle orme di s. Francesco di Assisi. In modi e forme diverse, ma in comunione vitale reciproca, essi intendono rendere presente il carisma del Poverello nella vita e nella missione della Chiesa.

2. In seno a detta famiglia, ha una sua specifica collocazione l'Ordine Francescano Secolare. Questo si configura come comunità di fraternità cattoliche sparse nel mondo e aperte ad ogni ceto di fedeli, i quali, spinti dallo Spirito a raggiungere la perfezione della carità nel proprio stato secolare, con la Professione si impegnano a vivere il Vangelo alla maniera di s. Francesco e mediante una regola autenticata dalla Chiesa.

3. L'applicazione ed interpretazione della presente Regola sarà fatta dalle Costituzioni Generali e da Statuti particolari.

Cap. II: "La Forma di Vita"

4. La regola e vita dei francescani secolari è osservare il Vangelo di Nostro Signore Gesú Cristo. Cristo, dono dell'amore del Padre, è la nostra via a Lui, è la verità nella quale lo Spirito Santo ci introduce, è la vita che Egli è venuto a dare in sovrabbondanza. Francesco d'Assisi fece del Cristo l'ispiratore e centro della sua vita con Dio e con gli uomini.

---

[1] The entire text of Francis' *Earlier Exhortation* in Italian is included here as a "Prologue" to the Rule. The text has not been included here since it is the Italian translation of the Latin text for which the English is given above pp. 31-33, and in *Chapter III*, pp. 144-161.

5. I francescani secolari, quindi, ricerchino la persona vivente di Gesú Cristo nell'Eucaristia, conformandosi a Lui, modello e forza della nostra esistenza, e diventandone lieti e fedeli portatori tra gli uomini. Essi si impegnino ad una assidua lettura del Vangelo, passando dal Vangelo alla vita e dalla vita al Vangelo.

6. Sepolti e risuscitati con Cristo nel Battesimo che li rende membri vivi della Chiesa, e ad essa piú fortemente vincolati per la Professione, si facciano testimoni e strumenti della sua missione tra gli uomini, annunciando Cristo con la vita e con la parola.

Ispirati da s. Francesco e con lui chiamati a ricostruire la Chiesa, si impegnino a vivere in piena comunione con il Papa, i Vescovi e i Sacerdoti in un fiducioso e aperto dialogo di creatività apostolica.

7. Quali "fratelli e sorelle della penitenza", in virtú della loro vocazione, sospinti dalla dinamica del Vangelo, conformino il loro modo di pensare e di agire a quello di Cristo mediante un radicale mutamento interiore che lo stesso Vangelo designa con il nome di "conversione", la quale, per la umana fragilità, deve essere attuata ogni giorno. In questo cammino di rinnovamento il Sacramento della Riconciliazione è segno privilegiato della misericordia del Padre, e sorgente di grazia.

8. Come Gesú fu il vero adoratore del Padre, cosí facciano della preghiera e della contemplazione l'anima del proprio essere e del proprio operare. Partecipino alla vita sacramentale della Chiesa, soprattutto all'Eucaristia, e si associno alla preghiera liturgica in una delle forme dalla Chiesa stessa proposta, rivivendo cosí i misteri della vita di Cristo.

9. La Vergine Maria, umile serva del Signore, disponibile alla sua parola e a tutti i suoi appelli, fu circondata da Francesco di indicibile amore e fu designata Protettrice e Avvocata della sua famiglia. I francescani secolari testimonino a Lei il loro ardente amore, con l'imitazione della sua incondizionata disponibilità e nella effusione di una fiduciosa e cosciente preghiera.

10. Unendosi all'obbedienza redentrice di Gesú, che depose la sua volontà in quella del Padre, adempiano fedelmente agli impegni propri della condizione di ciascuno nelle diverse circostanze della vita, e seguano Cristo, povero e crocifisso, testimoniandolo anche fra le difficoltà e le persecuzioni.

11. Sull'esempio di Cristo, fiducioso nel Padre, che per Sé o per la Madre Sua scelse una vita povera ed umile, cerchino di distaccarsi dai beni terreni, semplificando le proprie materiali esigenze; siano consapevoli, poi, di essere secondo il Vangelo, amministratori dei beni di Dio a favore dei figli di Dio. Cosí, nello spirito delle "Beatitudini" s'adoperino a purificare il cuore da ogni tendenza e cupidigia di possesso e di dominio, quali "pellegrini e forestieri" in cammino verso la Casa del Padre.

12. Testimoni dei beni futuri, e impegnati nella vocazione abbracciata all'acquisto della purità di cuore, si renderanno cosí liberi all'amore di Dio e dei fratelli.

13. Come il Padre vede in ogni uomo i lineamenti del Suo Figlio, Primogenito di una moltitudine di fratelli, i francescani secolari si sforzino di vedere Cristo negli altri, i quali per loro diventeranno autentici fratelli. In tale modo tutti gli uomini saranno accolti con animo umile e cortese come dono del Signore.

Il senso di fraternità li renderà lieti di mettersi alla pari di tutti gli uomini, specialmente dei piú piccoli, per i quali si sforzeranno di creare condizioni di vita degne di creature redente da Cristo.

14. Chiamati, insieme con tutti gli uomini di buona volontà, a costruire dal di dentro un mondo piú fraterno ed evangelico per la realizzazione del Regno di Dio, consapevoli che "chiunque segue Cristo, Uomo Perfetto, si fa lui pure piú uomo", esercitino con competenza le proprie responsabilità nello spirito cristiano di servizio.

15. Siano presenti con la testimonianza della propria vita umana ed anche con iniziative coraggiose tanto individuali che comunitarie, nella promozione della giustizia, ed in particolare nel campo della vita pubblica, impegnandosi in scelte concrete e coerenti alla loro fede.

16. Reputino il lavoro come dono e come partecipazione alla creazione, redenzione e servizio della comunità umana.

17. Nella loro famiglia vivano lo spirito francescano di pace, fedeltà e rispetto della vita, sforzandosi di farne il segno di un mondo già rinnovato in Cristo. I coniugati in particolare, vivendo le grazie del matrimonio, testimonino nel mondo l'amore di Cristo per la sua Chiesa.

Con una educazione cristiana semplice ed aperta, attenti alla vocazione di ciascuno, camminino gioiosamente con i propri figli nel loro itinerario umano e spirituale.

18. Abbiano, inoltre, rispetto verso le altre creature, animate e inanimate, che "dell'Altissimo portano significazione", e si sforzino di passare dalla tentazione di sfruttamento al francescano concetto di fratellanza universale.

19. Quali portatori di pace e memori che essa va costruita continuamente, ricerchino le vie dell'unità e delle fraterne intese, attraverso il dialogo, fiduciosi nella presenza del germe divino che è nell'uomo e nella potenza trasformatrice dell'amore e del perdono. Messaggeri di perfetta letizia, in ogni circostanza, si sforzino di portare agli altri la gioia e la speranza.

Innestati alla Resurrezione di Cristo, la quale dà il vero significato a Sorella Morte, tendano con serenità all'incontro definitivo con il Padre.

Cap. III: "La Vita in Fraternità"

20. L'Ordine Francescano Secolare si articola in gruppi o Fraternità a vari livelli: locale, regionale, nazionale, internazionale. Esse hanno singolarmente la propria personalità morale nella Chiesa. Queste fraternità di vario livello sono tra di loro coordinate e collegate a norma di questa Regola e delle Costituzioni.

21. Nei diversi livelli, ogni fraternità è animata e guidata da un Consiglio e Ministro (o Presidente), che vengono eletti dai Professi in base alle Costituzioni.

Il loro servizio, che è temporaneo, è un impegno di disponibilità e di responsabilità verso i singoli e verso i gruppi. Le fraternità al loro interno si strutturano, a norma delle Costituzioni, diversamente secondo i vari bisogni dei loro membri e delle loro regioni, sotto la guida del Consiglio rispettivo.

22. La fraternità locale ha bisogno di essere canonicamente eretta, e cosí diventa la cellula prima di tutto l'Ordine e un segno visibile della Chiesa, comunità di amore. Essa è l'ambiente privilegiato per sviluppare il senso ecclesiale e la vocazione francescana, nonché per animare la vita apostolica dei suoi membri.

23. Le domande di ammissione all'Ordine Francescano Secolare vengono presentate ad una fraternità locale, il cui Consiglio decide l'accettazione dei nuovi fratelli.

L'inserimento si realizza mediante un tempo di iniziazione, un tempo di formazione di almeno un anno e la professione della Regola. A tale sequenza di sviluppi è impegnata tutta la fraternità anche nel suo modo di vivere. Riguardo all'età per la Professione e al segno francescano distintivo, ci si regoli secondo gli Statuti.

La professione è di per sé un impegno perpetuo.

I membri che si trovino in particolari difficoltà, cureranno di trattare i loro problemi con il Consiglio in fraterno dialogo. Il ritiro e la definitiva dimissione dall'Ordine, se proprio necessario, è atto di competenza del Consiglio di Fraternità a norma delle Costituzioni.

24. Per incrementare la comunione tra i membri, il Consiglio organizza adunanze periodiche ed incontri frequenti, anche con altri gruppi francescani, specialmente giovanili, adottando i mezzi piú appropriati per una crescita, nella vita francescana ed ecclesiale, stimolando ognuno alla vita di fraternità. Una tale comunione prosegue con i fratelli defunti con l'offerta di suffragi per le loro anime.

25. Per le spese occorrenti alla vita della Fraternità e per quelle necessarie alle opere di culto, di apostolato e di carità, tutti i fratelli e le sorelle offrano un contributo commisurato alle proprie possibilità. Sia poi cura delle fraternità locali di contribuire alle spese dei Consigli delle fraternità di grado superiore.

26. In segno concreto di comunione e di corresponsabilità, i Consigli ai diversi livelli, secondo le Costituzioni, chiedano religiosi idonei e preparati per l'assistenza spirituale ai Superiori delle quattro famiglie religiose francescane, alle quali da secoli è collegata la Fraternità Secolare.

Per favorire la fedeltà al carisma e la osservanza alla regola e per avere maggiori aiuti nella vita di fraternità, il Ministro o Presidente, d'accordo con il suo Consiglio, sia sollecito nel chiedere periodicamente la visita pastorale ai competenti Superiori religiosi e la visita fraterna ai responsabili laici di livello superiore, secondo le Costituzioni.

"E chiunque osserverà queste cose, sia colmato in cielo della benedizione dell'Altissimo Padre e in terra sia colmato della benedizione del Figlio suo diletto con il santissimo Spirito Paraclito" (*Benedizione di San Francesco*).

Appendix IV

THE REDACTION OF THE RULE FROM APRIL 1977 THROUGH JUNE 1978

April 1977 Redaction[1]	*Final Redaction*	*Text sent to Curia*	*Rule of 1978*[2]
		PROLOGUE:	*PROLOGUE:*
		Exhortation of St. Francis to the Brothers and Sisters of Penance[3]	*Exhortation of St. Francis to the Brothers and Sisters of Penance*
I: The Secular Franciscan Order,	*I: The Secular Franciscan Order*	*I: The Secular Franciscan Order*	*I: The Secular Franciscan Order*
1. Among the many spiritual families	1. Among the many spiritual families	1. Among the many spiritual families	1. Among the many spiritual families

---

[1] The English translations of all four texts are that of the author. The original Italian versions of the first three texts are included within *Appendix III*, cf. above pp. 419-433. The Italian version of the *Rule of 1978* has been published in *Tertius Ordo* XXXIX (Dec 1978) 121-27.

[2] This English translation of the *Rule of 1978*, that of the author, differs from the officially approved English translation of the *Rule of 1978*. A more literal translation of the officially approved Italian text of the *Rule of 1978* has been given in order to demonstrate more clearly where the text was changed by the Sacred Congregration. These changes have been *italicized* within the text to facilitate a comparative overview.

[3] In this version of the Rule, submitted for approval by the Ministers General to the Sacred Congregation for Religious and Secular Institutes, the entire text of the *Earlier Exhortation* appears without explanation as a *Prologue*. The full text of the *Earlier Exhortation* has been omitted within this comparative analysis since it has been included within an extensive analysis in *Chapter III*.

April 1977 Redaction	*Final Redaction*	*Text sent to Curia*	*Rule of 1978*
raised up by the Holy Spirit in the Church, the Franciscan [family] unites all members of the people of God - laity, religious, and priests - who recognize that they are called to follow Christ in the footsteps of Saint Francis of Assisi.	raised up by the Holy Spirit in the Church[4], the Franciscan [family] unites all members of the people of God - laity, religious, and priests - who recognize that they are called to follow Christ in the footsteps of Saint Francis of Assisi.	raised up by the Holy Spirit in the Church, the Franciscan [family] unites all members of the people of God - laity, religious, and priests - who recognize that they are called to follow Christ in the footsteps of Saint Francis of Assisi.	raised up by the Holy Spirit in the Church, the Franciscan [family] unites all members of the people of God - laity, religious, and priests - who recognize that they are called to follow Christ in the footsteps of Saint Francis of Assisi.
In various ways and forms but in lifegiving union with each other, they make present the charism of the Poverello	In various ways and forms but in lifegiving union with each other, they make present the charism of the Poverello	In various ways and forms but in lifegiving union with each other, they intend to make present the charism of the Poverello	In various ways and forms but in lifegiving union with each other, they intend to make present the charism *of their common Seraphic Father*
in the life and mission of the Church.	in the life and mission of the Church.	in the life and mission of the Church.	in the life and mission of the Church.
2. The Secular Franciscan Fraternity holds a special place within this family.	2. The Secular Franciscan Fraternity holds a special place within this family.	2. The Secular Franciscan Order holds a special place within this family.	2. The Secular Franciscan Order holds a special place within this family.
It is a community of fraternities scattered throughout	It is a community of groups or fraternities scattered throughout	It is a community of Catholic fraternities scattered throughout	It is an *organic union of all* Catholic fraternities scattered throughout

[4] One of the changes introduced at this point in the process of redacting the new Rule was the addition of references. For example, at this point in the text a reference to *Lumen Gentium* 43 was added. Given that the references added within the *Final Redaction* sent to the Ministers General remain relatively unchanged throughout the remainder of the redactional process, those references have been omitted within this comparative overview in order not to obscurate unnecessarily the comparison of the texts themselves. The references which were added may be found in *Tertius Ordo* XXXIX (Dec 1978) 121-27; and in Z. Grant, ed., *The Rule of the Secular Franciscan Order*, Chicago 1980, 35.

April 1977 Redaction	*Final Redaction*	*Text sent to Curia*	*Rule of 1978*
the world and open to every group of the faithful who,	the world and open to every group of the faithful who,	the world and open to every group of the faithful who,	the world and open to every group of the faithful, wherein *the brothers and sisters,*
led by the Spirit, strive for perfect charity in their own secular state. They pledge themselves to live the Gospel in the manner of Saint Francis by means of a Rule approved by the Church, grouped together in fraternities under the direction of their respective leaders.	led by the Spirit, strive for perfect charity in their own secular state. They pledge themselves to live the Gospel in the manner of Saint Francis by means of a Rule approved by the Church.	led by the Spirit, strive for perfect charity in their own secular state. By their profession they pledge themselves to live the Gospel in the manner of Saint Francis by means of a Rule approved by the Church.	led by the Spirit, strive for perfect charity in their own secular state. By their profession they pledge themselves to live the Gospel in the manner of Saint Francis by means of a Rule approved by the Church.
			3. The present rule, succeeding the "Memoriale Propositi" (1221) and the rules approved by the Supreme Pontiffs Nicholas IV and Leo XIII, adapts the Secular Franciscan Order to the needs and expectations of the Holy Church in the changed conditions of the times.
		3. The interpretation	*Its interpretation belongs to the Holy See*
		and application of this Rule will be made by the General Constitutions and particular statutes.	*and its application will be made by the General Constitutions and particular statutes.*
II: The Way of Life	*II: The Way of Life*	*II: The Way of Life*	*II: The Way of Life*
3. The Rule and life of the Secular	3. The Rule and life of the Secular	4. The Rule and life of the Secular	4. The Rule and life of the Secular

April 1977 Redaction	*Final Redaction*	*Text sent to Curia*	*Rule of 1978*
Franciscans is to observe the gospel of our Lord Jesus Christ.	Franciscans is to observe the gospel of our Lord Jesus Christ.	Franciscans is to observe the gospel of our Lord Jesus Christ.	Franciscans is to observe the gospel of our Lord Jesus Christ *by following the example of Saint Francis of Assisi*,
		* *	who made Christ the inspiration and the center of his life with God and people.
Christ, the gift of the Father's love, is our way to him, the truth into which the Holy Spirit leads us, and the life which he has come to give us in abundance.	Christ, the gift of the Father's love, is our way to him, the truth into which the Holy Spirit leads us, and the life which he has come to give us in abundance.	Christ, the gift of the Father's love, is our way to him, the truth into which the Holy Spirit leads us, and the life which he has come to give in abundance.	Christ, the gift of the Father's love, is our way to him, the truth into which the Holy Spirit leads us, and the life which he has come to give in abundance.
		[Cf. 5, below]	Let the Secular Franciscans commit themselves moreover to a careful reading of the Gospel, going from Gospel to life and from life to the Gospel.
Thus, Francis of Assisi made Christ the inspiration and the center of his life with God and people.	Francis of Assisi made Christ the inspiration and the center of his life with God and people.	Francis of Assisi made Christ the inspiration and the center of his life with God and people.	* *
4. Let *us*, therefore, seek in the Gospel the living person of Jesus Christ,	4. Let the Secular Franciscans, therefore, seek in the Gospel the living person of Jesus Christ,	5. Let the Secular Franciscans, therefore, seek the living person of Jesus Christ	5. Let the Secular Franciscans, therefore, seek the living *and active* person of Christ *in their brothers and sisters, in Sacred Scripture, in the Church, and in liturgical activity.*

April 1977 Redaction	*Final Redaction*	*Text sent to Curia*	*Rule of 1978*
			The faith of Saint Francis, who often said "I see nothing bodily of the Most High Son of God in this world except his most holy body and blood", should be the inspiration and pattern of their eucharistic life.
		in the Eucharist,	
conforming *ourselves* to Him, the model and strength of *our* existence. And let *us* become joyous and faithful bearers of Him among people.	conforming themselves to Him, the model and strength of their existence, and becoming joyous and faithful bearers of Him among people.	conforming themselves to Him, the model and strength of their existence, and becoming joyous and faithful bearers of Him among people.	
	Let them commit themselves to a careful reading of the Gospel, going from Gospel to life and from life to the Gospel.	Let them commit themselves to a careful reading of the Gospel, going from Gospel to life and from life to the Gospel.	[Cf. 4, above]
10.[5] Members of the Church through Baptism,	10. *Having been buried and raised with Christ in Baptism which makes them living* members of the Church,	6. Having been buried and raised with Christ in Baptism which makes them living members of the Church,	6. Having been buried and raised with Christ in Baptism which makes them living members of the Church,
and more strongly	and more strongly	and more strongly	and more strongly

[5] The order of the paragraphs in both the "*April 1977 Text*" and the "*Final Redaction*" has *not* been preserved in this comparative analysis in order to demonstrate more clearly the parallels between these texts and the later versions. However, the number of each paragraph, as given in each of the respective Italian texts, has been preserved to indicate the paragraph's original placement within the text.

April 1977 Redaction	*Final Redaction*	*Text sent to Curia*	*Rule of 1978*
bound to her	bound to her	bound to her	bound to her
by profession,	by profession,	by profession,	by profession,
let them be witnesses	let them be witnesses	let them be witnesses	let them be witnesses
and instruments of her	and instruments of her	and instruments of her	and instruments of her
mission among the	mission among the	mission among the	mission among the
people, proclaiming	people, proclaiming	people, proclaiming	people, proclaiming
Christ by their life and	Christ by their life and	Christ by their life and	Christ by their life and
words.	words.	words.	words.
Inspired by St. Francis	Inspired by St. Francis	Inspired by St. Francis	Inspired by St. Francis
and with him called	and with him called	and with him called	and with him called
to rebuild the Church,	to rebuild the Church,	to rebuild the Church,	to rebuild the Church,
let *us*	let them	let them	let them
	commit themselves	commit themselves	commit themselves
live in full	to live in full	to live in full	to live in full
communion with the	communion with the	communion with the	communion with the
pope, bishops, and	pope, bishops, and	pope, bishops, and	pope, bishops, and
priests, in a trusting	priests, in a trusting	priests, in a trusting	priests, in a trusting
and open dialogue of	and open dialogue of	and open dialogue of	and open dialogue of
apostolic creativity.	apostolic creativity.	apostolic creativity.	apostolic creativity.
5. Let the "brothers	5. Let the "brothers	7. Let the "brothers	7. Let the "brothers
and sisters of penance",	and sisters of penance",	and sisters of penance",	and sisters of penance",
in virtue of	in virtue of	in virtue of	in virtue of
their vocation,	their vocation,	their vocation,	their vocation,
and motivated	and motivated	and motivated	and motivated
by the dynamic power	by the dynamic power	by the dynamic power	by the dynamic power
of the gospel,	of the gospel,	of the gospel,	of the gospel,
conform their way	conform their way	conform their way	conform their way
of thinking and acting	of thinking and acting	of thinking and acting	of thinking and acting
to that of Christ	to that of Christ	to that of Christ	to that of Christ
by means of a radical	by means of a radical	by means of a radical	by means of a radical
interior *reversal*	interior change	interior change	interior change
which the gospel itself	which the gospel itself	which the gospel itself	which the gospel itself
calls "conversion",	calls "conversion",	calls "conversion",	calls "conversion",
which because of	which because of	which because of	which because of
human frailty must be	human frailty must be	human frailty must be	human frailty must be
renewed daily.	carried out daily.	carried out daily.	carried out daily.
On this way	On this way	On this way	On this way
of *conversion*	of renewal	of renewal	of renewal
the sacrament of	the sacrament of	the sacrament of	the sacrament of
reconciliation is the	reconciliation is the	reconciliation is the	reconciliation is the
privileged sign of the	privileged sign of the	privileged sign of the	privileged sign of the

April 1977 Redaction	*Final Redaction*	*Text sent to Curia*	*Rule of 1978*
Father's mercy and the source of *new* grace.	Father's mercy and the source of grace.	Father's mercy and the source of grace.	Father's mercy and the source of grace.
11. As Jesus was the true worshipper of the Father, so *we will* make prayer and contemplation the heart of our being and acting. *We will* participate in the sacramental life of the Church,	11. As Jesus was the true worshipper of the Father, so let them make prayer and contemplation the heart of their being and acting. Let them participate in the sacramental life of the Church taking care to have a uniquely	8. As Jesus was the true worshipper of the Father, so let them make prayer and contemplation the heart of their being and acting. Let them participate in the sacramental life of the Church,	8. As Jesus was the true worshipper of the Father, so let them make prayer and contemplation the heart of their being and acting. Let them participate in the sacramental life of the Church,
above all the Eucharist; and *we will* join in liturgical prayer in one of the forms proposed by [the Church], thus reliving the mysteries of the life of Christ.	special devotion to the Eucharist; and let them join in liturgical prayer in one of the forms proposed by the Church herself, thus reliving the mysteries of the life of Christ.	above all at the Eucharist, and let them join in liturgical prayer in one of the forms proposed by the Church herself, thus reliving the mysteries of the life of Christ.	above all at the Eucharist, and let them join in liturgical prayer in one of the forms proposed by the Church herself, thus reliving the mysteries of the life of Christ.
12. The Virgin Mary, humble servant of the Lord, open to his word and to all his calls, was embraced by Francis with indescribable love and declared the Protectress and Advocate of his family. The *brothers and sisters will* witness to her their ardent love by imitation of her unconditional self-giving and by an out-pouring of faithful and conscious prayer.	12. The Virgin Mary, humble servant of the Lord, open to his word and to all his calls, was embraced by Francis with indescribable love and declared the Protectress and Advocate of his family. Let the Secular Franciscans witness to her their ardent love by imitation of her unconditional self-giving and by an out-pouring of faithful and conscious prayer.	9. The Virgin Mary, humble servant of the Lord, open to his word and to all his calls, was embraced by Francis with indescribable love and declared the Protectress and Advocate of his family. Let the Secular Franciscans witness to her their ardent love by imitation of her unconditional self-giving and by an out-pouring of faithful and conscious prayer.	9. The Virgin Mary, humble servant of the Lord, open to his word and to all his calls, was embraced by Francis with indescribable love and declared the Protectress and Advocate of his family. Let the Secular Franciscans witness to her their ardent love by imitation of her unconditional self-giving and by an out-pouring of faithful and conscious prayer.

April 1977 Redaction	*Final Redaction*	*Text sent to Curia*	*Rule of 1978*
7. Uniting themselves to the redemptive obedience of Jesus, who placed his will in that of the Father, let them faithfully fulfill the duties proper to their various circumstances of life. And let them follow the poor and crucified Christ, witnessing to him even amidst difficulties and persecutions.	6. Uniting themselves to the redemptive obedience of Jesus, who placed his will in that of the Father, let them faithfully fulfill the duties proper to their various circumstances of life. And let them follow the poor and crucified Christ, witnessing to him even amidst difficulties and persecutions.	10. Uniting themselves to the redemptive obedience of Jesus, who placed his will in that of the Father, let them faithfully fulfill the duties proper to their various circumstances of life. And let them follow the poor and crucified Christ, witnessing to him even amidst difficulties and persecutions.	10. Uniting themselves to the redemptive obedience of Jesus, who placed his will in that of the Father, let them faithfully fulfill the duties proper to their various circumstances of life. And let them follow the poor and crucified Christ, witnessing to him even amidst difficulties and persecutions.
6. Following the example of Christ, who trusting in the Father chose for Himself and His mother a poor and humble life,	7. Following the example of Christ, who trusting in the Father chose for Himself and His mother a poor and humble life,	11. Following the example of Christ, who trusting in the Father chose for Himself and His mother a poor and humble life,	11. Christ, trusting in the Father, chose for Himself and His mother a poor and humble life, *even though he valued created things attentively and lovingly*.
let them make sure	let them seek *to be detached from*	let them seek to be detached from	Thus, let the Secular Franciscans seek, *in a detachment from and in the use of, a proper relation to*
	temporal goods,	temporal goods,	temporal goods,
to simplify their own material needs to the advantage of the needy,	simplifying their own material needs.	simplifying their own material needs.	simplifying their own material needs.
conscious	Let them be mindful	Let them be mindful, then of being,	Let them be mindful then of being,
of the gospel	of the gospel	according to the gospel, stewards of the	according to the gospel, stewards of the
sense of goods.	sense of goods and the invitation to dispose of them to the advantage	goods of God for the benefit of God's children.	goods *received* for the benefit of God's children.

April 1977 Redaction	*Final Redaction*	*Text sent to Curia*	*Rule of 1978*
	of the needy, according to their possibilities.		
Let them strive in the spirit of "the Beatitudes" and as pilgrims and strangers on their way to the home of the Father,	Thus, in the spirit of "the Beatitudes", and as pilgrims and strangers on their way to the home of the Father, let them strive	Thus, in the spirit of "the Beatitudes", and as pilgrims and strangers on their way to the home of the Father, let them strive	Thus, in the spirit of "the Beatitudes", and as pilgrims and strangers on their way to the home of the Father, let them strive
to purify their hearts from every yearning for possession and power.	to purify their hearts from every yearning for possession and power.	to purify their hearts from every tendency and yearning for possession and power.	to purify their hearts from every tendency and yearning for possession and power.
8. Witnesses of the good yet to come, *we* will commit *ourselves*	8. Witnesses of the good yet to come and committed	12. Witnesses of the good yet to come and obliged	12. Witnesses of the good yet to come and obliged
to acquiring a purity of heart	to acquiring a purity of heart,	to acquire a purity of heart because of the vocation they have embraced,	to acquire a purity of heart because of the vocation they have embraced,
which will *make* *us* free amidst the cares of this world	they will set themselves free and will	thus, they will set themselves free	thus, they will set themselves free
and available for the love of God and of *our* brothers and sisters.	thus be available for the love of God and of their brothers and sisters	for the love of God and of their brothers and sisters.	for the love of God and their brothers and sisters.
9. As the Father sees in every person the features of his Son, the firstborn of many brothers and sisters, *we* too *will* make every effort to see Christ in others, whereby they will become for *us* authentic brothers and sisters.	9. As the Father sees in every person the features of His Son, the Firstborn of many brothers and sisters, let the Secular Franciscans make every effort to see Christ in others, who for them will become authenitic brothers and sisters. In this way all	13. As the Father sees in every person the features of His Son, the Firstborn of many brothers and sisters, let the Secular Franciscans make every effort to see Christ in others, who for them will become authenitic brothers and sisters. In this way all	13. As the Father sees in every person the features of His Son, the Firstborn of many brothers and sisters, let the Secular Franciscans

April 1977 Redaction	*Final Redaction*	*Text sent to Curia*	*Rule of 1978*
Therefore, with a humble and gentle spirit, *we* will accept all people as a gift of the Lord.	people will be accepted, with a humble and gentle spirit, as a gift of the Lord.	people will be accepted, with a humble and gentle spirit, as a gift of the Lord.	accept all people with a humble and gentle spirit as a gift of the Lord and an image of Christ.
Likewise, let them show respect towards other creatures, animate and inanimate, which "bear the imprint of the Most High".	Likewise, let them have respect towards other creatures, animate and inanimate, which "bear the imprint of the Most High".	[Cf. 18]	[Cf. 18]
The sense of community will make *us* happy to place *ourselves* on an equal basis with all people, especially with the lowliest, helping them to live with the dignity of creatures redeemed by Christ; and it will lead *us* to promote justice and peace and to work with others to eliminate every obstacle to a truly universal community.	The sense of community will make them happy to place themselves on an equal basis with all people, especially with the lowliest, for whom they will make every effort to create conditions of life worthy of creatures redeemed by Christ. Thus, they will be quick to commit themselves in service to the promotion of the human person and to work with all people of good will to realize peace and to eliminate every obstacle to a truly universal community.	The sense of community will make them happy to place themselves on an equal basis with all people, especially with the lowliest, for whom they will make every effort to create conditions of life worthy of creatures redeemed by Christ.	The sense of community will make them happy to place themselves on an equal basis with all people, especially with the lowliest, for whom they will make every effort to create conditions of life worthy of creatures redeemed by Christ.
13. Called, together with all people of good will, to build from within	13. Called, together with all people of good will, to build from within	14. Called, together with all people of good will, to build	14. Called, together with all people of good will, to build

April 1977 Redaction	*Final Redaction*	*Text sent to Curia*	*Rule of 1978*
a more loving and evangelical world for the realization of the kingdom of God and mindful that anyone "who follows Christ, the perfect human, becomes more human", let the Secular Franciscans	a more loving and evangelical world for the realization of the kingdom of God and mindful that anyone "who follows Christ, the perfect human, becomes more human", let them	a more loving and evangelical world for the realization of the kingdom of God and mindful that anyone "who follows Christ, the perfect human, becomes more human", let them	a more loving and evangelical world for the realization of the kingdom of God and mindful that anyone "who follows Christ, the perfect human, becomes more human", let them
competently exercise their own responsibilities in the Christian spirit of service.	competently exercise their own responsibilities in the Christian spirit of service.	competently exercise their own responsibilities in the Christian spirit of service.	competently exercise their own responsibilities in the Christian spirit of service.
Let them be active,	Let them be active *by the testimony of their own human life* and	15. Let them be active by the testimony of their own human life and	15. Let them be active by the testimony of their own human life and
even with courageous individual and communal initiatives, in the field of social justice	even with courageous individual and communal initiatives, in the promotion of justice *and in particular in*	even with courageous individual and communal initiatives, in the promotion of justice and in particular in	even with courageous individual and communal initiatives, in the promotion of justice and in particular in
and public life, committing themselves through concrete choices in harmony with their faith.	the field of public life, committing themselves through concrete choices in harmony with their faith.	the field of public life, committing themselves through concrete choices in harmony with their faith.	the field of public life, committing themselves through concrete choices in harmony with their faith.
We will esteem work both as a gift and as a sharing in the creation, redemption, and service of the human community.	Let them esteem work both as a gift and as a sharing in the creation, redemption, and service of the human community.	16. Let them esteem work both as a gift and as a sharing in the creation, redemption, and service of the human community.	16. Let them esteem work both as a gift and as a sharing in the creation, redemption, and service of the human community.
14. In *our* family *we will* live the Franciscan spirit,	14. In their family let them live the Franciscan spirit,	17. In their family let them live the Franciscan spirit of peace, fidelity and respect for life.	17. In their family let them live the Franciscan spirit of peace, fidelity and respect for life.

April 1977 Redaction	*Final Redaction*	*Text sent to Curia*	*Rule of 1978*
striving to make of it a sign of a world already renewed in Christ.	striving to make of it a sign of a world already renewed in Christ.	striving to make of it a sign of a world already renewed in Christ.	striving to make of it a sign of a world already renewed in Christ.
Aided by the community and			
living the grace of matrimony, the married members	Living the grace of matrimony, let the married members in particular	Living the grace of matrimony, let the married members in particular	Living the grace of matrimony, let the married members in particular
will bear witness in the world to the love of Christ for his Church. They will accompany their children on their	bear witness in the world to the love of Christ for his Church. Let them accompany their children on their	bear witness in the world to the love of Christ for his Church. Let them accompany their children on their human and	bear witness in the world to the love of Christ for his Church. Let them accompany their children on their human and
spiritual journey with a simple and open upbringing, being attentive to the vocation of each [child].	spiritual journey with a simple and open upbringing, being attentive to the vocation of each [child].	spiritual journey with a simple and open Christian upbringing, being attentive to the vocation of each [child].	spiritual journey with a simple and open Christian upbringing, being attentive to the vocation of each [child].
[Cf. 9]	[Cf. 9]	18. Likewise, let them have respect towards other creatures, animate and inanimate, which "bear the imprint of the Most High", and let them strive to move from the temptation of exploitation to the Franciscan concept of universal kinship.	18. Likewise, let them have respect towards other creatures, animate and inanimate, which "bear the imprint of the Most High", and let them strive to move from the temptation of exploitation to the Franciscan concept of universal kinship.
15. Bearers of peace and mindful that this [peace] must be built up unceasingly, let them seek out ways of unity and loving understanding	15. Bearers of peace and mindful that this [peace] must be built up unceasingly, let them seek out ways of unity and loving understanding	19. Bearers of peace and mindful that this [peace] must be built up unceasingly, let them seek out ways of unity and loving understanding	19. Bearers of peace and mindful that this [peace] must be built up unceasingly, let them seek out ways of unity and loving understanding

April 1977 Redaction	*Final Redaction*	*Text sent to Curia*	*Rule of 1978*
through dialogue, trusting in the presence of the divine seed in everyone and in the transforming power of pardon.	through dialogue, trusting in the presence of the divine seed in everyone and in the transforming power of *love* and of pardon.	through dialogue, trusting in the presence of the divine seed in everyone and in the transforming power of love and of pardon.	through dialogue, trusting in the presence of the divine seed in everyone and in the transforming power of love and of pardon.
Messengers of perfect joy in every circumstance, *we will* make every effort to bring joy and hope to others, fruits of the	Messengers of perfect joy in every circumstance, let them make every effort to bring joy and hope to others, fruits of the	Messengers of perfect joy in every circumstance, let them make every effort to bring joy and hope to others.	Messengers of perfect joy in every circumstance, let them make every effort to bring joy and hope to others.
		Since they are immersed in the	Since they are immersed in the
resurrection of Christ, which gives true mean- ing to Sister Death	resurrection of Christ, which gives true mean- ing to Sister Death	Resurrection of Christ, which gives true mean- ing to Sister Death, let them serenely	Resurrection of Christ, which gives true mean- ing to Sister Death, let them serenely
as	as	tend toward	tend toward
the ultimate encounter with the Father.	the ultimate encounter with the Father.	the ultimate encounter with the Father.	the ultimate encounter with the Father.
III: Life in Fraternity	*III: Life in Fraternity*	*III: Life in Fraternity*	*III: Life in Fraternity*
16. The Secular Franciscan Order is divided into groups or fraternities at various levels - local, regional, national, and international. These fraternities,	16. The Secular Franciscan Order is divided into fraternities at various levels - local, regional, national, and international. These fraternities, coordinated among themselves at each level, are united with those at a higher level.	20. The Secular Franciscan Order is divided into fraternities at various levels - local, regional, national, and international.	20. The Secular Franciscan Order is divided into fraternities at various levels - local, regional, national, and international.
each one having its own moral	Individually they have their own moral	Individually they have their own moral	Individually they have their own moral

April 1977 Redaction	*Final Redaction*	*Text sent to Curia*	*Rule of 1978*
personality in the Church,	personality in the Church.	personality in the Church. These various fraternities	personality in the Church. These various fraternities
are coordinated among themselves and united with those at a higher level.		are coordinated and united among themselves	are coordinated and united among themselves
		according to the norm of this Rule and of the Constitutions.	according to the norm of this Rule and of the Constitutions.
17. At various levels, each Fraternity is animated and guided by its respective Council and minister (or president) who are elected	17. At various levels, each Fraternity is animated and guided by its respective Council and minister (or president) who are elected	21. At various levels, each Fraternity is animated and guided by its respective Council and minister (or president) who are elected by the professed members	21. At various levels, each Fraternity is animated and guided by its respective Council and minister (or president) who are elected by the professed members
based upon appropriate approved norms.	based upon appropriate approved norms.	based upon the Constitutions.	based upon the Constitutions.
Their service, which is temporary, is a commitment of availability and responsibility to each member and to the community.	Their service, which is temporary, is a commitment of availability and responsibility to each member and to the community.	Their service, which is temporary, is a commitment of availability and responsibility to each member and to the community.	Their service, which is temporary, is a commitment of availability and responsibility to each member and to the community.
Within themselves the fraternities are structured in different ways	Within themselves the fraternities are structured in different ways	Within themselves the fraternities are structured in different ways according to the norm of the Constitutions,	Within themselves the fraternities are structured in different ways according to the norm of the Constitutions,
according to the various needs of their members and their regions, and under the guidance of their respective Council.	according to the various needs of their members and their regions, and under the guidance of their respective Council.	according to the various needs of their members and their regions, and under the guidance of their respective Council.	according to the various needs of their members and their regions, and under the guidance of their respective Council.

April 1977 Redaction	*Final Redaction*	*Text sent to Curia*	*Rule of 1978*
18. The local Fraternity, established canonically, is the basic unit of the whole Order and a visible sign of the Church, the community of love. It is the privileged place for developing a sense of Church and the Fran- ciscan vocation and for enlivening the apostolic life of its members.	18. The local Fraternity, established canonically, is the basic unit of the whole Order and a visible sign of the Church, the community of love. It is the privileged place for developing a sense of Church and the Fran- ciscan vocation, and for enlivening the aposto- lic life of its members.	22. The local Fraternity must be established canonically, and thus, it becomes the basic unit of the whole Order and a visible sign of the Church, the community of love. It should be the privileged place for developing a sense of Church and the Fran- ciscan vocation, and for enlivening the aposto- lic life of its members.	22. The local Fraternity must be established canonically, and thus, it becomes the basic unit of the whole Order and a visible sign of the Church, the community of love. It should be the privileged place for developing a sense of Church and the Fran- ciscan vocation, and for enlivening the apostolic life of its members.
19. The request for admission to the local Fraternity is made to the respective Council, which has responsibility for the Fraternity.	19. Requests for admission *to the* *Secular Franciscan* *Order* *are presented to* *a local Fraternity*, whose Council decides on the acceptance of new brothers and sisters.	23. Requests for admission to the Secular Franciscan Order are presented to a local Fraternity, whose Council decides on the acceptance of new brothers and sisters.	23. Requests for admission to the Secular Franciscan Order are presented to a local Fraternity, whose Council decides on the acceptance of new brothers and sisters.
One is admitted [into the Fraternity] through a time of initiation, a period of formation of at least one year, and profession of the Rule. The entire community is involved in this process of growth even by its manner of living.	Admission [into the Order] is accomplished through a time of initiation, a period of formation of at least one year, and profession of the Rule. The entire community is involved in this process of growth even by its manner of living. They may profess the	Admission [into the Order] is accomplished through a time of initiation, a period of formation of at least one year, and profession of the Rule. The entire community is involved in this process of growth even by its manner of living. The age for profession	Admission [into the Order] is accomplished through a time of initiation, a period of formation of at least one year, and profession of the Rule. The entire community is involved in this process of growth even by its manner of living. The age for profession

April 1977 Redaction	*Final Redaction*	*Text sent to Curia*	*Rule of 1978*
For admission one must be legally of age	faithful who are legally of age		
		and the distinctive Franciscan sign are regulated by the statues.	and the distinctive Franciscan sign are regulated by the statutes.
This profession of the life is by its nature a permanent commitment.	Profession of the life is by its nature a permanent commitment.	Profession is by its nature a permanent commitment.	Profession is by its nature a permanent commitment.
Members who find themselves in particular difficulties will deal with them in fraternal dialogue with the Council.	Members who find themselves in particular difficulties will take care to deal with their problems in fraternal dialogue with the Council.	Members who find themselves in particular difficulties will take care to deal with their problems in fraternal dialogue with the Council.	Members who find themselves in particular difficulties will take care to deal with their problems in fraternal dialogue with the Council.
		Withdrawal or	Withdrawal or
If it happens to come to a permanent dismissal from the Order, it	Permanent dismissal from the Order, if necessary,	permanent dismissal from the Order, if necessary,	permanent dismissal from the Order, if necessary,
is an act of the leaders at a higher level.	is an act of the leaders at a higher level.	is an act of the Fraternity Council	is an act of the Fraternity Council
		according to the norm of the Constitutions.	according to the norm of the Constitutions.
20. To foster communion among members, the Council, with the aid of individual [members],	20. To foster communion among members, the Council	24. To foster communion among members, the Council	24. To foster communion among members, the Council
organizes regular assemblies and frequent meetings,	organizes regular assemblies and frequent meetings [of the community],	organizes regular assemblies and frequent meetings [of the community],	organizes regular assemblies and frequent meetings [of the community],

April 1977 Redaction	*Final Redaction*	*Text sent to Curia*	*Rule of 1978*
		as well as with other Franciscan groups, especially with youth groups,	as well as with other Franciscan groups, especially with youth groups,
adopting the most appropriate means for growth in Franciscan and ecclesial life and encouraging everyone to the life of fraternity. This communion continues with deceased brothers and sisters praying for them.	adopting the most appropriate means for growth in Franciscan and ecclesial life and encouraging everyone to the life of fraternity. This communion continues with deceased brothers and sisters through prayer for them.	adopting the most appropriate means for growth in Franciscan and ecclesial life and encouraging everyone to the life of fraternity. This communion continues with deceased brothers and sisters through prayer for them.	adopting the most appropriate means for growth in Franciscan and ecclesial life and encouraging everyone to the life of fraternity. This communion continues with deceased brothers and sisters through prayer for them.
21. Regarding expenses necessary for the life of the Fraternity and those necessary for worship, the apostolate, and charity, let all the brothers and sisters offer a contribution according to their means. Furthermore, let it be a concern of the local fraternities to participate	21. Regarding expenses necessary for the life of the Fraternity and those necessary for worship, the apostolate, and charity, let all the brothers and sisters offer a contribution according to their means. Furthermore, let it be a concern of the local fraternities	25. Regarding expenses necessary for the life of the Fraternity and those necessary for worship, the apostolate, and charity, let all the brothers and sisters offer a contribution according to their means. Furthermore, let it be a concern of the local fraternities	25. Regarding expenses necessary for the life of the Fraternity and those necessary for worship, the apostolate, and charity, let all the brothers and sisters offer a contribution according to their means. Furthermore, let it be a concern of the local fraternities
in the higher level fraternities.	*to contribute to the expenses of the Councils* of the higher level fraternities.	to contribute to the expenses of the Councils of the higher level fraternities.	to contribute to the expenses of the Councils of the higher level fraternities.
22. As a concrete sign of communion and responsibility, let the Councils on various levels,	22. As a concrete sign of communion and coresponsibility, let the Councils on various levels,	26. As a concrete sign of communion and coresponsibility, let the Councils on various levels, in keeping with the Constitutions,	26. As a concrete sign of communion and coresponsibility, let the Councils on various levels, in keeping with the Constitutions,

April 1977 Redaction	*Final Redaction*	*Text sent to Curia*	*Rule of 1978*
ask for	ask for	ask for suitable and well prepared religious for	ask for suitable and well prepared religious for
spiritual assistance from the First Order and the Third Order Regular.	spiritual assistance from the superiors of the four religious Franciscan families, to whom the spiritual care of the Secular Fraternity has been entrusted by the Holy See.	spiritual assistance from the superiors of the four religious Franciscan families, to whom the Secular Fraternity has been united for centuries.	spiritual assistance from the superiors of the four religious Franciscan families, to whom the Secular Fraternity has been united for centuries.
To ensure growth in the observance of the Rule and to promote the life of the Fraternity, let the minister or president, with the consent of the Council, take care periodically to ask the responsible religious superiors for a pastoral visitation, and the lay ministers for a fraternal visitation.	*To promote fidelity to the charism* and observance of the rule and to receive greater support in the life of the Fraternity, let the minister or president, with the consent of the Council, take care periodically to ask the responsible religious superiors for a pastoral visitation, and the lay ministers *at a higher level* for a fraternal visitation.	To promote fidelity to the charism and observance of the rule and to receive greater support in the life of the Fraternity, let the minister or president, with the consent of the Council, take care periodically to ask the responsible religious superiors for a pastoral visitation, and the lay ministers at a higher level for a fraternal visitation, according to the norm of the Constitutions.	To promote fidelity to the charism and observance of the rule and to receive greater support in the life of the Fraternity, let the minister or president, with the consent of the Council, take care periodically to ask the responsible religious superiors for a pastoral visitation, and *the ministers*[6] at a higher level for a fraternal visitation, according to the norm of the Constitutions.

[6] Whereas the earlier texts specified "lay ministers" (*ai responsabili laici*), the official text omits wood "lay" (*ai responsabili*). However, this change was not indicated by the Sacred Congregation. Thus, it remains unclear why the change was introduced. Nonetheless, "ministers" does not necessarily exclude "lay" ministers.

April 1977 Redaction	*Final Redaction*	*Text sent to Curia*	*Rule of 1978*
"And may whoever observes all this be filled in heaven with the blessing of the most high Father, and on earth with that of his beloved Son, together with the Holy Spirit, the Comforter".	*"And may whoever observes all this be filled in heaven with the blessing of the most high Father, and on earth with that of his beloved Son, together with the Holy Spirit, the Comforter".*	*"And may whoever observes all this be filled in heaven with the blessing of the most high Father, and on earth with that of his beloved Son, together with the Holy Spirit, the Comforter".*	*"And may whoever observes all this be filled in heaven with the blessing of the most high Father, and on earth with that of his beloved Son, together with the Holy Spirit, the Comforter".*
(Blessing of St. Francis from the *Testament*),	(Blessing of St. Francis from the *Testament*)	(Blessing of St. Francis from the *Testament*)	(Blessing of St. Francis from the *Testament*)

INDEX

Stampato nel Giugno 1991
dalla tipografia Giovanni Greco
Casavatore (NAPOLI) - Tel.081 / 7364772